THE INNER JEFFERSON
Portrait of a Grieving Optimist

THE INNER JEFFERSON

Portrait of a Grieving Optimist

ANDREW BURSTEIN

University Press of Virginia
CHARLOTTESVILLE AND LONDON

THE UNIVERSITY PRESS OF VIRGINIA
Copyright © 1995 by the Rector and Visitors
of the University of Virginia

First published 1995

Frontispiece: Thomas Jefferson as secretary of state in 1791,
portrait by Charles Willson Peale. (Independence National
Historical Park, Philadelphia)

Library of Congress Cataloging-in-Publication Data
Burstein, Andrew.
    The inner Jefferson : portrait of a grieving optimist / Andrew
Burstein.
      p.   cm.
    Includes index.
    ISBN 0-8139-1618-6 (cloth)
    1. Jefferson, Thomas, 1743-1826.   2. Jefferson, Thomas, 1743-1826 —
Correspondence.   3. Sterne, Laurence, 1713-1768.   4. Presidents —
United States — Biography.   I. Title.
E332.B96   1995
973.4′6 — dc20

Printed in the United States of Ameria

To Hannah and Julius
for the love and the determination
And to David
for the spirit

Style has always some reference to an author's manner of thinking. It is a picture of the ideas which arise in his mind, and of the manner in which they rise there; and hence, when we are examining an author's composition, it is, in many cases, extremely difficult to separate the style from the sentiment.

— Hugh Blair, *Lectures on Rhetoric and Belles-Letters* (1783)

Time wastes too fast: every letter I trace tells me with what rapidity life follows my pen. the days and hours of it are flying over our heads like clouds of windy day never to return — more[.] every thing presses on — and every time I kiss thy hand to bid adieu, every absence which follows it, are preludes to that eternal separation which we are shortly to make!

— Thomas and Patty Jefferson's adaptation of a sentiment from Laurence Sterne's *Tristram Shandy,* written in the hand of both Jeffersons near the time of Patty's death in 1782. See fig. 5.

Contents

Preface   xi

Chronology   xvii

Introduction   1

1   The Well-Ordered Dreamworld   12

2   Sensitivity and Sterne   42

3   The Sensations of Europe   68

4   Letter Writing and Friendship   116

5   Friends, Neighborhood, and the Family Fireside   150

6   Obstructed Vision   196

7   Retirement, Religion, and Romantic Death   246

Conclusion   273

Notes   293

Index   327

Illustrations

Portrait of Jefferson by Charles Willson Peale, 1791   *Frontispiece*

Monticello, the well-ordered dreamworld   23

Letter: Jefferson to Robert Skipwith, 1771   27

Natural Bridge   37

Laurence Sterne, by Sir Joshua Reynolds   44

Patty Jefferson's deathbed adieu   61

Maria Cosway, by Richard Cosway   77

Letter: "My Head and My Heart," 1786   87

Engraving from Sterne's *A Sentimental Journey*   103

Letter: Jefferson to James Monroe, 1782   119

Letter: Jefferson to John Page, 1804   142

Preface

To APPRECIATE HOW Americans remain taken with Thomas Jefferson, one need only stand in line for the tour at Monticello. The visitors who wait to experience Jefferson's lost world regularly engage those standing with them in some speculation about Jefferson's reading habits, hobbies, or his feelings about slavery, anticipating some drama yet to come from study of the passionate democrat who roamed that splendid mountaintop. Jefferson attracts. President William Jefferson Clinton started his inaugural procession with an appearance at Jefferson's home and joked with inquiring schoolchildren that if Thomas Jefferson were alive he, the new president, would humbly step aside in favor of the founding father. Speaking at the University of Virginia on the occasion of Jefferson's 250th birthday on April 13, 1993, Mikhail Gorbachev stated that he had often sought inspiration from Jefferson's words in conceiving Russian political reform. Calling Jefferson "a magnet capable of attracting the hearts and minds of a new generation," the Nobel Peace Prize winner added that Jefferson was still "revealing hidden aspects of his personality." And septuagenarian Liu Zuochang, lone biographer of Jefferson in the People's Republic of China, supposed recently that it was a simple matter of his subject's character which made him most fitting as a model for late twentieth-century Chinese in their search for decency.

George Washington, Benjamin Franklin, and James Madison are equally admired for their contributions to and their leadership of the young America. But for some reason modern patriots do not embrace any of these figures with the sentiment, the emotional connection, that persists with Jefferson. Although Americans have ignored the two-dollar bill with his image on it, they come by the hundreds of thousands to Jefferson's home to experience Monticello as they imagine he did. Americans seem to need little prodding to gain the combined sense of esteem and compassion that Jefferson's life evokes. Only Abraham Lincoln compares in consciousness raising, in fixing on the spiritual essence of the nation.

In 1960 Merrill D. Peterson produced *The Jefferson Image in the American Mind* and set forth the uses of Jefferson's legacy — "a mixed product of memory and hope, fact and myth" — from the statesman's death in 1826 to the mid-twentieth century. Far less credibly, but more dramatically, Fawn M. Brodie made headlines in 1974 as a detective of sorts. In *Thomas Jefferson: An Intimate History,* she purported to have found what no previous scholars could, the telltale signs that Jefferson had fathered the children of a biracial slave named Sally Hemings, who might have been his deceased wife's half sister. In Brodie's enthusiasm to illustrate her point, she misread language, invoked currently fashionable psychological explanations to overinterpret unconscious patterns in Jefferson's writing, and construed psychic dilemmas without regard to eighteenth-century norms. In a profound work published in 1968, *White over Black: American Attitudes toward the Negro, 1550–1812,* Winthrop D. Jordan had maintained that miscegenation would have been a gross "lapse of character" for Jefferson. John Chester Miller further undercut Brodie's argument in *The Wolf by the Ears: Thomas Jefferson and Slavery* (1977), and Virginius Dabney made a separate effort to expose the flaws in her research in *The Jefferson Scandals* (1981). Yet some still consider Brodie's "intimate history" credible.

Others have since tackled the Jefferson "problem" from differing perspectives, with various degrees of creativity and investigative thoroughness. Professor Max Byrd's responsibly conceived fiction that depicts Jefferson in Paris (*Jefferson: A Novel,* 1993) ironically expresses the moral tone of Jefferson's world with greater consistency than more ambitious recent biographies. All of this merely proves that Jefferson studies can still excite the American imagination in the last quarter of the twentieth century, and that Jefferson the man still needs to be explored.

Once more, let us feed Americans' obsession to know the founding father with the passionate pen. But this work is distinctly different. What makes it different is the emphasis on Jefferson's sense of self, his self-fashioning. I aim to remove modern preconceptions as much as possible and re-create the mental world Jefferson knew. Based upon what he read and how he responded to it, what he wrote privately and what meanings he found in particular words and metaphors, the Jefferson resurrected in these pages is a man of an unfamiliar temperament, a man of his time, not ours.

To get under his skin, I do not chain myself to a strictly chronological approach, because my subject's most revealing and penetrating words did not necessarily spring from his mind in a predictable or linear way. Taking my cue from Jefferson's beloved *Tristram Shandy,* the eighteenth century's most controversial novel, "When a man is telling a story in the strange way I do mine he is obliged continually to be going backwards and forwards to keep all tight together in the readers' fancy." His politics are of interest insofar as they reveal his private impulses. I do not attempt to extract more personality than what is actually present in Jefferson's most heralded composition, the Declaration of Independence. That document was designed to be an amalgamation of the sentiment of a congress of men, not an expression of individuality. For individuality, I look to Jefferson's familiar letters.

This is neither a book which lavishly praises nor faithlessly scandalizes. I treat my subject with a sensitivity to the environment in which he lived and according to the assumptions his generation held. This Jefferson is not static; his mind develops over several convulsive decades. He becomes an energetic letter writer with a need for friends. He teeters back and forth, seeming at the same time to desire opposing values: monastic contemplation, the joys of family, and decisive public commitment. He examines life, nurtures an idealized vision of how it could be, and suffers from the knowledge that he may never break through the discord that persists among men. He is, in a certain sense, a lonely genius, a flawed poet.

This book addresses a range of related questions: How did the restless Jefferson cope with life's uncertainties? What was he like as a friend? Was his gift for words primarily the result of careful scholarship and clever self-presentation? Or can we crack the shell and find an internal energy, a man both imaginative and emotional, who stands up to dissection? Who was the thinking man behind the learned writer, policymaker, president? How did an essentially private person rally so many to his cause? Americans identify with Jefferson. With what emotional causes did Jefferson identify?

Answers are slow in coming, because the tremendous cultural changes that have taken place since Jefferson lived cloud any examination of him. Nevertheless, accepting what the passage of time has cost, I still believe it possible to uncover more of the inner Jefferson, or for that matter any historical figure who is complex or controversial enough to raise such challenges. One can retain a proper amount of scholarly detachment and still cherish the capacity to be astonished by what is possible.

This book has grown along with my son Joshua. Living in Jefferson's hometown, we drove to the mountaintop often, the way other families go on picnics. From the age of four, Josh came to feel that he had an investment of some kind in the shrine (aside from what he spent at the Monticello gift shop). His 1991 crayon portrait of Jefferson, after Charles Willson Peale's 1791 painting, suggests an identification. How much Jefferson's legacy will have a hold on my son as he matures, I cannot say. I can, however, recall his musing on his very first visit that Jefferson was bound to return and invite us to dinner. I told him there was a waiting list. We agreed we would be patient.

THE LARGEST SELECTION of Jefferson correspondence is at the Library of Congress, Washington, D.C. I have drawn on both this collection and the extensive holdings of the Manuscripts Division, Special Collections Department, University of Virginia Library when it was necessary to inspect originals. The Edgehill Randolph Papers and Ellen Wayles Coolidge correspondence, also at the University of Virginia Library, contain letters regarding Jefferson's life that were of value to this study. Although Jefferson began sentences with lowercase letters, I have capitalized these initial letters when quoting from unpublished documents, except when indicated. When quoting from various editions of Jefferson's published correspondence, I retain the usages employed by the respective editors.

I wish first and foremost to thank Peter S. Onuf, Thomas Jefferson Memorial Foundation Professor of History at the University of Virginia, for his contagious sense of intellectual adventure, probing questions, and consistent good nature over the course of this project. He has been a fabulous mentor and a thoughtful friend. Daniel P. Jordan, executive director of Monticello, and his staff have been exceedingly kind in opening Monticello's doors and cabinets. Merrill D. Peterson, too, has served as an inspiration. Catherine Mowbray was indispensable in providing a map of uncharted literary territory. Mark Nedostup offered artistic renditions of the Monticello Jefferson knew and provided enhancements of select letters. Special thanks to Lee Langston-Harrison, curator of the James Monroe Museum, to Jean J. Rousseau of Tours, France, and to Bill and Joan Witkin — for being there at crucial times.

The following scholars have read portions of the manuscript and have offered their particular expertise: Edward L. Ayers, Martin C. Battestin, Robert D. Cross, Joanne B. Freeman, Charles Fry, E. D. Hirsch, Jr., Rhys Isaac, Steve Kluger, David Levin, Jan Lewis, Kenneth Lockridge, Pan Petroff, Frank Shuffelton, Herbert Sloan, John Stagg, John Tinkler, and Douglas L. Wilson. I hope that their stimulating comments have resulted in making this a more solid and provocative book.

Portions of chapter 2 were previously published in "Jefferson and Sterne," *Early American Literature* 29, no. 1 (1994). Portions of chapter 4 appeared in "Jefferson and the Familiar Letter," *Journal of the Early Republic* 14, no. 2 (Summer 1994).

Chronology

1743	April 13	Born at Shadwell, Virginia
1745		Moves to Tuckahoe, Virginia
1752		Returns to Shadwell
1757		Peter Jefferson dies
1759		Publication of volumes 1 and 2 of Laurence Sterne's *Tristram Shandy*
1760		Enters the College of William and Mary, Williamsburg; meets John Page of Rosewell
1762		Graduates William and Mary, studies law with George Wythe, takes an interest in Rebecca Burwell; publication of the first volume of Macpherson's *Poems of Ossian*
1766		Travels to Annapolis, Philadelphia, and New York
1769		Breaks ground at Monticello; elected to House of Burgesses
1770		Shadwell burns; meets the widow Martha Wayles Skelton
1771	Aug.	Writes Skipwith letter
1772	Jan.	Marries Martha ("Patty")
	Sept.	Daughter Martha ("Patsy") born
	approx.	Makes Sterne entry in Literary Commonplace Book
1774		Acquires Natural Bridge
	July	Writes *A Summary View of the Rights of British America*
1775	March	Elected to the Continental Congress
	June	Arrives in Philadelphia
1776	June	Prepares Declaration of Independence
	July	Member of committee to design Great Seal of the United States
	Sept.	Departs Philadelphia
	Oct.	Attends Virginia assembly in Williamsburg, to take part in reform of laws over next three years; meets James Madison
1778	Aug.	Daughter Maria born
1779	June	Elected governor of Virginia

1780		Befriends law students William Short and James Monroe
1781	June	Leaves governorship at end of term, pursued by British troops
		Writes *Notes on the State of Virginia*
1782	April	Marquis de Chastellux visits Monticello
	May	Daughter Lucy Elizabeth born
	Sept.	Patty dies
	Nov.	Compelled to go to Richmond to answer charges of cowardice
	Dec.	Leaves Monticello for Philadelphia: lodges with Madison at House-Trist establishment
1783	May	Returns to Monticello
	Nov.	Attends Congress in Annapolis
1784	July	Sails for France
1785	Jan.	Learns of the death of Lucy Elizabeth the previous autumn
	May	Assumes post as minister to France, succeeding Benjamin Franklin; first publication of *Notes on Virginia*
1786	March	Travels to London (returns to Paris at end of April)
	Aug.	Meets Maria Cosway
	Oct.	Writes "My Head and My Heart" letter
1787	March	Departs for tour of southern France and northern Italy
	June	Returns to Paris
	July	Daughter Maria arrives
	Dec.	Angelica Church visits Paris
1788	March	Travels to Netherlands and along the Rhine (returns to Paris in April)
1789	April	Inauguration of George Washington
	July	Witnesses start of French Revolution
	Aug.	Learns he is to return to America
	Oct.	Sails to Norfolk
	Dec.	Offered position of secretary of state; arrives at Monticello
1790	Feb.	Daughter Martha marries Thomas Mann Randolph at Monticello

	March	Leaves Monticello for New York; visits Franklin in Philadelphia
	June	Agrees to Hamilton's funding and assumption plans
1791	Jan.	First grandchild, Anne Cary Randolph, born
	May	Tours upstate New York with Madison; Paine's *Rights of Man* published in America
1792	May	Feud with Hamilton heightens in letters; by September occasions Washington's deep concern
	July	Hamilton begins publishing newspaper attacks on Jefferson
	Sept.	First grandson, Thomas Jefferson Randolph, born
	Dec.	Congressional probe of Hamilton's Treasury Department launched
1793		France and Great Britain at war
	Dec.	Resigns as secretary of state; returns to Monticello after new year
1794		Becomes a farmer; nailery begins operation at Monticello
1795	June	Jay Treaty approved by Senate
1796	Feb.	Jay Treaty hailed by Washington
	Dec.	Adams elected president, Jefferson vice president
1797	March	Arrives in Philadelphia to assume vice presidency; also assumes presidency of American Philosophical Society; begins lively argument regarding religion with Benjamin Rush
	May	Mazzei letter of April 1796 reprinted in America
	July	Hamilton confronts Callender's revelation of Reynolds affair
	Oct.	Daughter Maria marries John Wayles Eppes
1798		XYZ affair; Alien and Sedition Acts passed; Jefferson and Madison team to write Kentucky and Virginia Resolutions
1799	Dec.	Washington dies bitter
1800	Dec.	Election results put Jefferson ahead of Adams, inadvertently tied with Aaron Burr
1801	Jan.	John Marshall named chief justice of Supreme Court
	March	Inaugurated as third president
1802	Sept.	Callender prints Sally Hemings story

1803		Louisiana Purchase
1804		Puts together "The Philosophy of Jesus"
	April	Maria Jefferson Eppes dies at Monticello
	July	Burr kills Hamilton in duel
1805	March	Second-term inauguration
1806		Learns of Burr conspiracy; begins construction at Poplar Forest
1809	March	After Madison's inauguration, retires to Monticello
1812		Recommences correspondence with John Adams; war with England
1814	Aug.	Writes Edward Coles in support of emancipation of slaves, without offering to do more to assist effort
1817		Undertakes design of future University of Virginia; visits Natural Bridge (with granddaughters) for the last time
1818		Compiles *Anas*
1820		Pastes together "The Life and Morals of Jesus"
1821		Writes *Memoir*
1823		Solicits "history of parties" from Justice William Johnson
1824	Nov.	Lafayette visits Monticello
	Dec.	Daniel Webster visits Monticello
1825		University of Virginia opens
1826	Feb.	Lottery bill passes, intended to alleviate Jefferson's debt
	July 4	Dies at Monticello

THE INNER JEFFERSON
Portrait of a Grieving Optimist

Introduction

THOMAS JEFFERSON'S MODERN biographers have uniformly praised their subject's intellectual energy and expressed frustration in trying to sort out his personal life. John Dewey hailed him "most universal," "far too above the average to be called a typical or representative American." Noting the statesman's preference for early retirement, for an unceremonious private life devoted to farming and book collecting, Dewey concluded that to be credited for public acts and little known as a human being "is just what he would have wished for himself."[1]

Echoing Dewey's characterization, Dumas Malone, author of six peerless volumes on Jefferson, affirmed that his subject was, and remained, a hard man to know intimately. Merrill Peterson wrote of an individual who "concealed his inner feelings behind an almost impenetrable wall of reserve" and lamented that even among his contemporaries Jefferson was the "least self-revealing and the hardest to sound to the depths of being." Wilson Carey McWilliams observed in his study of Americans' elusive pursuit of stabilizing values that Jefferson presented "a character which seems to be made up of warring antitheses." Bernard Bailyn termed him a "culture hero," a "luminous presence," whose real personality has vanished in history.[2] It is impossible to understand the public Jefferson without first understanding the private Jefferson. Yet, as these comments all suggest, those who have aspired to write of the person within have been blocked.[3]

This book does not try to supersede the two most thorough Jefferson biographies of the second half of the twentieth century, Malone's six-volume *Jefferson and His Time* (1948–81) and Peterson's single-volume *Thomas Jefferson and the New Nation* (1970). These works trace Jefferson's public career with analytic clarity for readers who desire to understand what Jefferson did, how and when and why. They comment meaningfully on the private Jefferson but subordinate private to public motives. Together, Malone and Peterson have sifted through the original and secondary literature as no other scholars, to transcend earlier Jefferson biographies, heroic epics, and polemical treatments.

Distinguished contributors to *Jeffersonian Legacies,* published in 1993 for the 250th anniversary of Jefferson's birth, reexamined Jefferson's character in the context of a mental world once presumed to relate somehow to our own and now regarded as strikingly unfamiliar. Other recent scholarship has probed Jefferson's bank of knowledge, described as a mix of traditional and antitraditional views. Of these, Charles A. Miller's *Jefferson and Nature* and Jay Fliegelman's *Declaring Independence* are particularly profound works that offer insights into the eighteenth-century way of reasoning. They lead the reader closer to what it was that Jefferson contended with and thrived on.[4]

We study physical representations of the past because we have no more direct access to the basic impulses or the historical memory of earlier peoples. It is difficult to say we know them. We read their writings, restore their homes, touch the objects they owned, and try to conjure a sense of their reality. The art of physiognomy may hint at certain powers of observation beyond the norm: in the case of Thomas Jefferson, there are numerous portraits made from life. But these teach us as much about the painter as the subject, especially of an era during which art ritually sought to capture so-called natural emotions that had "standard" expressions.[5]

We do know that Jefferson's perception of the world was significantly formed through reading and writing. His socialization occurred in a culture which prized the word. Walter J. Ong has written extensively about the sensorium as a focus for cultural studies, showing the receptivity of particular people in particular cultures to sensory stimuli. The eighteenth century, he noted, was the great age of English dictionaries, a time in which printed works received especially close attention. John Locke's influential conception of human understanding, as striking evidence of this fact, associated the mind with alphabetic (over vocal) images. "The eighteenth century," Ong pointed out, "was a significant watershed dividing residually oral culture from typographical culture." An analyst of Jefferson's art who also took note of that gradually devocalizing society compared the state of writing and oratory during Jefferson's formative years: the first gave substance to an American ideology, the second exhorted the people to take action. Jefferson's mind was more comfortably applied to that force of culture which "lived on paper rather than in the momentary quivering of air."[6]

It is language that allows human beings to exercise their distinctive intellectual faculties, and language that allows us, stepping carefully and observing changes in meanings over time, to make greater sense of the eighteenth century. What Jefferson wrote and the way he wrote tell us a great deal about who he was. Language—symbol of the soul's affections, as Aristotle put it—can bring us closer to Thomas Jefferson. But language is not an empirical science; it is mysterious and uncertain. It may help us to decide what is real, but it is also subject to misuse (most demonstrably in the conduct of politics).

Thomas Jefferson wrote deliberately, for posterity, for his state and nation—but not only in this one fashion. He kept account books and scrapbooks for his private use. The Literary Commonplace Book, for example, an individualized collection of excerpts from great poets and authors, strongly suggests the influences on Jefferson throughout the decade of his twenties. He wrote upwards of eighteen thousand letters to family, friends, experts on the varied subjects of his interest, and many people he did not even know who wrote soliciting his opinion. He kept an epistolary record, in his own hand, which runs 656 pages and lists chronologically every letter written and received from November 1783 until his death on July 4, 1826.[7] This familiar letter writing holds the greatest potential for revealing our subject's character. "Sheer copiousness testifies to a sense of vocation," one modern specialist has written, "a feeling that letter-writing is not merely a stopgap enterprise, but rather a campaign for intimacy with the other." Jefferson instructed his eighteen-year-old grandson, who was away at school: "Independent of the wish to hear from you, I would advise you, as an exercise, to write a letter to somebody every morning, the first thing after you get up. As most of the business of life, and all our friendly communications are by way of letter, nothing is more important than to acquire a facility of developing our ideas on paper." According to the memoirs of Jefferson's slave Isaac, the master "wouldn't suffer no one to come in his room" while he was absorbed in letter writing.[8]

Jefferson's letters show in varying degrees free expression, self-censoring, and sensitivity to the recipient. They serve as a window to personality development in the eighteenth century. They help us understand how friendships were maintained, how people took account of their own lives and the lives of others. They are at once art and history, social and psychological documents.

Jefferson's legacy has come to be associated not just with noteworthy documents but with the individual thought and style of writing that characterized them. Jefferson is best known to us as the penman of the American Revolution who helped give shape to the rhetoric of a proud democracy. Though an aristocrat, he was the nation's first "man of the people," fighting privilege, embracing the rights of and placing trust in the ordinary citizen. He first distinguished himself in 1774, as the author of a bold pamphlet he did not intend for publication, *A Summary View of the Rights of British America*. This eloquent challenge to the power of Parliament demanded the intercession of King George III on the colonists' behalf. A paper aimed merely to encourage the members of a Virginia convention, it proved to be the prophetic, unifying expression of thirteen distinct colonies. It rang with such vintage Jeffersonian statements as "The God who gave us life gave us liberty at the same time." *A Summary View* provided the rationale for Jefferson's selection two years later to voice the will of a new nation by drafting the Declaration of Independence for the Continental Congress meeting in Philadelphia.

Jefferson's first and persistent focus was the fate of Virginia, "my country," as he commonly called it. From 1776 to 1784 he sought to rewrite Virginia's criminal code, structure a system of public education, and ensure religious freedom. For two of those years, 1779–81, he served as Virginia's governor while his imperiled state contended with the invading British army. Yet he found time to pursue his writing vocation by enlarging on the twenty-three queries posed by the marquis de Barbé-Marbois, secretary of the French legation in Philadelphia. America's French allies wished to understand the physical features, population, and laws of Virginia, and Jefferson responded with *Notes on the State of Virginia,* the one book he published in his lifetime. Inevitably, the way *Notes* emerged, it expressed not only the setting of Virginia but also the controversial thought of Thomas Jefferson.

Jefferson returned to the Continental Congress, to a national forum, in 1783 and served as his nation's representative in France for the years leading to the French Revolution, 1784–89. In Europe he mingled with scientists and liberal thinkers, arranged for publication of his *Notes,* and immersed himself in the subject of international commerce. Recalled home and pressed to serve George Washington's administration as the first United States secretary of state, Jefferson reacquainted himself with an America in flux. Pitted against Treasury Secretary Alexander Hamilton, an ambitious, charismatic statesman who was both his political and his temperamental opposite, he rediscovered a need to elaborate the passionate principles of 1776. He feared a retreat from republicanism if Hamilton's men of privilege had their way. Worn from that highly visible conflict, Jefferson retired from active politics at the end of 1793 and in becoming a full-time planter applied his mind to the design of a superior moldboard plow and the reconception of his Monticello home. Privately he was always absorbed in design and redesign, putting up and pulling down, ordering and reordering; but the call of his growing constituency separated him from such mental exertions and lured him back into national politics. He served as vice president under John Adams (1797–1801) and two terms as president (1801–9) before returning his attention to the books and ideas that had stimulated him at the start of his public career. He could at last survey the world from atop his private mountain and satisfy his many component parts, tinkering with nature, with science, with classical literature and political theory. Once again, the printed word that had sparked his inner drive so many decades earlier compelled him in a productive retirement.

A common thread in this brief recapitulation of Jefferson's activities over several decades is the outward projection of an inner energy. We think of Jefferson as a creator. Indeed, given the amount of energy he devoted to letter writing and the pains he took in copying and preserving letters, it seems beyond question that this exercise was central to his self-creation and therefore useful in understanding his public creations. The book-loving Jefferson channeled his "light," his erudition, into letter writing and applied his letter writing toward enlivening his conversations with the world, toward expanding friendships. Letter writing, friendship, and his evolving sense of mission were all closely related.

He carried on his conversation essentially by conceiving an orbit of friends that circled the intimate "core" in which he placed himself and his immediate family, primarily his wife and daughters and later his grandchildren. This core circle embodied the highest degree of love and responsibility. To Jefferson, qualitative circles of affection could be constructed; their associated "connections" comprised an individual's life. He assured his daughter Maria a year after her marriage, "The circle of our nearest connections is the only one in which a faithful and lasting affection can be found, one which will adhere to us under all changes and chances." When he wrote to James Madison about buying land near Monticello, as Jefferson protégés William Short and James Monroe were also meant to do, Jefferson declared, "What would I not give you could fall into the circle."⁹ The vicissitudes of life made these circles his chief means of drawing emotional support.

Just beyond the core circle loomed the close friends of youth, especially John Page and Dabney Carr. With these people he shared visions as well as self-doubt and reacted to uncertainties. His pursuit of peace of mind, his nostalgia for happy times, returned him to this circle time and again.

In the colonial capital of Williamsburg, Jefferson formed another important circle, that of his mentors. Here Jefferson received a college education, became a lawyer, and later served as governor. Mentors William Small and George Wythe and the enlightened and forthcoming colonial governor Francis Fauquier helped shape young Jefferson's mental outlook. We do not possess a record of Jefferson's letter-writing conversation with any but Wythe; in that one case it seems clear that Jefferson wished to be a mirror of the accomplished lawyer and statesman. Wythe's wisdom and humanity were universally applauded. His scholarly thoroughness, versatility, and principled calm in public life represented, to Jefferson, the ideal temperament.

From another circle, his knowledgeable elders — notably Benjamin Franklin, John Adams, and George Washington — Jefferson was able to obtain a forum in order to display his talents. The Revolutionary leaders whose experience outweighed that of the young author of the Declaration of Independence were able, simply by dint of their reputations, to help establish a broader credibility for the untested Virginian. Jefferson did not forget the primacy of their historic actions and believed it was only proper for him to defer to them. Knowing his time would come, he did not compare his talents to theirs or seek to supplant them. This is how, after Adams bested him in the election of 1796, Jefferson could write Madison: "I can particularly have no feelings which would revolt at a secondary position to mr. Adams. I am his junior in life, was his junior in Congress, his junior in the diplomatic line, his junior lately in the civil government." [10]

By carrying on the style of his own advancement and becoming a mentor to others, Jefferson consciously invested in the future. He sought intellectual companionship with Madison, Monroe, and Short, as he sought political and emotional allies. His sense of duty to younger men reconfirmed the active nature of his own moral sense. His letters to these three show regard for their innate talents, which he felt made them worthy of not just his but the public's trust. To a lesser but still significant degree, Jefferson advised a number of other young men, sons of Virginia gentlemen of his generation who looked to him as a man of superior knowledge and taste.

The men of philosophy and science Jefferson so eagerly cultivated when he came to Philadelphia infused him with a kind of energy that was very necessary to him. These — whom Jefferson borrowed in part from Franklin's circle — consisted of astronomer David Rittenhouse, the inventive Francis Hopkinson, the philosophic Charles Thomson, the painter and natural historian Charles Willson Peale, and the physician and widely published educator Benjamin Rush. Their circle provided him with conversation concerning the practical application of ideas and formulas that guided Jefferson in his eager reading of natural history and pure science. He relied on the organization to which they belonged, Franklin's American Philosophical Society, to ground him in the American Enlightenment.

The next circle was that of the Europeans whose conversation helped expand his sense of identification — and purpose — beyond America's borders. In France, Thomas Jefferson was, after Benjamin Franklin, the best America had to offer. He was a cosmopolitan whose moments of utopian fancy seemed entirely compatible with his political sophistication and delighted everyone. Largely self-taught in the languages of French, Spanish, Italian, Latin, Greek, and Anglo-Saxon, Jefferson adapted to the European scene while retaining the relative simplicity of American manners. He possessed well-informed opinions and was resolute and convincingly unpretentious. From the marquis de Lafayette, Jefferson sought entry into the world of the liberal French nobility and received every possible kindness. The two dined together not infrequently and, on the eve of the storming of the Bastille, discussed the tense situation with fraternal trust. Thirty-five years later, in 1824, they saw one another again, embracing before the portico of Monticello. In the intervening years their friendship and mutual esteem remained undiminished. In an exchange of letters during 1815, for example, they wrote about their historical roles, about tyranny, democracy, and patriotism. Jefferson wished "wisdom and moderation" for France; Lafayette confirmed that if his countrymen had "deplorably Erred in the Means," they had "Steadily persevered in the primary object of the Revolution." The marquis then announced the birth of his eleventh grandchild, a boy named Thomas: "He is born to freedom."[11] The marquis de Chastellux, before he died during Jefferson's tenure in Paris, was another dutiful correspondent, philosophic spark, and personal advocate. The learned economist Du Pont de Nemours, though first known to Jefferson in an official capacity during commercial negotiations, became, after his resettlement in America, a devoted correspondent and willing collaborator in Jefferson's efforts to improve the system of education in America.

To the European women Jefferson wrote with a particular flair. They regarded him as a refreshing example of masculine gentility. They enjoyed his appreciative manner and sympathetic wit, took interest in his widowed state and the seeming uncertainty of his romantic future; and he in turn relished their company and the exposure to high culture their friendship afforded. Knowing what interested a woman, he made that interest his own, as in the repeated discussions concerning horticulture with Lafayette's aunt, Mme de Tessé, and his attempts to provide her with examples of American plants.

The women of America recognized in Jefferson a rare conversational prowess and, again, sympathetic wit. He could be called upon for a favor: something as small as forwarding a package or as large as negotiating matters of estate. Philadelphian Eliza House Trist, in whose home he and Madison boarded, felt Jefferson's compassion. "I cou'd give you as many reasons were I to enumerate your Virtues as wou'd fill a Volume folio," she wrote.[12] New Yorker Angelica Schuyler Church, who fell into his circle in Paris, saw a sweet, paternal figure and good listener who made her feel at ease. Abigail Adams and Jefferson wrote long, gracious, heartfelt letters to each other. She appreciated his agreeable manner and his generous support of her emotionally complex husband. As a mentally astute woman who understood that a woman's role was to comfort her husband while he engaged in public battle, she saw Jefferson as an ally who, with an almost feminine sensitivity, sought to promote the happiness of others.

In the circle of Jefferson's political friendships, resolute supporters in the age of the first party system, Jefferson wrote to build a usable consensus. He capitalized on years of preparation in public life in order to advance his aims, long nurtured in thought, without appearing to stifle the inventiveness of others. He wished, in a sense, to pilot the republican vessel without hands, to convince others (and perhaps himself as well) that nature (men's natural inclinations) and not he, a single individual, was their guide. Possessing such a following no doubt soothed Jefferson, though he wanted the world to think that he had done little or nothing to encourage its coalescence. Republicans were, he presumed, like the image he had of himself, men of conscience, disinterested citizens, who prized education and gave definition to a society in which rational arguments took place and calm prevailed.

We are fortunate to possess an extensive written record of Jefferson's life. He was a master record keeper, a political revolutionary with a strong compulsion to preserve personal order, a father who espoused the value of self-discipline. He strove for the predictable in his own life, for that sensible regulation which would make life durable, even undramatic. To Thomas Jefferson "pursuit of happiness" implied the erection of a sturdy framework. His "pursuit" was not the manifestation of active desire, as twentieth-century American more readily construe his most famous turn of phrase; its primary meaning was the potential to be independent and creative. And nothing gave Jefferson as great a sense of creative independence as sitting with pen in hand.

His quest was as quiet as he could make it. His artistry lay in the means by which he nourished his mind. Books and the pleasing society of compatible souls were life-giving. To James Madison and John Adams he often shared the stimulating thoughts that newly digested readings provoked in him. No less, he found satisfaction in the reproducible pleasure of gardening, writing to Charles Willson Peale, "No occupation is so delightful to me as the culture of the earth, and no culture comparable to that of the garden."[13] Monticello was the place Jefferson most associated with a sense of self, the perfect symbol of his inner life: the practical, well-ordered dreamworld. At home he was a gentleman gardener, amateur musician and scientist, wine connoisseur — a thinker, experimenter, collector — and letter writer. Perusing records of his habits and routine and how he addressed himself to whom, when, and why, we can observe, like a gardener attuned to the elements, Jefferson's growth.

The self that he projected in his correspondence both preceded and continuously shaped the historic lover of liberty, the publicly evolving Jefferson. We can characterize his sensitive aspect, the passion that occasionally surfaced, the heart of an amicable, philosophic man given to rational concerns. We can describe the social being who could not still his thoughts when it came to projecting a vision for America. The letter-writing Jefferson, private or public, was a man who required emotional fulfillment. Neither his moral philosophy nor his political doctrine could have evolved independent of the sense and sensibility his letters reveal. That during most of his adult life he spent only a few months out of each year in search of rural simplicity amid a loving family at Monticello suggests — despite his words to Peale and others — that Jefferson was more bound to worldly conflict than he would have cared to admit.

We must discover what made Jefferson respond, what linked his bookishness with a compulsion to express himself so forcefully in writing, privately and publicly. As we dissect his letters, a curious picture emerges. Writing was both a means of reaching out to others and a mechanism for creatively shaping, expanding, and embellishing contemporary idiom (and not without profound political implications). He embraced an unorthodox Americanized English and was a self-acknowledged "friend to neology" because he saw in inventive word-play an abundance of images and sounds.[14] Qualities of eloquence could not be fixed by rule but had to be progressively redefined according to their popular reception. This was how he assessed political developments as well. America could not be complacent. No aristocracy could be allowed to form, to limit the creative, productive potential of all (white) individuals of talent. America was destined to expand west, to republicanize vast territories. America's future beckoned.

Our task, then, is to recover the process by which Jefferson sought to apply his self-constructed vision to the larger world around him. We do this, of course, by interpreting his language. Writing to intimates, reflecting on his experience, he recorded his thoughts in a way that still vibrates for us in a recognizably Jeffersonian rhythm. We see Jefferson the letter writer conscious of self and sensitive to others, committed to realizing a certain effect. Sometimes he revealed struggle or doubt; often he rejoiced in the progress of civilization. In every case he exposed an urge, left a mark, expressed will. His ideas and expressions may not always have been original, but he was individual in his impulses and insights when he made self-conscious adjustments of intelligence that he accepted from sources outside himself.

At different moments in life, all individuals must improvise. Careful as he might have been to circumscribe his behavior, the letter-writing Jefferson accentuated certain images, modified the uses of certain words, supplied individuality to his eloquence. Thus he is penetrable. We can neatly describe the outside, the public persona, as earlier biographers have done; but to find the inner Jefferson, we must collect the combined outpourings of heart and intellect and identify personal crises. In the end, once we have properly located the man in his time and uncovered something more of the life of the mind, we have only to react to the vulnerable inhabitant of that place from which all our Jefferson documents ultimately derive.

I The Well-Ordered Dreamworld

THOMAS JEFFERSON BELIEVED that he did his most effective thinking and writing at Monticello. Here he organized, tabulated, cataloged, and filed, kept records of daily temperatures and the growth of fruits and flowers, and inventoried the letters he wrote and received. Here he established such daily routines as bathing his feet in cold water to prevent colds and riding on horseback for exercise. Here he built the most impressive library in America, raised his family, and entertained his friends. Monticello brimmed with life, yet it was the image of escape as well. As a structure it expressed its architect's creative spirit. It was for Jefferson, as Jack McLaughlin has written, "a dwelling that mirrored himself."[1]

Monticello did not arise spontaneously. Like everything else in Thomas Jefferson's life, it was carefully planned. It was begun only after Jefferson had proceeded far enough in life to bring it forth and fashion it as part of his self-fashioning. To appreciate Monticello, the mirror of Jefferson's inner life, we must appreciate the world it occupied, the geographic and psychological limits of its owner's early socialization.

JEFFERSON'S ALBEMARLE

THE YOUNG JEFFERSON, raised on Virginia's western frontier in the 1740s and 1750s, was exposed to the tidewater aristocracy at the colonial capital of Williamsburg in the 1760s and returned to his native Albemarle County to reestablish himself. From that point on, the master of Monticello brought the world to him, first by forming an unrivaled private library and then, as the frontier receded, by attracting ambitious travelers and Enlightenment intellects. Though he spent much of his life away from home fulfilling public obligations, he consistently wrote of his yearning for the peace and tranquillity that it offered.

Thomas Jefferson's father, Peter Jefferson, was an accomplished, strong-minded, self-reliant frontiersman. He had been among the first, in 1737, to settle in Albemarle County. His wife, Jane Randolph Jefferson, was of a distinguished Virginia family. The daughter of a sea captain and born in England, she gave him two daughters before their first son, Thomas, was born on April 13, 1743, at Shadwell, in a one-and-a-half-story farmhouse set on a small prominence. There were four large downstairs rooms and "garret chambers" above.[2] Two years later Peter Jefferson removed his family some sixty-five miles east to assume responsibility for the lands of his deceased friend William Randolph of Tuckahoe. Young Thomas enjoyed the company of his mother's relatives for six or seven years before the Jeffersons returned to Shadwell.

A few hundred yards south of the Jeffersons' clearing ran the Rivanna River (across it, two miles southwest, was the little mountain that would become Monticello), and looking north, Thomas could see the Southwest Mountains. As a teenager he hunted in these mountains and came to know the plantations of Dr. Thomas Walker of Castle Hill and Scottish-born John Harvie, men of substance who lived beyond the 2,600 contiguous acres owned by Peter Jefferson.[3]

The only organized religious life in the county centered on the parishes of St. Anne's in the south and Fredericksville in the north. Neither had a regular minister during extended periods before the Revolution, when there was frequent turnover in any case. Throughout the colony religious observance was informal. Baptisms and funerals commonly took place in the home. Unlike New England, where Harvard- and Yale-educated ministers assumed an active role in sustaining their well-ordered towns, here amid the sprawling plantation culture, community spokesmen were generally secular rather than religious voices, sociable men with a talent for public discourse. Jefferson in retirement reflected in a letter to John Adams, "Our clergy, before the revolution, having been secured against rivalship by fixed salaries, did not give themselves the trouble of acquiring influence over the people."[4]

Albemarle's founders lived their lives as tobacco planters, militiamen, road builders; they were ambitious, practical, businesslike individuals. Planters large and small transported their tobacco or wheat on tied-together canoes along the Rivanna River (three feet deep in most places during the navigable months of November to June) and eastward along the James. Most roads were forest paths, such as the Richmond-Albemarle passage skirting Shadwell that was called Three-Notched Road for the tree notches chopped by early trailblazers to keep travelers from becoming lost in the wilderness.

The first turnpike in the county was not constructed until Jefferson's second term as president. In 1797 Jefferson advised James Madison in advance of a scheduled trip to Monticello: "I write this to inform you that I have had the Shadwell & Secretary's ford both well cleared. If you come the lower road, the Shadwell ford is the proper one. It is a little deepened but clear of stone & perfectly safe. If you come the upper road, you will cross at the Secretary's ford, turning in at the gate on the road soon after you enter the 3. notched road. The draught up the mountain that way is steady and uniform." Horses could always ply the roads, but carriages were commonly waylaid by poor drainage, which caused ruts and impassable mud. As late as the summer of 1828, Margaret Bayard Smith could find herself lost over "a wild, woody track of ground" the day she and her husband traveled from Jefferson's to Madison's estate; "the road was so rugged and broken, that the carriage passed it with difficulty."[5]

In colonial times rural taverns, or "ordinaries," dotted the primary routes, far enough apart that the lack of competition meant lodgers had to endure wretched conditions. The rough way of life Jefferson's contemporaries knew is also borne out by punishments recorded in Albemarle's court records: a pillory and stocks were built, debtors whipped, and grand juries called to investigate "fighting, stabbing and stealing" in addition to adultery, selling liquor without a license, and related threats to the public order. Thomas Jefferson knew no town of any consequence until he went off to college. In fact, at the time he sat down to write the Declaration of Independence in Philadelphia, the largest town of Albemarle, Charlottesville, still contained only a dozen houses. Albemarle was, as Dumas Malone has described it, "a silent country of far-flung patriarchal seats" without architectural pretension.[6]

Well-to-do planters were distinguished from common farmers by their crafted furniture, fine linen and woolen clothes, silver buckles and satin shoes, the sugar, coffee, tea, and wine on their tables, and the books on their shelves. John Harvie, who died in 1768, bequeathed 189 titles to his beneficiaries; in his will Peter Jefferson left 24 titles, including Addison's works, *Instructions for Indians,* a history of England, and Anson's *Voyage round the World.* Such a collection indicated a lively interest in affairs of the day. Peter Jefferson and Joshua Fry, an Oxford-educated professor of mathematics, together surveyed and published a well-regarded map of Virginia in 1751. Three years later Colonel Fry commanded young Lieutenant Colonel George Washington in the French and Indian War.[7]

While Albemarle's first settlers struggled to establish themselves, hostile Indians still inhabited the county to the west. The Jefferson house was a popular way station for the friendly Cherokees whose embassies were bound for Williamsburg. Jefferson long after reflected on his early attachment to Indians, writing to John Adams of his presence in the warrior-orator Outasette's camp on the eve of that Indian's journey to England: "The moon was in full splendor. . . . His sounding voice, distinct articulation, animated action, and the solemn silence of his people at their several fires, filled me with awe and veneration, altho' I did not understand a word he uttered." Jefferson was impressed by the Indian's use of words to make a noble display of his humanity, to move others.[8]

In contrast to Albemarle stood the manors of the coastal plain or tidewater, the symbols of high culture in pre-Revolutionary Virginia. Sturdy brick homes and orderly gardens lent urbanity to rural life, and expanding libraries supported dignified dinner discussions. Country gentlemen conceived that they were living like the English aristocrats on whom their lives were modeled. As Rhys Isaac has written, the great houses "served to replicate in the colony certain established European architectural norms that were expressive of social position." The "strong sense of gradations of dominance and submission" in architecture corresponded with the owners' consciousness of their stature in the extended community. The tidewater gentry were sociable people in periwigs and ruffles who self-consciously practiced the courtesies of gentlefolk in order to separate themselves from the boorish people who lacked means. In idealizing their role at the pinnacle of a hierarchical society, they cultivated virtue through responsible public service in the governor's council, the General Court, and the House of Burgesses. During the first half of the eighteenth century, some had sent their teenage sons to England to be educated; after midcentury the College of William and Mary in the colonial capital came to be viewed as a proper alternative to Virginians increasingly proud of their native institutions.[9]

Virginia gentry, in a certain sense, lived on the edge. In the decade and a half leading up to the Revolution, they came to fear for their honor as they amassed great personal debt. Producing and shipping tobacco to England in a time of fluctuating prices, they nonetheless fashionably indulged themselves, importing the finest of the mother country's manufactures through their tobacco brokers. They remained close to their land — Virginia's dispersed settlement pattern owing in part to the nature of tobacco cultivation — and sought to increase their wealth without displaying a too obvious interest in commerce. As debt came to compromise their personal independence, they kept up appearances, continuing to relish their extensive familial and social ties, acting to inspire confidence in their social lessers.[10]

Because distances held greater significance in a time of few good roads, impressions of Virginia, beyond its northern boundaries, were formed by word of mouth contacts and were necessarily vague. New Englanders for the most part considered Virginians wilderness people, rough and unrefined, and Virginians themselves were conflicted about what kind of people they were and would become. When Princeton-educated Philip Fithian arrived in the Old Dominion in 1773 to tutor the children of tidewater planter Robert Carter, he wrote in his journal that at church "Almost every Lady wears a red Cloak; and when they ride out they tye a white handkerchief over their Head and face. . . . I was distress'd whenever I saw a Lady, for I thought She had the Tooth-Ach!" Despite such strange habits, young Philip encountered only polite, hospitable, good-humored Virginians. He had previously heard "that this country is notorious for Gaming" but found no evidence even of a pack of cards or dice. To the Reverend Enoch Green of Philadelphia, he wrote: "As to what is commonly said concerning Virginia that it is difficult to avoid being corrupted with the manners of the people, I believe it is founded in a wholly mistaken notion that persons must, when here frequent all promiscuous assemblies; but this is so far from the truth. . . . I believe that the virginians have of late altered their manner very much."[11]

Jefferson later noted that he himself had not been immune to temptations. As a grandfather advising his eldest grandson, he wrote, referring to the early loss of his father: "When I recollect that at 14. years of age, the whole care and direction of my self was thrown on my self entirely, without a relation or friend qualified to advise and guide me, and recollect the various sorts of bad company with which I associated from time to time, I am astonished I did not turn off with some of them, and become as worthless to society as they were. . . . From the circumstances of my position I was often thrown into the society of horseracers, cardplayers, Foxhunters." Fortunately, "characters of high standing" had entered his life and served as proper models so that he could shun gambling for the "steady pursuits of what is right."[12]

Thomas Jefferson's education was begun at the Latin school of the Reverend William Douglas in Goochland County (between Shadwell and Tuckahoe), where he boarded during the school year from the age of nine. His exposure to the classics continued at James Maury's log-house school in 1758–59 after Peter Jefferson's death. Maury was the financially pressed rector of Fredericksville Parish in the northern part of Albemarle, and Jefferson was able to travel home on weekends. At the College of William and Mary, where he matriculated in 1760, he formed important connections among the tidewater gentry, "a more universal Acquaintance, which may hereafter be serviceable to me," as Jefferson predicted in his first extant letter.[13] His determined pursuit of knowledge made him stand out in college. The patronage of two distinguished men, first the philosophical Scotsman William Small and then George Wythe, lawyer in the General Court and member of the House of Burgesses, pointed Jefferson toward a legal career. While in Williamsburg (the better part of the years 1760 to 1765), he socialized with the well-to-do, danced at the Raleigh Tavern, and met the political leaders of the day. His closest friend and guide to the tidewater social scene was classmate John Page of Rosewell, who was descended from some of Virginia's most illustrious names and lived in a stately mansion. (Page's aunt was the wife of Peter Jefferson's friend William Randolph of Tuckahoe.) Jefferson's correspondence with Page in 1763–64 suggests that he felt he was missing out on events of importance during the months each year he spent back in Albemarle.

It was not until 1766, at age twenty-three, that Jefferson ventured outside Virginia for the first time, traveling to Annapolis, Philadelphia, and New York. In the Maryland capital he witnessed celebration of the Stamp Act repeal, which Malone has categorized as Jefferson's first reckoning of the "community of colonial interests."[14] But, even if for a time he considered his origins provincial, he always was drawn back to the red soil and pristine images of that part of Virginia his father had first explored.

In 1767, as a new attorney, Jefferson began to appear in Williamsburg, before the General Court, whose proceedings he had watched as a student four years earlier. In addition to work on behalf of his Albemarle neighbors, he traveled across the Blue Ridge Mountains to Augusta County to represent the property interests of clients there. As one of the few General Court lawyers with a western clientele, Jefferson met people from all walks of life when the rural county courts were in quarterly session and brought their problems before the seat of authority in Williamsburg, where inferior court decisions were appealed.[15]

Jefferson broke ground at Monticello in 1769, a year in which he was involved in 198 law cases, significantly more than in any other year of his practice. In the same year he entered the House of Burgesses and began his political career by drafting what Malone characterized as "stereotyped resolutions" suited to the pomp and circumstance dictated by the colonial governor. Jefferson remained silent in formal sessions of the legislative body, expressing himself more forcefully in small group meetings.[16] In February 1770 his mother's Shadwell home — his birthplace — burned, destroying his already valuable collection of books. This personal tragedy hastened Jefferson's move to his mountain.

PALLADIO AND PLINY

WE MUST VIEW the importance of Jefferson's dwelling in two ways: as a practical symbol of its architect's spirit and as the sanctuary he established for those he loved. The story of Monticello itself is a fluid one, as the mountaintop estate was remodeled and restored time and again over a period of forty years. The interior seen today was completed in 1809. The exterior porticoes were not finished until 1823, when Jefferson was eighty.[17]

Jefferson did not build on property his father had bequeathed him along the Rivanna River, the logistically convenient and commercially prudent choice. He chose instead to level the top of an 867-foot mountain, a process requiring as well the clearing of dense forest for roads. One visitor in 1815 wrote, "The ascent of this steep, savage hill, was as pensive and slow as Satan's ascent to Paradise."[18]

Site selection was not the only way in which Jefferson differed from other Virginia plantation owners. He summed up his dismissive attitude toward standard building practices in the one book he wrote, the fact-filled (and argument-prone) *Notes on Virginia,* which he put together largely in 1781. Declaring architecture an "elegant and useful art," Jefferson wrote: "The genius of architecture seems to have shed its maledictions over this land. Buildings are often erected, by individuals, of considerable expence. To give these symmetry and taste would not increase their cost. . . . But the first principles of the art are unknown, and there exists scarcely a model among us sufficiently chaste to give an idea of them."[19] In what is arguably Jefferson's most self-revealing letter, his "My Head and My Heart" dialogue, he disclosed that his sensible, rational Head typically conjured architectural "diagrams and crotchets" (jointed wood used as building supports) to lull his restive mind to sleep.[20]

Jefferson the independent country gentleman was impressed with two related aesthetic traditions that he translated into a lifestyle: the Palladian, rooted in the monuments of Western antiquity, and the classical Roman itself. He fashioned his home from both his Head and his Heart, believing that he could know nature through mathematical formulas and through the delight of the senses in imitating the divine work of creation.

Andreas Palladio was a sixteenth-century Italian architect whose work was popular in England during the first half of the eighteenth century. Jefferson owned the manual Palladio wrote, providing simple rules for building that the classically educated nobleman could follow. He preferred to work directly from Palladio's text than to follow the Georgian adaptation of Palladio visible in Williamsburg. Palladio's villas had symbolized rural retirement in Palladio's own time, and they tended to be built in "elevated and agreeable places," to use Palladio's words. They featured harmony of proportion and offered choices of column styles according to the desired effect, masculine, feminine, or rustic. McLaughlin has written, "The grammar of the orders is as prescriptive as the syntax of language."[21]

Jefferson's early drawings, based on the illustrated books he owned, show a compulsiveness in mechanical effort and a fascination with numbers. He carried out his measurements to four or five decimal places at a time when carpenters and bricklayers were rarely able to keep to the inch, let alone fractions. Before Monticello, in fact, few homes in colonial Virginia had been built from anything more than sketches. The original house, before the dome, featured a vintage Palladian double portico (one atop the other). The underlying concept was twofold: to consolidate functions — covered passageways provided access to kitchen, stables, and storehouse — and to make a statement of the occupant's social status. Stately rising columns framed an airy, many-windowed manor. The choice of octagon rooms in Jefferson's expansion of the house represented a gifted amateur's decision to tinker with Palladian plans and, as some have suggested, to create an enclosed, protected place, a "nest" or "bosom," by this changed geometry.[22]

Jefferson, the neoclassicist architect, did not stop in his historic reverie with the sixteenth-century Palladio. Indeed, the classic example was to him more chaste and at once more vital, more majestic, than the

Palladian refinement of the original. The quintessential Roman villa conjured that vision of rural urbanity which Jefferson embraced. He owned the illustrated *Villas of the Ancients* by Robert Castell, published in 1728, which stressed the taste of Pliny. Pliny wrote often of his surroundings; no one had better expressed the classical art of living well.

Even at the end of his life, Jefferson was found absorbed in Pliny's letters. Two of these go on at length about the beauty and repose his villas afforded, the first being at Laurentinum: "The landscape on all sides is extremely diversified, the prospect in some places being confined by woods, in others extending over large and beautiful meadows, where numberless flocks . . . fatten in the warmth of this rich pasturage. My villa is large enough to afford conveniences, without being extensive."²³

Pliny described the interior of the home, from porch to drawing rooms, where the family was "sheltered from all winds except those which are generally attended with clouds." The dining room was "exceedingly warmed and enlightened not only to the direct rays of the sun, but by their reflection from the sea." The reader is led from room to room, reaching a terrace "perfumed with violets, and warmed by the reflection of the sun from the portico, which as it retains the rays, so it keeps off the northeast wind." We can imagine Jefferson reading and responding to Pliny's orchestration of nature and the elements, for Jefferson was similarly sensitive to the time of day each room received sun, a concern shared as well by Palladio. There was at Monticello, as at Laurentinum, only one "defect," the absence of a running stream. Pliny's wells, however, proved more reliable than Jefferson's.²⁴

The second of Pliny's villas described in his correspondence was in Tuscany, far from the sea and with a commanding view. Its prospect was nearly that of Monticello:

> The winters are severe and cold, so that the myrtles, olives, and trees of that kind which delight in constant warmth will not flourish here; but it produces bay trees in great perfection. . . . The summers are exceedingly temperate, and continually attended with refreshing breezes, which are seldom interrupted by high winds. . . . The disposition of the country is the most beautiful that can be imagined: figure to yourself an immense amphitheater; but such as the hand of nature could only form. Before you lies a vast extended plain bounded by a range of mountains, whole summits are crowned with lofty and venerable woods, which supply variety of game . . . fertility is nothing inferior to the lowest ground . . . from

the top of our neighboring mountains, you would imagine that not a real, but some painted landscape lay before you, drawing with the most exquisite beauty and exactness; such an harmonious and regular variety charms the eye which way soever it throws itself. My villa is so advantageously situated that it commands a full view of the country round.[25]

The attention Pliny gave his fertile and scenic mountain-bounded estate is mirrored in Jefferson's garden record keeping and loving descriptions of "my native woods and feilds." To the much-heralded Philadelphia botanist William Hamilton, he wrote: "Of prospect I have rich profusion and offering itself at every point of the compass. Mountains distant and near, smooth & shaggy, single & in ridges, a little river hiding itself among the hills so as to shew in lagoons only, cultivated grounds under the eye and two small villages."[26]

Jefferson's eclectic vision, combining antique and Palladian concepts, was accomplished with mechanical precision and represented, in Karl Lehmann's words, "the law of nature in architectural terms." Absorbed in expressing an innate sense of beauty and bringing system to nature, Jefferson was typical of eighteenth-century philosophers who sought a "universal intelligibility" in man's surroundings.[27] Classic style at once represented the power of symmetry and order (natural simplicity) and a time in history when the human spirit rose to great heights.

Beauty and function were inseparable in Jefferson's mind. For the government buildings he would design, he tampered less with the classical effect: imposing columns symbolized the grand scale of legislative decisions and inspired awe. Creating a place for cultivation of his own self entailed more modest expression and emphasized comfort over nobility. This explains the unobtrusive stairways and dumbwaiters and such clever touches as skylights and triple-sash windows for seasonally adjusted ventilation.[28] As a further expression of his desire to reach beyond what he could actually touch, Jefferson thought to incorporate as many of the world's cultures as could fit into his well-ordered dreamworld, including the Chinese lattice railings that skirt the house.

Of course, a very visible — and permanent — part of Jefferson's Monticello was the presence of slaves and hired laborers. Jefferson's earliest memory, according to family lore, was of being carried to Tuckahoe on a pillow by a mounted slave. His much younger brother Randolph would later fiddle and dance in the slave quarters, but to what extent Jefferson himself cared for — or even knew — the stories and songs of that culture, we cannot be certain. Among the more than twenty slaves he inherited from his father was his coachman Jupiter, born at Shadwell the same year as Jefferson, who traveled almost everywhere with his master until his death in the year Jefferson was elected president. In the months before Jefferson's wedding, he was often dispatching Jupiter to purchase staples: butter, bread, corn, candles. To the slaves Jefferson inherited soon were added 135 from his father-in-law, including domestic servants Ursula, who would nurse his children, her husband, the blacksmith known as King George, and the Hemingses, a large family of "bright" mulattoes. Though he referred to his slaves when he made written accounts as "my family," Jefferson did not consciously, in moral terms, register their contribution to his happiness. It was not expected that he should. He separated himself emotionally from them and — while considering them inferior to whites in the exercise of reason — intellectually celebrated their humanity. His 1771 Account Book paints a picture: Jefferson distantly fantasized a "Burying place" on his mountain where, in the midst of his family, he proposed to inter "a favorite and faithful servant" beneath a pyramid of "rough rock-stone," with a pedestal "made to receive an inscription." Jefferson did erect a cemetery not long after, but he ultimately reserved it for white friends and family. He was a fair master but not uncomfortable in the role of master. He wished that his slaves would live "without want" and intermarry with others on the estate so that he could keep families intact; but they were still in his mind part of an inheritance and no greater part of his vision than the white laborers he hired to lay bricks.[29]

Jefferson loved to doodle with numbers and lines and seemed never to be without some plan for Monticello. He sketched everything from parquet floors to hanging blinds between the columns of porticoes, designed the grounds, and when at all possible supervised construction personally. He preserved private spaces more than most eighteenth-century home builders, which some commentators have related to his willingness to accommodate guests. He set apart and restricted access to his own bedroom, study, and library, placing guests in the front two bedrooms on the other side of the main entrance hall and upstairs. Friends and learned acquaintances visited regularly, and Jefferson became known for his hospitality (fig. 1).

In envisioning the world of Monticello, Jefferson did not confine his thought to the man-made. God had to place, too. Jefferson had familiarized himself with the Bible at an early age and, though he did not express enthusiasm about his religious training, occasionally re-

1. The well-ordered dreamworld in 1825. Watercolor of Monticello by Jane Braddick Peticolas. (Monticello/Thomas Jefferson Memorial Foundation)

ferred to its lessons. On his own he consulted religious texts periodically to refine his philosophy of life, while he unequivocally shunned all mystical suggestions. To be acceptable God had to be perceived as a Workman-Creator, as a builder of order. Jefferson did not look to God for guidance in public affairs; like a majority of the Virginia gentry, he articulated the sense that his countrymen's safety and prosperity would be secured by the force of knowledge, by scientific inquiry, by man's moral sense.[30]

He thought of the grounds of Monticello in comparable terms, stopping to marvel at what was beyond human manipulation. God's genius appeared in the visible forms of nature and elicited respect from the philosophical Virginian, who, in the Newtonian tradition, sought an understanding of the infinite through scientific observation and experimentation: he emulated his Creator as a nurturer as well as a builder. Or as Ernst Cassirer has written of the Enlightenment understanding as it developed from Spinoza, "Just as surely as nature is a work of God, so too it radiates the image of the divine spirit; it mirrors God's immutability and eternity."[31] Jefferson was infinitely patient with natural processes. Monticello was first an attempt to display sensitivity to the natural prospect and, next, a reflection of Jefferson's desire to give life to something distinctive and durable. He was drawn to the idea of a home that was as solid as the great tidewater manors, mathematically consonant, supportive of invention and convenience, and reminiscent of the grandeur of antiquity. Transcending all this was the sublime genius that made the land bear fruit. As yet, Jefferson had not traveled widely, except through his books; but it was primarily those imaginative excursions which had led him to this point. He made his home an attraction and delighted in its aesthetic variations. Tasteful in its day, Monticello became a monument to one man's expansive mind ever after.

There were two dramatic periods, architecturally speaking, in which Monticello was built. The first was its initial construction, as the designer readied his home for his bride, Martha ("Patty") Wayles Skelton Jefferson. The second period of great activity was the decade of the 1790s, once Jefferson had returned from five years in Europe, a traveler who had ventured toward the lands of Roman greatness. He was inspired by firsthand contact with the Old World to double the size of the original house and to add the distinctive dome, though this visually appealing feature where some of his grandchildren later bunked may have been the least useful of Jefferson's creative compulsions.[32]

"Thou, Good Young Man, Persevere"

Jefferson associated the construction of Monticello with the life he dreamed for Patty and himself and their offspring. We cannot analyze their love story through Jefferson's written words, because this private man, deeply shaken by his wife's untimely death in 1782 at the age of thirty-three, destroyed (in what was, for many at this time, a customary means of carrying on with life) a rich and no doubt revealing correspondence. Having restored his emotional system over the next decade, Jefferson projected his retirement from politics and his return to Monticello in 1793. By then he had conceived this second spurt of building in terms of a sanctuary for the family who remained for him to dote upon. His elder daughter Martha was to see all but one of her twelve children reach adulthood. Younger daughter Maria, resembling her mother in looks and in spirit, was a teenager when her father reestablished himself on the mountain. Visitors from the 1790s through Jefferson's last years all recorded the constant activity of the grandchildren growing up, and the grandchildren described Jefferson as a highly attentive grandfather.

We must probe the provocative beginnings of Monticello, the marriage of Thomas and Patty Jefferson, if we are to move beyond the aesthetics of the architect and approach an understanding of the emotion of the husband and father. After watching his adolescent friends wed early and undertake their family responsibilities, Jefferson, not quite twenty-seven, fell in love with the musical young widow Martha Wayles Skelton. The courtship apparently began early in 1770, judging from a hint in one of Jefferson's letters to happily married John Page, wherein he noted that "I am become an advocate for the passion: for I too am coelo tactus [touched by heaven]." This was close to the time when Jefferson changed the name of his home from "The Hermitage" to the more clever "Monticello," Italian for "little mountain."[33]

He was living there in February 1771 when he wrote to James Ogilvie, a Virginia friend gone to London, whose stunted career Jefferson was attempting to improve by soliciting letters attesting to Ogilvie's character. As the letter writer turned to gossip, his subject became the trials of a mutual friend "wishing to take himself a wife," who was at odds with his prospective father-in-law. This led to mention of Jefferson's own situation. "I too am in that way; and have still greater difficulties to encounter not from the frowardness of parents, nor perhaps want of feeling in the fair one," but from the destructive fire that had claimed Shadwell and most of his possessions. With "a very few books . . . I have lately removed to the mountain from whence this is dated and with which you are not unacquainted. I have here but one room, which, like the cobler's, serves me for parlour for kitchen and hall. I may add, for bed chamber and study too. My friends sometimes take a temperate dinner with me and then retire to look for beds elsewhere. I have hopes however of getting more elbow room this summer."[34]

Jefferson worked hard to make his mountain livable, seeking grafts and seeds for the planting of garden vegetables, fruit trees, and flowers. Mrs. Drummond, a Williamsburg acquaintance of George Wythe, procured some of these things for her "Amiable freind" Jefferson. In March she wrote a spirited reply to a letter from Jefferson, long lost, in which she took pleasure in his match. Praising his "Romantic, Poetical" description, no doubt of his bride-to-be, she commented: "Thou wonderful Young Man, so piously entertaining, thro out that, exalted Letter. Indeed I shal' think, Spirits of a higher order, Inhabits Yr. Aerey Mountains, — or rather Mountain, which I may contemplate, but never can aspire too." Taken with his enthusiasm, Mrs. Drummond urged him to "persever thou, good Young Man, persevere," that he might achieve "the full completion, of all Yr. wishes, both as to the Lady and every thing else."[35]

In June, Jefferson wrote from Monticello to his tobacco broker, Thomas Adams, then in London, to change his order for a clavichord to a pianoforte, for he was "charmed" with one he had recently seen. Spare nothing in procuring the best quality, Jefferson implored; "let the case be of fine mahogany, solid, not vineered . . . worthy the acceptance of a lady for whom I intend it." Adding India cotton stockings and "a large Umbrella with brass ribs covered with green silk," for all of which he would compensate with tobacco, Jefferson reiterated his urgent priority. Send these things "as soon as you receive this . . . particularly the Forte-piano for which I will be very impatient."[36]

Henry S. Randall related an anecdote passed down through the family. As a vivacious young woman, Patty had more than just the one suitor. When two young bachelors appeared on her doorstep one day, they were treated to the sounds of Patty's harpsichord and Jefferson's violin and the two harmonizing voices. Perceiving real romance in these melodic strains, the would-be suitors took their hats and promptly left.[37]

Jefferson's letter of August 1771 to Robert Skipwith, who had married Patty's half sister Tabitha, displayed a convivial regard for one connected to his "new family" (fig. 2). Addressing merely "Thomas Jefferson Esquire" (without a destination) and depositing the envelope "to the care of Miss Wayles," Skipwith had requested a list of books "suited to the capacity of a common reader who understands little of the classicks and who has not leisure for any intricate or tedious study." The total cost was not to exceed £30. In his enthusiastic reply Jefferson revealed a lot about his self-cultivation. Citing the contributions of literature to improvement of the mind, he extolled the merits of pure storytelling: "We never reflect whether the story we read be truth or fiction. If the painting be lively, and a tolerable picture of nature, we are thrown into a reverie, from which if we awaken it is the fault of the writer." In another natural metaphor he referred to the "spacious field of the imagination," approving a view of nature by which the mind is free

2. Jefferson to Robert Skipwith, August 3, 1771. (Thomas Jefferson Papers, Special Collections Department, Manuscripts Division, University of Virginia Library)

to wander. But literature bore a decisive moral responsibility as well. Shakespeare's *King Lear* better exemplified "a lively and lasting sense of filial duty" than "all the dry volumes of ethics and divinity." History was a "moral exercise" which needed literature to help "excite . . . the sympathetic emotion of virtue." As Jay Fliegelman has observed, reading in the post-Lockean age had become "a primary emotional experience itself, a constituent of identity, a way of understanding and making one's self." And Jefferson, exemplifying this theme, was faithful to a definition of truth as "truthfulness to feelings rather than to facts."[38]

The letter to Skipwith contains rare insight into the consciousness of the young Jefferson, the Jefferson who had yet to apply his passion for reading to the composition of written documents of public import. The sociable, soon-to-be-wed Virginian perceived in the study of the Greek and Roman classics, Shakespeare, and the Bible critical lessons of moral conduct. Beyond this, he firmly rejected any dogma which abandoned common sense to faith in miracles. Thus, under the heading "History, Antient," he listed the Bible, along with Livy, Tacitus, Plutarch, and Charles Rollin's popular multivolume history of the Babylonians, Egyptians, Persians, and Greeks. Under "Religion," he placed at the top "Locke's conduct of the mind in search of truth," then listed several non-Christian examples from the ancient world: Cicero, Xenophon, Epictetus, and Seneca. These titles were followed by Bolingbroke's "Philosophical works," the essays of David Hume, and Lord Kames's *Principles of Morality and Natural Religion,* three authors who rejected those Christian beliefs which contradicted "sense" and the laws of nature.[39] Also under "Religion," however, was one near contemporary, and the only collection of Christian sermons on the list: those of the Anglican clergyman and novelist Laurence Sterne (1713–1768).

The seven-volume set of Sterne's *Sermons,* which Jefferson so admired, were not unusual as sermons, but they repeatedly stressed the individual's obligation both to self and to others. Jefferson's list of religious books, insofar as it represented an everyday course in moral-philosophical judgment, shows a certain earnestness in approaching his own obligations as a friend. The common theme on Jefferson's list is enlightenment, whether produced through literature's ability to excite the "sympathetic emotion of virtue" or through some other moral authority. In either case it reveals an inner voice which binds reason and sentiment in Jefferson.

During these intoxicating months of courtship, then, Jefferson continued to carry on his legal practice, never one to lose his Head; but he was particularly attentive to moral matters governed by the Heart, as he was aroused by the sudden opportunity to be of use to a charming, available lady. Enclosing for Skipwith his carefully tabulated list of books, "a general collection" costing thrice the £30 proposed, the at once dreamy and lucid Jefferson was careful not to hold himself at too great a distance from his less scholarly correspondent. He extended to Skipwith a warm invitation: "Come to the new Rowanty, from which you may reach your hand to a library formed on a more extensive plan. Separated from each other but a few paces, the possessions of each would be open to the other. A spring, centrically situated, might be the scene of every evening's joy. There we should talk of the lessons of the day, or lose them in Musick, Chess, or the merriments of our family companions. . . . Come then and bring our dear Tibby [Tabitha] with you; the first in your affections, and second in mine. Offer prayers for me too at that shrine to which, tho' absent, I pay continual devotion. In every scheme of happiness she is placed in the foreground of the picture, as the principal figure. Take that away, and it is no picture for me."[40]

His invitation to the "new Rowanty" was Jefferson's lighthearted manner of expressing good-fellowship. Rowantee was the name of an old Nottoway Indian village, by which Skipwith referred to his own home in Dinwiddie County that Jefferson perhaps had never visited. For Jefferson this was a playful way to equate the lives and aspirations of the two of them, brought together by their attraction to half sisters.[41] The spring he alluded to, never built, was to be a cascade whose reservoir would sit within a storied temple.[42] The "shrine" to which Jefferson paid continual devotion, of course, was Patty. Happiness was a "scheme," a state of affairs subject to design and (one might imagine) even "diagrams and crotchets" such as he had dreamed of in planning his happy shelter on the mountain. He visualized that happiness by placing Patty in his mental pictures.

The construction of Monticello was meant to support Jefferson's dual ideal of intellectual enjoyment and amiable society. As his later friendships with James Madison and others would make even clearer, he consistently pursued a life in which he could daily occupy himself with literary and philosophical interests to be shared with others, challenging conversation, music, chess, and, after Paris, exquisite dining. Having discussed "the lessons of the day," this ideal society of friends would have time for "the merriments of our family companions." And the combination of activities, as he assured Skipwith, would lighten the heart.

According to family tradition Patty was "distinguished for her beauty." She was not tall (Jefferson stood 6 feet 2½ inches), with "large, expressive eyes of the richest shade of hazel" (as were Jefferson's). She was "frank, warm-hearted and somewhat impulsive." In his reply to Jefferson's book suggestions, Robert Skipwith described Patty's quality glowingly. She had "the greatest fund of good nature . . . all that sprightliness and sensibility which promises to ensure you the greatest happiness mortals are capable of enjoying."[43]

Prophetically, her mother had died young, a week after Patty's birth in the autumn of 1748. Martha Eppes had married John Wayles in 1746 and bore twins who died and then Patty, her only child to survive. Patty's father, a successful lawyer whom Jefferson found to be "a most agreeable companion, full of pleasantry and good humor," outlived a second wife and married for a third time in 1760. In 1766, at the age of eighteen, Patty married Bathurst Skelton, then twenty-two, and gave him a son a year later. But Skelton, a college acquaintance of Jefferson, died in 1768. Presumably, this widow of two years, with a three-year-old son, met Thomas Jefferson at a party in Williamsburg. In courting her at the Forest, her father's estate located between Williamsburg and Richmond, Jefferson was fully prepared to become stepfather to the boy, who, however, died in June 1771, six months before the marriage.[44]

The wedding was held on New Year's Day, 1772, at the Forest. After the ceremony it was Jefferson, not the bride's father, who paid the Reverend Mr. Davies the marriage fee of five shillings and gave a fiddler ten. Leaving the Wayles place "after a fall of snow not very deep," the newlyweds found rougher going each mile, gave up their carriage for horseback, and arrived at a snowbound Monticello late at night, where "one of the Pavillons only was tenantable."[45] Nine months later, their first daughter, Martha ("Patsy"), was born.

This must have been a time of domestic tranquillity—to use a term of which Jefferson was fond—for it was not until Patsy was a toddler that her father began to devote considerable time to politics. In the first few years he gave attention to the productivity of his land, experimenting with new plants, such as rice. He harvested his first fruit in 1772 and added fruit trees the following year. In 1773, the year before he gave up his law practice, his receipts totaled more than the previous four years combined; he was ordering massive quantities of bricks as well as glass and glass windows.[46] Having surrounded himself with a family, Jefferson was absorbed in expanding Monticello in all directions.

THE JOY OF GRIEF

PRESUMABLY JEFFERSON HIMSELF burned the letters that he and his wife exchanged. We can only imagine what messages passed between them. We do know, however, that Jefferson's taste for poetry, later by his own assessment abandoned, was very much alive at this time. In February 1773 he wrote to a London merchant he had met in Virginia, requesting the Gaelic originals of the epic poetry of Ossian, bard of the third century A.D., that he might teach himself the ancient language. The merchant was Charles Macpherson, cousin to noted translator James Macpherson, a former classmate of Jefferson's college mentor Dr. William Small, who was reputed to have labored over the authentic reconstruction of this Celtic Homer.

But Ossian, it turned out, was a fraudulent creation. Samuel Johnson unmasked Macpherson and called him "a Ruffian" in a blunt letter of 1775. Jefferson, like the Scottish rhetorician Hugh Blair who published a commentary on the works, was not merely duped but completely overtaken by the one he admiringly termed the "rude bard." Eighteen-year-old John Quincy Adams noted in his diary in 1785, "Spent the evening with Mr. Jefferson, who is a great admirer of Ossian's poems: which he thinks are indisputedly genuine."[47]

The images of Ossian never entirely receded from Jefferson's imagination. The lengths to which he would go to explore Ossian's world, the fact that this self-demanding student who had undertaken to read Homer in the original now desired to learn Gaelic for this one purpose, indicates the depth of his interest. The dark and mysterious heroic tale stayed with him from colonial times through old age. At a point between 1768 and 1772—when he was either contemplating a home or already living at Monticello—Jefferson copied several haunting passages from his 1763 edition into his Literary Commonplace Book, so we might imagine that he read them aloud in Patty's presence. In 1773, when he buried his boyhood friend and brother-in-law, Dabney Carr, at Monticello, Jefferson contemplated lines from Ossian for Carr's tombstone inscription. He transcribed a long passage from Ossian's *Carthon* in the margin of his 1789 copy of Edward Gibbon's *The History of the Decline and Fall of the Roman Empire*. In 1799 he would write his daughter Maria that a letter of hers conjured visions of Ossian to him, "like the bright beams of the moon on the desolate heath."[48] Even later he would give the Ossianic poems as a gift to his eldest granddaughter when she was still in her teens.[49] Most revealing are the memoirs of the marquis de Chastellux, soldier and philosopher who had figured prominently at the battle of Yorktown in the fall of 1781 and arrived at Monticello on Jefferson's thirty-ninth birthday in 1782.

Describing Jefferson's home as unique and calling Jefferson "the first American who has consulted the Fine Arts to know how he should shelter himself from the weather," Chastellux praised Mrs. Jefferson, "a gentle and amiable wife." After she, eight months pregnant, had gone to bed, the men remained to converse over a bowl of punch. "We happened to speak of the poetry of Ossian," the marquis related in his memoirs. "It was a spark of electricity which passed rapidly from one to the other; we recalled the passages of those sublime poems which had particularly struck us, and we recited them for the benefit of my traveling companions, who fortunately knew English well and could appreciate them, even though they had never read the poems. Soon the book was called for, to share in our 'toasts': it was brought forth and placed beside the bowl of punch. And before we realized it, book and bowl carried us far into the night." In one of the greatest tributes ever made to Jefferson in his lifetime, Chastellux concluded that "no object has escaped Mr. Jefferson; and it seems indeed as though, ever since his youth, he had placed his mind, like his house, on a lofty height, whence he might contemplate the whole universe."[50]

Ossian spun a tale of woe and overpowering grief, of the grim-faced warrior-king who could not take pleasure in his conquest and killing. Behind the story of sword fights, gold-studded shields, and rattling armor was a manipulative purpose: to inspire readers of this sentimental suffering to uphold eighteenth-century morals, to find compassion and benevolence, to celebrate the noble human spirit and the affectionate bonds of husbands, wives, and children. By promoting the work, Scottish professor Hugh Blair, whose *Lectures on Rhetoric and Belles-Lettres* was to become a standard for Jefferson, lent his illustrious name to a cult of masculine gallantry that spread quickly to the Continent and to America.[51]

For Blair, Ossian was consistently "prompted by his feelings; and to speak from the abundance of his heart." The king's manner was simple and unforced, his sufferings "virtuous," his plaint animated with nostalgic images. With the crash of weapons in the awful tumult of battle, he found his humanity. Pathos reigns in Ossian, and natural metaphors abound. Two dark streams meet as factions collide. A retreating force is compared to clouds receding. Men and oaks fall. And the narrator Ossian's solemn voice "remains, like a blast, that roars lonely on a sea-surrounded rock, after the winds are laid." Perhaps too melancholy, wrote Blair in his final assessment of the epic, but always moral.[52]

Jefferson's response to Ossian sheds light on his overall reading of the lessons of history. In addition to imbibing the pleasures of melancholy, the "joy of grief" that Blair invoked in his *Dissertation,* the Virginian identified with the sense of manly independence associated with former ages, whether the British isles in the third century or the Romans before that. Ancient societies presented, beyond the mere events recorded in their preserved literature, a perfect picture of human manners, in Blair's words "the history of human imagination and passion." Progress could not remove what lay at the core of the human soul. Over the centuries "the understanding gains ground upon the imagination," "language advances . . . from fervour and enthusiasm to correctness and precision," and human nature is invariably "pruned according to method and rule."[53] And yet the spirit that the ancients possessed, and that animated Ossian's dark, threatening world, could be a vital element reaffirming eighteenth-century morals. The ennobling energy of the ancients, now hidden behind the poise, the cultivated tone, of the Enlightenment, was every bit retrievable.

Empathic feeling lay at the core of Jefferson's civic humanism and his commitment to the cause of a people striving for full expression through political liberty. The Enlightenment mind was restless, pursuing a sense of historic mission. On a personal level Jefferson took up the cult of feeling, the sentimental morality of Ossian, to find in literature a quality of vulnerability that was otherwise hard to embrace. Marshall Brown has observed that eighteenth-century sentiment was not productive but reactive: "Intense feelings for nature and humanity were accompanied by the intense anxieties about the integrity of the self that can be discerned . . . in the feelings of incapacity and sterility that beset so many" writers. The "drastic character of most of the best writing of these decades" was not so much "an expression of power but of debility . . . a kind of inverse solipsism, a belief that everything is real except oneself." Brown referred to a "void in the heart" which conditioned both the idealization of the past and the melancholy approach to feeling.[54]

While the cult of Ossian seemed to contrast with eighteenth-century polish, it nicely expressed the Enlightenment ideal. As one scholar has put it, "Ossian's warriors represented the best qualities of the past and present. They were surprisingly refined and polite; yet they were tenacious fighters. Their shining masculine independence was not tarnished by their appreciation of social intercourse."[55] In Jefferson polish and primitivism coexisted without apparent tension. One was of the refined moral sense, the other of the budding imagination. The exercise of reason, in other words, did not exclude the joys of imagination; indeed, the imagination could be put to the task of improving the moral character in human actions. That is what Macpherson did in writing with melancholic persuasion. And it is what Jefferson would do in his writing as well, excelling at the imaginative and the affecting, if not always self-probing or necessarily conscious (in the manner Brown described) of the self his words revealed. The noble Celtic savage opened the mind to new possibilities in liberal thought. The Jefferson who could become fired up about the poetry of Ossian could become excited about the heroic possibilities for nature-bound Americans artificially subject to an unwholesome, "effeminate" kind of British rule.

By the 1770s the image of the Scottish Highlands had come to be associated with romantic plainness and pastoral pleasure. Fearing degeneration as the land became more integrated with England, James Macpherson had sought to give his people a new historic identity by portraying the heroic deeds of their ancestors. He achieved much more, of course. The emphasis the Greeks and Romans had placed on their gods, he (in the guise of Ossian) placed on his human heroes. When the mighty Fingal displayed his power to heal, for instance, it was not through divination but through pharmacology: he understood the properties of plants. This made converts of men like Jefferson, who preferred the human realm to the supernatural. Ossian believed not in celestial intervention but in his father's memory.[56]

Chastellux's characterization of that night of Ossianic revelry suggests, too, that Jefferson was capable of intimacy during a guests's short stay. When, that autumn, he first accepted the appointment by Congress to join Franklin and Adams in France, Jefferson looked forward to making the voyage with Chastellux. He wrote to Madison of the prospect: "No circumstance of a private nature could induce me to hasten over the several obstacles to my departure more unremittingly than the hope of having the Chevalr. de Chattlux as a companion in my voiage." Outside events were to make this plan impossible. But once in Paris, Jefferson quickly looked up Chastellux, who, like John Adams, was nine years his senior. With both men Jefferson mixed warmth and deference; that is to say, deference did not inhibit warmth.[57]

Chastellux encountered Jefferson during a critical time. It was the culmination of ten years of marriage, ten years of building up the mountain, ten years of balancing private and public, combining scholarly and state enterprise; it was, in sum, the formative period in Jefferson's life. At that point, before his introduction to Europe, Jefferson the Virginian had completed his self-construction as a social being as he engaged in construction of his home on the little mountain. The night with Chastellux and his companions beside the punch bowl is important because it reveals that Jefferson was responsive to a sentimental world spawned by enigmatic forces and overcome with images of death, in which man's moral duty prevails. It shows, too, that his inner state was significantly formed by a poetic sense, a facet of his creative mind subsequently repressed, or at least not shared with many outside the family circle.

PET TREES AND MOCKINGBIRDS

THOUGHTS OF MONTICELLO brought out the most poetic of Jefferson's visions. In the autumn of 1786, from Paris, he penned a nostalgic song to his native Virginia, with emphasis on his own private mountain:

> She [Maria Cosway, the artist to whom he writes] wants only subjects worthy of immortality to render her pencil immortal. The Falling spring, the Cascade of Niagra, the Passage of the Potowmac thro the Blue mountains, the Natural bridge [near Lexington, Virginia, that Jefferson had purchased in 1774; fig. 3]. It is worth a voiage across the Atlantic to see these objects; much more to paint, and make them, and thereby ourselves, known to all ages. And our own dear Monticello, where has nature spread so rich a mantle under the eye? mountains, forests, rocks, rivers. With what majesty do we there ride above the storms! How sublime to look down into the workhouse of nature, to see her clouds, hail, snow, rain, thunder, all fabricated at our feet! And the glorious Sun,

when rising as if out of a distant water, just gilding the tops of the mountains, and giving life to all nature![58]

Twice more in the same letter, Jefferson used the word *sublime* in describing either the heights of nature or heights of feeling. The concept of a "natural sublime" had developed in England during the late seventeenth century as men journeyed through the Alps. They described a new aesthetic experience which combined delight and terror, beauty and awe. This sense of the sublime was intensified by poets, who speculated about "the infinite," and came to be associated with extremes of the imagination.[59]

In his *Lectures on Rhetoric and Belles Lettres,* Hugh Blair devoted the better part of one lecture and the entirety of another to this subject. After sections on "Genius" and "Pleasures of the Imagination," he divided the sublime into that of objects and that affecting human life. In either, he stated, the emotion raised was the same. The "moral or sentimental sublime" arose from "certain affections, and actions of our fellow creatures," in heroism, for example. The man who was above passion, above fear, "animated by some great principle to the contempt of popular opinion, of selfish interest, of dangers, or of death," struck others with a sense of the sublime. The sublime expressed "grandeur in its highest degree."[60]

Sublime writing, Blair explained, citing the classics, was not that which, like Caesar's *Commentaries,* displayed purity, simplicity, and elegance but that which, like Homer's *Iliad,* thundered with superhuman passions due to the unleashing of unusual power. The sublime needed no ornament. Nature, after all, was in dire tumult. Neither could a general description be sublime, only the specific, striking circumstance of something terrifyingly impressive. The sublime could not exist in a "middle state" but must "transport us" or "leave us greatly disgusted and displeased . . . the imagination is awakened and put upon the stretch." Citing the phrase "God said let there be light, and there was light," Blair concluded, "The main secret of being sublime is to say great things in few and plain words."[61]

Blair repeatedly cited the works of Ossian for examples of the sublime. Jefferson had read Blair's *Dissertation* when, in his 1773 letter to Charles Macpherson, he predicted that Ossian's poems would "during my life continue to be to me, the source of daily and exalted pleasure. The tender and sublime emotions of the mind were never before so

3. Natural Bridge, painting by Frederic Edwin Church, 1852. (Bayly Art Museum of the University of Virginia)

finely wrought up by human hand." Despite the questionable authenticity of the poems, Jefferson long praised Macpherson's Ossian. The volume of *Temora* that he inscribed to his eldest grandchild, Anne Cary Randolph, begins with the awe-inspiring description of a landscape before battle: "The blue waves of Ullin roll in light, the green hills are covered with day. Trees shake their dusky heads in the breeze. Grey torrents pour their noisy streams." And in a different dramatic vein, Jefferson copied into his Commonplace Book what one recent Ossian scholar has called "a sublime articulation of grief" in the episode of a father who unknowingly kills his son and dies upon the realization: "O thou that rollest above, round as the shield of my fathers! whence are thy beams, o sun! thy everlasting light? thou comest forth in thy awful beauty and the stars hide themselves in the sky; the moon, cold and pale, sinks in the western wave, but thou thyself movest alone. . . . thou lookest in thy beauty from the clouds, and laughest at the storm. But to Ossian thou lookest in vain; for he beholds thy beams no more."[62]

The sun is youth, strong and exultant, and human beings bravely but inefficiently walk the earth. Here we find a picture of the sublime which appealed to Jefferson and which he wished to invoke in his letter to Maria Cosway. Jefferson was hoping to write — if not claiming sublimity himself — in such a way as to cause that young artist to share his heart-thumping sense of the potential of human sentiment and sensuality. He sought to produce this effect, in part, with a description of that corner of nature which was his and which remained close to his heart during the years he resignedly left his memories of Patty and public-spiritedly (and with intellectual curiosity) agreed to serve abroad. It was his Heart and not his Head that wrote of Monticello, attempting a description which, in Blair's words, "raises the mind much above its ordinary state, and fills it with a degree of wonder and astonishment."[63] Jefferson sought to convey both delight and seriousness, to show that he could feel beyond his powers of description. On yet another level he employed language designed to produce visual images (for the recipient was a painter) and described the sun "gilding the tops" of the mountains.

Jefferson saw as sublime a vision which straddled the neoclassical and romantic sensibilities. It was at once awe and fear and the beginning of wisdom. Thomas McFarland has defined the difference between the two sensibilities with his own metaphor from nature: the "sun of Reason" and perfectible human nature that classicism embraced versus a paradisal external nature, "the moonlit realms of Imagination" in which romanticism would seek refuge. Henry Steele Commager has observed that Americans alone could merge classicism with romanticism without contrivance.[64] They lived at once amid rational order and virgin forest, the quantifiable and the immeasurable.

A tradition of primitivism had preceded Thomas Jefferson, and an even more articulate manifestation would succeed him. Writers of the Middle Ages had been the first to associate the wilderness with spiritual harmony and a healthy sensuality, in contrast to the conflict and immorality of markets and towns. Montaigne added to the literary convention with his essay "Of Cannibals," as did Daniel Defoe in 1719 with *Robinson Crusoe.* Jean-Jacques Rousseau was similarly inclined, and a series of late eighteenth-century European visitors to America celebrated the country's forests and the wondrous sense of abandonment in being so surrounded by nature. Other than the Ossianic reverie, Jefferson referred to the sublime exclusively in American terms. Scenes of order and calm he encountered in his European outings were merely "beautiful," insufficient to transcend human manipulation.[65] Nothing was quite so majestic, even dizzying, as Monticello or the Natural Bridge, the elevations that he had made his own.

In a further application of the concept, Jefferson called the Natural Bridge "the most sublime of Nature's works. . . . It is on the ascent of a hill, which seems to have cloven through its length by some convulsion." Crossing on foot over the "abyss" along its narrow way and looking down the more than two hundred feet to the water below, Jefferson admitted to the sensation of a violent headache. But recovering and descending into the valley, he found a new delight, that is, the beginning of wisdom. Then he added: "It is impossible for the emotions, arising from the sublime, to be felt beyond what they are here: so beautiful an arch, so elevated, so light, and springing, as it were, up to heaven, the rapture of the Spectator is really indescribable!"[66] While married to mechanical order in his cerebral pursuits, Jefferson at heart understood external nature as stormy and unruly.

The Natural Bridge that George Washington had once surveyed and Thomas Jefferson purchased from King George III, with 156 surrounding acres, was a wonder of nature its owner marveled at throughout his life. He appealed in vain not only to Maria Cosway but painter friends John Trumbull and Charles Willson Peale to capture it on canvas and led the marquis de Chastellux part way there for a visit in 1782. The last trip Jefferson made to the Natural Bridge was at age seventy-four, accompanied by two of his granddaughters.[67]

That same year, 1817, a British lieutenant named Francis Hall paid a visit at Monticello. Jefferson took him on a walk around the grounds "to visit his pet trees, and improvements of various kinds." As they stood looking at a pyramidlike mountain forty miles distant, Jefferson enraptured his guest by describing how the mountain "looms, or alters its appearance, becoming sometimes cylindrical, sometimes square, and sometimes assuming the form of an inverted cone." The host wondered aloud why such a phenomenon had yet to be named by philosophers, as *looming* was "applied by sailors, to appearances of a similar kind at sea." The Virginian had described the same phenomenon in his *Notes* thirty years before. As an old man he had not gotten — and still sought — his explanation. Others in America would cultivate a similar sense. In 1792 Harvard graduate Jeremy Belknap wrote of the White Mountains of New Hampshire as a wilderness which appealed to the "contemplative mind." He found the "wild and rugged scenes" poetic and marveled at "aged mountains, stupendous elevations, rolling clouds, impending rocks, verdant woods" able to "amaze, soothe and to enrapture."[68]

Jefferson relied on external nature to inspire man's productivity and sensitivity. According to his Account Book, he bought and kept pet mockingbirds during the first period of Monticello life. In 1793 he urged his daughter Martha to teach her young children "to venerate it as a superior being in the form of a bird." And in the President's house, he enjoyed the company of a mockingbird, of which Margaret Bayard Smith wrote: "Whenever [Jefferson] was alone he opened the cage and let the bird fly about the room. . . . Often when retired to his chamber it would hop up the stairs after him and while he took his siesta, would sit on the couch and pour forth its melodious strains. How he loved this bird! How he loved his flowers! He could not live without something to love, and in the absence of his darling grandchildren, his bird and his flowers became objects of tender care."[69]

At Monticello he took great interest in the growth of trees and shrubs, so that the cover they furnished might attract more birds, and he fed his tame deer in an enclosure on the grounds. At one time he even gave thought to inviting every wild animal "except those of prey," planning to "court" them by "laying food for them in proper places."[70] To Jefferson that part of nature which he could systematize was a friendly sanctuary, conducive to thought and worthy of his assiduous attention.

In the 1780s and 1790s Jefferson had opportunity to compare his native Albermarle, where he aimed to construct an oasis of learning in the heart of nature, with great cities as well as those rare scenes of sublimity he had encountered in his travels. Though comfortable in the court of Versailles and in the salons of Paris, he did not in any way view the pomp associated with such refinement as essential to his way of life. On the contrary, he preferred the serenity of his home, ideally surrounded by learned friends and farmers. To Jefferson, American's future as well required a strong rurally based society, free of city-bred corruptions.[71] That is, civilized man needed to assume an active role in avoiding those vices which afflicted him when "progress" placed him where his newly aroused wishes would begin to detach him from his nature-given happiness. Simplicity of character was true dignity, and the ideal state lay somewhere between the wild and the luxury-loving. In an age of self-evident truths, the most basic truth originated with the benevolence of nature. The legend of Daniel Boone was celebrated as early as 1784 and in the 1820s began to define the paradoxical requirement that the American extol both civilized refinement and a love of uncorrupted nature. With the works of James Fenimore Cooper and Henry David Thoreau, wilderness life and morality would be further joined.[72]

Jefferson had conceived the world of Monticello for himself both as a mathematical puzzle to solve and a love sonnet to past glory and present amusement. Implicitly, nature itself was at once scientifically measurable and evocative of pure poetry. In his mind Jefferson meandered from place to place from his perch atop Monticello, tempted to construe nature's symbols into delights and mysteries. It was a lifelong source of satisfaction to him that he could plant and harvest from here, provide his guests with extraordinary conversation, and scan the skies in wonder.

2　*Sensitivity and Sterne*

THOMAS JEFFERSON'S APPETITE for reading and book collecting was unmatched by his contemporaries. From an early period one author in particular symbolized Jefferson's introspection and self-defining sociability. It is through that influential figure, Englishman Laurence Sterne, that we shall continue in quest of the inner Jefferson.

In 1772 the newly wedded Jeffersons gave attention to the productivity of their mountain. According to Jefferson's Garden Book, they enjoyed its spring peas, cucumbers, Irish potatoes, and "plumb-peaches." In 1773 Patty's father, John Wayles, died, leaving a sizable inheritance which, Jefferson reported, "doubled the ease of our circumstances."[1] Patty became pregnant with their second child.

It was in 1772 or 1773 that Thomas Jefferson turned to his Literary Commonplace Book, a scrapbook of significant quotations which he had been keeping since his college days in Williamsburg, and made an entry from one of the final chapters of Sterne's popular and highly risqué novel *The Life and Opinions of Tristram Shandy, Gentleman*.[2] In the satirical tradition of Rabelais and Cervantes, this self-promoting cleric, known as much for his flirtations with women as for his affecting *Sermons*, told the sometimes bawdy, sometimes haunting story of Tristram, a man best described as a student of thought and feeling. It deals too little with action and too much with sense and reflection to be reviewed in traditional terms. Written inelegantly close to the manner of real speech, filled with comic similes such as "He pick'd up an opinion, Sir, as a man in a state of nature picks up an apple" (vol. 3, chap. 34), it is always reaching out to the reader with self-conscious sentimentalism.[3]

Near the beginning the character Tristram purposefully announces: "I have undertaken, you see, to write not only my life, but my opinions also; hoping and expecting that your knowledge of my character, and of what kind of a mortal I am, by the one, would give you a better relish for the other. As you proceed farther with me, the slight acquaintance, which is now beginning betwixt us, will grow into familiarity; and that, unless one of us is in fault, will terminate in friendship." Along with Tristram come his father, Walter Shandy, whose "vexations" with life are established "in a drollish and witty kind of peevishness," and the less apprehending Uncle Toby, "of a peaceful, placid nature" and "patient of injuries," who could not hurt a fly, literally.[4]

Yet *Tristram Shandy* is less a "story" than a deft manipulation of the reader's attention, "a grab-bag of digressions, accidents and interruptions," as two modern critics have expressed.[5] For our portrait of Jefferson's thinking, the importance of Sterne's narrative lies even more in its effect than in what it says. It is a way of looking at life, an exercise in self-definition which obscures the line between fiction and autobiography. It is a vehicle for establishing the author's principle that thought without feeling is as useless as feeling without reason (that all-encompassing Enlightenment byword, denoting the mind's vital energy in pursuing truth). The first two volumes of *Tristram Shandy* were published in 1759, the ninth and final volume in 1767. Jefferson most probably had read the first as a student at William and Mary and owned the rest by the time he began building at Monticello.

Laurence Sterne, like Thomas Jefferson, hungered for books and alluded to other authors in all he wrote (fig. 4). Like Jefferson, he amused himself by playing the violin. He sought and relished fame, but as a clown might; he performed for his public. After meeting Sterne in 1760, James Boswell composed a "poetical epistle" describing Sterne's contagious laughter, his fiddling, and his "extreamly neat" drawing. The author of *Tristram Shandy* immersed himself in what is called "the tradition of learned wit." He particularly enjoyed Shakespeare, Swift, and Pope and turned repeatedly to Locke's great epistemological work, *An Essay concerning Human Understanding* (1690). Taking Locke's dictum that nothing is in the intellect which is not first in the senses — that all ideas are derived from experience — Sterne approached his sentimental comedy with gravity. Lockean knowledge, language, and reality absorbed Sterne as much as his title character in *Tristram Shandy* and produced a suggestive blend of tragedy and comedy which, to Sterne, mirrored life.[6]

Sterne was the herald of a counterculture, who perhaps requires a mid-twentieth-century comparison to make better sense to today's reader: Sterne combined Joseph Heller's social satire with John Lennon's playful and sometimes sexual lyric. Or, as Ian Jack has suggested, "*Tristram Shandy* stands to the eighteenth-century novel much as *Waiting for Godot* stands to the well-written play."[7] Sterne sought to shock; it was his means of prompting contemporaries to be fearless in facing up to what they did not always care to speak about, their flawed humanity, their common weaknesses.

LAURENCE STERNE, A.M.
Prebendary of York &c.&c.

4. Laurence Sterne, engraving from the 1760 portrait by Sir Joshua
Reynolds, frontispiece to Sterne's *Works,* 4 vols. (London, 1808)

Moreover, Sterne was an exhibitionist. After *Tristram Shandy* had brought him fame, he unabashedly wrote a long series of sentimental letters to Eliza Draper, a much younger married woman.[8] He seemed to stand for everything that opposed modesty and virtue. Why the generally undemonstrative Jefferson thrilled to read and reread Sterne and called his writings "the best course of morality that ever was written" is a fascinating question that deserves closer scrutiny.[9]

The novel's structure defied all eighteenth-century literary conventions. In addition to the impediment to progress occasioned by the author's intrusive voice, there are chapters totally and intentionally blank, strange marks and drawings, strong sexual innuendo, and a hero who is not born until midway through the narrative. Amid this comic confusion, Sterne used words indecorously while cleverly expanding what words can do. As just one example, this is how the reader first encounters the "man-midwife" who is meant to bring Tristram into the world: Dr. Slop, "a little, squat, uncourtly figure . . . with a breadth of back, and a sesquipedality of belly," while "waddling through the dirt upon the vertebrae of a little diminutive pony," is about to have an accident with "a strong monster of a coach-horse." In crossing himself the doctor "let go his whip; — and in attempting to save his whip betwixt his knee and his saddle's skirt, as it slipped he lost his stirrup, in losing which he lost his seat: — and in the multitude of all these losses (which, bye the bye, shows what little advantage there is in crossing), the unfortunate Doctor lost his presence of mind." In the "explosion of mud" that followed, "never was a Doctor Slop so beluted, and so transubstantiated, since that affair came into fashion."[10]

There are images of falling, flying, and shifting objects. Things and ideas come at all angles, such as "Nothing is more dangerous, madam, than a wish coming sideways in this unexpected manner upon a man" (vol. 3, chap. 1). As a devoted reader and careful student of words, Thomas Jefferson appreciated Sterne's message: all that which lay behind his anarchy concerned the precariousness of language, the dual problem of literary characters — particularly Walter and Toby — failing to make themselves properly understood to one another and the author of the text frequently questioning whether he was reaching the reader as he intended.[11]

As Jefferson was and would remain keenly aware, words used in self-presentation had the potential both to enlighten and confuse. Tristram asserts: "Writing, when properly managed, (as you may be sure I think mine is) is but a different name for conversation: As no one, who knows what he is about in good company, would venture to talk all; — so no author, who understands the just boundaries of decorum and good breeding, would presume to think all: The truest respect which you can pay to the reader's understanding, is to halve this matter amicably, and leave him something to imagine, in his turn, as well as yourself."[12] Halving responsibility is typical of Sterne's disarming approach. People both give and withhold knowledge of themselves, a condition which for this author had to do not only with the understanding of words but with affections.

Astute readers were aware of the book's earthier imagery, such as a key turning in a keyhole while the subject of procreation was under consideration. Fingers and thumbs were employed as agents of pleasure. A "thing" could belong to either male or female. And by calling such attention to the literal meaning of "nose," Sterne made certain that every reader would conjure a phallus. Entering the most "pensive and melancholy" part of his writing, Tristram, generally given to "rash jerks and hair-brained squirts," noted that for once he was not "dropping thy pen — spurting thy ink about thy table and thy books."[13]

Sterne's intention was to taunt, to stop short of completing the innuendo; again, halving the responsibility in order to allow the reader to feel he had drawn his own conclusion from it. Sexuality belonged to the human condition; it was a natural part of man's curiosity and an important source of energy. In the final volume one of the characters observes ironically that "the act of killing and destroying a man" in war can be discussed without society taking umbrage, but that which creates human life is "so held as to be conveyed to a cleanly mind by no language, translation or periphrasis whatever."[14]

Tristram Shandy is playful and impulsive, gossipy and speculative, rich with fallibility when the very human characters stumble as they set forth their thoughts. But words are only one explanation for the novel's impact. Elizabeth Harries has examined the historic penchant of great authors to use blank spaces for effect, to cling to incomplete forms by intent. She averred that Sterne was aware of the manner in which Petrarch, Rabelais, Cervantes, and Swift all associated their scattered fragments with some phenomenon of chaos and disintegration — of the self, the text, or the world. Sterne wanted to destabilize the world of the narrative. His artistic purpose in this regard was "like the artificial ruins that were constructed in many eighteenth-century gardens," to emphasize "the interplay of chance and design, of the work of nature and the work of the artist." He found incompleteness energizing. Believing he could communicate certain thoughts better without words, Sterne expected the sympathetic reader to engage his imagination and provide missing (and unwritable) emotion.[15]

Seeking to uncover truths about the workings of the human mind, Sterne presumed to emulate the candid self-revelatory purpose of one of his favorites, the French essayist Montaigne (1533–1592). Both were extremely self-conscious writers who retreated into the potentially embarrassing core of personal experience in order to reach original conclusions about self-expression, conscience, private compulsions, worldly justice, and the mysteries of being and dying.[16] Sterne's detractors did not appreciate a clergyman-writer who mentally undressed in public, however. There were many who considered Sterne a ridiculous embarrassment to polite society and sought to censure him. This did not seem to bother the unconventional cleric, who thrived on ambiguity and challenge.

Then why the appeal to a man like Jefferson? Because the Virginian was eager to comprehend the human condition, and Sterne, on many levels, through dignified persuasion as much as adolescent mischief, represented invention and imagination—liberation.[17] Moreover, his digressive tendencies and unorthodox punctuation combine to unnerve the reader, to undercut all expectation of what narrative is meant to do: reach a timely conclusion. In volume 4, for example, Tristram requires five chapters to transport Toby and Walter down a staircase. The compelling effect of the narrative is to amplify time as Tristram ruminates about a life which drifts toward death.

There are throughout the book, as in Jefferson's lifelong familiar letters, potent allusions to nostalgic feeling. Obsessively, Sterne painted himself into *Tristram Shandy* as the character Yorick ("Alas, poor Yorick!" the text exclaims, the mournful words enclosed in a death-black border). Marshall Brown has written that "free speech is shadowed by death." In killing off Yorick, the authentic or "canonical Sterne," early in the work, the author left "a kind of posthumous novel. . . . The narrator becomes a ghostly ventriloquist."[18] Sterne was battling tuberculosis, which would defeat him a year after he completed the ninth volume. He imagined in fiction (at the opening of volume 7) that writing two volumes each year would bend the natural course of time and prolong his very life.

Everything could be treated with comic spirit except the very real experience of death. "Philosophy has a fine saying for everything," Tristram narrates. "For Death, it has an entire set." The primitive state of medicine in the eighteenth century resulted in high rates of infant mortality. Tristram's nose was deformed by an imperfect gadget of science, his brother Bobby died without warning; the Jeffersons' second child, born at Monticello in 1774, would live but a year and a half, and their only son, born three years later and apparently unnamed, survived less than a month. Jefferson had lost his father in 1757 and his favorite sister, Jane, in 1765. His best friend and brother-in-law, Dabney Carr, was struck down in his prime and was the first to be interred in Monticello's cemetery. Patty herself would die of complications resulting from childbirth. The comic mode in *Tristram Shandy* was designed to attract enough interest so as to relieve the tension of mortality. Remarkably, with its combination of sex, laughter, and death, the book has no ending. It is a sensory flight of fancy, time-transcendent in a way that Enlightenment rationalism proscribed, but which nonetheless affected the Heart of Jefferson.[19]

Sterne and Jefferson, in their respective media of personal self-expression, wrote with an understanding of human limitations, though the invalid Sterne felt pressed by time. The long-lived Jefferson, outwardly so durable and writing publicly with America's political inheritance in mind, was assaulted from within by an unstoical weakness he could not deny in attempting to face the losses of those he loved. In the case of his sister Jane, pain was transformed into nostalgia. He spoke of her often in his later years, commenting that "some sacred air" in church brought back her "sweet voice" and "sweet visions."[20] He would admit to his feelings in personal correspondence and unquestionably appreciated Sterne's contribution to that sensibility which provided him with the outlet.

Whether the subject was sex or mortality, Laurence Sterne helped to release pent-up emotions in affected readers. It is possible that two of his American readers needed less prompting than most. Virginia's most voracious book collector, in the process of building the elegantly imaginative Monticello, wanted to include his wife in everything that fed his dream realization. While men alone were treated to an education in the socially prescribed languages of Latin and Greek, women were encouraged to read morally uplifting fiction such as Samuel Richardson's epistolary novels and to teach their children. Patty may not have pored over the newspapers with her husband, but there seems little doubt that the Jeffersons shared, through the extensive poetry and literature they owned, a world of the imagination more developed than most, one well suited to the mountain sanctuary. As a woman not expected to look beyond beautiful sentiments in what she read, Patty Jefferson probably missed a good deal of Sterne's bawdy suggestiveness; but she would have, with her husband, picked out vignettes that highlighted the affecting potential of the human spirit.

CONSCIOUSNESS AND CONSCIENCE

THE PASSAGE FROM *Tristram Shandy* that Thomas Jefferson copied into his Commonplace Book in the early part of his marriage was not one of earthy humor, though he remembered and even repeated some of those in later years to both men and women.[21] It was rather a tender and nostalgic verse, a moving and sorrowful drama: "Time wastes too fast! every letter I trace tells me with what rapidity life follows my pen. the days & hours of it are flying over our heads like clouds of a windy day never to return more! everything presses on: and every time I kiss thy hand to bid adieu, every absence which follows it, are preludes to that eternal separation which we are shortly to make!" In his transcription Jefferson used exclamation marks in place of Sterne's colon and dashes, to dramatize the sentiment further.[22]

This passage from the ninth and final volume of Sterne's masterpiece acquired renewed value at the end of what Jefferson in his 1821 autobiography called "ten years of unchequered happiness" with Patty, as the shared sentiment of two lovers about to bid adieu.[23] In the early 1770s, of course, he was not able to anticipate this premature parting. That he was impelled to commonplace the late, controversial Laurence Sterne in a notebook otherwise filled with classical wisdom and noble verse such as Shakespeare and Milton, provides a hint of Jefferson's romantic inclinations and his open-mindedness at the time he was learning to appreciate the company of an agreeable wife.

Another side of Sterne that appealed to Jefferson came in a more standard form of moral-philosophical writing. Indeed, it has been argued that the passage which Jefferson copied into his Commonplace Book had "biblical echoes" and exemplified the quality and writing style of Sterne's *Sermons*.[24] The tone of the *Sermons* tended to reflect not torment, or death and desire, but duty toward the living and an ultimate optimism about life.

Tristram Shandy introduced the conflict between science and religion. Sterne's final book, *A Sentimental Journey,* had Yorick discovering the existence of his soul. And the *Sermons* confirmed that Sterne sought from his religious life what he called an "ounce of practical divinity" to correspond to a recognition of the limits of reason.[25] Having followed Sterne's career closely, Jefferson was doubtlessly aware that the clergyman-author, while writing with strict adherence to a biblical mode appropriate for an Anglican service, had been in close contact with the French philosophes known for their materialist views. The only way that Christianity could be compatible with Jefferson's thought was to emphasize human values over miracles and to be presented democratically. Sterne had so complied.

Sterne extensively addressed matters of moral obligation, writing that every thinking man understood whether or not he possessed a good conscience. In other matters he might be deceived, but "here the mind has all the evidence and facts within herself: — is conscious of the web she has wove." Because "conscience is nothing else but the knowledge which the mind has within itself of this," a person can know and judge himself.[26]

Note first, as Sterne's conflation of these two related words suggests, *conscience* and *consciousness* were undergoing conceptual change. During the half century before Jefferson's birth, they often traded meanings, a process which would continue well into the nineteenth century. James Buchanan's *New English Dictionary* of 1757 defined *conscious* as "self-convicted" and "inwardly persuaded," *consciousness* as the morally more demanding "guiltiness, inward conviction."[27] Samuel Johnson's 1783 *Dictionary* associated *consciousness* with Locke, as "the perception of what passes in a man's own mind," and *conscience* from Edmund Spenser, "the knowledge or faculty by which we judge the goodness or wickedness of our own actions." Dr. Johnson's second definition for *conscience* listed "justice." Subsequent lines gave "real sentiment," "difficulty," "reason," and, most notably, "consciousness; knowledge of our own thoughts or actions." Richard Steele's sentimental comedy *The Conscious Lovers* (1722) was performed in England as late as 1791 and associated the title with a mode of behavior. His "conscious" characters found "how laudable is love when born of virtue!"[28]

Jefferson himself generally favored the construction of conscience in the manner of the Scottish philosophers, as "moral sense . . . given to all human beings in a stronger or weaker degree." In the same letter he described "consciousness" as the perception that one acted under the eye of a god.[29] Writing John Adams on Socrates, he remarked that the Greek had "considered the suggestions of his conscience, or reason, as revelations, or inspirations from the Supreme mind, bestowed . . . by a special superintending providence." Rousseau was of a similar mind and stressed that conscience belonged to nature as "the voice of the soul, just as the passions are the voice of the body." Man's contentment was assured by his moral sense, aided by reason, and enacted by the freedom to choose right behavior. Whichever definition we stress, it remains that in the late seventeenth and eighteenth centuries, man was discovering his consciousness (in the modern sense of the word), his self-awareness, by examining his conscience.[30]

Moreover, the poets of this period whom Jefferson was reading in his teens and twenties (Dryden and Pope, for example) used the adjective *conscious* to express awareness both of self and one's surroundings. *Consciousness* celebrated an intimacy or communion between nature and the self. Thinkers such as Rousseau, Henri de Boulainviller, and Etienne Bonnot de Condillac addressed methods of communicating self-knowledge and modes of introspection. They emphasized verbs of perception and feeling, metaphors that noted the impossibility of escape from the self.[31] In *Don Quixote*, Frederick Garber has written, the adventures spawned by an autonomous inner life become "the adventures of a consciousness that claims the fullest self-sufficiency." *Tristram Shandy* goes further. Consciousness is the primary reality, all that is whole in the novel. "The energies of the imagination are so fully internalized that they turn in upon themselves, use themselves as characters, and shape the narrative out of their own capacity for shaping." The only order in the novel is supplied by the processes of consciousness. And, as Martin Battestin has explained, with *Tristram Shandy* "reality is now no longer something external to the individual—something 'out there' to which he must relate in prescribed ways; it has become internal and subjective, a world, as it were, of his own involuntary creating whose tenuous order, imposed by the mechanical operations of the mind organizing a multiplicity of sensations, is for each man private and arbitrary and unique."[32]

For educated and publicly active Americans of Jefferson's day, the concept of self-knowledge owed most to Locke. In *An Essay concerning*

Human Understanding, the English philosopher gave structure to personal identity. He wrote, "*Self* is that conscious thinking thing . . . which is sensible or conscious of pleasure and pain, capable of happiness or misery, and so is concerned for *itself,* as far as consciousness extends." Locke's "consciousness," the interior nature of experience from which knowledge was derived, in certain usages corresponded with the French *sentiment intérieur.* Boulainviller and Denis Diderot, dramatist-encyclopedist and good friend of Sterne, considered *sentiment* to be one of the important sources of knowledge and self-knowledge.[33]

Jefferson was expressing sentiment when he responded to Ossian and acquired the Natural Bridge. The eighteenth-century sensitivity to feeling, to beauty in nature and in moral man alike, has become known as *sensibility,* the defining ideal of the age. Poetry and literature were meant to convey sensibility not through a subtle elegance of description but by directly producing an emotional effect on readers. Sensibility, or the ethic of sentiment, became a sentimental affliction for those who possessed it; they believed themselves cursed by "finely fashioned nerves." So while the mid-eighteenth-century understanding of sentiment involved the notion of a pleasurable self-consciousness, reverie, self-enjoyment, it could be broken by the realization of sentimental "affliction." The mind was more conscious than ever before of its tremendous vulnerability before "the formative influences of uncontrollable impressions, distractions, and random events." Sentiment, in any case, led a person to a fuller appreciation of his or her humanity.[34]

The interiority of Sterne's writings, this consciousness which grips the self and energizes the self, led the author to place paramount value on moral sentiment. The external world could not be controlled, though the internal world could be if carefully nurtured. Passion constantly tested reason, as impulse challenged conscience.[35] Sterne had decided views on how the world should be; it hinged on the need for people to attain heightened self-awareness before striving for intimacy with another. The man of feeling originated with his inner voice. The self was made and remade over time as sense experience continuously begot ideas and enlarged the commitment to pursue happiness. Jefferson construed this process as a moral exercise, as he read and taught himself and fashioned himself into a model eighteenth-century gentleman.

Self-fashioning, the generation of one's identity, has been described as a "manipulable, artful process" as it came about during the Renaissance. It was part of a dialectic in which individual will was locked in continuous contest with power outside the self, that is, family and society. *Fashioning,* as the word was employed from the sixteenth century, related to the work of parents and teachers, to acts of willing deception, but also to the "representation of one's nature or intention in speech or action."[36] We can say, using this historically relevant term, that Jefferson not only absorbed what was around him but took part in fashioning himself, with the wide range of possibilities and all the tensions the word implies.

So when Jefferson recommended Sterne's *Sermons,* the one contemporary Christian text placed under "Religion" in his list for Robert Skipwith, he presumably was thinking of the natural inclinations of the private self. But he was also highly sensitive to the complexity of living in a society preoccupied with public reputation, a society in which the private self was presumed to be the same as the sincere images others saw. Jay Fliegelman has written of the "fantasy of total divulgence" and the "anxieties about self-control and self-revelation" that underlay "the creation of a new self-consciousness in an age of criticism."[37] Unquestionably, society held dominance over the individual. The self-conscious pursuit of private virtue could not be separated from one's sociability.

Sterne probed these problems. In the sermon "Self-Knowledge," he wondered how it could be that "the only creature endowed with reflection" so often and so easily deceived himself. How readily men censured others for shortcomings and transgressions they were blind to in themselves. One proceeded to discover good conscience by "retiring into ourselves, and searching into the dark corners and recesses of the heart, and taking notice of what is passing there." Sterne urged the seeker to uncover his "unsuspected passions" and the "many secret turns and windings in his heart to which he was a stranger."[38]

In "Vindication of Human Nature," he tried to harmonize the clearheaded individual with his "social virtue and public spirit." The Creator, as "all-wise contriver," intended man for "the love of society and friendship." In returning often to the biblical proposition that "no man liveth to himself," Sterne asserted that God made man in his own image "not surely in the sensitive and corporeal part of him" but in "moral rectitude" and "benevolent affections." In "Time and Chance," Sterne expressed his ultimate conviction that God seeks the "best and greatest ends for the happiness of his creatures."[39]

Sterne examined principles and motives. He believed in acts of charity, the impulse of generosity he so happily found in his fellows. He embraced obligations, civility, that which he felt placed man closer to God. He and Jefferson shared that concern with the workings of man's innate moral sense in public affairs. No reader can miss—and Jefferson surely did not fail to note—the opening sentence of Sterne's first published sermon, "Inquiry after Happiness," introducing words Jefferson later made familiar: "The great pursuit of man is after happiness; it is the first and strongest desire of his nature;—in every stage of his life, he searches for it, as for hid treasure."[40]

JUDGMENT AND WIT

IN JEFFERSON'S PRAISE of Sterne as "the best course of morality," we can link *Tristram Shandy* with the *Sermons* on the basis of the two men's shared conviction that in a world of inconstancy and turmoil, human beings are given to compassionate understanding. *Tristram Shandy* provided Jefferson with a sympathetic picture of the life he knew in which pleasures sought were frequently opposed by circumstances of human fallibility or mortality, and the *Sermons* invested the individual consciousness with the strength required to endure in a world of passions and temptations.

To attain this sensibility both Sterne and Jefferson had intellectualized Locke's celebrated discussion of the roles played by reason and emotion in thinking and self-fashioning. Locke had juxtaposed judgment and wit. The former defined the mind's capacity to analyze, to take things that seemed similar and reveal their difference. The latter defined the mind's capacity to synthesize, to take dissimilar things and reveal their compatibility.[41] Locke, like Dryden in this instance, rendered judgment, founded on experience, a mechanical operation. It is key as well to Samuel Johnson's conception of the improvability of the mind, needing memory to complete its labors. The romantic imagination would come to replace memory as that which gives stability to perception; but from Locke to Johnson, imagination, like fancy, was disparaged as an "inferior version of experience."[42] Sterne and Jefferson (most notably in the dialogue he wrote between "my Head and my

Heart") insisted that cold, mechanistic judgment cannot produce in human beings the desirable quality of compassionate understanding.

Sterne took up the theme of judgment and wit in the preface to *Tristram Shandy* (which, characteristically, appears not at the outset but in volume 3), using a playful image of these two concepts functioning as opposite knobs on the back of a chair. Both knobs — "top ornaments of the mind of man" — are necessary, he declared in the Lockean mode. While agreeing that judgment and wit together comprise intelligent thinking, Sterne challenged Locke's implication that judgment is the superior faculty. He wrote, "The great *Locke,* who was seldom out-witted by false sounds, — was nevertheless bubbled here."

Sterne's novel repeatedly demonstrates judgment's failing. The characters' differences inhibit genuine communication. Rather than engage in provocative dialogue, they voice their intellectual obsessions, which causes them to speak at cross-purposes: Toby talks incessantly of fortifications, Walter of noses. It is only when the characters emerge from their self-absorption, even for brief moments, that, aided by wit (here meaning sentiment or imagination), they become cognizant of qualities they possess in common with others. For example, in the course of an argument, Walter is able to reconcile with Toby when their gazes suddenly meet and his brother's goodness "penetrated [Walter] to his heart."[43] It is precisely at such moments that they come to represent the moral heights to which dignified human beings can ascend. Absorbing the message of Sterne, the sensitive and sociable Thomas Jefferson, who understood writing as an inherently moral activity — as a test of character — was able to communicate with a strong consciousness of his duty to humanity; indeed, it was his sympathetic emotion, his idea of compassionate understanding for others, that drew him into public debate.

Sterne ended his preface with the printer's fist and its pointed finger to signal an ironic injunction. He wrote not for "great wigs" and "long beards," for those self-important men who take themselves and their ideas too seriously; he knew they could not appreciate his wit. The democratic Jefferson, speaking of friendship, was similarly predisposed in "My Head and My Heart": "Wealth, title, office, are no recommendations to my friendship. On the contrary great good qualities are requisite to make amends for their having wealth, title and office." Even as a nineteen-year-old student Jefferson was skeptical of the powdered wig, the "old-fellows," the type who "parfumes most, embroiders most"; yet he accepted the requirement that he read their works to gain that knowledge which provided a young man the tools to compete in colonial society.[44] Jefferson embraced Sterne's moral lessons no less than the elders' orthodoxy, but he valued Sterne's that much more for their lack of pretentious judgment and for that certain vehicle — sympathetic and imaginative wit — which conveyed them.

Jefferson believed that "style, in writing or speaking, is formed very early in life, while the imagination is warm, and impressions are permanent."[45] To judge from this statement, and by what he read, we must assume that he considered the greatest influence on (at least) his public writing style to have been the ancients, adding, not insignificantly, the English rationalist Lord Bolingbroke (1678–1751), whose philosophical beliefs exceed all others on the pages of the Commonplace Book. Moreover, Bolingbroke's defense of liberty against parliamentary corruption figured prominently in the American Revolutionaries' political rhetoric. His was "a style of the highest order," which Jefferson in his late years compared to the "lofty, rhythmical, full-flowing eloquence of Cicero. Periods of just measure, their members proportioned, their close full and round . . . His writings are certainly the finest samples in the English language of the eloquence proper for the senate."[46] For poetic inspiration the young Jefferson had turned to the epics of Homer and Ossian. He appreciated, too, the soulful imagery of Alexander Pope, noted translator of the *Iliad* and an intimate of Lord Bolingbroke. But to sustain his moral tone without being didactic, to enhance his emotional appeal in a world whose order might be threatened with disintegration at any time, he drew philosophically on the wit of Sterne.

"Time Wastes Too Fast!"

LIFE BEGAN TO follow Jefferson's pen. In the spring of 1774 he became intensely involved in Virginia's effort to support its sister colonies in opposing Parliament's authority. That summer he wrote *A Summary View of the Rights of British America,* a document addressed to the king "with that freedom of language and sentiment which becomes a free people." Considered too bold or premature by most in the Virginia legislature, this resolution caused a stir in England and led American leaders on a national scale to take notice of the thirty-one-year-old Virginian who had composed it.[47]

Jefferson's *Summary View* represents the imaginative expression of its author to a greater degree than the subsequent Declaration of Independence. It is premised on the notion that Americans had always been a distinct people, and that like the Saxons before them, they had left one country to resettle freely in another without giving up their natural right to choose their government. Jefferson's premise rests more on a moral than a legal foundation and is directed at the king himself. Hidden in language of conciliation ("fraternal love and harmony") is an open-ended threat: "The god who gave us life, gave us liberty at the same time: the hand of force may destroy, but cannot disjoin them. This, Sire, is our last, our determined resolution." The buildup to this resolution is a heartrending progression, quintessential Jefferson, who, midway through the document, affectingly shifted the emotional refrain from third person singular ("his majesty" or "his majesty's governor of the colony of Virginia") to the second person singular ("your majesty or your Governors"). "Open your breast Sire, to liberal and expanded thought," Jefferson declared as he neared his final appeal. "Let not the name of George the third be a blot in the page of history. . . . The whole art of government consists in the art of being honest." Moral sentiment and sensitivity, in Jefferson's view, must command the hearts of all human beings, but especially public servants such as his sovereign, whom he reminded directly that "kings are the servants, not the proprietors of the people."[48]

As a founder of the Virginia Committee of Correspondence at about this time, Jefferson clearly embraced national concerns from the start of his political writing career. When in 1775 failing health obliged Peyton Randolph, recently replaced by John Hancock as chair of the Continental Congress, to return to Virginia, Jefferson was elected to succeed him. He took to those responsibilities which utilized his ability to write, carefully producing each paper with an emphasis on moral issues, as he began to move in the circle that included Benjamin Franklin and John Adams.[49]

Jefferson was away in Richmond, Williamsburg, and Philadelphia for several months in the spring and summer of 1775, returning to Patty only briefly. He remained in Philadelphia again from October 1 through Christmas. During this time he wrote to his wife often, as attested by repeated shorthand injunctions to Patty's brother-in-law Francis Eppes: "For the particulars of that melancholy event I must refer you to Patty," or, "To her therefore for want of time I must refer you." As Jefferson's responsibilities enlarged and time passed, the unreliability of the post caused him much concern. He reported to Eppes that he had been trying unsuccessfully to obtain news of his wife and family. "The suspence under which I am is too terrible to be endured."[50]

In the fateful year 1776, Jefferson was at home when his mother died on March 31, but he left on May 8 for Philadelphia, giving Patty £10 for expenses. He purchased paper, toothbrushes, and a half pound of tea and had his watch repaired.[51] On June 7 Richard Henry Lee of Virginia introduced a resolution of independence, and on June 11 Congress appointed a committee of five — Jefferson, Adams, Franklin, Roger Sherman of Connecticut, and Robert Livingston of New York — to produce a text expressive of the already unanimous decision to separate from Great Britain.

Unlike the self-inspired *Summary View,* the Declaration that Thomas Jefferson was called upon to draft was meant as a composite of the thought of many, the joint resolve of thirteen culturally distinct, independent states. In undertaking this monumental task, Jefferson drew equally from a reasoning mind and a sensitive heart to synthesize, with a particular lyrical intensity, both the sentiment and vision of his countrymen. Congress deleted certain language reminiscent of his *Summary View,* such as that concerning the voluntary population of North America "at the expence of our own blood & treasure, unassisted by the wealth or the strength of Great Britain." Depiction of the Americans as "a people fostered & fixed in principles of freedom" was apparently deemed redundant. Congress also expunged from the draft Jefferson's "acquiescence" to the "necessity" of *"eternal separation,"* a significant (if perhaps unconscious) borrowing from the Commonplace Book entry of Sterne's nostalgic passage of two lovers shortly to be separated by death. In spite of these changes, and writing with precision and fluency, Jefferson achieved the logical and stylistic balance that makes the Declaration a still powerful expression of America's determination to stand out in a world of disturbances, political and moral.[52]

On July 4, 1776, the day Congress adopted his Declaration, Jefferson bought a thermometer, gave money to charity, and purchased seven pairs of women's gloves.[53] He remained in Philadelphia through early September, discussing the terms of confederation. Almost immediately after his return, Patty became pregnant for the third time; but on this occasion he only stayed at Monticello a fortnight before riding to Williamsburg. Once again he did not return until Christmas. He was present in May 1777 when Patty bore his only son, who survived less than three weeks.

Throughout this period of excitement and danger, Jefferson juggled responsibilities. Letters, of course, framed his day and affected his state of mind. As public affairs took him away from Monticello, he was obliged to rely on the mails to sustain emotional connections. He would have reason, now and throughout his life, to despair over a lack of security in the system of delivery. Regular correspondents were careful to acknowledge letters received and sometimes recapped their most recent letter before proceeding. This was the only means to clear up confusion arising from undelivered letters. From Congress, Jefferson used irony to reflect on the ways of the post: "I have set apart nearly one day in every week since I came here to write letters. Notwithstanding this I never had received a scrip of a pen from any mortal breathing. I should have excepted two lines from Mr. Pendleton to desire me to buy him 24. lb of wire from which I concluded he was alive."[54]

Personal pressures heaped upon the nature of communications and the uncertainty of the Revolution's course made life for the author of the Declaration of Independence constantly unnerving. Jefferson was a man who prized self-control, whose emotional makeup was such that any perception of disorder had to be opposed with heightened mental (ordering) activity. He thus immersed himself immediately in legislative affairs back in Williamsburg, reconceiving laws and seeking consensus among his fellows. When daughter Maria was born during the summer of 1778, he was enjoying a certain amount of leisure at Monticello, planting fruit trees and manufacturing tens of thousands of bricks to resume building his home. He had time for music and to correspond on the event of a solar eclipse. In early 1779 British and German prisoners of war were quartered in Jefferson's neighborhood, affording his family the unexpected company of their polite, musical officers and wives who rented a nearby estate.[55]

From June of that year until June 1781, he served as governor of Virginia, a time of financial weakness for his state and an emotional low point for his people. Many of Virginia's sons were fighting outside the state when the British determined to carry the war there. Jefferson, at least, was able to stay close to his family during these years, settling them first in the stately Governor's Palace in Williamsburg and then at a humbler residence in less vulnerable Richmond, to which Jefferson had urged the state government to relocate. The governor proved himself far better at constructive tasks over which he exercised his creative power (restructuring the professorships at the College of William and Mary in 1779 and researching and writing his *Notes on Virginia* from 1780 on) than in marshaling meager resources to defend the vast war-torn territory under his administration. In his 1821 *Memoir* Jefferson chose not to recall his years as governor in any detail, referring readers to a "public history" by Girardin and denying history any personal reflections of the time.[56] While making a favorable impression on the courageous marquis de Lafayette, who commanded the army that faced the encroaching forces of Cornwallis in Virginia, Jefferson was chased from office in June 1781 at the end of his two one-year terms by a raiding party under Colonel Banastre Tarleton. The erstwhile governor took his family to his remote Poplar Forest property in the vicinity of the Natural Bridge as redcoats climbed to Monticello itself. He only returned to the protected retreat of his mountain world when the threat of British occupation ended.

The death of Patty Jefferson in September 1782 marked a turning point in the history of Monticello and in the manner in which Thomas Jefferson expressed prospects for his personal future. As early as July 1776, he had shown concern for his wife's fragile constitution, writing John Page from Philadelphia that "every letter brings me such an account of her state of health, that it is with great pain I can stay here." A few days later he wrote Page again with war news, adding fresh concern: "I am under the painful necessity of putting off my departure, notwithstanding the unfavorable situation of Mrs. Jefferson's health."[57] Cornwallis had surrendered in October 1781, at the start of Patty's sixth and final pregnancy, and Jefferson's official responsibilities were few. It was, he thought, the end of his active political life. He had plans to enjoy his growing family.

The Jeffersons' firstborn, Martha, was ten years old when she lost her mother. She later wrote: "He [Jefferson] nursed my poor mother in turn with aunt Carr [Dabney Carr's widow, Jefferson's sister] and her [Patty's] own sister—sitting up with her and administering her medicines and drink to the last. For four months that she lingered he was never out of calling; when not at her bedside, he was writing in a small room which opened immediately at the head of her bed. A moment before the closing scene, he was led from the room in a state of insensibility by his sister, Mrs. Carr, who, with great difficulty, got him into the library, where he fainted, and remained so long insensible that

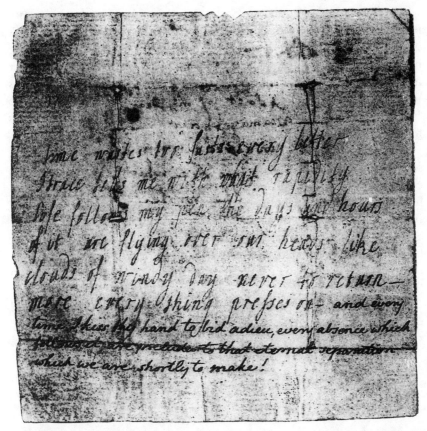

5. Note written by Thomas and Patty Jefferson before September 6, 1782. Jefferson kept this precious souvenir close at hand for the remainder of his life. (Courtesy of James Monroe Museum and Memorial Library, Fredericksburg, Va.)

they feared he never would revive." Martha reported that her father remained to himself for weeks, walking "almost incessantly, night and day," until he fell exhausted. When at last he emerged from this stupor, Jefferson rode horseback with his daughter five or six miles a day, "rambling about the mountain," occasionally bursting into tears.[58]

Before she died, Patty Jefferson either copied from the Commonplace Book or wrote from memory the first part of the passage from Sterne: "Time wastes too fast: every letter I trace tells me with what rapidity life follows my pen. the days and hours of it are flying over our heads like clouds of windy day never to return — more [.] every thing presses on" (fig. 5). This is one of only a few surviving samples of her writing, showing a clear hand. Each sentence is begun with a lowercase letter, in the manner of her husband. But she did not complete Sterne's quote. She raised her pen, and presumably right then, at her bedside, her husband finished the passage for her. Conceiving it at that particular moment to be set as a dialogue between a husband and wife, Thomas Jefferson took his cue, continuing on the same line: "— and every time I kiss thy hand to bid adieu, every absence which follows it, are preludes to that eternal separation which we are shortly to make!"[59]

The paper on which these lines were written was found after Jefferson's death forty-four years later "in the most secret drawer of a private cabinet which he constantly resorted to," together with a lock of Patty's hair and the golden curl of a daughter who died in infancy, and "various other souvenirs of his wife, and each of his living and lost children . . . all arranged in perfect order, and the envelopes indicated their frequent handling." On the back of the 4½-inch-square note, the mature Martha recorded: "A lock of my Dear Mama's Hair inclosed in a verse which She wrote."[60]

Mrs. Jefferson was buried in the Monticello cemetery. Her husband inscribed a long epitaph:

To the Memory of
MARTHA JEFFERSON
Daughter of John Wayles;
Born October 19th, 1748, O.S.;
Intermarried with
THOMAS JEFFERSON
January 1, 1772;
Torn from him by Death
September 6, 1782:
This Monument of his Love is inscribed.

Below, Jefferson added a Greek epitaph taken from the *Iliad* of Homer, honoring the unbanishable memory of the best friend of a lifetime: "Nay if even in the house of Hades the dead forget their dead, yet will I even there be mindful of my dear comrade."[61]

We can understand what love they had, what love Jefferson lost (or, in his revealing words, had "Torn from him"), and what life on the mountaintop was like by the empathic picture Jefferson painted for James and Elizabeth Monroe shortly after they were wed. He suggested, before having met her, that Mrs. Monroe "will find that the distractions of a town, and waste of life under these, can bear no comparison with the tranquil happiness of domestic life. If her own experience has not yet taught her this truth, she has in it's favor the testimony of one who has gone through the various scenes of business, of bustle, of office, of rambling, and of quiet retirement, and who can assure her that the latter is the only point upon which the mind can settle at rest. Tho not clear of inquietudes, because no earthly situation is so, they are fewer in number, and mixed with more objects of contentment than in any other mode of life."[62]

Within weeks of Patty's death, Jefferson wrote feelingly to Elizabeth Wayles Eppes, one of his wife's half sisters. He noted that his daughters were in good health and "as happy as if they had no part in the immeasurable loss we have sustained." He termed his own existence "miserable," "too burthensome to be borne," with "all my plans of comfort and happiness reversed by a single event." He vowed to delay his visit to the Eppes home until he could "support a countenance as might not cast a damp on the chearfulness of others." Recovering, he explained to Chastellux in November that he had been rendered "as dead to the world as she was whose loss occasioned it. Your letter [unanswered for over a month] recalled to my memory, that there were persons still living of much value to me." He apologized for failing to answer the Frenchman's earlier letter, received during Patty's illness, reiterating how affected he had been by "the dreadful suspence in which I had been kept all the summer and the catastrophe which closed it." He made it clear that if his wife had remained healthy, he had been unshakably determined to retire permanently to Monticello, shunning all other pursuits and content with his contribution to American independence.[63]

This question of his public commitments must have been a long, running battle between Jefferson and his wife and within Jefferson himself. In the summer of 1776, Edmund Pendleton had expressed "lament that it is not agreeable and convenient to you" to serve longer in Congress. He suggested that if Jefferson could be joined by his wife, "I hope you'l get cured of your wish to retire so early in life from the memory of man." It would have been acceptable, by the classical standard of leadership, for Jefferson to have retired at this time, just as George Washington would retire in 1783 at war's end, a moral hero as well as a military one.[64] He and Patty each had suffered from his long absences. If it was true that he had finally, firmly yielded to a life committed to "domestic and literary objects," then Patty's loss alone forced

Jefferson to heed his friends' call to return to affairs of state. Merrill Peterson has assessed Jefferson's growth during the period of his withdrawal. Reemerging after the process of mourning, he could now "take adversity in stride, stoically shore up his feelings, and view the favored life of retirement with more becoming modesty." Jefferson's character did not change but was improved in "balance and resiliency." He was "stronger and wiser" when he returned to public life.[65]

He stabilized his mind by thinking of his children's education. He placed four-year-old Maria and the infant Lucy Elizabeth in the Eppeses' charge while he accepted an overseas posting. Only Patsy would accompany him, in December 1782, on his journey to Philadelphia and beyond. By rejoining Congress, Jefferson spent only limited time at the home whose construction and maintenance now brought to mind his irreparable loss.

In the two years between Patty's death and his setting sail for Europe, Jefferson was at Monticello only from May to October 1783. Upon departure from Monticello at this latter date, he began his Summary Journal of Letters, an orderly index of all the letters he wrote and received, a means of remaining in touch with people while away from his well-ordered home. His letters during those five months of residence on the mountain evince little of emotional content, except for one to James Madison, recently jilted by a young woman.

Sixteen-year-old Kitty Floyd, Madison's intended, was an acquaintance of eleven-year-old Patsy Jefferson during the stay in Philadelphia in 1782–83; the two girls on at least one occasion used Madison as a courier for their letters. Before returning to Monticello that spring, Jefferson had taken a close interest in the match. An encouraged Madison recounted to his friend in April "pleasing proof that the dispositions which I feel are reciprocal." When Jefferson subsequently received Madison's unhappy news in August, not quite eleven months after he lost Patty, he lamented "the misadventure which has happened from whatever cause it may have happened. Should it be final however, the world still presents the same and many other resources of happiness, and you possess many within yourself. Firmness of mind and unintermitting occupations will not long leave you in pain."[66] Jefferson was articulating what his own recourse had been, the need to steel oneself to the experience of loss by becoming immersed in public affairs. In Madison's case he raised the prospect that other amorous opportunities would present themselves, but he granted himself no early release of the pain he was enduring.

A letter to Eliza House Trist at the end of 1783 showed another side of Jefferson during this awkward period. This sensitive, good-hearted Philadelphia friend was pining for her absent husband and had determined to search the area of the Mississippi where he was last seen. As Jefferson's and Madison's landlady, she had seen the widower of three months upon his arrival at Congress the previous year and no doubt had occasion to hear of his sorrow. Now he was writing to her, commiserating, "I hope the day is near when Mr. Trist's return will make amends for the crosses and disappointments you complain of." Convinced that hers was only a temporary parting, he urged her to appreciate that she was not one of "the many wretched" who were barred from the consolation of a prospective reunion. "They [the wretched] will tell you it is from heaven you are looking down on them," he related in transparent imagery. "It is not easy to reconcile ourselves to the many useless miseries to which Providence seems to expose us." It certainly seems that Jefferson's words were at once meant to soothe the recipient of his letter and suggest a partial reprieve for his own troubled soul. But in the next breath, he took a fanciful turn. Projecting Mrs. Trist into the Mississippi wilderness, he supposed: "If you chuse to live in the woods, you may find them nearer. I have much to say in favour of those of my own country, and particularly of that part of it in which I live." He would be on the lookout for "some of the tallest and most recluse I can find. I have now in my eye a mountain where nothing but the eagle can visit you which I think would suit your present taste for retirement. It looks down on mine as a giant does on a dwarf. It wants but one circumstance to render it perfect, which is that it should be placed within a dozen miles of Philadelphia, or rather Philadelphia within a dozen miles of it."[67] Perhaps by this vision Jefferson meant to describe a state of peace and tranquillity, which he still associated with a reclusive mountaintop. As a modest friend, he placed hers above his and, understanding her attachment to Philadelphia, brought that city to the vicinity of her mountain. Or there may be more to Jefferson's words. In his eye, he stated, was a place too high for any but the eagle, thus very close to heaven. With a fantastic bent, he conjured a mountain which was poised to challenge the supremacy of nature's forces, and he introduced a bird which symbolizes wisdom and virtue.[68] The association may be seen to reflect on his dejected state, his still fresh memory of Patty's flight from the mountaintop he had now left behind.

Moreover, from Paris in 1785 he would write a letter to Abigail Adams, combining a reference to Ovid's story of Phaeton, racing uncontrolled across the sky in the Sun's chariot, with the metaphor "learn us the way to heaven on wings of our own." With hardly a breath, he then gave an account of a recent visit to the home of a French noblewoman wherein he compared the French nightingale to the "superior" American mockingbird. And to Maria Cosway, not long after, he would write, "I wish they had formed us like the birds of the air, able to fly where we please." The repetition of such imagery—birds, wisdom, and the way to heaven—could hardly be accidental. Wishing to be where there was love, Jefferson envied (at least rhetorically) the winged creatures of nature. While fantasizing a means to fly from personal problems, he did not cease to find frustration in invoking such imagery; his note to Maria Cosway continues: "When clambering a mountain, we always hope the hill are on is the last. But it is the next, and the next, and still the next."[69] It was to women that he typically addressed such fanciful notions, presumably because he felt that they would understand outpourings of emotion, whether these were intentionally self-probing or unintendedly self-revealing. Like Laurence Sterne, he longed for feminine sympathy. Like Sterne, he was absorbed with chaos and consciousness.

In Sterne's enigmatic Shandean world, as in Locke's theory, there is no consistent, commonly understood reality. In Sterne's manipulation of Locke, as in Jefferson's literary flights of fancy, isolation of the self and the insufficiency of reason—in short, the uncertainty that prevails in reality as perceived by each writer—elicit expressions of sentiment and imagination. These represent an effort to control events that may in fact be beyond control. "The order we impose on the world and in terms of which we govern and solace our lives," Martin Battestin has written, thinking of Sterne, "is equivalent to Truth, that our private ontologies may substitute for Reality."[70]

The writings of Sterne had given to Jefferson first an imaginative counterweight to the workaday requirements of his law practice, then a pleasing format for the acquisition of moral lessons, and finally a precedent to draw on in expressing sentiment. Sterne had helped him to recognize and to deal philosophically with the human condition. Jefferson was impressed by Sterne's creative manipulation of words to startle, awaken, and sensitize readers.

Jefferson was not alone among sophisticated Americans in pursuing a creative outlet through the artistic manipulation of Sterne's world. New Jersey–born William Dunlap (1766–1839), sometimes called the father of American drama, left his native shore the same year Jefferson did, 1784, to study portrait painting under Benjamin West, the accomplished Pennsylvanian who had established his studio in London in 1763. Perhaps, as in Jefferson's case, Dunlap had been taken with Sterne earlier and became more intensely smitten during his time abroad. In any event, on his return home in 1787–88 he wrote a play which he called *The Father: or American Shandy-ism*. It was performed before enthusiastic audiences in New York the next year. The characters have Shandean names and peculiarities: Doctor Quiescent, familiarly called "Quizzy," is a clownish, half-witted man claiming to have received his degree at Edinburgh (where talented Americans like Benjamin Rush went to study medicine) after writing "a thesis upon recovering drowned kittens." He tells a story about a "concatenation" of broken bones. There is in Dunlap's play a Widow Grenade, to correspond to Sterne's Widow Wadman, and an opening scene in which Mr. Racket sports a "patch across his nose" and reads a newspaper while his wife berates him for his inattention to her. Soon the audience learns that his nose was injured by a fall from a cow, yet the sexual suggestion is sustained by the appearance of the villainous British captain Ranter, who makes known his intention of seducing Racket's wife. At one point Cartridge, aide to the prominent Colonel Duncan, even invokes Sterne directly, saying, "When his honour was wounded, I used to set by his bed side and read to him his favourite stories out of *Tristram Shandy* till he forgot his long confinement, and his pain." In order to illustrate the colonel's benevolence, Cartridge recasts the encounter of Tristram's uncle Toby and the fly he refused to harm. "I'll not hurt thee," Toby remarks in the novel. "This world surely is wide enough to hold both thee and me." In Dunlap's play the fly becomes a mosquito, and the colonel is quoted, "'I can forgive thee,' says he, 'thou actest up to thy nature.'"[71]

The popular acceptance of Sterne among his American readership produced a rich idiom for expressing a range of emotions.[72] During his upcoming five years in Europe, Jefferson would have occasion to uncover new meaning in Sterne, prompted by that author to undertake imaginative exercises in writing.

3   The Sensations of Europe

AT THE END of a month's transit through Connecticut, Rhode Island, and Massachusetts, Jefferson sailed to Europe from Boston on July 5, 1784, aboard the *Ceres;* it was only the second crossing for this vessel named for the golden-haired Roman goddess of agriculture. He was accompanied by his daughter Martha ("Patsy"), Monticello slave James Hemings, Colonel Tracy, who owned the vessel, and just three other "select" passengers. The voyage to England was a brisk nineteen days under pleasant skies. Jefferson dined well and recorded in his Account Book each noon the temperature, wind direction, and such "miscellaneous circumstances" as sightings of a whale and a Portuguese man-of-war. After a brief stopover in Portsmouth, England, for the feverish Patsy to see a doctor, the Jeffersons crossed the Channel, rode over an impressively fertile landscape near harvest time ("a perfect garden," Patsy wrote), and arrived in Paris in early August.[1]

John Dos Passos has described the city that Jefferson saw from his carriage: "Narrow thoroughfares that skirted huddles of medieval dwellings packed around Gothic churches and abbeys and huge fortifications like the Bastille. . . . Driving through one of the crowded thoroughfares that cut through the city, hemmed by blocks of tall houses of pale stucco, the traveler was occasionally refreshed by the sight of trees in a paved open space, or a fountain set about with market stalls." Jefferson would become intrigued with new structures rising in Paris, such as the Palais Royal, which contained a covered promenade, shopping arcade, restaurants, and a salon where he might challenge the local chess masters. The nearby Halle aux Bleds, municipal grain market, was a celebrated rotunda whose wood-ribbed dome allowed sunlight to stream through its radiating glass sections. Here the Virginian received inspiration for the design of public buildings he would propose after his return home.[2]

He renewed acquaintances with Benjamin Franklin and John Adams, his esteemed colleagues who had remained in Europe after negotiating the 1783 Treaty of Paris, which acknowledged American independence. Together they now aimed to promote America's commercial interests, hoping to defeat the monopolistic policies of smug European governments. After two months in temporary lodgings, Jefferson rented a modest, unfurnished townhouse on the cul-de-sac Taitbout. While Patsy attended school at the exclusive Panthémont convent, he resided here for precisely one year from October 1784, hiring servants and a coachman, ordering ample bookshelves built, and entertaining fellow Americans regularly. William Short, his protégé from Virginia and soon-to-be private secretary, arrived just as Jefferson was getting his place in order and lived here with him, as did Colonel David Humphreys, the dour but intelligent former aide to Washington who was serving as secretary of the congressional commission. Young John Quincy Adams was a regular visitor, too.[3]

It was here in January 1785 that the marquis de Lafayette, arriving from America, delivered word to Jefferson of the death of his toddler, Lucy Elizabeth, of whooping cough in Virginia.[4] In all, his first six months of residence in Paris were neither smooth nor triumphant. In December 1784 Jefferson wrote Madison that he looked "with fondness to the moment when I am again to be fixed in my own country." To Monroe, at the same time, he aired his frustration over inordinate delays in delivery of mail to and from France, owing to backward postage collection procedures in New York. He anguished, in cipher, about housing and travel expenses, for which he hoped he would not be held personally responsible. A few weeks later he wrote Monroe again, anxious because the keys to their ciphers did not work, rendering messages to one another incoherent. "We are as yet quite uninformed whether Congress has met, where they are sitting, who is their president, what they are doing, how long they expect to sit, and every thing else relative to them." Jefferson seemed disheartened. "It seems as if all the powers had become torpid with the winter." And to Monroe once more in March, "I have had a very bad winter, having been confined the greatest part of it. A seasoning as they call it is the lot of most strangers: and none I beleive have experienced a more severe one than myself. . . . We have had for three weeks past a warm visit from the sun (my almighty physician) and I find myself almost reestablished."[5]

Jefferson's move in October 1785 to the more impressive Hôtel de Langeac on the Champs Elysées near the city gate that led to Versailles was occasioned by his succession of Franklin as American minister at the court of Louis XVI. As Malone has written, Franklin had been a marvel to the French, "first citizen of the world," "the embodiment of science, philosophy and simplicity." This cult hero, whose name had been linked with those of Voltaire and other great minds, effortlessly managed to charm the French into presuming that he, as much as Washington, had clinched victory for the new Republic. At his villa in Passy on the road to Versailles, Franklin surrounded himself with admiring neighbors, including uninhibited women whom he enjoyed teasing.[6]

Franklin returned to America in July. Adams had learned of his own appointment as envoy to Great Britain in May and departed shortly, leaving Jefferson to conquer Paris quietly. At the Hôtel de Langeac he cultivated his own garden with vegetables reminiscent of life in Albemarle. Short continued with him. The American minister entertained fellow countrymen passing through and from time to time members of the French nobility. The thirty-year-old Connecticut-born painter John Trumbull, studying under Benjamin West in London, became a favorite of Jefferson in 1786 and lived with him for a time. After nine-year-old Maria's arrival in the summer of 1787, joining her sister at the convent school, happy children's voices were added periodically to intimate, conversational, wine-accented dinners. Martha recorded that her father's "habits of study in Paris &c were very much what they were else where."[7]

Becoming More Useful to the World

Even before he achieved national prominence as the author of the Declaration of Independence, Jefferson had sought out European correspondents and attempted to build cosmopolitan connections. He had welcomed Lafayette to Virginia in the heat of war and so impressed the young war hero that he predicted the Virginian would one day accept a foreign appointment. He had entertained Hessian officers Baron de Riedesel and Baron de Geismar at Monticello during their months of captivity, enjoying music and merriment with these French-speaking prisoners. And he had acquired an Italian neighbor, the entrepreneur Philip Mazzei, in 1773.[8]

This effusive Florentine, a half generation older than Jefferson, was touring America with Jefferson's tobacco broker, Thomas Adams, whom he had met in London. During a walk with the owner of Monticello at dawn the day after he arrived, Mazzei's magnetic host convinced him to purchase four hundred acres next door. Mazzei's retinue of laborers were astonished by Jefferson's ability to converse in Italian, a language he had taught himself to read but had had no occasion to speak. Soon Mazzei attempted a bold venture in the cultivation of grapes for wine and mulberry trees for silk, aided by investments from Jefferson, John Page, George Washington, and other Virginians. The company might have succeeded had war not intervened. Nevertheless, Mazzei found the people of Albemarle County intelligent and kind, fell in love with America, and gladly represented the commercial and political interests of his adopted country on return trips to Europe. He wrote in his memoirs that after 1782 "in Jefferson's house I had been greatly saddened by the memory of his angelic late wife, a sadness that solitude made even more deeply felt." The vacuum left by Jefferson's departure led Mazzei to follow his friend to Europe, where, after one dinner together, he noted of his sensitive friend that "Mr. Jefferson read on my face what I felt in my heart."[9]

Mazzei had prepared for his erstwhile neighbor a detailed memorandum describing the personalities Jefferson was likely to encounter and those whom he should seek out in Paris for intellectual stimulation. Heading that list was Louis Alexandre, duc de La Rochefoucauld, "one of the greatest and most singular geniuses of the age." Writing Jefferson on the eve of his departure, another Americanized European, St. John de Crèvecoeur, called that aristocrat "the pearl of all the Dukes a Good Man and a most able Chemyst. His House is the Cente[r] of [reunion] where Men of Genius and abilities Often Meet. You have therefore a great Right To Share his Friendship." The French-born writer then concluded: "I wish you health and plenty of friends. I hope you'll be pleased with our Social Scène, which is the shining side of our nation."[10]

At first Jefferson was hampered by what he recognized as his deficiency in spoken French. It was not until mid-1786, when he had been in France nearly two years and minister for one, that he appeared truly comfortable. Official negotiations had met with mixed results, but his personal life certainly had become more fulfilling. Convivial John Trumbull was enjoying Jefferson's hospitality, as the American minister wrote his predecessor, Dr. Franklin, in August: "Nothing worth reading has come through the press, I think, since you left us. . . . Europe enjoys a perfect repose at present. . . . Your friends here, within the circle of my acquaintance, are well, and often enquire after you. No interesting change that I recollect has taken place among them." Jefferson had at last settled in. He had visited John Adams and family in London that spring, an experience which deepened the cooperative sentiment shared by those two men. To David Humphreys, Jefferson wrote gaily: "Lafayette is on summer holiday and the rest of the beau monde are also vanished for the season. We give and receive them you know in exchange for the swallows." A year earlier Jefferson had written Abigail Adams that he loved the French "with all my heart," comparing them favorably to the "proud" and "carnivorous" English. When he wrote her in August 1786, he observed, "Here [in Paris] we have singing, dancing, laugh, and merriment."[11]

He took advantage of his connections and frequented the philosophic salons, that unique Paris institution responsible for spreading the Enlightenment. Salons had begun as *salons de compagnie,* where friends gathered for games, music, and conversation. Their celebrated role in the Enlightenment came about because the knowledgeable, cultivated women who founded them orchestrated each performance and transformed diversion into an ever-growing public discourse. The salons brought men of letters together with men of power and position. All were immersed in the effort to raise the consciousness of a generation, to establish centers of serious social reform and virtuous self-cultivation where once there had been only the frivolous amusements of fawning monarchists.[12]

In these assemblies the dictates of eighteenth-century sociability conditioned the free play of ideas. Alan Charles Kors has written, "It was impolite to challenge the vague religiosity of the ladies; it was impolite to offer in the midst of a pleasant afternoon or evening a view of man and the universe that was without inherent charm, inherent warmth, inherent light. . . . it was impolite to quarrel and, above all, to quarrel sincerely and doggedly." Men of manners, sentiment, and wit met to delight each other, to say things well. The intellectual served the social.[13]

Jefferson spent time among the friends of Mme Helvétius, a Franklin admirer, at Auteuil. As a nature lover he may have been attracted to her menagerie, her well-known passion for flora and fauna. Deer roamed the property, along with ducks, chickens, pigeons, and "a variety of birds housed in huge aviaries." It was "a vibrant, somewhat chaotic household," a place of great merriment, which shocked the straight-laced Adamses. Abigail associated Mme Helvétius with the overall moral decadence she and her husband found in France. Yet, after the Adamses had moved to London, Jefferson wrote Abigail of his anticipation of possibly being welcomed into yet another group of notables:

"I took a trip yesterday to Sannois and commenced an acquaintance with the old Countess d'Hocquetout. I received much pleasure from it and hope it has opened a door of admission for me to the circle of literati with which she is environed."[14]

Jefferson appears to have been most stimulated, as both Mazzei and Crèvecoeur had predicted, by the circle that gathered about the duc de La Rochefoucauld and his mother, the duchesse d'Enville. Here congregated such notables as Condorcet, born the same year as Jefferson and called "last of the philosophes," who would write at the end of Jefferson's five-year stay, "Monsieur Jefferson will always be the friend of the philosophers and of the free men of all countries."[15]

Lafayette's aunt, Mme de Tessé, lived at the spectacular Chaville, near Versailles. She was quite fond of the American minister, as was her unmarried companion, portrait painter Mme de Tott (the honorific Mme owed to her family's standing). To Tessé, Jefferson would write in 1803 that "the friendship with which you honored me in Paris was among the circumstances which most contributed to my happiness there." He was thankful to this woman for having helped him refine his aesthetic sense; he made repeated efforts to transport American species of plants for her and, well into retirement, corresponded with her on botanical subjects. There were in addition charming and attractive women like Mme de Corny, who had married a liberal aristocrat, friend of Lafayette, and who appreciated the company of the chivalrous Jefferson when her husband was away. Gilbert Chinard has written that Mme de Corny in particular was very much conscious of Jefferson's widowed status and possessed thoughts she "probably would not have wanted to admit to herself." Upon Jefferson's return to America, she wrote regretfully, doubting that he would remember her with as much feeling as she would him: "Je vais vous prédire votre sort. Vous vous remarierez, oui, c'est sûr, et votre femme sera heureuse." [I will predict your fate for you. You will remarry, yes, it's certain, and your wife will be happy.][16]

Jefferson certainly had not forgotten the poetic experience he had enjoyed at Monticello with the marquis de Chastellux. It was the Frenchman's correction of an error in his conception of harmony in English verse that caused Jefferson to take up his scholarly "Thoughts on English Prosody," which he completed in Paris and termed "a tribute due to your friendship." The aristocrat had long been a distinguished participant in the most fashionable salons. His historical work

De la félicité publique (1770) had received Voltaire's praise and was noteworthy in its thematic search, comparable to Jefferson's, for definable public and private "pursuits of happiness." In his writing the marquis censured organized religion for economically oppressing the people and the martial rulers of Europe for exhausting their treasuries on war and expansion simply to sustain the myth of civilizing wealth. He urged instead adoption of the progressive philosophic spirit.[17]

Chastellux proved to be a reliable correspondent and ready resource for Jefferson, particularly in transmitting to the celebrated naturalist the comte de Buffon, in late 1785, both an American panther skin and a copy of the *Notes on Virginia*. Buffon's disparagement of Indians' innate abilities helped to reinforce the European prejudice that America was a less hospitable place for development of species. Jefferson's organized contributions to anthropological and zoological controversy thus announced his intent to defend the New World against the Old.[18]

Jefferson composed the *Notes* after his term as governor, in the last year of Patty Jefferson's life. The book had grown from a questionnaire sent him in 1780 by the marquis de Barbé-Marbois, secretary of the French legation in Philadelphia. If the *Notes* was conceived in order to satisfy the curiosity of America's wartime allies as to local circumstances, it was equally an effort to satisfy Jefferson's own lively interest in Virginia's natural endowments and to philosophize about people and manners. The manuscript he forwarded to Barbé-Marbois during the spring of 1782 was evidently the subject of discussion between Jefferson and Chastellux during the latter's Monticello visit that April. Taking a revised and greatly enlarged manuscript with him to Europe, Jefferson consulted again with Chastellux and, through a printer presumably recommended by Franklin, arranged for publication in France of 200 copies (intended for private distribution) in early 1785. Chastellux enthusiastically endorsed Jefferson's *Notes*, disappointed only by the limited number the author had ordered. Jefferson commented in turn on the first edition of Chastellux's *Voyages de M. le marquis de Chastellux dans l'Amerique septentrionale*, embarrassed by the complimentary portrait of himself, "a lively picture of what I wish to be but am not."[19]

Thus Jefferson was welcomed into Europe's republic of letters, his emerging stature augmented by authorship of the *Notes*, the definitive text of which would be published in London in 1787. If not a character like Franklin, he gravitated just as naturally to that cosmopolitanism

whose adherents thrived on philosophical abstractions, universal principles, ideological concerns. They aimed to be, as Diderot proclaimed
in the *Encyclopédie,* "strangers nowhere in the world," reaching beyond
the narrowness of intolerant nationalism. They were interested in natural wonders and natural science and in doing good for humanity; they
embraced eclecticism, they upheld civilization. They comprehended
their own novelty while claiming intellectual modesty, open to the wisdom of many ages, many nations. If French, they shared the late Voltaire's anticlericalism and wit; possessing no other power over the
direction of their as yet unrepublican government, they actively encouraged the intellectual class of different countries to come to them. If
English, they were alienated liberals, dissidents like Thomas Paine and
Richard Price, who extolled America's virtues. If Scottish or American,
they regarded England as the bully of nations and suffered London's
special contempt for provincialism.[20] Though soon to diffuse, the
Parisian-centered cosmopolitan ideal still thrived during Jefferson's
Paris tenure. Jefferson was there to obtain, in this sense, a kind of cultural conditioning. Chastellux had said of him in 1782 that he was a
man of intellectual attainments "without ever having quitted his own
country," who was above political ambition and who "loves the world
only insofar as he can feel that he is useful." Now, in 1786, as the most
distinguished American on the Continent, comfortable in lacking the
desire to compete with Franklin's legacy, Jefferson saw his opportunity
to become more useful to the world.

My Head and My Heart

JEFFERSON WAS NOT unresponsive to the temptations of Europe. He
had an eye for both man- and nature-made beauty. While his secretary,
William Short, was embarking on an affair with "Rosalie," the young
wife of the duc de La Rochefoucauld, Jefferson became entranced with
a golden-haired English painter.

Jefferson, who very much enjoyed the company of well-bred, articulate women, adopted a strict moral code amid what he perceived as
a laxness among the French. He found himself uniquely challenged,
however, during the late summer of 1786. He had been widowed four
years by this time, when his young painter friend John Trumbull accompanied him on an outing to inspect the domed Halle aux Bleds

and introduced Jefferson to Mr. and Mrs. Richard Cosway of London, friends, too, of M. and Mme de Corny.

Maria Louisa Catherine Cecilia Hadfield Cosway was a talented twenty-seven-year-old, born in Florence, Italy, of English parents. Helen Duprey Bullock has described her as "the embodiment of the eighteenth-century ideal of grace and beauty—a slim, graceful figure, fashionably, almost extremely dressed," her voice "musical and soft— her speech an appealing mélange of five or six languages which she spoke fluently but somewhat imperfectly." She was the survivor of a strange and sensational childhood tragedy, having escaped the murderous hands of her nursemaid, who did away with four of her siblings. Maria then grew up in a convent, where her talent in art and music blossomed. At age nineteen she was elected to the Academy of Fine Arts in Florence.[21]

She was a Roman Catholic who had contemplated taking her vows. But then she had moved to London with her ambitious mother, who prodded Maria into marrying the foppish but highly successful miniaturist Richard Cosway. He was seventeen years her elder, one year older than Jefferson, but a vain, undignified little man, who flirted openly and was the butt of jokes. Still, Cosway introduced his wife to the society of titled gentlemen and ladies and was, at least indirectly, responsible for prominent exhibitions of her work. In addition to formal portraits, she painted imaginative subjects, such as a detail from the poems of Ossian, displayed at the Royal Academy. She also composed love songs.[22] One of her husband's sketches of her presents a faintly smiling, rather engaging figure, more comfortable, it seems, than in the self-portrait that shows her arms tightly folded and eyes unyielding. A full-length portrait, undated, suggests her delicacy (fig. 6). As her future correspondence with Thomas Jefferson would reveal, Maria Cosway preferred the warmth and bright skies of Italy to the dampness of London. Like Jefferson, she was enchanted by nature, requiring periodic escape from cosmopolitan society.

The day of their first meeting, Jefferson found that he could not be torn from this captivating woman, petite and musical as Patty had been. He canceled a rendezvous with the elderly duchesse d'Enville by fabricating the excuse of pressing diplomatic business, or as Jefferson wrote in his reflection on that day, "lying messengers were to be dispatched into every corner of the city with apologies for your [his own Heart's] breach of engagement." On subsequent days and weeks, as Richard

6. Maria Cosway, painting by Richard Cosway. (Courtesy of Cincinnati Art Museum, Museum purchase)

Cosway went about his business seeing clients, his young wife saw Thomas Jefferson; how many times and whether they were generally alone are not known. They went sightseeing, and they spent evenings at the theater. A one-act play they attended, *Les Deux Billets,* was, tauntingly, a comedy about an intriguing suitor who had stolen a love letter from his rival.[23] It was quite possibly in Mrs. Cosway's company that Jefferson, on September 18, vaulted a fence along the Seine and dislocated his right wrist.[24] Jefferson himself wrote to William Stephens Smith, John and Abigail Adams's son-in-law: "How the right hand became disabled would be a long story for the left to tell. It was by one of those follies from which good cannot come, but ill may."[25]

It was a painful injury, improperly set, and troubling for one whose routine depended so much on letter writing. Jefferson dictated his official correspondence to William Short. When Maria Cosway and her husband surprisingly resolved to return to London in early October, Jefferson wrote on October 12 with ardor and his left hand and entrusted his most private communication to the discreet John Trumbull, rejoining the Cosways en route home.

The twelve pages Trumbull carried represented the thoughtful occupation of at least one entire day of Jefferson's life. His dialogue between Head and Heart is a self-consciously constructed but nonetheless inspiring work of tender sentiment. The intellectual wrote in spirited, sensuous language, as one who wishes it were possible in his world to incline toward the spontaneous, artistic, and natural. Although he destroyed the letters he and his wife had exchanged, Jefferson willingly preserved the letterpress copy of "My Head and My Heart." (The recipient's copy has not been found.) Malone has called "My Head and My Heart" a less playful letter than some of Jefferson's to Abigail Adams and as a love letter "full of vexing qualifications." Bernard Mayo described it as an "affectionate letter in the form of an essay on friendship."[26] Exploring Jefferson's use of language and placing "My Head and My Heart" in the context of his other familiar letters can serve to uncover more of the inner Jefferson.

Jefferson began the twelve-page letter by recounting his emotion at the moment he saw off Maria and Richard Cosway on the day they left Paris. At the Pavillion de St. Denis, a squat, pillared gatehouse near the city wall, he "performed the last sad office of handing you into your carriage," staying to see "the wheels get actually into motion." And then, "I turned on my heel and walked, more dead than alive," to his own carriage. The mood is set for melancholy.[27]

This is a visual performance, as well as an evocation of Jefferson's thoughts (allowing room for a conventional compulsion to paint outward emotions artificially). At his coach, Jefferson reported next, he looked for the missing gentleman who had also accompanied the Cosways to the gatehouse. He was a sixty-seven-year-old scholar of Greek art, named d'Hancarville (which Jefferson spelled "Danquerville"), who likely did not sense his momentary companion's torment. D'Hancarville had breakfasted with Trumbull and the Cosways on August 11 and accompanied them to the Louvre that day and Versailles the next. When Jefferson joined the Cosway party on August 19 (and "almost daily" thereafter), he frequently ran into the Frenchman, though he may not have known a great deal about him. In 1786 d'Hancarville was assisting Richard Payne Knight in the compilation of a book on the "mystic theology of the ancients," which contained sexually explicit illustrations. He had a spotty reputation in Europe, moreover, having languished more than once in debtor's prison. One recent commentator has written that d'Hancarville ingratiated himself "by a deft combination of the forbidden and the exotic." What this cataloguer of the erotic in antiquity had to do with the Cosways is not entirely clear. He was expelled from Maria's native Italy some years earlier for publishing pornography, but in these years she was constantly expressing concern for his state of mind. He would forward to Jefferson a letter from Maria Cosway, "l'aimable," as he called her, the following February, regretting not delivering it in person owing to a leg as infirm as Jefferson's wrist. When Maria Cosway invited the yet ill-feeling d'Hancarville to dinner at Jefferson's at the end of her second visit to Paris late in 1787, he begged off.[28]

In any event, the wayward d'Hancarville was found nearby and "dragged down stairs," and together they "crammed into the carriage, like recruits for the Bastille." After a while, "silence was broke with a 'je suis vraiment affligé du depart de ces bons gens.' [I am truly aggrieved at the departure of these good people.] This was the signal for a mutual confession [of dis]tress."

Perhaps it was the Frenchman who uttered these words. The images Jefferson offered to this point are suggestive of a loss of control, confinement, and the desire for release: "dragged down," "silence was broke," "crammed," "Bastille," and finally the "confession" through which his release would ultimately come. Presently, before the conversation could proceed far enough for Jefferson to sense catharsis, d'Hancarville was delivered to his home, and then the lonely Jefferson to his. He now paused meaningfully[29] and concluded the first paragraph of his letter: "Seated by my fire side, solitary and sad, the following dialogue took place between my Head and my Heart."

The format persists until the eleventh page of the letter:

> *Head.* Well, friend, you seem to be in a pretty trim.
> *Heart.* I am indeed the most wretched of all earthly beings. Overwhelmed with grief, every fibre of my frame distended beyond it's natural powers to bear, I would willingly meet whatever catastrophe should leave me no more to feel or to fear.

In the Heart's first expression, the dominant metaphor is that of an unwell body, an out-of-control creature of sensation. Jefferson introduced words of measure that he often used to add feeling to nouns; here it is "every fibre of my frame," fiber being an elemental component of being. Later in the letter he contributed "a grain of prudence" and "every cell of my composition." In his autobiography he would express pride that the bills he introduced in the Virginia assembly in 1779 formed a system by which "every fibre" of aristocracy would be eradicated. In a letter to James Monroe, in which Jefferson decisively wrote of his resolve to remove himself from political strife, there was "no lurking particle" of ambition left in him, "every fibre of that passion" for public life was gone, his spirit wounded in such a way that only "the all-healing grave" could cure him. Jefferson knew, too, what it meant "to lose every species of connection which is dear to the human heart: friends, brethren, parents, children."[30] Thus, when Jefferson wrote anything heartfelt, incorporating words of measure gave him a means of dramatizing an event or the sense that life was fleeting. Here in "My Head and My Heart," Jefferson was willing, rhetorically speaking, to encounter a "catastrophe," if that extreme solution would bring an end to the unpleasant sensations produced by his own thoughts ("feel" and "fear" are verbs of thought).

> *Head.* These are the eternal consequences of your warmth and precipitation. This is one of the scrapes into which you are ever leading us. You confess your follies indeed: but still you hug and cherish them, and no reformation can be hoped, where there is no repentance.

Thus ends page 1 of Jefferson's letter. He was attempting to represent a conflict of towering proportions, one of "eternal consequences." The Heart's "warmth and precipitation" can connote exertions that are not under proper control (Dr. Johnson's 1783 *Dictionary* gives "blind haste" for *precipitation*). The body is torn by activity — "scrapes" — while the moral dimension of action and thought is combined in "hug" (action) and "cherish" (thought). The Heart will not repent, or mediate, its tendency toward precipitous acts.

> *Heart.* Oh my friend! This is no moment to upbraid my foibles. I am rent into fragments by the force of my grief! If you have any balm, pour it into my wounds: if none, do not harrow them by new torments.

"Rent" and "harrow" are further expressions for the torn body, laid waste by grief. In its next rejoinder the Head rationally observes that the Heart only listens when suffering as a result of follies. When such "paroxyzm" — Dr. Johnson's "periodical exacerbation of a disease" — ends, the Heart will always vow that it has learned its lesson: "You fancy it can never return." Following this, the Head relates having whispered to the Heart, in advance of Jefferson's introduction to the Cosways, that friendship always poses a danger to "tranquillity." That danger is "the regret at parting," the prospect of loss.

The Heart disputes the Head's interpretation of the first meeting, asserting that the "desire" originated with the Head's fascination with Parisian architecture. "I never trouble myself with domes or arches. The Halle aux bleds might have rotted down before I should have gone to see it. . . . You then, Sir, and not I, have been the cause of the present distress."

This concludes page 2. At the top of page 3, the Head picks up, excoriating the Heart's "dilating [speaking exuberantly] with your new acquaintances, and contriving how to prevent a separation from them." The Head "knew" its companion was "getting into a scrape" as soon as the "lying messengers" were called for, and "I would have nothing to do with it."

> *Heart.* Oh! my dear friend, how you have revived me by recalling to mind the transactions of that day! How well I remember them all, and that when I came home at night and looked back to the morning, it seemed to have been a month agone. Go on then, like a kind comforter, and paint to me the day we went to St. Germains. How beautiful was every object. . . . [Jefferson went on to recount physical structures they

saw.] Every moment was filled with something agreeable. The wheels of time moved on with a rapidity of which those of our carriage gave but a faint idea, and yet in the evening, when one took a retrospect of the day, what a mass of happiness had we travelled over. . . . The day we went to St. Germains was a little too warm, I think was not it?

The movement of time oriented Jefferson emotionally, though not with a uniform result. Time is a comfort, a healer, as in his words of consolation to Eliza Trist when she finally discovered herself a widow: "I hope your mind has felt the good effects of time and occupation. They are slow physicians, indeed, but they are the only ones." But just as profoundly, time is impotent. Continuing his advice to Mrs. Trist, Jefferson noted that the "opiate influence" of time and occupation "lessens our sensibility tho their power does not extend to dry up the sources of sorrow."[31] Metaphorically aligning the wheels of time and the wheels of the carriage, he was able to reckon that "every moment was filled with something agreeable." Even so, this view of time as connected mechanically to emotional well-being was another way of denying himself control over events in his own life. For time to "fly" (one month went by, it seemed to him, in one day), it must be bound to fortune. This will correspond to the Heart's acceptance, on page 11, near the conclusion of the dialogue, that "we are not immortal. . . . We have no rose without it's thorn; no pleasure without alloy," no means of seizing control of destiny. This Heart is no optimist, surely not in matters of love. While the Heart claims to be "revived" by the Head's mention of the first day with the Cosways, the fact of mortality is an ever-present check on the natural effusions of the Heart; even the "mass of happiness" Jefferson momentarily projected is succeeded by the oblique and possibly sexual inference that the day was "a little too warm" for the comfort of not just the cautious Head but the imprisoned, embattled Heart as well.

Head. Thou art the most incorrigible of all beings that ever sinned! I reminded you of the follies of the first day, intending to deduce from thence some useful lessons for you, but instead of listening to these, you kindle at the recollection, you retrace the whole series with a fondness which shews you want nothing but the opportunity to act it over again. I often told you during it's course that you were imprudently engaging your affections under circumstances that must cost you a great deal of pain: that the persons indeed were of the greatest merit, possessing good sense, good humour, honest hearts, honest manners, and eminence in lovely art: that the lady had moreover qualities and accomplishments, belonging to her sex, which might form a chapter apart for her: such as music, modesty, beauty, and that softness of disposition which is the ornament of her sex and charm of ours. But that all these considerations would increase the pang of separation: that their stay here was to be too short: that you rack your whole system when you are parted from those you love, complaining that such a separation is worse than death, inasmuch as this ends our sufferings, whereas that only begins them: and that the separation would in this instance be the most severe as you would probably never see them again.

The Head recognizes the Heart's desire to turn back the clock and develops its counterargument rationally. It does not dispute that Mrs. Cosway is attractive, worthy of the Heart's attention. She is accomplished, and she is virtuous, possessing "the softness of disposition which is the ornament of her sex." That is not the point: the sinning, folly-prone Heart "kindles," i.e., becomes warm and impassioned by mere recollection. This change in temperature and temperament is the first step on the road to ruin. Again invoking the metaphor of the unwell body, the Head sternly reminds its often-tempted companion that it is imprudent—the key word here—to open itself to the inevitable hurt occasioned by "the pang of separation." To "rack your whole system" is unquestionably self-destructive.

And yet temptation remains, for, as the Heart next protests, Maria Cosway had "told me they would come back again the next year." When the Head observes, "in the mean time see what you suffer," advising "a grain of prudence" in the likely chance that the Cosways in fact would not return to Paris, the Heart stumbles a moment, and the Head follows up: "Perhaps you flatter yourself they may come to America?" It is now that the Heart launches into its celebration of the sublime recounted in chapter 1.

Winding down from this passage, in which Jefferson's Heart suggests that there would be no better place than America "for the exercise of their enchanting art," the language returns to its first melancholy premise: "Deeply practiced in the school of affliction, the human heart knows no joy which I have not lost, no sorrow of which I have not drank! Fortune can present no grief of unknown form to me! Who then can so softly bind up the wound of another as he who has felt the same wound himself?"

It is worth noting that Jefferson's personal testament to loss of love immediately follows his description of Monticello, where Patty lay buried. This is where the sun "when rising as if out of a distant water, just gilding the tops of the mountains," gave life to all nature, where the human heart could both soar to its highest point and sink to its lowest. The Heart's concluding sentiment here is an affirmation of the power of empathy; and so, after lamenting for five pages its failure to contend with mortality, it is conceiving a new and forceful argument: without the investment of Heart, there is no progress and no happiness.

"Let us turn another leaf, for this has distracted me," wrote Jefferson, from the Heart's perspective, at the bottom of page 5 of the letter.

The Heart having assigned sublimity and enchantment to the American landscape, the Head now turns to the way in which London's "lying newspapers" slandered the young nation as the home of "lawless banditti, in a state of absolute anarchy." Why would any "reasonable creature . . . venture among us?"

The Head is allowing the Heart to muster its strength (and ultimately prevail in the debate). With that last question it has yielded in the smallest way, setting the stage for the Heart to do what both acknowledge it is most adept at doing, coming to America's defense: "There is not a country on earth where there is greater tranquillity . . . where strangers are better received, more hospitably treated, and with a more sacred respect."

If the initial purpose of this digression was to convince Maria Cosway to visit America, the full result was to be the Heart's ascension from its earlier melancholy to a state of patriotic pride. This transformation — the reminder that the American Revolution was a victory for the Heart — would then make it possible for the Heart to revel in its ability to overcome long odds in personal, as well as national, affairs.

As "sensible people who think for themselves," the Cosways would see clearly that America, far from anarchy, was in the process of building roads and canals and schools and making humanistic laws such as Jefferson's own Statute for Religious Freedom.

The Head sees it is beginning to lose ground and immediately reminds its companion that the issue at hand is not America's progress but the very personal notion that the Heart has been "imprudent" to "place your affections, without reserve, on objects you must soon lose and whose loss when it comes [end of page 6] must cost you such severe pangs." On the Cosways' last night in Paris, "you tossed us from one side of the bed to the other. No sleep, no rest. The poor, crippled wrist too." The Heart is asked to "mend your manners. This is not a world to live in random as you do."

This is perhaps the quintessential statement of the Head. Jefferson had grown up ordering and organizing, measuring, maintaining lists, and observing closely before deciding upon an action. Part of him begged for release, that the spirited imagination might to be allowed to take flight. If "to live in random" is to surrender order and accept the torment that seems inevitably to follow any foray beyond the predictable, then Jefferson was still to be convinced. "Everything in the world is a matter of calculation," insists the reasoning Head. "Advance then with caution, the balance in your hand. Put into one scale the pleasures which any object may offer; but put fairly into the other the pains which are to follow, and see which preponderates. The making of an acquaintance is not a matter of indifference."

It is at this point that the Head speaks in the metaphor of the sea to strengthen its message: "Do not bite at the bait of pleasure till you know there is no hook beneath it. The art of life is the art of avoiding pain: and he is the best pilot who steers clearest of the rocks and shoals with which it is beset." Although Thomas Jefferson's mother was the daughter of sea captain Isham Randolph, her son was never comfortable with the risks of any sea voyage. His father's brother, after whom he was named, died at sea under Isham Randolph's command. In an early letter to John Page, Jefferson described his feeling after fording a river in the rain: "I confess that on this occasion I was seised with a violent hydrophobia." In a rare display of anger, the mature Jefferson was crossing another river by ferry when the two ferrymen, in the midst of a personal quarrel, stopped midstream. Their normally placid passenger became unsettled and threatened the men's lives if they did not push on.[32] As an avid classicist Jefferson must have been keenly aware of the symbolism: in Greek mythology the ferryman represented Death, agent of passage along the river Styx. Yet the sea also brought up the image of infinity, the source of creation, and of ultimate repose.

In the eighteenth century the sea was the primary link among the world's cultures. Its real perils were known to all.[33] One of the few books that Peter Jefferson owned, and bequeathed to his son, was Anson's *A Voyage round the World*, published in 1748. This large, illustrated volume responded to a public that had "never failed to be inquisitive about the various accidents and turns of fortune" of long voyages, as the author's introduction explained. The genre remained popular; over the years Jefferson himself acquired dozens of such works: *Ledyard's Journal of Cooks's Last Voyage, Mortimer's Voyage to the Asiatic Islands, and Canton, Voyage de Le Gentil dans les mers de l'Inde, Hakluyt's History of the West Indies*, and *Phipp's Voyage in 1773, towards the North Pole*, to name but a few. While sea metaphors are still used — a confused person can be "out to sea" — they were more potent in Jefferson's day. Jefferson's anxiety was apparent when he wrote to Eliza House Trist a mere two months after "My Head and My Heart": "Living from day to day, without a plan for four and twenty hours to come, I form no catalogue of impossible events. Laid up in port, for life, as I thought myself at one time, I am thrown out to sea, and an unknown one to me. By so slender a thread do all our plans of life hang!"[34]

Fearing his daughter Maria's transatlantic crossing, Jefferson researched the history of various ships and decided upon the age at which a vessel was safest. Only then did he write to the Eppes family in Virginia with his reasoning and recommendation. Returning from Europe in 1789, the Jeffersons would encounter treacherous conditions at sea, which Martha recorded: "At ten o'clock at night the wind rose the vessel drifted down dragging her anchors one or more miles, but we had got within the capes whilst a number of vessels less bold were blown of the coast some of them lost. . . . we had to beat up against a strong head wind which carried away our topsails and were very near being run down by a brig coming out of port." To St. George Tucker, Jefferson would write in 1793: "What an ocean is life! And how our barks get separated in beating through it!" To Philip Mazzei in 1796, he would write of political opponents who preferred "the calm of despotism to the boisterous sea of liberty." Here Jefferson made clear that the boisterous sea was his friend in politics, though it might be his nemesis as a symbol of inner turmoil, wherein he was much less confident of his ability to weather life's storms.[35]

If the sea of passion posed dangers, then what did the Head, continuing its argument, define as pleasure? The intellectual. "Ever in our power, always leading us to something new, never cloying, we ride, serene and sublime,[36] above the concerns of this mortal world, contemplating truth and nature, matter and motion, the laws which bind up their existence, and the eternal [end of page 7; for page 8, see fig. 7] being who made and bound them up by these laws. Let this be our employ." If this explanation of the value of disengagement was not compelling enough, the Head prescribed further: "Leave the bustle and

7. Jefferson to Maria Cosway, October 12, 1786. Page 8 of the twelve-page "My Head and My Heart" letter, written left-handed after Jefferson fractured his right wrist. (Library of Congress)

tumult of society to those who have not talents to occupy themselves without them. Friendship is but another name for an alliance with the follies and misfortunes of others. Our own share of miseries is sufficient: why enter then as volunteers into those of another?" For if we become too involved when a friend's "fortune is shipwrecked" (again a sea metaphor), then "we must mourn the loss as if it was our own."

The Head had not dictated friendship to Thomas Jefferson in the past. Letters evidence the generous Virginian's yearning to share his mind with such "antient" countrymen as Page, Madison, and Monroe and to share his Heart with such women as Eliza House Trist and Abigail Adams. At the time of his preoccupation with Maria Cosway, Jefferson had told Eliza Trist, "The happiest moments it [my heart] knows are those in which it is pouring forth it's affections to a few esteemed characters." He was selective in letting others into his heart but always eager to do so, accepting physical separation as part of the bargain. To Albert Gallatin, his loyal secretary of the treasury and adviser, he declared, "No one feels more painfully than I do, the separation of friends."[37] The Head appears to be exaggerating for effect in this particular passage, suggesting that the "bustle and tumult of society" are fine for those made tough enough to withstand them; but for one of Thomas Jefferson's makeup, "serene and sublime" occupations are more suitable.

This, as things turn out, is the last opportunity for the Head to speak. The Heart now takes over, in the longest unobstructed passage of the letter (three and a half pages):

> *Heart.* And what more sublime delight than to mingle tears with one whom the hand of heaven hath smitten! To watch over the bed of sickness, and to beguile it's tedious and it's painful moments! To share our bread with one to whom misfortune has left none! This world abounds indeed with misery: to lighten it's burthen we must divide it with one another.

At this moment of ecstasy, Jefferson chose not "happiness" or "pleasure" but "delight" to express the sublime sense achieved in the compassionate commitment to another. "Happiness" is a too general word in his vocabulary, reduced in energy and authority by its varied uses. "Pleasure," brought up several times in this letter (pages 7, 9, and 11), is coupled with "pain," "misfortune," monkish unsociability, or "alloy," meaning diminution. He generally recognized that "pleasure" does not come free. Jefferson preferred the use of "delight" in the context of undiminished, unabased satisfaction, of pure friendship or pure intellectual enjoyment. "Delight" was spiritually potent for him, employed in Homeric depictions or other references to awe and wonder that captured his mind. Composing to Abigail Adams a tribute to the collection of Greek figures he had acquired for her, Jefferson referred to the deities who commanded song and the chase as "our supreme delight." To Pierre Samuel Du Pont, he explained his own purpose on earth with the same phrase: "Nature intended for me the tranquil pursuits of science, by rendering them my supreme delight." Jefferson expressed "delight" when Joseph Priestley, the preeminent Unitarian thinker whose work he admired more than that of any other living theologian, proposed coming to America to continue his controversial writing undisturbed. In the same letter Jefferson termed his reading of Homer in the original Greek "this rich source of my delight."[38]

Jefferson's distinctive use of "pleasure" and "delight" curiously relates to Edmund Burke's remarks in the first part of his treatise on the sublime and beautiful. "Pleasure," Burke noted, "quickly satisfies; and when it is over, we relapse into indifference . . . tinged with the agreeable colour of the former sensation." It is not "pleasure," he added, but "delight" that arises from the removal of pain or danger. In a subsequent section of the work, entitled "The Effects of Sympathy in the Distresses of Others," Burke elaborated, "Whenever we are formed by nature to any active purpose, the passion which animates us to it, is attended with delight, or a pleasure of some kind . . . and as our Creator has designed we should be united by the bond of sympathy, he has strengthened that bond by a proportionable delight; and there most where our sympathy is most wanted, in the distresses of others." "Misfortune," he went on, "always touches with delight. This is not unmixed delight, but blended with no small uneasiness."[39] Jefferson's "delight" is unmitigated, but that does not always mean pleasurable. He acknowledged in this epic passage the sublime nature — the awful emotional torment — when his Heart would "mingle tears with one whom the hand of heaven hath smitten."

The Heart enthusiastically proceeds to chronicle its "delight" in a series of further exclamations. "When languishing then under disease, how grateful is the solace of our friends! How we are penetrated with their assiduities and attentions!" The "solace of our friends" thus penetrates — an active, dynamic, enduring sensation. "How much are we

supported by their encouragements and kind offices!" Jefferson capitalized the word "Heaven"—he frequently did not—as he continued:
"When Heaven has taken from us some object of our love, how sweet
it is to have a bosom whereon to recline our heads, and into which to
we may pour the torrent of our tears! Grief, with such a comfort, is
almost a luxury!"

To the Head's contention that life is smoother when one insulates
himself from others, the Heart nods knowingly, as if to say, "Ah yes!
but . . . ," and observes that "nobody will care for him who cares for
nobody." Retreat from friendship was surely not a desirable way of life
for the sociable and ultimately optimistic Jefferson to pursue. He may
have become guarded with respect to remarriage, given the depth of
his love for Patty and the long term of misery he had served after her
death; but he was convinced that the value of friendship far outweighed
the countervailing pain of loss. As Jefferson's pen reached the bottom
of the eighth page of the letter and he began a new sheet, the Heart
rejoices that friendship is "precious not only in the shade but in the
sunshine of life: and thanks to a benevolent arrangement of things, the
greater part of life is sunshine." The pathetic fallacy by which weather
phenomena are associated with human emotions is quite common in
the English language. Two and a half years earlier, Jefferson had conversed with a young friend about the future; his view was then still
clouded by the loss of his wife, as he wrote, "The sun of life having
with me already passed his meridian, with you he is ascending."[40]

By the time of this writing, however, his sunny disposition had been
restored. The Heart continues graphically: "I will recur for proof to the
days we have lately passed. On these indeed the sun shone brightly!
How gay did the face of nature appear! Hills, vallies, chateaux, gardens,
rivers, every object wore it's liveliest hue! Whence did they borrow it?
From the presence of our charming companion. They were pleasing,
because she seemed pleased."

This is flattery, of course, but Jefferson's Heart is arriving at a cre-
scendo in the composition.

> Let the gloomy Monk, sequestered from the world, seek unsocial
> pleasures in the bottom of his cell! Let the sublimated philosopher grasp
> visionary happiness while pursuing phantoms dressed in the garb of
> truth! Their supreme wisdom is supreme folly: and they mistake for hap-
> piness the mere absence of pain. [Here, Jefferson seems to mock Burke's

distinction.] Had they ever felt the solid pleasure of one generous spasm
of the heart, they would exchange for it all the frigid speculations of their
lives, which you [the Head] have been vaunting in such elevated terms.

The Head's "pleasure" has been termed "unsocial," while the Heart's
"pleasure" is, for once, "solid." What the Head calls "happiness" is
merely "visionary," made unwholesome by its pointless pursuit of unnatural entities.[41] The "garb of truth" suggests a metaphorical covering,
a "garb" which hides reality or diverts understanding. The crowning
contrast, though, is the "generous spasm of the heart," a warm, natural
convulsion supplying elemental power to the human organism, and the
"frigid speculations," cold, inanimate schemes, which may supplement
a person's existence with useful notions but do not help sustain it.

The Heart, so emboldened, conclusively determines that it is "miserable arithmetic which would estimate friendship at nothing." The or-
gan of sensation has been compelled to endure the Head's plodding
"principles uttered which I detest and abjure." The time has come in
the debate to dismiss finally the pretentions of the overcautious Head:
"When nature assigned us to the same habitation, she gave us over it a
divided empire. To you she allotted the field of science, to me that of
morals. . . . In denying to you the feelings of sympathy, of benevolence,
of gratitude, of justice, of love, of friendship, she has excluded you from
their controul. To these she has adapted the mechanism of the heart."
And now the final disengagement: "Morals were too essential to the
happiness of man to be risked on the uncertain combinations of the
head. She laid their foundation therefore in sentiment, not in science."

To prove that the Head is not fit to decide moral questions, the
Heart offers two instances from Jefferson's life. First, "when the poor
wearied souldier, whom we overtook at Chickahominy with his pack
on his back, begged to let him get up behind our chariot, you began to
calculate that the road was full of souldiers," and that the horses would
"fail in their journey" if overburdened. After some distance, "becoming
sensible you had made me do wrong, that tho we cannot relieve all the
distressed we should relieve as many as we can," the Heart overruled
the Head's command and turned around, but too late. The soldier was
gone, and Jefferson could not "find him out to ask his forgiveness."
Second, in Philadelphia, "when the poor woman came to ask a charity,"
the Head "whispered that she looked like a drunkard." Jefferson made
a token offering, presuming the money would be spent promptly on

ale. "When I sought her out afterwards, and I did what I should have done at first, you know that she employed the money immediately towards placing her child at school."[42]

These two incidents refer directly to transforming moments within the main character's consciousness in Laurence Sterne's *A Sentimental Journey,* set in France. Sterne's fictional encounter with a beggar was drawn to illuminate the internal conflict between judgment and wit (read: Head and Heart). It is sentiment, the sympathetic imagination, that produces generosity, empathy, moral behavior in *A Sentimental Journey,* as in *Tristram Shandy.*

In the opening scene of this book, the sentimental traveler Yorick refuses to give alms to a monk. He pronounces first the rationalization that the unfortunate of his own country had first rights to his mercy ("I have left thousands in distress upon our own shores") and then insults the monk by distinguishing between those who are poor for lack of work and those who "have no other plan in life, but to get through it in sloth and ignorance, *for the love of God.*" Afterward, Yorick confines himself to a broken-down *desobligeant,* or carriage-for-one, acknowledging his words and actions as evidence of his own self-absorption. Upon meeting a beautiful woman (as Jefferson meant to suggest in his affecting encounter with Maria Cosway), he discovers in himself the power of his magnanimous, generous side. Yorick is moved to a reconciliation with the monk he has snubbed. He offers a pinch of snuff and then offers the snuffbox itself as "the peace-offering of a man who once used you unkindly, but not from his heart." The monk accepts and "with a stream of good nature in his eyes" exchanges his own snuffbox for Yorick's. On a subsequent trip to the same area, the sentimental traveler seeks out his friend, only to learn that the monk had been dead three months by this time. But he feels the irresistible desire to visit his resting place and sits fingering the monk's snuffbox before "plucking up a nettle or two" at the head of the grave. Finally, Yorick "bursts into a flood of tears."[43]

In his 1771 letter to Robert Skipwith, after observing that reading fiction elevated sentiment, Jefferson had explained: "We neither know nor care whether Lawrence Sterne really went to France, whether he was there accosted by the poor Franciscan, at first rebuked him unkindly, and then gave him a peace offering; or whether the whole be not fiction. In either case we are equally sorrowful at the rebuke, and secretly resolve *we* will never do so: we are pleased with the subsequent atonement, and view with emulation a soul candidly acknowledging it's fault, and making a just reparation."[44] Fifteen years later, in the self-probing "My Head and My Heart," Jefferson wished to illustrate a certain responsiveness, and his moral regard for Mrs. Cosway, by reconstituting vignettes of Sterne. His Account Book shows that he often gave small sums to indigent people. Patsy's letter to Eliza Trist portrays what it was like as they first arrived on the Continent: the "singularity of the phaeton carriage" transported from America had "attracted the attention of all we met, and when ever we stopped we were surrounded by beggars. One day I counted no less than nine where we stopped to change horses." Jefferson was at his most Sternean when he wrote to Madison of an encounter forty miles outside Paris. A poor woman had patiently responded to his questions about labor conditions, after which he presented her with an unsolicited twenty-four sous. "She burst into tears," he reported, "of a gratitude which I could perceive was unfeigned, because she was unable to utter a word."[45]

Jefferson met Sterne on the plane of consciousness, sentiment, and morality. His principles were ever consistent with the English author's. Both men were deeply concerned with the place generosity occupied in the formation of character and in being a friend to others. From the point at which he makes amends with the monk, Sterne's Yorick plainly finds pleasure in opening himself up to his natural emotions to establish deeper communication with the people who come into his life. Jefferson seems to have known Sterne's intent in writing *A Sentimental Journey,* as the author described in a letter, "I told you my design in it was to teach us to love the world and our fellow creatures better than we do now."[46] After relating the touching story of the woman in Philadelphia, Jefferson's Heart could be speaking as well for the newly enlightened Yorick when it asserts, "Those who want the dispositions to give, easily find reasons why they ought not to give" and then adds, "I do not know that I ever did a good thing on your [the Head's] suggestion, or a dirty one without it."

Jefferson knew, too, that America's just war for independence could not have been conducted had not the patriots been governed by their Hearts. The Head had calculated and compared and found Britain's "wealth and numbers" alarmingly superior; the Heart had supplied "enthusiasm" against wealth and numbers, and in doing so, "we saved our country." This justified belief in a "Providence, whose precept is to do always what is right, and leave the issue to him."

The top of Jefferson's eleventh page begins: "But leave me to decide when and where friendships are to be contracted. You [the Head] say I contract them at random, so you said the woman in Philadelphia was a drunkard. I receive no one into my esteem till I know they are worthy of it. . . . You confess that in the present case I could not have made a worthier choice. You only object that I was so soon to lose them. We are not immortal ourselves, my friend; how can we expect our enjoiments to be so? We have no rose without it's thorn; no pleasure without alloy. It is the law of our existence; and we must acquiesce."

This passage appears to be an unprovoked retreat from the rapturous testament to the delight of compassionate friendship. The Heart answers the Head's plaint — but not without confusion — by insisting that friendship is worth the pain of enduring loss. For all the acceptance of human mortality, the Heart speaks of "the law of our existence," a concept better invoked by the Head. Spontaneous, instinctive emotions — relationships that spring from the sympathetic imagination — hardly seem verifiable by any law. The Head still has a claim on the Heart, it would seem again, for the Heart goes on, "I feel more fit for death than life," before recovering. "But when I look back on the pleasures of which it [Jefferson's pitiable condition] is the consequence, I am conscious they [the pleasures] were worth the price I am paying. . . . Hope is sweeter than despair." This hope is the hope of the Cosways' promised return. Mr. Cosway had predicted summer, Mrs. Cosway spring. "I should love her forever," the Heart exudes, "were it only for that!"

The dialogue devolves from this point, and the twelfth and final page of the letter, the "nightcap," as Jefferson termed it, asks conventionally for her reply: "If your letters are as long as the bible, they will appear short to me. Only let them be brim full of affection. I shall read them with the dispositions with which Arlequin [Harlequin] in les deux billets [the play they attended together] spelt the words 'je t'aime' and wished that the whole alphabet had entered into their composition." From here, Jefferson engaged in chitchat until giving a final report on his condition: "As to myself my health is good, except my wrist which mends slowly, and my mind which mends not at all, but broods constantly over your departure." He signed the epic letter below "sentiments of sincere affection and esteem."

Most analysts of "My Head and My Heart" have called the debate a draw or insisted that Jefferson simply obeyed his Head.[47] But it seems clear that in giving the Heart the last word, as well as the longest uninterrupted speech, Jefferson was attempting to convince himself that the Heart was right. He had feelings, rich and pulsating, alive within him. The Head could not provide him with the metaphorical sunshine he yearned for. Only through the Heart could Jefferson achieve the optimistic state that he, as an inheritor of Enlightenment thinking, required for sustenance.

The Heart is most convincing in sounding the rhythmic suggestion to exchange "one generous spasm of the heart" for "all the frigid speculations" of the monks and "sublimated" philosophers. This is the cause Jefferson took up inside himself, the seemingly uncomplicated delight he craved in extending himself outward. He knew he was driven by book reading, by calculations; he could never lose that. But what he feared—what he knew he was capable of depriving himself of—was the self-affirming feeling that strikes when one opens his heart and allows another into his life. Maria Cosway's melodic voice, artistic sensitivity, and feminine charm—and her special regard for him—had caused Jefferson to conceive a picture of intimacy with another such as he had only known once before in his adult life. This tempting scenario may have been intensified for Jefferson by the frustration that either she expressed to him on one of their outings or he instinctively understood, of her loveless marriage to a self-centered man who may have come to resent her talent. "My Head and My Heart" was Jefferson's attempt to lay down the battle lines in this murky conflict, this foray into uncharted moral territory.

In Jefferson, as in Sterne, the Head contrives to convince a man that he is content when he remains isolated from others: but in each case, though the writer accepts that portion of the Lockean system by which judgment, or the Head, reigns supreme in constructive enterprise, judgment is not superior to wit, and the Head cannot beat back the Heart's advance. The Heart is best suited to resolve questions of morality, to do good and produce genuine happiness. What more telling guide could there be for Jefferson than the assertion that the Heart had "saved" the American Revolution?

So, to give coherence to Jefferson's life story, finally to seal his long letter to Maria Cosway, we must say that the Heart won. But the Head ultimately would have to rule in this relationship, because Jefferson had too much constructive enterprise at stake to sacrifice public considerations for private pleasure—with a married woman. And while that may be the visible result, he would not hesitate to use his imagination again.

Maria Cosway's reply to Jefferson's dialogue was altogether unrevealing. Wishing she had the ability to answer his irresistible sentiment with something of comparable worth, she resignedly expressed what she could, gratitude that he had befriended her at all. The first part of her October 30 letter was in English, the rest in Italian. Her handwriting was of varying thickness, sweeping and angular, generally unhurried. The lowercase *t* was crossed with a long line; words beginning with *c*, whether they were properly capitalized, as "Cosway," or lowercase, as "cause" and "company," were announced with a great curling *C*. She had shown, in the Italian postscript she appended to John Trumbull's October 9 letter to Jefferson, that she could let go of precision; in contrast to the uniform character of Trumbull's artistic hand, her words were spaced widely and spread across the page. The force of her pen evidenced a lighter touch than Jefferson's typically slow, thick, earthy cursive. His characters were low and more rounded and entirely unpretentious, consistent with his later advice to his grandson: "Take pains at the same time to write in a neat round, plain hand, and you will find it a great convenience through life to write a small and compact hand as well as a fair and legible one."[48]

Subsequent letters to Jefferson showed that she yearned for his news. On November 17, in Italian, she imagined "a thousand misfortunes." On November 27, again in Italian, she complained that she had written twice, without his reply. "I wait," she appealed, "with great concern, I fear that your arm may be worse, but even this would not prevent you from writing me." He wrote one page on November 19, announcing that it was she who deservedly was to receive the "first homage" of his long unoccupied right hand. Though he described the letter as necessarily short, this was "good news for you; for were the hand able to follow the effusions of the heart[,] that would cease to write only when this should cease to beat." He exited dramatically, punctuated by a pained "Mercy cramp! that twitch was too much. I am done, I am done—Adieu ma chere madame." The letter was unsigned.[49]

Jefferson's next two letters, of November 29 and December 24, were also unsigned, and in the former he explained at some length why that was: "My letters which pass thro' the post offices either of this country or of England being all opened, I send thro' that channel only such as are very indifferent in their nature. This is not the character, my dear madam, of those I write to you. The breathings of a pure affection would be profaned in the eye of a Commis of the poste. I am obliged then to wait for private conveiances. I wrote you so long ago as the 19th of this month by a gentleman who was to go to London immediately, but he is not yet gone. . . . Could I write by the post I should trouble you too often: for I am never happier than when I commit myself into dialogue with you, tho' but in imagination." A bit further down, Jefferson pronounced: "I am determined when you come next not to admit the idea that we are ever to part again. But are you to come again? I dread the answer to this question, and that my poor heart has been duped by the fondness of it's wishes. What a triumph for the head! God bless you! May your days be many and filled with sunshine! May your heart glow with warm affections and all of them be gratified! Write to me often, write affectionately and freeiy, as I do to you. Say many kind things, and say them without reserve. They will be food for my soul." Ironically, Jefferson was unable to find a reliable messenger and added a P.S. to the unsigned letter: "No private conveiance occurring I must trust this thro' the post-office, disguising my seal and superscription."[50]

We can understand why Thomas Jefferson Randolph, in editing the four volumes of Jefferson's memoirs and correspondence shortly after his grandfather's death, resolved to include "My Head and My Heart" but not the subsequent Cosway correspondence. The contrived dialogue fit a certain literary form which dated back to the Greeks and which other eighteenth-century correspondents, including Benjamin Franklin, had employed. In it Jefferson paid at least lip service to Mr. Cosway, referring to "these good people," speaking repeatedly in the plural when he meant to be understood in the singular, and ending, "Present me in the most friendly terms to Mr. Cosway." The letters of November and December, however, were of a decidedly different, perceptibly passionate tone. Naturally, Jefferson was sensitive to this when he refused to put his signature on them. And his grandson prudently gave the later correspondence to his personal attorney, in whose firm's possession the letters remained until their first publication in the mid-twentieth century.[51]

In the November 29 letter, Jefferson urged his friend to write affectionately and "freely, as I do to you," to say things "without reserve"; her sentiments could sustain him as "food for my soul." There appears to be no question that, at parting, the two knew how each felt about the other. Nowhere else in Jefferson's letters do we find this intense desire for a correspondent to write "without reserve." Surely he desired to do so. In Paris he had opened himself up to this woman, no doubt explaining how his wife's death had left him so long insensible. Revived, distant from the scene of his married life, and after four years' mourning capable of feeling passion for a woman, he had regaled the artist with fantastic notions about their traveling together through the forests of America.

On December 24 Jefferson extended the fantasy. This is the letter in which he envied the power of birds to fly where they pleased. For the power to fly to her side, he, speaking with rhetorical license, would have "exchanged . . . many of the boasted preeminencies of man." Jefferson had read as a youth the myth of Fortunatus. "He had a cap of such virtues that when he put it on his head, and wished himself anywhere, he was there." The Head of Jefferson's dialogue could be so much more manageable, Jefferson must have been thinking, were this airborne fantasy real. "I have been all my life sighing for this cap," he went on. "Yet if I had it, I question if I should use it but once. I should wish myself with you, and not wish myself away again. En attendant [awaiting] the cap, I am always thinking of you. If I cannot be with you in reality, I will in imagination."[52]

It is interesting to examine for a moment the linear rhythm Jefferson created in this passage. This is how it appears on the first of his two pages:

> he was there. I have been all my life sighing for this cap. Yet if I had
> it, I question if I should use it but once. I should wish to be with you,
> and not wish myself away again. En attendant the cap, I am always
> thinking of you. If I cannot be with you in reality, I will in imagination.

He compressed the two words "with you" on the second line to maintain the fullness of the phrase on one line, then left space after "always" on the third line in order to keep "thinking of you" together on the next. The tender thought comes to a natural close at the end of the fourth line with "imagination."

He went on to discuss the hopeful logistics of her packing for Paris and, before finishing, reminded her of what he had set forth in "My Head and My Heart": "I am determined not to suppose I am never to see you again. I believe you intend to go to America, to draw the Natural bridge, the Peaks of Otter &c. that I shall meet you there, and visit with you all those grand scenes. I had rather be deceived, than live without hope. It is so sweet! It makes us ride so smoothly over the roughnessess of life." These lines bring Jefferson to the closing thought of his letter and run on to the top of page 2. "I had rather be deceived," ends the last line of the first page, before the second page opens dramatically: "than live without hope." He had said as much as he wished to on this date and filled the largely unused sheet with a sweet Italian farewell — "Addio la mia cara ed amabile amica!" — and a short postscript.

A Sentimental Journey

BEFORE HE SAW Maria Cosway again, Jefferson embarked on a three-and-a-half-month journey to the south of France and to northern Italy, near where she had spent her youth. He left Paris the end of February, traveling to the medicinal waters of Aix-en-Provence in hopes of healing his wrist through natural therapy. He passed time in the celebrated vineyards of Burgundy and Beaujolais. During the third week he found poetic delight in the "most perfect remains of antiquity which exist on earth" in Nîmes.[53] Aix was the cleanest city he had ever seen, though he was disappointed in his main purpose there, bathing his wrist with "40 douches, without sensible benefit." He paid close attention to the changing landscape and to the agricultural pursuits of the French and Italians on his tour. Writing William Short regularly, he called Marseilles "charming," comparing its bustle to London and Philadelphia. From Toulon he wrote of the countryside, "Nothing can be ruder or more savage . . . nothing more rich and variegated." From the "handsome city" of Nice, he crossed the Alps on the back of a mule and went as far into Italy as Turin, Milan, and Genoa in April, before returning to Nice along the Italian Riviera. Then he took the long route from Aix to Avignon and west two hundred miles on the Canal de Languedoc. He had wanted to inspect this engineering work, built by Louis XIV, which had no American equivalent. He declared: "Of all the methods of traveling I have ever tried, this is the pleasantest. I walk the greater part of the way along the banks of the canal, level and lined with a double row of trees which furnish shade. When fatigued I take seat in my carriage, where, as much at ease as if in my study, I read, write, or observe." At a leisurely two to three miles per hour, as he informed his daughter, the canal method of travel enabled Jefferson to enjoy the sounds of nightingales "in full chorus" and the sights of villages and farms, which he found quaint. He reached Bordeaux, the canal terminus, after nine days and stayed four more days inspecting the wine country before proceeding to Nantes, Tours, Orléans, and finally Paris on June 11.[54]

One month before his departure, preoccupied with Sterne, Jefferson had written a London bookseller for the five-volume 1780 complete works in duodecimo, saying: "I name this edition because it brings all his works into the smallest compass of any one I have seen. If you know of any edition still smaller I would prefer it, elegantly bound." Jefferson had owned *A Sentimental Journey* as early as 1768; he again would seek the pocket-size Sterne before he returned to America in 1789, and once more in 1804, as president.[55]

He wanted Sterne at hand during his travels, which shows how routinely the consciousness of that author crept into Thomas Jefferson's energetic pursuit of new understandings. The evidence is unmistakable. In *A Sentimental Journey* Sterne was quick to inform the reader that there are many kinds of travelers. Heading his list are "simple" ones, which include the "Idle," "Inquisitive," "Lying," "Proud," "Vain," and "Splenetic." Then there are "Travellers of Necessity," "The delinquent and felonious Traveller," "the unfortunate and innocent Traveller," and then, at last, his alter ego Yorick, "The Sentimental Traveller."[56]

Jefferson saw himself as just such a traveler. He wrote on April 5 from Marseilles: "The plan of my journey, as well as my life, being to take things by the smooth handle, few [objects] occur which have not something tolerable to offer me. . . . 'A traveller, sais I, retired at night to his chamber in an Inn, all his effects contained in a simple trunk, all his cares circumscribed by the walls of his apartment, unknown to all, unheeded and undisturbed, writes, reads, thinks, sleeps, just in the moments when nature and the movements of his body and mind require. Charmed by the tranquillity of his little cell, he finds how few are our real wants, how cheap a thing is happiness, how expensive a one pride.'" Compare the tone in Sterne's opening scene, in which Yorick arrives in France, goes to his lodgings at a Calais inn, and takes account of his circumstances: "Just God! said I, kicking my portmanteau aside, what is there in this world's goods which should sharpen our spirits, and make so many kind-hearted brethren of us, fall out so cruelly as we do by the way? When man is at peace with man, how much lighter than a feather is the heaviest of metals in his hand! he pulls out his purse, and holding it airily and uncompressed, looks round him, as if he sought for an object to share it with." Jefferson was using a narrative style that is unusual for him, one that could only have come to him self-consciously from his reading of Sterne. Indeed, transcribing his press copy of this letter during his retirement years later, Jefferson even substituted Sterne's word "portmanteau" for "trunk."[57]

The following week, writing Lafayette, Jefferson rejoiced in his communion with commoners: "I am never satiated with rambling through the fields and farms, examining the culture and cultivators with a degree of curiosity which makes some take me to be a fool, and others to be much wiser than I am. . . . You must ferret the people out of their hovels as I have done, look into their kettles, eat their bread, loll on their beds under pretense of resting yourself, but in fact to find if they are soft. You will find a sublime pleasure in the course of this investigation, and a sublimer one hereafter when you shall be able to apply your knowledge to the softening of their beds or the throwing a morsel of meat into their kettles of vegetables." Sterne's chapters "The Supper" and "The Grace" present Yorick in a comparable situation, finding "a little farmhouse surrounded with about twenty acres of vineyard . . . full of everything which could make plenty in a French peasant's house." He delights in the "joyous genealogy" of this earthy family: "They were all sitting down together to their lentil-soup; a large wheaten loaf was in the middle of the table; and a flagon of wine at each end of it promised joy thro' the stages of the repast—'twas a feast of love . . . my heart was sat down the moment I enter'd the room; so I sat down at once like a son of the family; and to invest myself in the character as speedily as I could, I instantly borrowed the old man's knife, and taking up the loaf cut myself a hearty luncheon; and as I did it I saw a testimony in every eye, not only of an honest welcome, but of a welcome mix'd with thanks that I had not seem'd to doubt it."[58] The idiom that Sterne created in *A Sentimental Journey* Jefferson routinely adopted in his personal correspondence while in Europe.

He quoted Sterne directly. To Maria Cosway he opened one letter: "Hail, dear friend of mine! for I am never so happy as when business, smoothing her magisterial brow, says 'I give you an hour to converse with your friends.' And with none do I converse more fondly than with my good Maria: not her under the poplar, with the dog and string at her girdle: but the Maria who makes the Hours her own." Sterne's Maria first appears in *Tristram Shandy,* a young beauty forsaken by her lover and overwrought. In *A Sentimental Journey* she is a melancholy wanderer, not having regained her mind. Yorick encounters her under a poplar, with her elbow in her lap, and dressed in white, much as Tristram had described her to him. The sentimental traveler sits beside her and wipes her tears, then his own, then hers, and feels "such undescribable emotions within me" that "I am positive I have a soul" (fig. 8). Knowing Jefferson's fondness for the Sternean idiom, Abigail Adams, "surfeited with Europe" and longing for "the rural cottage, the purer and honester manners of my native land," announced to her Virginia friend: "I hope one season more will give us an opportunity of making our escape. At present we are in the situation of Sterne's starling."[59] In *A Sentimental Journey* a starling in a cage complains, "I can't get out — I can't get out." Yorick attempts to free him, without success; the bird is destined to spend its entire existence being passed from owner to owner, unappreciated.[60]

It is more than incidental that Jefferson wrote of Sterne and like Sterne primarily in letters to women. Sterne's own passion and imagination makes this understandable. In his waning years the tubercular Sterne longed for feminine sympathy. Appreciation for women was what made him love life and what made him write. He required the presence of a woman to elicit the sympathetic reactions of Yorick in his encounter with the monk. Later in the journey a humble *fille de chambre* buying from a bookseller *The Wandering of the Heart* causes Yorick to express generosity anew with the unpremeditated gift of a coin, which she sews into a satin purse.[61]

In the last year of his life, Sterne carried on an extensive sentimental flirtation through the mails with a young married woman, twenty-three-year-old Eliza Draper. He wrote to her unabashedly, "[My passions] flow, Eliza, to thee — and ebb from every other Object in this world — and Reason tells me they do right." In a letter not long after he declared, "I want to have you ever before my Imagination — and cannot keep You out of my heart or head — In short thou enterst my Library, Eliza!"[62] He introduced her to the world on the first page of *A Sentimental Journey*.

Possibly, Sterne and Jefferson were more in love with the lively art of their composition than with the particular women to whom they wrote such fantastic sentiments. Yet we cannot entirely dismiss as playful fiction the suggestions of sexuality that appear in both. Beyond the permissive world of his literature, Sterne was accused of indiscretions with women, warned by friends and censured by critics for his lascivious behavior. And Jefferson, though the very picture of social grace and

8. Sterne's character Maria with her dog on a string, attended by Yorick.
From the London, 1780, edition of *A Sentimental Journey*.

public virtue, teased Maria Cosway: "At Strasbourg I sat down to write to you. But for my soul I could think of nothing at Strasbourg but the promontory of noses, of Diego, of Slawkenburgius his historian, and the procession of the Strasbourgers to meet the man with the nose. Had I written to you from thence it would have been a continuation of Sterne upon noses, and I knew that nature had not formed me for a Continuator of Sterne: so I let it alone till I came here and received your angry letter. It is a proof of your esteem, but I love better to have soft testimonials of it. You must therefore now write me a letter teeming with affection: such as I feel for you."[63] The reference to noses is an unmistakable sign. This double entendre in *Tristram Shandy* is perhaps the best known example of sexual innuendo in all of Sterne. Jefferson, despite the prudishness attributed to him by William Short, could not have meant anything else. In Sterne's writing sex is nearly always present as part of the author's friendly conspiracy with his reader, so much so that the understanding reader of Sterne cannot remain passive; he or she must forfeit any pretense of innocence with regard to the sexual message.[64] Yet Tristram's sexual self-definition in the novel is problematic. He, like Jefferson, lacks masculine models for sexual assertiveness. Despite all the innuendo Tristram never discovers himself as a sexual being but operates under the notion that sex is fraught with danger. The story of Slawkenburgius results in "riot and disorder."[65] Jefferson's writing to Maria Cosway, in much the same tone as *Tristram Shandy,* seems conscious in wanting to arouse, and yet there is no real sex. Intentionally or not, both Jefferson and Sterne presented to posterity a provocative, perhaps unanswerable question about their personal relations with women: "Did they or didn't they?"

The two even employed a common metaphor, that of taking a mistress, to express enthusiasm for intellectual pursuits: what a book by Bruscambille is to Walter Shandy and a fortification is to Toby, architecture was to Jefferson. The first "solaced himself with *Bruscambille* after the manner, in which 'tis ten to one, your worship solaced yourself with your first mistress." Delighting in the secrecy contrived by his uncle in reenacting the battle in which he was wounded, Tristram observes, "Never did a lover post down to a belov'd mistress with more heat and expectation, than my Uncle *Toby* did, to enjoy this self-same thing in private." From Nîmes, Jefferson wrote a celebrated letter to Mme de Tessé, in Paris: "Here I am, Madam, gazing whole hours as the Maison quareé, like a lover at his mistress. . . . This is the second time I have been in love since I left Paris. The first was with a Diana at the Chateau de Laye Epinaye in the Beaujolois, a delicious morsel of sculpture, by Michael Angelo Slodtz. This, you will say, was in rule, to fall in love with a fine woman: but with a house! It is out of all precedent!"[66] Late eighteenth-century convention expected a certain warm-bloodedness or sensual indulgence in a gentleman's writing to his female friends and undoubtedly helped Jefferson release certain tensions. But as much as the twentieth-century mind-set urges us to answer "Did they or didn't they?" with "They must have," we have no way of being certain.[67]

Enlightenment orthodoxy recognized the primacy of the sexual in human thought, as an undeniable element in human happiness. Sex was treated substantially and respectably in medical treatises and guides such as *The Art of Getting Beautiful Children*, first published in 1712. Essays in the form of poetry tempered what might otherwise have been too delicate for some readers. Fantastic stories of monstrosities resulting from unusual pairings added spice to the general interest. Jefferson surely knew of the existence of this literature and of the environment it nourished, enough to be amused by Sterne's volumes-long narration of the course of procreation resulting in Tristram's birth. Throughout the eighteenth century the pregnant woman was a "highly sensitive conductor of impressions, sensations, shocks and emotions." Jefferson himself made jokes about pregnancy, though he was averse to discovering humor in infidelity.[68]

Sex could lead to good or ill. From Steele's *The Conscious Lovers* to Samuel Richardson's novels, to Philadelphian Charles Brockden Brown, eighteenth-century writers idealized maidenly virtue and displayed distrust of the libidinous suitor. After marriage, women shone brightest in the private sphere of the home where their handiwork and other talents could be expressed. Though they might become more imaginative and assertive by reading extensively, outside the home women were expected to adopt an apologetic pose, to be passive and compliant, keeping all forcefulness within.[69] They should be "sensible," aware that nature had made them for giving birth and rearing children. They might write and publish verse, even histories, but public speaking remained strictly a male occupation. Men reserved their strength for the public; getting about in this age of sociability, they inevitably had occasions to become acquainted with the domestic lives led by others. Infidelity was known not to be unusual and was generally accepted. But men understood the female sexual imagination somewhat less well than their own and portrayed it mysteriously, as Sterne did in *Tristram Shandy*.

A publicly acclaimed woman such as Maria Cosway was less under the control of her husband than the great majority of women, and while her name had been linked with the Prince of Wales before Jefferson met her, there is nothing really to substantiate this charge. Furthermore, because her husband had the reputation of an eccentric, such gossip struck within fashionable society can be discounted. Everything we know about Thomas Jefferson suggests that as he conversed with her about beauty and natural wonders, music and other forms of sensory delight, he scrupulously reminded himself that however undeserving a husband Richard Cosway may have been, he was still her husband. And he was nearby. In the early autumn of 1786, Jefferson may have found in moments of physical closeness with Maria Cosway an irresistible urge to caress this captivating female who seemed almost to have sprung from his imagination (and in writing to her as he did, he allowed his imagination to magnify her appeal). Yet, owing to the constant presence of his cautionary Head, he probably did not share full intimacy with her. That he was smitten at the time he wrote "My Head and My Heart" and in the correspondence that followed is unmistakable, yet when Maria Cosway returned to Paris for the last four months of 1787, leaving Mr. Cosway at home in London, the fire anticipated so strongly in correspondence apparently did not rekindle.

Just before he departed for Aix, Jefferson had written Trumbull in London and instructed that friend to "scold" Maria for failing to announce her imminent return to Paris, though as Jefferson scolded, he was just as certain to lay all his "affections at her feet." On his return to Paris, he wrote her a brief recap of Italy, woodenly explaining his failure to do more by invoking an extended classical comparison, that like the ancient hero Aeneas, he had been out of communication with the living. His letter of July 1 opened: "You conclude, Madam, from my long silence, that I am gone to the other world. Nothing else would have prevented my writing to you so long. I have not thought of you the less, but I took only a peep into Elysium. I entered it at one door and came out the other." He seemed to be suggesting, too, that the lack of communication could have been resolved had she earlier made the effort to return to Paris. "Why were you not with me?" he prompted. "So many enchanting scenes which only wanted your pencil to consecrate them to fame." In typical fashion he next sketched a romantic scene: "Imagine to yourself, madam, a castle and village hanging to a cloud in front, on one hand a mountain cloven through to let pass a gurgling stream." Then, asking her again when she planned to come, he projected, "Come then, my dear Madam, and we will breakfast every day à Angloise, hie away to the Desert, dine under the bowers of Marly, and forget that we are ever to part again."[70]

Their flirtation drove them to become master and mistress of one of the flattest and least revealing of epistolary forms of the age, the tease and chastisement. To Jefferson's insufficiently apologetic letter, Maria Cosway replied, pouting: "Do you not deserve a longer letter, my dear friend? No, certainly not, and to avoid temptation, I have a small sheet of paper." Professing her unhappiness in having waited so long for him to write, she pressed, "And you felt no remorse?" Glad to know he was well and back in Paris, she went on to "lament I was not a castle hanging to a cloud" in Italy, and "oh! if I had been a shadow of this *Elysium* of yours! how you would have been tormented! I must excuse you a little, since you tell me you thought of me, and Italy was your Object." With a twinkle Jefferson wrote to Trumbull, saying: "My love to Mrs. Cosway. Tell her I will send her a supply of larger paper."[71]

She did come at last, for the opening of the Grand Salon of the Louvre at the end of summer. It appears that she was daily occupied with the artists' circle, and that she and Jefferson, after such long anticipation, did not spend a great deal of time together.[72] He wrote Trumbull that there were numerous times when he had called on her only to find her away from home, and that from "the meer effect of chance," she had encountered the same when calling on him.[73] She remained in Paris through early December. After her return to London, Jefferson was not inspired to write her until mid-January. Their subsequent correspondence was certainly friendly but, on his part, much subdued. It is possible that both parties were resigned to this turn of events, though Mrs. Cosway's continuing anxiety about Jefferson's letters suggests a strong need at least for his attention.

Near the time that Maria Cosway returned to London, John Trumbull arrived back in Paris, accompanied this time by Angelica Schuyler Church, whose sister Elizabeth had married Alexander Hamilton. Mrs. Church was herself married to a member of Parliament, John Barker Church; she and her English husband had been well acquainted with Trumbull during the Revolutionary War as newlyweds living in New England. Mrs. Church and Mrs. Cosway were good friends, the latter writing to Jefferson: "She Colls' me her Sister. I coll' her my My dearest Sister. If I did not love her so Much I would fear her rivalship. But no, I give you free permission to love her with all your heart and I shall be happy if you keep me in a little corner of it."[74]

Jefferson claimed that he did not spend very much time with Angelica Church during the few months she spent in Paris, but on the eve of her return to London, he wrote to her fancifully about the means he might employ to prevent "dejection of mind" on any future parting: "When you come again, I will employ myself solely in finding or fancying that you have some faults, and I will draw a veil over all your good qualities, if I can find one large enough. I think I shall succeed in this. For, trying myself to-day, by way of exercise, I recollected immediately one fault in your composition. It is that you give all your attention to your friends, caring nothing about yourself." Envisioning a time when they might travel through America together, he added, "I have been planning what I would shew you: a flower here, a tree there; yonder a grove, near it a fountain; on this side a hill, on that a river."[75]

Mrs. Church's daughter Catherine ("Kitty"), staying at the home of Mme de Corny, had become close with Maria Jefferson. This friendship strengthened the bond between the parents, who exchanged thoughtful gifts for the children through the mail. Meanwhile, it appeared to Maria Cosway that Jefferson was ignoring her. In March 1788 she opened a letter: "I have waited some time to trie if I could recover my usual peace with you, but I find it is impossible yet, therefore Must adress Myself to you still *angry*. Your long silence is impardonable." And in June she closed another, "Tho' you neglect me, I force myself to your recolection." The next month Jefferson wrote a letter to Mrs. Cosway which began "My dear dear friend" and insisted that after a tour through Holland and the Rhine, "the only letter of private friendship I wrote on my return, and before entering on business, was to you. . . . Of voluntary faults to you I can never be guilty, and you are too good not to pardon the involuntary. Chide me then no more; be to me what you have been; and give me without measure the comfort of your friendship." Somewhat mollified, she replied in August, announcing her joy in receiving a portrait of Jefferson painted by Trumbull. Writing while in the company of Mrs. Church, she implored Jefferson to visit her before his return to America.[76]

Angelica Church had revealed to Jefferson a few weeks earlier that she and Maria were "enjoying the quiet of the country, she plays and sings, and we very often wish that Mr. Jefferson was here, supposing that he would be indulgent to the exertions of two little women to please him." Jefferson urged Mrs. Church on August 17 to join him at Le Havre once he had found "a good ship," that they might coordinate their voyage together back to America. "Think of it then, my friend," he wrote, "and let us begin a negociation on the subject. You shall find in me all the spirit of accomodation with which Yoric began his with the fair Piedmontese." Here again was Sterne, at his most sexually charged. In the final scene of *A Sentimental Journey,* Yorick and his traveling party are inconvenienced one "wet and tempestuous night," the parson obliged to share his room at the roadside inn with a Piedmontese, a lady "with a glow of health in her cheeks" accompanied by her *fille de chambre.* The two principals engage in "a two hours negociation" before arriving at a "treaty of peace," wherein sleeping arrangements in the tiny room are agreed. Yorick's bed is separated from the lady's by only a flimsy curtain. The two toss and turn, unable to sleep, and Yorick finally speaks out, "no more than an ejaculation," which the lady maintains is "an entire infraction of the treaty." The *fille de chambre* attempts to slip in the narrow passage between the disputants just as Yorick stretches out his hand, catching "hold of the fille de chambre's — "[77]

With Angelica Church, Jefferson was very much at ease, solicitous, yet without the pronounced passion that rose and receded so dramatically with Maria Cosway. That was not to be repeated with any other woman. Jefferson, so often coming into contact with attractive married women, adopted a warm, indulgent style, playful to the point of hinting at amorous possibilities, yet morally secure and nonthreatening. It seems he was too reserved to be sexually forward in person; even the allusion to Sterne on noses was a lighthearted reference, which in any case was beyond the comprehension of Maria Cosway, to judge by her confused reply: "But how could you led me by the hand all the way [through his journey], think of me, have Many things to say, and not find One word to write, *but on Noses?*"[78]

In the case of the artist Mme de Tott, Mme de Tessé's friend and protégé, Jefferson wrote appealingly, though it might as well have been in the third person. His Head monopolized all conversation with this unmarried woman. Here was Jefferson's passionless attempt to draw her into his tour of the south of France: "I presume that you think, as most people think, that a person cannot be in two places at one time. Yet is there no error more palpable than this. You know, for example, that you have been in Paris and it's neighborhood, constantly since I had the pleasure of seeing you there: yet I declare you have been with me above half my journey. I could repeat to you long conversations, word for word, and on a variety of subjects. When I find you fatigued with conversation and sighing for your pallet and pencil, I permit you to return to Paris a while, and amuse myself with philosophizing on the objects which occur."[79]

Jefferson amused himself with "objects." Contrast Sterne's brief but more convincing invocation, bringing Eliza Draper to bed with him: "I was not deceived Eliza! by my presentiment that I should find thee out in my dreams; for I have been with thee almost the whole night, alternately soothing thee, or telling thee my sorrows." A more celebrated use of this technique occurs in *Tristram Shandy,* in which the main character explains: "I have been getting forward in two different journeys together, and with the same dash of the pen. . . . I have brought myself into such a situation as no traveller ever stood before me; for I am at this moment walking across the market-place of Auxerre, with my father and my uncle Toby, in our way back to dinner; — and I am at this moment also entering Lyons, with my post-chaisse broke into a thousand pieces; — and I am, moreover, this moment in a handsome pavilion, built by Pringello, upon the banks of the Garonne . . . where I now sit rhapsodizing all these affairs."[80]

It may be correctly said that as Jefferson composed, the act of writing composed him. To women he was capable of creating an unreal, sensual, sentimental world, pretending to be escaping the sober obligations he imposed upon himself, which ruled his life. Sterne's emphasis on thought and feeling profoundly affected Jefferson throughout his formative years, culminating in the expressions chronicled in this chapter. But Jefferson, though rich in the number of imagination-prompting volumes that he owned, could never take things as far as his beloved Sterne. For example, while attempting to preserve for eternity the memory of an imagined happiness with Eliza Draper, the dying author had written in his journal, "I have brought your name *Eliza!* and Picture into my work — where they will remain — when You and I are at rest forever — some Annotator or explainer of my works in this place will take occasion, to speak of the Friendship which Subsisted so long and faithfully betwixt Yorick and the Lady he speaks of." Detailing how they had met and what their circumstances were, he continued to project their love story.

Mrs Draper had a great thirst for Knowledge — was handsome — genteel — engaging — and of such gentle dispositions and so enlightened and
understanding, — That Yorick, (whether he made such Opposition is not
known) from an acquaintance — soon became her Admirer — they caught
fire at each other at the same time — and they would often say, without
reserve to the world, and without any Idea of saying wrong in it, That
their Affections for each other were *unbounded* — Mr Draper dying in the
Year ***** — This Lady return'd to England, and Yorick the year after
becoming a Widower — They were married — and retiring to one of his
Livings in Yorkshire, there was a most romantic Situation — they lived
and died happily. — and are spoke of with honour in the parish to this
day."[81]

This audacious statement, recording the deaths of those who stood in
their way — Sterne's wife and Eliza's husband — exposed a selfish fantasy
the more Head-principled Jefferson would never have dared to indulge,
at any point, with Mrs. Cosway.

Jefferson never met Sterne, not having left American shores until
sixteen years after the author's death. However, one final connection
does seem worth noting. The miniature portrait of Eliza that Sterne
kept with him during the waning months of his life, showed proudly
wherever he went, and referred to on the opening page of *A Sentimental
Journey,* was inspired by a miniature owned by Sterne's close friends the
Jameses and painted by Richard Cosway.[82]

"THAT HE DOTH NOT CHANGE HIS COUNTRY MANNERS"

ONCE OVER HIS drawn-out flirtation with Maria Cosway and the
European style of life for which she stood, Jefferson was able to caution
restraint — by way of a diversionary grand tour — to William Short,
whose romance with the married duchess Rosalie persisted. At the
same time Jefferson began to write his most affecting letters of reminis-
cence. He emerged from his five years abroad convinced that Virginia
was where love, "a consolatory thing," "is felt in it's sublimest degree."
Refreshing in its relative simplicity and untainted by the ills of European society, America was the best place on earth to promote morals
and develop the mind. To his Albemarle neighbor Dr. George Gilmer,
he wrote wistfully, "All my wishes end where I hope my days will end,
at Monticello."[83]

Encompassing both his nostalgia for Monticello and his belief that he was best suited to the life of an enlightened farmer, Jefferson wrote meaningfully to another friend whose company he had shared in pre-Revolutionary times: "Your letter has kindled the fond recollections of antient times; recollections much dearer to me than anything I have known since. . . . No attachments soothe the mind so much as those contracted in early life; nor do I recollect any societies which have given me more pleasure, than those of which you have partaken with me. I had rather be shut up in a very modest cottage, with my books, my family, and a few old friends, dining on simple bacon, and letting the world roll on as it liked than to occupy the most splendid post which any human power can give."[84] This prose, while intended as hyperbole, still shows the cosmopolite yearning to retrieve a familiar part of his life from which official duties had separated him. Only the onset of the French Revolution the following year would lure Jefferson to desire to be present at the creation of what he was predicting as a new and better Europe. His Heart now centered on what only retirement would convey, while his Head, predictably, would determine the value of witnessing a political transition. Jefferson, this man constructed of both Head and Heart, consistently searched for a healthy balance between worldly concerns and provincial comforts.

From the beginning of his European experience, Jefferson had expressed his belief that an American education was most apt for his countrymen. To Virginian Walker Maury, son of his early teacher James Maury, he wrote after his melancholy first year in Paris: "Of all the errors which can possibly be committed in the education of youth, that of sending them to Europe is the most fatal. I see [clearly] that no American should come to Europe under 30 years of age: and [he who] does, will lose in science, in virtue, in health and in happiness, for which manners are a poor compensation, were we even to admit the hollow, unmeaning manners of Europe to be preferable to the simplicity and sincerity of our own country." He had already hinted at this sentiment in a letter to Charles Thomson: "I have always disapproved of a European education for our youth from theory: I now do it from inspection."[85]

In a letter to young John Banister, Jr., the son of a Virginia friend and a onetime student of George Wythe who was then traveling in the south of France, Jefferson summed up his feelings with a sensuousness and drama reminiscent of the resounding voice he gave to his Declaration nine years earlier.

Let us view the disadvantages of sending a youth to Europe. To enumerate them all would require a volume. I will select a few. If he goes to England he learns drinking, horse-racing and boxing. These are the peculiarities of English education. The following circumstances are common to education in that and the other countries of Europe. He acquires a fondness for European luxury and dissipation and a contempt for the simplicity of his own country; he is fascinated with the principles of the European aristocrats, and sees with abhorrence the lovely equality which the poor enjoys with the rich in his own country: he contracts a partiality for aristocracy or monarchy; he forms foreign friendships which will never be useful to him, and loses the season of life for forming in his own country those friendships which of all others are the most faithful and permanent.

Jefferson was recalling his own impressionable youth, just as he would later tell his teenage grandson that he felt fortunate in having narrowly escaped the vices that had claimed some of his mates. The list of the moral depradations and sinister seduction that Europe had come to represent to him crystallizes in the continuation of this paragraph:

He is led by the strongest of all the human passions into a spirit for female intrigue destructive of his own and others happiness, or a passion for whores destructive of his health, and in both cases learns to consider fidelity to the marriage bed as an ungentlemanly practice and inconsistent with happiness: he recollects the voluptuary dress and arts of the European women and pities and despises the chaste affections and simplicity of those of his own country; he retains thro' life a fond recollection and a hankering after those places which were the scenes of his first pleasures and of his first connections.[86]

Jefferson did not wish Banister to fall prey to that power over the mind which alone could defeat the purity of an American. Inordinately suspicious of women who did not conform to his standard of gentility, he seemed assured of his own immunity.

Anne Willing Bingham was a singularly beautiful American woman, much taken with Parisian fashions, who, along with her husband, visited Jefferson in mid-1786 and some months later returned to Philadelphia. Ten days before writing an effusive letter to her, Jefferson disdainfully reported to Madison that her husband, a would-be diplomat, was much taken with himself and "had a rage for being presented to great men," which he accomplished only when such notables were "susceptible of impression from the beauty of his wife." Though disgusted by the husband's pretensions, Jefferson, whether he liked it or not, was himself in some manner affected by Mrs. Bingham.[87]

He addressed her with accustomed ease and fancy, painting an unflattering portrait of Paris. "You are then engaged to tell me truly and honestly," Jefferson cajoled, "whether you do not find the tranquil pleasures of America preferable to the empty bustle of Paris. For to what does the bustle tend? At eleven o'clock it is chez Madame. The curtains are drawn. Propped on bolsters and pillows . . . she writes to some of her acquaintances and receives the visits of others." He continued with a day in the torpid life of a spoiled Parisian matron, concluding that nothing mattered to her but the gluttony of the present. "If death or a bankruptcy happen to trip us out of the circle, it is a matter for the buz of the evening, and is completely forgotten by the next morning." Jefferson then contrasted this with the meaning of life in America: "Every exertion is encouraging, because to present amusement it joins the promise of some future good. The intervals of leisure are filled with the society of real friends, whose affections are not thinned to cob-web by being spread over a thousand objects."[88]

Mrs. Bingham replied to Jefferson's "candor" with "a sincere declaration" of her own opinions. Acknowledging that some Parisians were consumed by the "frivolous" in their "fashionable pursuits," she protested that his picture was "rather overcharged." To her, French women were "more accomplished" in social intercourse and "the happy Art of making us pleased with ourselves." She marveled at the salons, whose coordinators could on the one hand lead "in all the fashionable Dissipation of Life, and at more serious moments" gather "an assembly of the Literati." Mrs. Bingham was duly impressed with these "Arts of Elegance" which made the mind "continually gratified with the admiration of Works and Taste."[89] Jefferson, of course, knew better than she the stimulations of the social scene; his hyperbole, for which she took him to task, was merely a design to enliven the composition. Whether we read his letter as a ritual show of regard for one he may have held in no particular esteem or the quasi-flirtatious challenge he reserved for attractive, married women, Jefferson consistently praised the virtues of his native land.

At the start of the momentous year of 1789, he wrote his younger brother Randolph, a man of lesser talents with whom he corresponded infrequently: "Nothing in this country can make amends for what one loses by quitting their own." Despite his taste for the arts of the Continent, his "frame of reference," as Merrill Peterson has written "was America, not Europe. . . . Europe had made him more profoundly American."[90] A year after his arrival in Paris, Jefferson had written Charles Bellini, an Italian who had made his home in Virginia, that he was "a savage from the mountains of America" who had "brought with me all the prejudices of country, habit and age." Years afterward, writing to John Adams, Jefferson remained adamant: "Before the establishment of the American states, nothing was known to History but the Man of the old world, crouded within limits either small or overcharged, and steeped in the vices which that situation generates." Europe, he believed, would follow America's lead, if, indeed, it could escape these circumstances of "ignorance, poverty and vice."[91] It certainly does not appear, in any case, that Jefferson's immersion in the social scene and his infatuation with Maria Cosway forced any compromise of the searing words he had for young Banister in 1785. William Short, who missed America less, wrote Jefferson from the exciting capital of Rome in March 1789 of the temptation to run through one's fortune purchasing "rare and curious things." After his shopping spree he was at wit's end and chose a moral his mentor would appreciate: "Sterne says the best way of resisting temptation is to fly it. This is what I am about to do."[92]

Maria Cosway wrote Jefferson in February 1789 that as he returned to America, she would join in spirit, "walk thro' the beautiful acres you will describe to me by letter." She ached for him to stop by London and visit en route: "T'is cruel not to do it." Complaining of the "self-interested sentiments," the "black and malicious hearts" in British politics at that moment, she went on, "Oh why am I never to achieve my great desire of finding myself in solitude with a small number of friends?" Though she seemed to miss him still, unhappy with the shortness of his letters, Jefferson perhaps had made his peace with his season of desire and longed only for home. Or he might have arrived at the same understanding Francis Bacon had reached in his essay "On Travel." On return home, Bacon advised, "let his travel appear rather in his discourse than in his apparel or gesture . . . and let it appear that he doth not change his country manners for those of foreign parts, but only prick in some flowers of that he hath learned abroad into the customs of his own country."[93]

4   *Letter Writing and Friendship*

JEFFERSON'S LETTERS WHILE he was on the Continent demonstrate the manner in which he applied his Heart, his imagination, to his relationships. Of interest, too, are the intellectual and cultural influences that gave shape to his most notable means of self-expression, his familiar letter writing. An understanding of this medium will make it easier to chart the course of Jefferson's friendships and ultimately to distinguish his most private thoughts from more "affected," ritually controlled and highly rationalized, communications.

Jefferson spent his life reaching out to others. He struggled anxiously, along with everyone else in the eighteenth-century world, to sustain reliable communications across distances. Throughout the colonies the pursuit of knowledge required careful attention and frequent stimulation. People like Jefferson and John Adams, whose aspirations extended beyond what local society could provide, ached to become acquainted with like-minded people, for intellectual male companionship. They had no more efficient means than letter writing. Noted a young John Adams, "We are seldom so happy, as to find Company much inclined to Speculation, and as some of us, can find no Company at all, the only Method left, is that of Correspondences." Letters had "all the Advantages of Conversation, with the Additional ones of searching deeper into subjects." Seventeen years later he would add to this statement, detailing what perceptive study over the course of time had brought him to understand about different writing styles. Amid excitement over the proclamation of the Declaration of Independence, he wrote to his wife: "The epistolary is essentially different from the oratorical and the historical style. Oratory abounds with figures [i.e., figurative speech]. History is simple, but grave, majestic, and formal. Letters, like conversation, should be free, easy, and familiar."[1]

While the character of the two dynamic colonies of Virginia and Massachusetts differed, they had in common a generation of rising lawyers, assertive men who possessed the tools to hold their own in political discourse, who maintained what Richard Brown has called "quasi-fraternal networks" by frequent letter writing. It was this group who would assume the advocacy for the colonies as a whole and translate elite notions of liberty and tyranny to inspire less wellborn men to enlist in the American cause. Buoyant personalities, self-confident activists, had acquired refined language, concepts of civic virtue and classical dignity, knowledge of history and political philosophy, oratorical skills, and clever reasoning.[2] These attributes enabled them to set aside differences in customs and outlook and find commonality of purpose in the 1770s. As individuals, their reputations rose to a large extent with their production of pamphlets and public documents. And, in order to personalize their cooperation, share confidences, or simply stay in touch between gatherings, the genteel Revolutionaries relied on the medium of the familiar letter.

The Ciceronian Ethos

Familiar letter writing already had a considerable history by this time. Jefferson and like-minded men actively applied its inherited conventions. Rhetoric and the epistolary form owe their origin to the ancients, to Cicero, Quintilian, Seneca, and Pliny, whose works Jefferson owned in Latin and in translation. Few in America equaled him in devotion to a classical education. He wrote in his *Notes on Virginia:* "The learning of Greek and Latin, I am told, is going into disuse in Europe. I know not what their manners and occupations may call for: but it would be very ill-judged in us to follow their example in this instance."[3] Furthermore, he collected Indian vocabularies and never ceased to be fascinated by the logic, structure, and pronunciation of language.[4] In proposing names for the new American territories to be established when Virginia ceded its western lands in 1784, Jefferson preferred classical designations such as Cherronesus, "the peninsula," for what would eventually become northern Michigan; Metropotamia, "the land measured by the rivers," for southern Michigan/northern Ohio; and Polypotamia, "the land rich in streams," for the area of southern Illinois/northern Indiana/western Kentucky.[5]

For Jefferson the foremost authority was Cicero, who linked masculine virtue, self-control, self-improvement, and the dignified expression of character through epistolary eloquence. After a youth devoted to study of the classics, Jefferson reread the many volumes of Cicero's letters during his retirement at Monticello. He described Cicero as "able," "learned," and "honest," the "first master" of style.[6] Cicero epitomized the accomplished early writers who published their largely uncensored thought, moral-philosophical exposition, disguised in familiar correspondence.

In the *Epistolae ad Atticum,* Cicero wrote his beloved friend Atticus through times of personal and political trial. "Who can prefer speaking to writing?" he once asked. "How much more did I learn from your letters, than from [the letter-bearer's] conversation?" Going into exile, Cicero showed how expressive words can enrich friendship and humbly support one's public reputation at the same time: "All I beg of you is, that as you have ever loved me personally, you will continue in the same affections. I am still the same man. My enemies have robbed me of all external comforts but not of my internal peace and satisfaction."[7]

Compare Jefferson. In June 1781, during his troubled wartime governorship, he was personally and politically wounded when Virginians accused him of cowardice in evading capture by the British.[8] He attempted to uphold the Ciceronian ethos the following spring in a letter to friend and protégé James Monroe, in which he explained his decision to leave politics: "Before I ventured to declare to my countrymen my determination to retire from public employment I examined well my heart to know whether it were thoroughly cured of every principle of political ambition, whether no lurking particle remained which might leave me uneasy when reduced within the limits of mere private life. I became satisfied that every fibre of that passion was thoroughly eradicated" (fig. 9). Sensuous language and statement of principle combined to fortify outer dignity and restore inner ease. As he continued to express his thoughts through this medium, Jefferson curiously crossed out the word "esteem" and substituted the more personal "affection" in declaring what it was that he sought from his countrymen. At the hands of the "well-meaning but uninformed," "I had been suspected and suspended in the eyes of the world without the least hint then or afterwards made public which might restrain them from supposing I stood arraigned for treasons of the heart and not mere weaknesses of the head. And I felt that these injuries, for such they have been since acknowledged, had inflicted a wound on my spirit which will only be cured by the all-healing grave." These revelations were mingled with anxiety over his wife's final illness. Yet a hearty expression of friendship was not lost in the composition. In closing, he invited Monroe to visit Monticello: "It will give me great pleasure to see you here whenever you can favor us with your company. . . . you will find me to retain a due sense of your friendship."[9]

Dear Sir   Monticello May 20 1782

    I have been gratified with the receipt of your two favours of the 5th & 11th inst. ~~which~~ ~~~~ ~~the~~ ~~~~ it, that your county has been wise enough to en--list your talents into their service. I am much obliged by the kind wishes you express ~~and you~~ of seeing me also in Richmond, and am always mortified when anything is expected from me which I cannot fulfll, I more especially ~~where~~ if it relate to the public service. before I ventured to declare to my countymen my determination to retire from public employment I examined well my heart to know whether it were thoroughly cured of every prin--ciple of political ambition, whether no lurking particle remained which might leave me uneasy ~~~~ when reduced within the limits of mere private life. I became satisfied that every fibre of that passion was thoroughly eradicated. I examined   also in ~~~~ other views my right to withdraw. I considered that I had been thirteen ~~twelve~~ years engaged in public service. that during that time I had so totally abandoned all attention to my private af--fairs as to permit them to run into great disorder and

While most men of consequence dictated to scribes, Cicero revealed that he wrote Atticus in his own hand. Their friendship was repeatedly put in such terms as these: "I know how much you are my friend; I know how solicitous, how anxious, your affections are"; "It gives me pleasure to hear from you, were it only to know that you have nothing to say." Lamenting that "I cannot ˋenjoy life without you," Cicero said, "Scribbling and writing do not sooth my sorrows, but they stupify my brain." To his brother Quintus, Cicero wrote of his "anxiety, and, as always happens when one's affections are engaged, I never cease imagining what I least desire to imagine."[10] For Cicero, and mirrored in Jefferson's letters, writing to a friend was undertaken to alleviate tension and effect emotional release.

But writing did not simply satisfy private needs. Friendship was associated with public virtue. Elsewhere Cicero wrote of its cultivation: "Friendship was given by nature as a helper in virtue . . . because virtue cannot reach the greatest heights in solitude."[11] He believed that individuals were responsible for their own destinies, their minds illuminated by constant desire for self-improvement through knowledge of nature. Virtue (nature carried to perfection) was the thinker-statesman's constant concern, applied equally to writing and to social activity.

The dignity of great writing could be expressed no more convincingly than in familiar letters. In the preface of his 1751 translation of *Epistolae ad Atticum,* William Guthrie revealed how the mid-eighteenth century was incorporating the ancient worldview into its own. He and his contemporaries were searching for greater personal intimacy:

> They [the Epistles] are written in the language of friendship, a language which friends alone understand. If there is any material difference between human nature in that age and this, it lies in the conception of virtue. The following pages evince, there was a time, when friendship in the human breast could rise into a passion strong as their love, and sacred as their religion, but without the impurities that sometimes debased the one, and the superstitions that always polluted the other. The friendship of our author for Atticus, is full of nice suspicions, delicate jealousies, kind fears, and fond endearments. It has every characteristic of violent, but virtuous, passion. It breathes every tender grace that delights the mind, and awakens every soft emotion that affects the heart.[12]

In other words, what may appear to the late twentieth-century ear as highly stylized and conventionally repressive of emotion offered the eighteenth-century reader a meaningful glimpse of the inner life. Translator Guthrie recognized that the greatness of letters lay in the unintended revelation of human nature, "in all its beauties, and with all its blemishes; with all its virtue, and with all its weaknesses." Cicero's love of Atticus "triumphs in his soul; sparkling amidst his affections, and unextinguished by his calamities."[13] This is the height to which Jefferson aspired in emulation of the masters of eloquence.

The letters of Pliny offer another classical model of epistolography demonstrating friendship, honor, and social advancement.[14] Recommending a friend for a military position, Pliny wrote: "Our friendship began with our studies, and we were early united in the closest intimacy. . . . In his conversation, and even in his very voice and countenance, there is the most amiable sweetness. . . . He has so happy a turn for epistolary writing, that were you to read his letters, you would imagine they had been dictated by the Muses themselves." William Melmoth, the eighteenth-century translator-editor of Pliny, followed this text with instructive comments from Locke's *Treatise on Education:* "The writing of letters enters so much into all the occasions of life, that no gentleman can avoid shewing himself in compositions of this kind. Occurrences will daily force him to make this use of his pen, which lays open his breeding, his sense, and his abilities, to a severer examination than any oral discourse." When Thomas Jefferson wanted to convey to James Madison his impression of John Adams's son-in-law William S. Smith, he noted, "You can judge of Smith's abilities by his letters."[15]

Without insisting that a candidate's letter-writing talent was always the key to advancement, we can still point to the sentiment and style of Pliny's example in letters of introduction that travelers and office seekers carried in the new American Republic. Jefferson's in 1781 on behalf of then law student William Short is typical: "The bearer Mr. William Short purposing to Philadelphia for the prosecution of his studies, I do myself the honor under authority of the acquaintance I had the pleasure of forming with you in Philadelphia, of introducing him to your notice, persuaded that you should give him an opportunity of being known to you, you will think it a circumstance not merely indifferent to add to the number of your well wishers a gentleman of very uncommon genius, erudition and merit."[16]

Medieval Italians taken with rhetoric and law were first to revive the Ciceronian form. They devised rules for every *epistole,* including a fixed greeting, or *salutatio,* followed by a statement designed to create a favorable impression, then the body of the letter or petition and a proper conclusion.[17] But the familiar letter in Italy took on an entirely new complexion in the fourteenth century, when the prolific Petrarch imbued his epistles with a new spirit of individuality. Jefferson's century was indebted to that Italian for his refinement of classical epistolography.

Petrarch declared his style to be "plain, domestic and friendly," asserting that the value in letter writing lay in communicating in "ordinary speech." To "know the mind and heart of one's interlocutor," he stated, "is not a difficult art." In another letter he protested that "whatever I say to friends is in large measure spontaneous. . . . Great love needs no artificial eloquence." He was referring to the love of a friend, with whom one can "dare express everything as though to yourself." He eschewed ornamentation, repeatedly invoking the example of Cicero. Like the Roman, who wrote to his friend Atticus that there was nothing "sweeter" than to correspond without constraint, Petrarch delighted in his own inconsistency. "I strive for the truth by hesitating, pondering, and deliberating."[18]

Petrarch's contribution to the development of familiar letter writing was this emphasis on the mind at leisure, expressive of natural emotions, in a revival of the classical value that coupled friendship and writing. His fascination with Cicero was not so much with the celebrated orator whose talent he applauded but rather with the self-revelatory correspondent who provided insights into his time as he demonstrated an uncomplicated sense of fellowship in the leisurely nature of a letter's composition. There was, for Petrarch, a historical treat to be had in the close examination of familiar letter writing.

Seeing classical greatness in such terms, Petrarch and succeeding humanists deemphasized *contentio,* or political oratory, in favor of *sermo,* informal, more conversational, but nonetheless elegant discourse. They upheld the Ciceronian ideal, combining scholarly expertise with worldly engagement. As teachers or public servants, they straddled the line that separated the spiritual or contemplative from more practical pursuits, balancing their ancient and modern allegiances. As John F. Tinkler has said of Renaissance humanism, the intellectual was "essentially contemplative and tied to the past, while the life of practical affairs [was] active and tied to the present."[19]

Jefferson knew Petrarch's poetry and went out of his way to visit Petrarch's villa in Avignon, France,[20] but there is no direct evidence of his having read the Italian's epistles. Nevertheless, we can see Jefferson as an heir to the Petrarchan humanist tradition. Writing apart from official duties, and often removed to pastoral settings, the humanists were ambivalent about the public system they claimed to honor. Petrarch's successors in the art of self-expression embodied an independent and even defiant spirit which was conducive to later notions of political liberalism.[21]

There are clear Petrarchan elements in Jefferson's familiar letter writing. For example, at a time of escalating partisan debates, he wrote from Monticello to his faithful republican companion William Branch Giles: "I shall be rendered very happy by the visit you promise me. The only thing wanting to make me completely so, is the more frequent society with my friends. It is the more wanting, as I am become more firmly fixed to the glebe. If you visit me as a farmer it must be as a condisciple: for I am but a learner; an eager one indeed, but yet desperate, being too old now to learn a new art. However, I am as much delighted & occupied with it, as if I was the greatest adept. I shall talk with you about it from morning till night, and put you on very short allowance as to political aliment."[22] Here, a resigned manner mixes with the pastoral theme in the expression of friendship. Jefferson's mock-embarrassment does not make him appear any less the master of his self. A disinterested, even self-deprecatory tone surfaces without diminishing the overall effect of self-confidence that makes him available as a political leader. The Ciceronian ethos stands behind such expression, the idea that authority is established and dignified actions flow from constancy of character. Jefferson appears now a virtuous example of neoclassical contentment, the philosopher-citizen in retreat, and a cultivator of the sort he idealized in his *Notes on Virginia*.[23]

SELF-REVELATION AND SELF-CULTIVATION

THE FAMILIAR LETTER advanced in the form of Montaigne's profound and introspective *essais* in the sixteenth century, which Jefferson read in French and numerous times quoted in correspondence.[24] Montaigne implied in a 1588 appendix that the *essais* would have taken the form of personal correspondence had not the intended recipient of all this knowledge, his dear friend La Boëtie, died. Thus he wrote "to find in himself what he had lost in his friend."[25]

In the process of opening himself up, Montaigne made obligatory references to Cicero: "I also like reading the *Letters to Atticus,* not only because they contain a very ample education in the history and affairs of Cicero's time, but much more because in them I discover his personal humors. For I have a singular curiosity, as I have said elsewhere, to know the soul and natural judgment of my authors." The "soul and natural judgment," that which mattered most in conversation, appeared not in self-edited texts but in uncensored expression. Montaigne referred to Brutus's lost book on virtue: "I would rather have an exact report of the conversations he held with some of his close friends in the tent on the eve of battle than the speech he delivered the next day to his army. I had rather know what he did in his study and his chamber than what he did in the Forum and before the Senate."[26]

Montaigne did not doubt that his way of writing departed from classical rhetoric, being a more natural form of self-expression, "free and irregular in its arrangement" [*dispositions libres et dereglées*], spontaneous and subjective. He regarded Cicero as pretentious and self-promoting. Jefferson shared this critical perspective, recognizing, in Karl Lehmann's words, "a lack of conscience, charity, and philanthropy" in the Roman example. Classical antiquity provided a conceptual framework but by no means a model of perfection. To Joseph Priestley, Jefferson wrote that he conceived of progress in forward-looking terms rather than the "Gothic idea" of seeking "improvement of the human mind" or "perfect" government or religion by recurring to the past. Montaigne was likewise forward-looking; his "book of the self" was the first to celebrate the individual experience leisurely, experimentally, anecdotally — a milestone in familiar letter writing and self-expression.[27]

Montaigne distrusted extreme eloquence. In his own work form surrendered to content. His approach to friendship and the private self exemplified what would become an integral part of the modern familiar letter. "Our free will," he wrote, "has no product more properly its own than affection and friendship." Friendship was a "harmony of wills," "bred, nourished and increased only in enjoyment, since it is spiritual, and the soul grows refined by practice."[28]

Ultimately, though, Petrarch remained in Montaigne's humanist conscience. Both believed that learning improved character and introspection brought knowledge of man's truest potential. It was by means of learning and introspection that man could take possession of himself. Both appreciated the illuminating use of familiar letters — as intimate conversation—in the process of self-knowledge. Indeed, through to Jefferson's day, *conversation* itself contained a wider range of meaning than the word does today. The 1783 edition of Dr. Johnson's *Dictionary* defined *conversation* first as "familiar discourse," while still retaining the Renaissance sense of "behavior; a manner of acting in common life."[29]

The British Whigs and French and Scottish philosophes who preceded Jefferson all profited from this rich tradition. They were aided by the expansion of a discriminating reading public. Men of letters no longer necessarily required, as in Petrarch's day, prominent people to serve as their patrons.[30] Ideas circulated more freely, and writing became a more widely practiced pleasure, celebrating individuality.

Naturally, as a product of his times, Jefferson was influenced by the letter-writing manner of his contemporaries. Perhaps none of these was so absorbed in the transforming power of the familiar letter as the English novelist Samuel Richardson (1689–1761), who referred to letter writing as "the cement of friendship . . . friendship avowed under hand and seal." He achieved tremendous popularity with his epistolary novels *Pamela: or Virtue Rewarded* (1740) and *Clarissa* (1747), sentimental works that praised virtuous behavior in a world of corrupt influences. In the list Jefferson prepared in 1771 for Robert Skipwith, he recommended both of these, which is not surprising; they were among the most popular books of the age. With Richardson, the nature of reading had come to be understood "not as a substitute for experience but a primary emotional experience itself, a constituent of identity, a way of understanding and making one's self."[31]

Richardson saw the medium of the letter as a precipitant to dramatic action. A letter was something to comment on, a document which demanded care and time and, he might say, formed the heart of life's activities. As his characters were absorbed in the contemplation and production of soulful personal letters, Richardson himself wrote to an admiring lady in 1748 that letter writing was friendship "more pure, yet more ardent, and less broken in upon, than personal conversation can be amongst the most pure, because of the deliberation it allows, from the very preparation to, and action of writing."[32]

In contrast stood the erudite Samuel Johnson (1709–1784). Jefferson owned the groundbreaking *Dictionary* from an early age, thought the two men otherwise had little in common in outlook. Most notably, Johnson opposed Enlightenment rationalism and stressed revealed religion.[33] A vivid and versatile and at times flippant letter writer, he professed to view leter writing as hardly more than utilitarian. When he had something to communicate, he did so in a proper and businesslike manner. Yet he softened from time to time, to ask his favorite correspondent, Mrs. Thrale, whether she kept his letters: "They will, I hope, always be in some degree the records of a pure and blameless friendship, and in some hours of languour and sadness may revive the memory of more cheerful times." Once he provoked her by declaring, "Some, when they write to their friends, are all affection; some are wise and sententious; some strain their powers for efforts of gaiety; some write news, and some write secrets; but to make a letter without affection, without wisdom, without gaiety, without news, and without a secret, is, doubtless, the great epistolick art." He then added to this sprightly critique: "In a man's letters, you know, Madam, his soul lies naked, his letters are only the mirrour of his breast; whatever passes within him is shown undisguised in its natural processes; nothing is inverted, nothing distorted; you see systems in their elements; you discover actions in their motives." Johnson's standard for epistolary virtuosity demanded knowledge and command of words, imagination ("to place things in such views as they are not commonly seen in"), and presence of mind.[34]

Letters were the "life blood" of the Enlightenment. From the 1760s, prompted by the diffusion of creative ideas from Parisian salons, letter writers sought to converse with a wider audience, willingly putting writers and readers on a more nearly equal footing. Through the copied letter, the circulated letter, the open letter, readers became writers and contributed to this age of sociability and cosmopolitanism. The salons not only brought together provocative minds who then entered into private correspondence; they also produced philosophic newsletters that made the republic of letters an ever-expanding community and elevated the letter into a celebratory form for human aspirations.[35]

On the eve of the romantic age (which some date from the start of the French Revolution in 1789), letter writing allowed an imaginative diversion from traditional social constraints and ultimately a complete surrender to impulse and passion. In the process it opened the mind to "natural" sources of inspiration, metaphoric possibilities that engaged the writer with the natural world or simply prompted a bolder expression of human nature.[36] The taste for cultural primitivism that Ossian represented (sentiment) replaced the authority of Johnson's *Dictionary* (reason). The liberated imagination could now produce a more forceful picture of one's thought. Someone like Jefferson could write with the social consciousness, the "self-adaptation," of Francis Bacon (the self checked by society) or the ardent "self-unfolding" and "self-reflection" of Montaigne. Indeed, like Bacon, whom he termed, with Newton and Locke, one of "the three greatest men the world had ever produced," Jefferson combined theoretical themes with concrete, businesslike plans; and, like Montaigne, he was conscious of his autonomous self. Man, more than ever, was in control of his moral universe, free to cultivate himself through the creative use of words.[37]

Hugh Blair, professor of rhetoric of Edinburgh University, published a series of his lectures in 1783, two decades after promoting Macpherson's Ossian. His *Lectures on Rhetoric and Belles Lettres* quickly became preeminent at universities in Great Britain and America and remained so for at least the next half century. Jefferson repeatedly recommended this author to students and honored Madison's request in 1784 to procure a copy. Blair's work is not only representative of the age in which Jefferson wrote but also of that influence on Jefferson's development as a stylist of language which was not strictly classical or legal.[38]

Blair said of his time that whereas "improvements in every part of science, have been prosecuted with ardour," none of the liberal arts had been more favored than "the beauty of language, and the grace and elegance of every kind of writing. The public ear is become refined." Invoking (though not by name) the discourse begun by Locke, he defined reason, the Enlightenment's venerable standard for development of thought, as "that process of mind which in speculative matters discovers truth, and in practical matters judges the fitness of means to an end." Reason, however, only enhanced pleasure; intuition produced it. Taste, "the power of receiving pleasure from the beauties of nature and of art," though not instinctive, belonged to the most fundamental of sensations, even closer than reason to human nature.[39]

In its most profound manifestation, taste, to Blair, revealed a person's moral superiority: "Wherever the affections, characters, or actions of men are concerned . . . there can be neither any just or affecting description of them, nor any thorough feeling of the beauty of that description, without our possessing the virtuous affections. He whose heart is indelicate or hard, he who has no admiration of what is truly noble or praiseworthy, nor the proper sympathetic sense of what is soft and tender, must have a very imperfect relish of the highest beauties of eloquence and poetry."[40]

Taste could be taught, and man was improvable. Blair's optimism is clearly reflected in Jefferson, so attuned to man's educability. As one who popularized the beliefs that human beings were naturally endowed with both talents (intellectual energy) and political rights, Jefferson accepted that beyond the force of reason, qualities of human nature (sense) motivated progress. He relied upon Locke's epistemological writings and, as Charles Miller has noted critically, "distrusted or was willing to ignore what he could not sense." As a thinker Jefferson saw reason as an aid to the senses; he perceived that both combined in the act of writing. Karl Lehmann has written as well of Jefferson's Lockean understanding: taste was a natural endowment, and language, as the vehicle of ideas, was a sensual vehicle whose "very life was expanding imagination, by the sole means of which reason as well as memory could become articulate and the moral sense could crystallize principles."[41]

For Blair, style in writing, "the peculiar manner in which a man expresses his conceptions," was something beyond mere choice of words. He cited, for example, the importance of sound, the musicality of words used to "facilitate certain emotions." To avoid monotony, short sentences should be mixed with "long and swelling ones, to render discourse sprightly." Yet, to apply too much effort to producing harmony was to exceed "proper bounds." Blair settled for moderation: "Sense has its own harmony, as well as sound; and where the sense of a period is expressed with clearness, force, and dignity, it will seldom happen but that the words will strike the ear agreeably." Late in life, in keeping with his comments to John Adams and the grammarian John Waldo, Jefferson wrote to the oratorical Edward Everett, a Boston Unitarian about to embark on a distinguished political career, "I readily sacrifice the niceties of syntax to euphony and strength."[42]

This view seems consistent with Jefferson in his prime, too. In "Thoughts on English Prosody," which he completed in Paris in 1786, Jefferson revealed how he regarded the structure of poetry and prose. The twenty-seven-page effort is a technical analysis of rhythm and accent, in which he emphasized the musicality of words: no matter if written in prose form or in stanzas, poetry contains intentional, built-in pauses and emphases, the "charms of music," which any person who

owns "a well-organized ear" can discern.[43] Jefferson was probably be-
holden to Blair's "The Nature of Poetry," "Versification," and the chapter on Homer and Virgil for support, if not directly for structure, of his
thesis. "Man," wrote Blair, "is both a poet and a musician by nature."
His assessment of the superiority of blank verse as a "noble, bold, and
disencumbered species of versification . . . particularly suited to subjects of dignity and force" contrasts with the "strict regularity of rhyme"
better suited to works that have no need for strong emotion. This is
mirrored in Jefferson's decisive statement toward the end of his essay:
"What proves the excellence of blank verse is that the taste lasts longer
than that for rhyme. The fondness for the jingle leaves us with that for
the rattles and baubles of childhood, and if we continue to read rhymed
verse at a later period in life it is such only where the poet has had the
force enough to bring great beauties of thought and diction into this
form. When young any composition pleases which unites a little sense,
some imagination, and some rhythm." If Jefferson concluded that only
Homer and Virgil remained the standards for immortality in poetry
(echoing Blair's refusal to class anything other than the *Iliad* and the
Aeneid as epics), he was at the same time implicitly suggesting that all
sophisticated writing is orchestrated, conditioned by its rhythmic
force.[44]

Jefferson frequently praised the sound of the Greek language, to
which Lehmann has attributed the "vigorous, rich, and beautiful" in
Jefferson's writing style. Never "scrupulous about words when they are
once explained," Jefferson liked the flexibility of Greek, its built-in poetic license. He once speculated in a letter to his friend John Page (albeit
with political overtones) that "the modern Greek is not yet so far departed from it's antient model, but that we might still hope to see the
language of Homer and Demosthenes flow with purity from the lips
of a free and ingenious people."[45] It was the vitality and imagination
of the language that influenced his thoughts about the modern Greeks'
potential as a self-governing people.

In Hugh Blair's prescription for effective writing, the Roman masters were worthy of study but insufficient in imagination for the
eighteenth-century mind. "Language is become a vehicle by which the
most delicate and refined emotions of one's mind can be transmitted,
or, if we may so speak, transfused into another."[46] Since nature endowed the writer with ability, method and rule—even Blair's own—
were of secondary importance. No figure of speech could bring beauty

or elegance to a composition which lacked those qualities. Merit lay in animation, what at one point he called "spirited conciseness."

On the subject of the epistolary medium, Blair thought traditionally: "Even if there should be nothing very considerable in the subject; yet if the spirit and turn of the correspondence be agreeable; if they be written in a sprightly manner, and with native grace and ease, they may still be entertaining." He expressed a guarded view about the contents of letters: "It is childish indeed to expect, that in letters we are to find the whole human heart of the author unveiled. Concealment and disguise take place, more or less, in all human intercourse. But still, as letters from one friend to another make the nearest approach to conversation, we may expect to see more of a character displayed in these than in other productions, which are studied for public view."[47]

There are thus two kinds of epistolary history, the kind over which the subject exercises control and the kind which chronicles a truer intimacy between writer and recipient. Lord Bolingbroke, whom Jefferson esteemed both as a writer and as a political philospher, contrasted Cicero with Pliny. The former was the more self-revelatory, his imperfections visible in the letters to Atticus; the latter wrote his letters for the public. Both were close-up views of history, but qualitatively different. Horace Walpole, a man of letters and near contemporary of Jefferson, writing to a friend who was considering collecting his own correspondence for publication, remarked, "Familiar letters written by eyewitnesses, and that, without design, disclose circumstances that let us more intimately into important events, are genuine history; and as far as they go, more satisfactory than formal premeditated narratives."[48]

We can appreciate the tension between "genuine history" deliberately compiled by the subject and "genuine history" reconstructed from letters not necessarily selected by the letter writer for publication. Walpole did not regard the sanctity of the genre in the same way that Bolingbroke apparently did, the latter professing no desire for "Epistolary fame" and expressing preference for the "pleasure" of reading history though the discovery of letters that were written without the public in mind, to "pry into a Secret which was intended to be kept from us."[49]

Jefferson did not write, even his most personal letters, without reserve. He did not gush. He adhered largely to the conventions of his time. On the other hand, he had little desire to publish his personal letters and had a limited audience in mind when he wrote them.[50] In a letter which reveals much about his tendency to experiment with his thoughts when writing his friends, Jefferson castigated the Quaker George Logan for having exposed their earlier correspondence to the public, using Jefferson's name. A writer must defend his words when he sets out to debate a public issue, Jefferson asserted, but "this is not our purpose when we write to a friend. We are careless, incorrect, in haste, perhaps under some transient excitement, and we hazard things without reflection, because without consequence in the bosom of a friend."[51]

For Jefferson, the act of writing contained an implied trust. Perhaps the best way to characterize his letters is: part history, part art; intention and invention. They show the range of his interests, the amount of time he spent in reflection, and—both as public and private communications—the quality of what emerged.

MENTORS AND FRIENDS

FRIENDSHIP IS A wonderful mystery of time. It is, in any age, a prime social relation, universally understood to be an important source of entertainment and emotional fulfillment, an intellectual outlet, a desirable instrument for acquiring images of all that exists beyond the self. It can offer a convenient (and sometimes crucial) sounding board for one's own thoughts, more powerful than family by its voluntary nature. Indeed, it may compete with, or even substitute for, family in a person's developing sense of trust, responsibility, and expectation. Friendship is conditioned by chance—opportunity—and what we sometimes call "chemical" attraction. It acquires a strong moral dimension as it grows and, by the simple nature of the sharing of confidences, involves the risk of self-disclosure. It makes the demand of a person that he or she be willing to communicate vulnerability.[52]

Examining Jefferson's use of the written word and applying these universal qualities to his friendships show that he relied greatly on his emotional connections. He displayed his trust in often subdued but nonetheless emotionally rich language. But friendship must also have, like language itself, a temporal and social context. Discovering the particular nature of eighteenth-century friendship leads to a better understanding of personal and political alignments in the early American Republic.

Jefferson's friendships can be divided into categories according to his and his friends' ages and cultural backgrounds. In addition to forming friendships with his peers, he recognized the crucial importance of cultivating knowledgeable elders to gain initiation into American elite society, and even before being dispatched to Paris in 1784, he wanted to form connections with the luminaries of Europe. Jefferson profited as well from the mentoring process, first as a student and later as a mentor himself.

Dr. William Small, professor of mathematics, had arrived from Scotland two years before seventeen-year-old Thomas Jefferson matriculated at the College of William and Mary. Dr. Small's "enlarged and liberal mind," his communicative manner, and his particular attachment to young Jefferson, made the first-year student feel as passionate about mathematics as he did the classics. In his memoir, written in 1821, Jefferson asserted that Small had "probably fixed the destinies of my life." He described how the professor "made me his daily companion when not engaged in the school; and from his conversation I got my first views of the expansion of science, and of the system of things in which we are placed."[53]

Sometime after their relationship began, Small was appointed to fill a temporary vacancy in the chair of philosophy. He "was the first who ever gave, in that college, regular lectures in Ethics, Rhetoric, and Belles-lettres." Perhaps equally as important, in 1762, before he left for Europe, Small introduced Jefferson to the dinner table of the enlightened colonial governor Francis Fauquier and to George Wythe, the legal scholar who would carry on the direction of this devoted student.[54]

Wythe was Jefferson's second mentor, who later became his good friend and political ally in critical times. An impressionable Jefferson found in Wythe, nearly twice his age when they met, those qualities of mind which he would strive to express with his pen: a healthy balance between classical scholarship for an understanding of the human heart and the use of the law for taking practical, public action. Judging from Jay Fliegelman's account of eighteenth-century pedagogical tendencies, the fatherless Jefferson might also have found in his mentor, like the Greek Telemachus, "the ideal parent of one's disposition." From Paris in 1787, enclosing books, Jefferson wrote to Wythe "with every possible sentiment of esteem and respect" of "my debt to you for whatever I am myself." Time did not lessen this sentiment. In 1820 Jefferson addressed the author of a proposed biography of Wythe, comparing his late teacher's "exalted virtue" to a "polar star." Recalling that the statesman had never made a single enemy, he further praised: "No man ever left behind him a character more venerated." This just and temperate man, devoted to human rights, was "the honor of his own, and the model of future times." Jefferson was not blindly expressing the lifelong gratitude of an accomplished student, for Benjamin Rush echoed the sentiment: 'I have seldom known a man to possess more modesty, or a dovelike simplicity and gentleness of manner."[55]

A humane man with philosophical purposes, Wythe taught Jefferson mental discipline, including an early morning regimen which Jefferson maintained throughout his life. (His daughter Martha described him as an "early riser." A visitor to Monticello in 1809 observed that even in retirement the sun never sees him in bed, and his mind designs more than the day can fulfill.") Wythe helped nurture an already growing love of books and is said to have influenced even his pupil's democratic orthographical style, by which nouns were not capitalized; Wythe went even further than Jefferson, lowercasing the word *I*. And as Jefferson years later would find himself accused, Wythe was often criticized for being too erudite, too philosophically minded. It was Wythe who prodded Jefferson to read Homer in the original Greek.[56] Jefferson would strongly advise that those in his charge—his nephew Peter Carr and later his grandson Thomas Jefferson Randolph—do the same. Curiously, while Wythe and Jefferson were both lawyers of exceptional quality, they were poor orators. This does not suggest any necessary correlation; during the 1790s Wythe was mentor to another lawyer-in-training, the captivating speaker Henry Clay.

According to modern literature on the subject, the mentor has several related functions that come into play according to the needs of the protégé at certain stages of development. He or she can be teacher and trainer, resource and consultant, host and guide, sponsor and career role model, informal counselor, and friend and confidant(e). It appears that George Wythe served Jefferson in all of these capacities at one time or other, a parent and peer combined. Moreover, in eighteenth-century America it was common practice for a young man who aspired to advance himself in society to seek, often but not always through familial connections, a patron to make the way easier.[57] In Jefferson's case familial connections did not precede the student's arrival in Williamsburg; but during his long stay there, his familial attachment to the Wythes became in fact more pronounced than Jefferson's actual blood ties.

Mentoring differs from apprenticeship. It is not an arbitrary process imposed on any student but rather an elective process over which the student exercises personal control. Once he projects his receptivity to a potential mentor, the mentor can significantly and dramatically influence the process of his protégé's accession to adulthood, providing a vision which serves to alter the latter's potentially static self-perception. He may use his influence to conserve and deepen traditional values, or he may break with tradition, offering the younger person the fruits of his own mind and experience. Whichever path is taken, the student tends to internalize the ideology of the trusted mentor and employ it as a framework for adult expression.[58]

Adolescent rebellion was not a natural part of life's processes in the mid-eighteenth century; society had the dominant role in defining the adult identity of the individual. Thus, entrusting a mentor with responsibility for one's direction came somewhat easily. Possibly seeing as merely rhetorical Jefferson's statement in later years that he faced the real temptations of gambling and other irresponsible pastimes during college, Malone has observed that Jefferson's particular attraction to the older generation at that time is a sign that he was intellectually precocious, restrained, and of a serious humor.[59]

In George Wythe, Thomas Jefferson found a model of intellectual purity, a steadfast will and liberal mind to affirm the correctness of his own course. In 1765, during the Stamp Act crisis, Wythe and the older members of the House of Burgesses adopted a principled but conciliatory approach to the problem of taxation, while the fiery young Patrick Henry made his reputation by accelerating the challenge to the crown. Jefferson stood by and listened intently, and later defended the more conservative Wythe as having "begun the opposition on the same grounds." Agreeing ultimately with Henry's approach in this instance, Jefferson noted that the two generations were able to find a pace of resistance comfortable to all. Jefferson recognized that the mentor could influence, without binding.[60]

After Jefferson had completed his studies, Wythe brought him to the General Court. Later they teamed to rewrite Virginia's laws; it was Wythe who introduced Jefferson's proposed Virginia constitution in June 1776 and then worked closely with his former student to revise Virginia's laws: 126 bills were presented in all.[61] As a friend Wythe demonstrated his sentiment in tireless devotion rather than sweet words. When Jefferson's Shadwell home burned down in 1770, incinerating his library, Wythe sent useful items, life-sustaining gifts of nectarines, apricot grafts, and grapevines for the orchard Jefferson was planning for

Monticello. When the teacher died in 1806, he willed his former student the whole of his library, perhaps not worthy of "a place in his museum, but, estimated by my good will to him, the most valuable to him of anything which I have the power to bestow." Jefferson, in turn, planned to erect a monument to his teacher amid a grove of trees atop Monticello.[62]

Both Wythe and Jefferson were conscious of the power that one generation could exercise over the next. Jefferson wrote to his grandson years later how his own life might have taken a different course without the intercession of his early models. He recalled that he had felt the "incessant wish that I could even become what they were. Under temptations and difficulties, I could ask myself what would Dr. Small, Mr. Wythe, Peyton Randolph [a cousin who served prominently in the Virginia House of Burgesses] do in this situation? What course in it will ensure me their approbation? I am certain that this mode of deciding on my conduct tended more to it's correctness than any reasoning powers I possessed."[63]

As teenage rebelliousness had no place in the 1760s, so determining one's own identity as an adolescent was absent of today's emotionality. Despite his independence of thought and spirit, Jefferson as a young adult entrusted his professional training to Wythe, subordinating his own reason to the wisdom of another's experience. He did not feel that he was inhibiting the exercise of his creative faculty, rather that he was submitting himself to a proper examination, as a socially responsible man of his time was obliged to do. He knew that nothing was freer, as David Hume wrote, than the imagination of man. The mind had authority over all its ideas; the firm beliefs it produced were "excited by nature like all other sentiments."[64] Yet, for one aspiring to gentility, training necessitated self-restraint. Jefferson, as protégé, was ready to profit equally from intellectual and moral example. While under Wythe's tutelage he was likely assuring himself that the quality of the man he was to become was a direct consequence of the quality of his mentor.

Of those people in whom Thomas Jefferson confided, none was more intimate than John Page of Rosewell. Page was the closest thing in Jefferson's life to Cicero's Atticus. In the letters they exchanged, there is undisguised affection and a mutual appreciation. Born the same month, April 1743, Jefferson and Page met as students at William and Mary and corresponded regularly until the latter's death in 1808. They shared amateur scientific interests and exposure to the great minds of the colony. They were together inspired by William Small, whom Page called "illustrious." Despite equal opportunity Page compared himself unfavorably to his friend, saying "I was too sociable, and fond of the conversation of my friends, to study as Mr. Jefferson did, who could tear himself away from his dearest friends, to fly to his studies."[65]

The threads of friendship were woven not just by shared scholarship, for in the earliest record of the Jefferson-Page correspondence, the future author of the Declaration of Independence fretted over his inability to win the heart of the orphaned Rebecca Burwell of the tidewater county of York. The letter was boyish chatter, but it reveals the trust on which their relationship was based. "If there is any news stirring in town or country," Jefferson appealed on Christmas Day, 1762, "such as deaths, courtships, or marriages, in the circle of my acquaintance, let me know it. Remember me affectionately to all the young ladies of my acquaintance, particularly the Miss Burwells, and Miss Potters, and tell them that though that heavy earthly part of me, my body, is absent, the better half of me, my soul, is ever with them."[66]

Jefferson was hopeful that Rebecca Burwell might respond to his interest in her. When she apparently refused to offer any encouragement, he suggested to Page a short time later that they travel to Europe in a vessel Jefferson would build and call the *Rebecca*. "This, to be sure, would take us two or three years, and if we should not both be cured of love in that time, I think the Devil would be in it."[67]

A half year later Jefferson was still at Page's side in the society of Williamsburg, forlorn but not yet having given up on Miss Burwell. He told Page of his resolve to confront her with his feelings, while appealing to his friend to make the first approach: "I never can bear to remain in suspence so long a time." Jefferson seemed resigned to defeat and yet unable to quiet his agitated state: "Perfect happiness I beleive was never intended by the deity to be the lot of any one of his creatures in this world. . . . The most fortunate of us all in our journey through life frequently meet with calamities and misfortunes which may greatly afflict us; and to fortify our minds against the attacks of these calamities and misfortunes should be one of the principal studies and endeavors of our lives." The would-be suitor closed fearfully, "If this letter was to fall into the hands of some of our gay acquaintance, your correspondent and his solemn notions would probably be the subjects of a great deal of mirth and raillery, but to you I think I can venture to send it."[68]

These free and almost self-mocking ruminations show that the otherwise self-reliant Jefferson was receptive to those confidences which make an often lonely existence bearable. His letters to Page may have been his first flirtation with feelings about the realities of an unstable — whether or not tamable — world. Consciously or unconsciously, Jefferson was early preparing himself for the kind of struggle that would later crystallize in politics, and for which friendship would become increasingly important to his creative capacity.

It is significant that at twenty-one and lovelorn, Jefferson thought about employing codes to communicate intimate thoughts. Given the insecurity of the post, and even the miscarriage of letters sent through personal messengers, Jefferson proposed to his confidant Page, "We must fall on some scheme of communicating our thoughts to each other, which shall be totally unintelligible to every one but ourselves."[69] He favored at this time a tachygraphical alphabet, a form of Latin and Greek shorthand; in later years, devising strategies to prevent the spread of gossip to hostile political circles, he, Madison, and Monroe would rely on a system of numerical ciphers to exchange views with less restriction on issues both national and personal. In any case, Jefferson's sensitivity about private notions and heartfelt admissions, his suspicions about the malicious purposes of outsiders, was evident when he was young.

He reckoned that he had inherited a world of uncertainty and potential hostility, yet Jefferson was far from gloomy. A sardonic side emerges from time to time in his letters to Page. In 1766, on the first day of his first journey beyond Virginia's boundaries, Jefferson wrote that his horse had "run away with me and greatly endanger[ed] the breaking my neck." He mocked himself: "Surely never did small hero experience greater misadventures than I did." That comical "small hero" was Tristram Shandy, in Sterne's very words. While reporting the loss of virtually all his books in the Shadwell fire of 1770, Jefferson could yet chide his friend Page for failing to keep up his part of the correspondence: "Why the devil don't you write? But I suppose you are always in the moon, or some of the planetary regions. I mean you are there in idea, and unless you mend, you shall have my consent to be there de facto."[70] The two of them studied the stars; Page may have been the more addicted to this avocation.

Good-natured ribbing was atypical of Jefferson in letters, except with those few with whom he shared a particular "chemistry" — and history. Now, having just started construction of Monticello, he could even cherish "treasonable thoughts of leaving [thes]e my native hills," if it meant moving near Page's Rosewell. Hyperbole was to become a favorite means for Jefferson to add power to his phrases in his familiar letters; his use of "treasonable" here is an early example of Jefferson seemingly satisfying his own imagination. Blair observed that hyperbole prevailed in language "according to the liveliness of the imagination," characteristic of the young. "Correct" and "phlegmatic" Europeans shunned hyperbole. For the reserved Jefferson, this was one of his outlets (and would long be) for that "warmth of passion" which he otherwise tended to repress in person—certainly among men.[71]

He continued protesting to Page: "However, the gods I fancy were apprehensive that if we were placed together we s[houl]d pull down the moon or play such devilish prank with their works." Describing his recent visits to Rosewell as "philosophical evenings," Jefferson praised the "charms irresistible" of Mrs. Page and the other ladies in attendance and finished this sentimental letter with playful Latin word games. Though involved in the weighty affairs of the Virginia House of Burgesses, they were ever the schoolboy-correspondents.[72]

While Thomas Jefferson was being dispatched to Congress in Philadelphia in June 1775, John Page prepared to do his share as a member of the Virginia Committee of Safety. An ardent patriot, he kept Jefferson updated on military preparations, writing that autumn, "I can declare without boasting that I feel such Indignation against the Authors of our Grievances and the Scoundrel Pirates in our Rivers and Such Concern for the Public at large that I have not and can not think of my own puny Person and insignificant Affairs." The following spring he implored, "For God's sake declare the Colonies independent at once, and save us from ruin." Jefferson, of course, did his part, eliciting Page's delightful postscript to a news-laden July 20 letter: "I am highly pleased with your Declaration. God preserve the united States. We know the Race is not to the swift nor the Battle to the strong. Do you not think an Angel rides in the Whirlwind and directs this Storm?"[73]

Their unbreakable friendship weathered the Virginia gubernatorial election of 1779, in which Jefferson bested Page, the then lieutenant–governor. Jefferson wrote a well-measured note in which he suggested that "the difference in number which decided between us [67 to 61 in the assembly] was too insignificant to give you a pain or me a pleasure [had] our dispositions towards each other been such as to have admitted those sensations." Obliged to leave town a short time after the results had come in, Page alerted his friend that he was not to infer "low, dirty feelings" from that act: "I have such Confidence in your good Opinion of my Heart that were it not for the World who may put a wrong Construction on my Conduct I should scarcely trouble you with this Apology." Jefferson appropriately responded: "I know you too well to need an apology for any thing you do. . . . As this is the first, so I hope it will be the last instance of ceremony between us." The letter was signed, "Your affectionate friend."[74]

Time changed little. The two remained as brothers. In 1785, in his first season in Paris as the American minister, Jefferson received a letter from the now less diligent correspondent Page which must have compensated in emotion for any loss of time. Protesting first his demanding schedule as a public man and plantation owner, Page sighed: "What Time then have I to dedicate to my absent Friends? Believe me, next to the Conversation of my Friends, I enjoy the Satisfaction of writing to them, and you may be assured Jefferson, I have not a Friend whose Friendship I value more, or whose Conversation I esteem so much as yours. I must repeat what I told you in my last, that I am the more obliged to you for your Attention to me." It appeared that his other friends had given up on Page, all save for the dutiful Jefferson, who wrote back, "This correspondence is grateful to some of my warmest feelings, as the friendships of my youth are those which stick closest to me, and in which I most confide."[75]

There was never any pretense or formality between them, hardly a "dear Sir " (which Jefferson did use when writing Madison) but generally "dear Page" or "My dear Jefferson." When their politics clashed, as they did on the subject of church and state, their dialogue remained friendly and sensitive. Page was a firm supporter of the Episcopal church and wished to see it kept healthy through a general assessment. He feared that relying wholly on voluntary contributions would allow an opinionated few to manipulate its leaders, and this, in turn, might cause "Tumult and Anarchy," which would strengthen the "rich, proud, and aristocratical gentry." Jefferson's Bill for Establishing Religious Freedom presupposed that any such assessment was an infringement on individual liberty. This bill had been presented to the Virginia assembly first in 1779 and in 1785 was about to pass. Page lamented the event to his diplomat friend: "I have said the more on this Subject because I have just read an outrageous Piece against the Assessment, in which your Opinion is quoted and referred to, as authority against the Arguments for an Assessment, and because I have heard that you had altered your Opinion, having found that the most rational Sects bear up with Difficulty under the unequal Burthen of supporting their Teachers."[76]

Jefferson did not receive the letter until three months had gone by. He was not inspired to reply right away, most likely because he could not have said anything to alleviate Page's discomfort. He had made his true feelings known when writing to Madison in cipher: "I am glad the Episcopalians have again shewn their teeth and fangs. The dissenters had almost forgotten them." His next allusion to religion in a letter to Page was subtle rather than confrontational. Enclosing a copy of his ambitious *Notes on Virginia,* which spelled out his religious views eloquently and at length, Jefferson referred to the unpleasantness of London, a subject he and Page surely agreed upon. Calling that city's extravagance "a more baneful evil than toryism," he added significantly, "Would a missionary appear who would make frugality the basis of his religious system, and go thro the land preaching it up as the only road to salvation, I would join his school tho' not generally disposed to seek my religion out[side] of the dictates of my own reason and feelings of my own heart."[77]

With veiled language Jefferson was playing upon the sensibilities of the church-minded Page. He could not disguise, however, that he equated all religion with "systems," and "systems" were either conducive to or subversive of a spirit of independence. Later, Jefferson would comment with a sense of personal honor: "I never considered a difference of opinion in politics, in religion, in philosophy, as cause for withdrawing from a friend."[78]

Page at first opposed the Constitution but became a fervent supporter before the final votes were cast. He went on to serve in the House of Representatives during Washington's administration, while Jefferson served as secretary of state, and was a frequent companion of James Madison as the division between Federalists and Republicans recast national politics. In 1794 Page was prominent among those who called for a congressional investigation of Hamilton's Treasury Department, and he further proved his commitment to the Jeffersonians in opposing Jay's Treaty during the debate of 1796. In 1798, when Jefferson came under criticism for material he had included in his *Notes,* he appealed to Page to help him set the record straight: "You & I were so

much together about the year 1774, that I take for granted that whatso-
ever I heard you heard also, & therefore that your memory can assist
mine."[79]

Page was turned out of office by a Federalist upsurge in the tidewater
in 1797 and began to encounter financial difficulties at home. Jefferson
not only lent a sympathetic ear but uncharacteristically used his prerogative, while he occupied the President's House, to appoint Page collector of customs in Petersburg with a substantial salary. He cautioned the
amiable Page not to be too trusting, which he evidently considered his
friend's most pronounced fault.[80] Though he knew Page might not be
the best candidate for the job, Jefferson wanted to help his oldest
friend, who recovered politically and served for three years as governor
of Virginia (1802–5, succeeding James Monroe).

Personal warmth resurfaced in times of personal agony; true friends
needed few words to convey profound meaning. In 1804, when Page
and Jefferson had known one another over forty years, and the president lost his delicate twenty-six-year-old daughter Maria, Governor
Page sent a warm letter of condolence. He called earth "a Vale of Sorrow" from which Maria had escaped. Jefferson responded from the
President's House:

> Others may lose of their abundance, but I, of my want, have lost even
> the half of what I had. My evening prospects now hang on the slender
> thread of a single life [his remaining daughter Martha]. Perhaps I may
> be destined to see even this last cord of parental affection broken! . . .
> When you and I look out on the country over which we have passed,
> what a field of slaughter does it exhibit. Where are all the friends who
> entered it with us, under all the inspiring energies of health and hope?
> As if pursued by the havoc of war, they are strewed by the way, some
> earlier, some later, and scarce a few straglers remain to count the
> numbers fallen, and to mark yet by their own fall the last footsteps of
> their party.

As he reread the latter part of the passage, Jefferson inserted the phrase
"under all the inspiring energies of health and hope" in the narrow
space between lines, presumably to produce the ironic counterposition
that better brought out his heartfelt thoughts (fig. 10).[81]

That Jefferson reserved such drama for the trusted Page gave cre-
dence to his earlier assurance that "the friendships of my youth are
those which stick closest to me, and in which I most confide." Letter

Washington June 25, 1804

Your letter, my dear friend, of the 25th ult. is a new proof of the goodness of your heart, and the part you take in my loss marks an affectionate concern for the greatness of it. it is great indeed others may lose of their abun--dance, but I of my want, have lost even the half of what I had. my evening prospects now hang on the slender thread of a single life. perhaps I may be destined to see even this last cord of parental affection broken! the hope with which I had looked forward to the moment, when resigning public cares to younger hands I was to retire to that domestic comfort from which the last great step is to be taken, is fearfully blighted. when you and I look out on the country over which we have passed, what a field of slaughter does it exhibit. under all the inspiring energies of health and hope where are all the friends who entered it with us? as if pursued by the havoc of war, they are strowed by the way, some earlier, some later, and scarce a few straglers remain to count the numbers fallen, and to mark yet by their own fall the last footsteps of their party. is it a de--sireable thing to bear up thro' the heat of the action, to witness the death of all our companions, and merely be the last victim? I doubt it. we have however the traveller's consolation. every step shortens the distance we have to go; the end of our journey is in sight, the bed wherein we are to rest and to rise in the midst of the friends we have lost. 'we sorrow not then as others who have no hope,' but look forward to the day which 'joins us to the great majority.' but whatever is to be our destiny, wisdom, as well as duty, dictates that we should acquiesce in the will of him whose it is to give and to take away, and be contented in the enjoyment of those who are still permitted to be with us. of those connected by blood the number does not depend on us, but friends we have if we have merited them. those of our earliest years stand nearest in our affections, but in this too you and I have been unlucky. of our college friends (and they are the dearest

Governor Page

10. Jefferson to John Page, June 25, 1804 (image enhanced). The grieving father surveys "a field of slaughter." (Library of Congress)

writing indeed helped Jefferson preserve old relationships and restore a sense of harmony during times of personal crisis. He could seek, with Page, the comfort that came to mind upon retrieving the less demanding images of a vibrant youth or the corresponding release that occurred as he railed against the torment of lost love. He could announce, without fear, the condition of his soul through such tactile images as "the last footsteps."

The next year, 1805, Page visited the president at Monticello. During Jefferson's last year in office, the two concluded forty-six years of friendship and correspondence with a poignant exchange. The president had heard that his friend was seriously ill. "'In the midst of life we are in death' so has said some great moralist," he began, certainly aware that his quote was from the *Book of Common Prayer*, "and so says truth even for the young, and how much rather for us who have closed our thirteenth lustre [a space of five years]!" Page was then serving as commissioner of loans for the state of Virginia, and Jefferson offered, as he was empowered while he remained president, to transfer the office to Page's son, *"for your use,* with an understanding that it should afterward, &, continue with him for the *benefit of the family.*" Page said that he preferred to "retain any Office till my last Moment." He went on, revealing his financial troubles to Jefferson, who, ironically, would also depart life in debt. "Rosewell is all I have left; & by Sales & Deaths of Negroes, I have not enough left to work *it!*" But he wished to conclude with a proper sentiment. "God bless you! then my dear Friend, for your Consolation. *As to Death,* I have long been prepared to meet it. . . . I am indeed so weak that I am ready to die this Minute, but I must make Efforts to live. & I declare to you my Friend! that no misfortunes[,] no certain approach of death, have I suffered to sink my Spirits." He closed, "That God Almighty may preserve & bless you my beloved Friend, is the fervent Prayer of your old Friend [signed] John Page." He died not quite a month later.[82]

Even before Page, there was Dabney Carr. Jefferson met Carr at the age of fourteen, at the Reverend James Maury's school, where they both boarded. According to Randall, this firm friendship was "founded on kindred feelings, tastes, principles, and pursuits. They were inseparable companions; read, studied, took their exercise, practiced their music, and formed their plans together." When Jefferson was twenty-two, Dabney Carr married his younger sister Martha. Jefferson wrote sublimely of Carr's simple virtues in a letter to John Page: "This friend of ours, Page, in a very small house, with a table, half a dozen chairs, and one or two servants, is the happiest man in the universe."[83]

In 1773 brothers-in-law Jefferson and Carr organized a meeting of men of "forwardness and zeal" to form committees of correspondence with sister colonies. Rather than keep the honor for himself, Jefferson urged that Carr, a new member of the Virginia House of Burgesses, move the resolution, "making known to the house his great worth and talents." These were Jefferson's fond recollections of his friend nearly a half century after Carr's death; for in the month following his public debut, Dabney Carr succumbed to a fever. He was laid to rest at Shadwell while Jefferson was away and disinterred shortly thereafter on Jefferson's instruction. His body was removed to the little mountaintop where the two friends had formerly spent time together, where they had made a pact that the survivor would bury under a particular oak tree whichever should die first. Thus was inaugurated the Monticello cemetery, conceived before there was a Monticello.[84]

Dabney Carr left six children, whom Jefferson willingly took in and helped raise. The eldest, Peter Carr, was a favorite, and Jefferson gave great personal attention to his education. Upon setting out for France in 1784, he named James Madison the teenager's guardian, attesting to the importance he placed on that young life and suggesting the ambition he had for him. The meaning of friendship to Thomas Jefferson comes through palpably in his request to Madison: "I have a tender legacy to leave you on my departure. I will not say it is the son of my sister, tho her worth would justify my resting it on that ground; but it is the son of my friend, the dearest friend I knew, who, had fate reversed our lots, would have been the father to my children." It is significant, too, that in coming to the defense of Dabney Carr's brother Overton in 1782 when the latter was suspected of toryism, Jefferson termed himself "religiously bound to respect" his departed friend's memory. He was inspired at that moment to recall Dabney Carr as "the dearest friend I possessed on earth, who had every excellence which good sense, learning, or virtue could give."[85]

"Something That Unlocked My Heart"

Benevolence, learning, and honesty were the qualities Jefferson consistently invoked when expressing appreciation for a friendship and issuing injunctions to the younger generation. As he wrote his nephew Peter Carr of masculine integrity: "Nothing is so mistaken as the supposition that a person is to extricate himself from a difficulty, by intrigue, by chicanery, by dissimulation, by trimming, by an untruth, by an injustice. . . . An honest heart being the first blessing, a knowing head is the second." Jefferson valued the Heart first, then the Head. To his grandson Thomas Jefferson Randolph, he advised honesty, prudence, a calm demeanor, and "good humor as one of the preservatives of our peace and tranquillity." He cautioned the teenager against being argumentative: "I never yet saw an instance of one of two disputants convincing the other by argument. . . . Conviction is the effect of our own dispassionate reasoning, either in solitude, or weighing within ourselves dispassionately what we hear from others standing uncommitted in argument ourselves." The grandfather ended this particular letter warning against the perils of politics, where "the habit of silence" serves one best in confronting zealotry.[86]

Reinforcing this sense of how a socially responsible person should comport himself, Jefferson had told Benjamin Rush only months earlier what he wished his grandson to be: "I am in hopes he possesses sound judgment and much observation; and, what I value more than all things, good humor. For thus I estimate the qualities of the mind: 1, good humor; 2, integrity; 3, industry; 4, science. The preference of the first to the second quality may not at first be acquiesced in; but certainly we had all rather associate with a good-humored, light-principled man, than with an ill-tempered rigorist in morality."[87] From this list comes Jefferson's truest standard for judging others and judging himself. Desire for self-improvement, diligently cultivated, would develop into a natural amiability.

Just as he believed in a vision of political liberty requiring a well-ordered, broadly understood structure, Jefferson also saw friendship as a blessing built upon a universally appreciated moral foundation. Mutual respect and consistent loyalty arose from self-conscious efforts to cooperate, modifying the individual's freedom to pursue selfish ends. Jefferson equated individual piety with patriotic spirit; the two operated on the same principle of self-effacement for the sake of community. Friendship first involved making choices based on natural affinities, then applying one's moral precepts (self-restraint, sensitivity to another's emotional needs) to keep that friendship on course over time.

Beyond this, Jefferson envisioned friendship in terms of a charmed, ever-widening circle of strong-minded, scholarly men and delicate, artistic women in the avid pursuit of new knowledge and appreciation of beauty. His was a rather sentimental vision, expressive of that softness and gentility, and optimism, which his eulogists have long attributed to him. Jefferson was contemplative, carefully weighing the value of words whenever he wrote, striving for expression that appealed to the emotional predispositions of his friends. If he was perceptive in appealing to their emotional needs, he must also have believed that they could see into his Heart as well. To confront the question of whether Jefferson meant to convey his own personality or employ language skillfully to imitate an ideal he had construed for his sociable purpose, we must judge whether he would have been able to rationalize the latter method within his own conscience. Would not a man of such moral purposes have set boundaries for himself, delimiting the point beyond which polite language became cheap? As his reading of Sterne or his letters to John Page, Maria Cosway, and Eliza Trist illustrate, he desired very much to confront his humanity and assuage his fears. He relied on his few trusted friends, as he relied on the written word, to clarify issues and resolve inner turmoil.

What, then, did Jefferson bring to his friendships? Though he did not evince ready emotion, he sought to understand what made people happy and responded generously to whatever sensibility that was. The most enamored with Jefferson was Margaret Bayard Smith, wife of Washington newspaper editor Samuel Harrison Smith. She recalled a man "so meek and mild, yet dignified in his manners, with a voice so soft and low [a moment later she described his voice again, this time "almost femininely soft and gentle"], with a countenance so benignant and intelligent." Jefferson's longtime overseer at Monticello, Edmund Bacon, similarly recorded that "his countenance was always mild and pleasant. You never saw it ruffled. No odds what happened, it always maintained the same expression." When Mrs. Smith first met Jefferson in 1800, she wondered: Could this be "the vulgar demagogue, the bold atheist and profligate man I have so often heard denounced by the federalists?" (Her father, John Bayard, was one of the latter.) She described her encounter with President-elect Jefferson, being as yet unaware of his identity, as the two of them sat alone in her parlor. Her appealing guest had "entered into conversation on the commonplace topics of the day, from which, before I was conscious on the commonplace topics of the day, from which, before I was conscious of it, he had drawn me into observation of a more personal and interesting nature. I know not

how it was, but there was something in his manner, his countenance
and voice that at once unlocked my heart." After Europe, his disarming
talent with people had been honed and his way with women had
grown relaxed.[88]

A Dutch visitor to the Continental Congress when it met in Annapolis in 1784, G. K. van Hogendorp, gave testament to the bearing of an
earlier Jefferson:

> Mr. Jefferson, during my attendance at the session of Congress, was
> more busily engaged than anyone. Retired from fashionable society, he
> concerned himself only with the affairs of public interest, his sole diver-
> sion being that offered by belles lettres. The poor state of his health, he
> told me, was the cause of this retirement; but it seemed rather that his
> mind, accustomed to the unalloyed pleasure of a lovable wife, was imper-
> vious since her loss to the feeble attractions of common society, and that
> his soul, fed on noble thoughts, was revolted by idle chatter. . . . He has
> a shyness that accompanies true worth, which is at first disturbing and
> which puts off those who seek to know him. Those who persist in know-
> ing him soon discern the man of letters, the lover of natural history, Law,
> Statecraft, Philosophy, and the friend of mankind.

Jefferson was impressed with Hogendorp as well and requested his address in the Netherlands that they might continue correspondence:
"Your thirst after knowledge, your capacity to acquire it, your dispositions to apply it to the good of mankind, with the ardent spirits of
youth necessary to support a man against the impediments opposed to
him, give your country much to hope from the continuance of your
life."[89]

The Jefferson whom Smith saw and the Jefferson whom Hogendorp
saw were two facets of the same man, of course. Jefferson valued his
national and international connections, but he was most comfortable
with those he had known, and who had known him, when he was
merely a Virginian. One of these marveled that of all the men he had
known in his life, Jefferson was "the most sincere" in the profession
of friendship.[90]

Men were attracted to his compelling range as a conversationalist,
women to his gentle manner. Those who knew both his inner strength
and his inner vulnerability recognized Jefferson as one who felt deeply.
Those who knew him less well considered him intensely private, a person who exhibited a mild exterior and hid his sensitive nature. As Hogendorp observed, this was shyness, not coldness. Henry Adams, who

wrote of Jefferson critically, commented: "He shrank from whatever was rough or coarse, and his yearning for sympathy was almost feminine. That such a man should have ventured upon the stormy sea of politics was surprising."[91]

In Jefferson's world people like him survived by proscribing limits on behavior. To a certain extent Jefferson's mask was a display of self-possession, a conscious attempt to be morally consistent. To be too obvious in one's self-presentation was to invite critical attention from one's peers and potentially harmful interest in private matters, diversion from that studied, neoclassical contentment Jefferson worked to achieve in his self-presentation through letters. He wished, at least rhetorically, to avoid conflict in the political sphere, where relationships were historically the most uneasy. Moreover, he believed in a cosmic sociability that accorded with his vision of domestic harmony in which selfish passions were suppressed. Family was, as Jan Lewis has written, "the prototype of society" for Jefferson.[92] But this ideal was not static. Just as his own children had to earn his love by diligent pursuit of right behavior, sociable friends had to reflect upon their personal qualities on a regular basis and continually monitor their own sociability.

Friends grounded Jefferson. Embracing a concept of man's virtuous potential relieved his troubled soul; the importance of human connections in providing sources of consolation and community thus was heightened. His desire to harmonize, to extend the family metaphor, led him to sustain a bucolic vision of his country and to seek every means to uphold and encourage moral sentiment. In this construct, human beings pursued happiness in life, blessed by the nature in which they were placed by a benevolent Creator; but as sociable beings they had to develop their innate capacities and to share what they learned with similarly inspired friends. It is not surprising, in this light, that Jefferson should have combined letter writing and a humanitarian public spirit with a love for designing, building, and improving Monticello and cultivating the grounds of his private mountaintop. Just as Sterne wrote to stay alive, Jefferson built and grew things and expanded his network of friends to preserve and maximize control over life that was fleeting.

Attentive to his larger social concerns, Jefferson resembled many letter writers of this period in maintaining a stronger consciousness of the recipient of his letters than later letter writers would. He endeavored to make emotions observable by "standing outside" himself, dramatically belittling himself, or composing comically pointed dialogue. Jefferson is an excellent example of one whose use of language varied in order to enhance the appeal of each effort to a correspondent. When, during his presidency, someone sent him original works of poetry and solicited criticism, he used poetic imagery to refuse the task. The "powers of fancy" had declined steadily since his early days, he insisted. "Every year seems to have plucked a feather from her wings till she can no longer waft one to those sublime heights to which it is necessary to accompany the poet." He openly addressed matters of the Heart to women who expressed themselves to him in a heartfelt way. He used religious metaphors with his Episcopalian friend John Page and to his own favorite interpreter of Christianity, Dr. Joseph Priestley, wrote, "I thank on my knees . . . ," in an otherwise secular mode.[93] Inducing George Washington to serve as president for a second term, he developed an irresistible argument pitting hope against tyranny and corruption, in deference to the president's classical consciousness. Cicero remained the model for correctness, for polite style, while the informality of Montaigne and the sentimental idiom of the eighteenth century each had an appreciable effect.[94]

The essential Thomas Jefferson was the private individual, an engaging and considerate friend. He was a member of the Virginia gentry first, an Enlightenment cosmopolitan second, and in either case possessed of a strong consciousness of personal honor and public obligation. The Virginian was independent but elevated the virtues of moderation and accommodation. The cosmopolitan contemplated a world of distinct but harmonizing elements. Jefferson attempted to epitomize civility in all of his personal encounters and foster reason and understanding in his letters. Ultimately, he would be repelled by the personal terms of engagement in political quarrels. Only his very personal fears for the fate of his vision of a benevolent republican society would place him at the center of controversy. These fears would cause him to rationalize behavior that others perceived as hostile. Nevertheless, as Wilson Carey McWilliams has written, Jefferson's concern "lay foremost with the lives of individuals, not the life of the nation or of the race." Fraternity for him was not a future goal but always a present need.[95] Friendship was so essential to his own pursuit of happiness that he could not have endured the natural world's challenges and politcal world's unkindnesses without it.

5   *Friends, Neighborhood, and The Family Fireside*

AS A LAWYER in his mid-twenties, traveling to and from Williamsburg, Jefferson found his niche and a recognizable personality. His mental discipline, meticulous preparation, and mastery of detail made him an effective advocate. Here he was all business, better suited to the appeals process than to the job of arguing emotionally before a jury, as his early acquaintance, the less studied but oratorically powerful Patrick Henry, did.[1] To his highly regarded (if extremely sympathetic) nineteenth-century biographer Randall, young Jefferson projected himself engagingly and beamed with intelligence and a "happy, hopeful spirit."[2] It is hard to know, though, whether this glorifying description equally portrays the ever-doodling architect of the early Monticello and the dogged young attorney on horseback.

As Jefferson aged, descriptions of him become more animated, better focused. According to those who encountered him in his prime, Jefferson's movements were "unrestrained, swinging and bold," but "calm authority sat in Jefferson's eye. . . . The impression which his looks conveyed was that of great firmness and gentleness combined—of powerful energy in perfect repose." Known in his maturity as a charming raconteur (at Monticello or dinners at the President's House), he was, however, unable to raise his voice "above the loudness of ordinary conversation"; it would "sink in his throat" and render him inarticulate.[3] This portrait suggests affability but does not quite come to life. More pronounced expositions from public commentators are not available because Jefferson did not go out of his way to ingratiate himself, though in person the Virginia gentleman could always please.

A variant of Randall's description was left by judgmental, often lyrical, William Maclay, a Pennsylvania senator who recorded in his journal personal observations of a 1790 Senate committee meeting presided over by the secretary of state. This was his first encounter with the Virginian:

> Jefferson is a slender man; has rather the air of stiffness in his manner; his clothes seem too small for him; he sits in a lounging manner, on one hip commonly, and with one of his shoulders elevated much above the

other; his face has a sunny aspect; his whole figure has a loose, shackling air. He had a rambling vacant look, and nothing of that firm, collected deportment which I expected would dignify the presence of a secretary or minister. I looked for gravity, but a laxity of manner seemed to shed about him. He spoke almost without ceasing. It was loose and rambling, and yet he scattered information wherever he went, and some even brilliant sentiments sparkled from him.[4]

Maclay's response is typical of those who did not penetrate Jefferson's undemonstrative veneer. Maclay did not perceive the fastness of his inner constitution, the intensity of his mental exertions. Jefferson's "loose, shackling air" is hard to gauge today but perhaps equates with what we call unprepossessing behavior.

He did not stand on his dignity, particularly after his return from Europe. His preference for informality in dress could unnerve the more orthodox of his class. At a dinner one month after he first saw Jefferson, Maclay contrasted the comportment of three cabinet members: Treasury Secretary Alexander Hamilton evinced a "boyish, giddy manner," the portly Secretary of War Henry Knox alone displayed dignity, and Jefferson "transgresses on the extreme of stiff gentility or lofty gravity."[5] Apparently the secretary of state had adjusted his "loose" manner in the ceremonial atmosphere of a formal dinner sponsored by the Senate. It is clear that Senator Maclay was not intimate with Jefferson, though he persistently censured Hamilton's policies and approved of the course Jefferson was shortly to pursue. Maclay was outside the circle of trusted friends who surrounded Jefferson and, in disseminating his ideas, gave Jefferson's individual voice the power it did not come by naturally.

"Partie Quarree"

Thomas Jefferson sought to promote his interests by establishing a consensus of compatible minds. When first undertaking public responsibilities, he cultivated friendships with men who could offer the wisdom and connections of their greater experience and initiate him into elite circles. Once established, comfortable among this elite, Jefferson looked to construct a community of younger friends whose potential was clear, whose eager acquisition of knowledge impressed him, and whose views he could help shape.

To construct that community, Jefferson literally sought to construct, or have his friends construct, estates in the neighborhood of Monticello. The three most noted rising young Virginians who fell into Jefferson's circle were James Madison, James Monroe, and William Short.

Of the three, the first Jefferson encountered was the one most complementary. James Madison, Jr. (he dropped the Jr. from his signature when his father died in 1801), was eight years younger than the author of the Declaration of Independence, when they met in the autumn of 1776. Much earlier, at James Maury's school, Jefferson had befriended Madison's cousin of the same name, the Reverend James Madison, who became president of the College of William and Mary in 1778. In 1776 his twenty-five-year-old namesake was a shy and as yet unheralded member of the Virginia House of Delegates. That season, Jefferson, notable but not yet nationally celebrated for his work in Philadelphia, was prominent in the debate on disestablishment of the church in Virginia; the young Madison was a member of the Committee on Religion. Madison biographer Irving Brant concluded that Madison's "reticence and diffidence formed a bar to an immediate recognition of the bond between" Jefferson and himself. The two did not begin to confer with any regularity until 1779, when Jefferson became governor and Madison prepared to take his seat in the Continental Congress. By 1782, the year Jefferson lost his wife, their friendship was firm; it was Madison who, it appears, most persisted in luring the widower back into public view. The two were together at Congress in Philadelphia in late 1782 and again in late 1783, sharing lodgings at the House-Trist establishment. This was time enough to speak of books and scholarship and to solidify their unique partnership, which neither time nor distance would disrupt. In 1783, the year Jefferson and Madison most often shared each other's company (or regularly wrote about such topics as the temperature and density of the earth, in addition to politics), Jefferson drew up the catalog of his already impressive Monticello library on the scheme devised by Francis Bacon. Other book collectors arranged their books by size and subject, Jefferson according to Baconian principles of memory (human and natural history), reason (moral philosophy, law, and pure science), and imagination (art and architecture, poetry and literature). The Library of Congress would later adopt this method.[6]

It was early in 1784, as Jefferson was anticipating his departure for Europe, that he delivered to Madison a warm proposal: "I hope you have found access to my library. I beg you to make free use of it. . . .

Monroe is buying land almost adjoining me. Short will do the same. What would I not give you could fall into the circle. With such a society I could once more venture home and lay myself up for the residue of life, quitting all it's contentions which grow daily more and more insupportable. Think of it. To render it practicable only requires you to think it so. Life is of no value but as it brings us gratifications. Among the most valuable of these is rational society. It informs the mind, sweetens the temper, chears our spirits, and promotes health."[7] The passage is revealing both of Jefferson's plan for a neighborhood and of his particular relationship to Madison. The friendship between the two men, to this point, was very much bound in books. Madison's company brought improvement of the mind, new knowledge achieved under circumstances of harmonious calm. Here, bearing in mind how Jefferson divided himself into Head and Heart, we read him urging Madison to "think of it," repeating "only . . . think it so." He did not (perhaps never did) bid Madison to "imagine" or "feel." While this does not have to suggest a lack of emotional concerns on the part of either man, it points to the language Jefferson employed to solicit a response from his friend and to make him feel at ease.

"Render it practicable," reduced friendship to calculation. It was a reasonable man (as Jefferson, of course, perceived himself) who understood what was "practicable." He used the word primarily when contemplating worldly events, as in speculating to George Washington in 1784 on the "practicability" of commercial navigation to the West. To Du Pont de Nemours, Jefferson generalized: "What is practicable must often controul what is pure theory." Yet, here, urging Madison to settle near him, the optimistic Jefferson eagerly asserted that a complex decision was in fact quite simple: "To render it practicable only requires you to think it so."[8]

It is also apparent that the thought of Madison's friendship and prospective company reminded Jefferson of the generally uncertain nature of the pursuit of "gratifications" (that which gives life value). His having written "venture home" in this hopeful context can be read as an admission that most connections in Jefferson's life were tenuous, susceptible, emotionally jarring. *To venture* in the eighteenth century connoted hazard and dare, as it does today. Dr. Johnson's 1783 *Dictionary* gives "to engage in or make attempts without any security of success." Jefferson, moreover, was on the verge of a major sea voyage and an open-ended tour abroad. Still acutely sensing the loss of his wife (an example of what might happen even at home with loved ones), his mental, if not physical, health concerned him; he saw Madison as one key to stability, as the friend with whom he could be "rational," whose company held for Jefferson the unmatched power to "inform," "sweeten," "chear," and in doing all this, ensure health.

Jefferson would not let up, trying repeatedly to bring Madison permanently closer, as a letter from Paris late that same year demonstrates: "I once hinted to you the project of seating yourself in the neighborhood of Monticello, and my sanguine wishes made me look on your answer as not absolutely excluding the hope. Monroe is decided in settling there and is actively engaged in the endeavor to purchase. Short is the same. Would you but make it a 'partie quarree' I should believe that life still had some happiness in store for me. Agreeable society is the first essential in constituting the happiness and of course the value of our existence: and it is a circumstance worthy great attention when we are making first our choice of a residence. Weigh well the value of this against the difference in pecuniary interest, and ask yourself which will add most to the sum of your felicity through life."[9] Once again, he endeavored to represent his need in terms of a rational and philosophical, rather than emotional, definition of friendship. "Weigh well the value," he phrased his proposal of what might otherwise have been a sentimental decision. The "partie quarree" refers to the French *carrée,* which connotes a mathematically sound four-way grouping. Jefferson's quantification of pleasure ("the sum of your felicity") informs much about the relationship.

Though Madison never took up Jefferson on his offer, neither did he waver in his commitment. His was a mind that was focused, that did not wander. He proved to be a most outstanding collaborator who gave to Jefferson, time and again, the comfort of constructive friendship, consideration, and loyalty.[10]

Jefferson had greater success luring James Monroe to Albemarle County, though it took more than a decade to settle him there, at what is now known as Ash Lawn. Monroe was an enthusiastic patriot who had joined the Third Virginia Infantry in Williamsburg while Jefferson was laboring over his Declaration in Philadelphia. During his service he met future notables Alexander Hamilton, Aaron Burr, and the marquis de Lafayette. Returning to civilian life under strained financial circumstances, he very much needed someone to unburden himself to, a sponsor and friend, a mentor. Jefferson guided him through the law, sent him on a wartime mission to set up a channel of communications from Richmond to North Carolina, and paved the way for Monroe's entry into state politics.[11]

Early in the effort to convince this protégé to become his neighbor, Jefferson sent books from France, including "the plan of your house." He appealed with an undisguised fervor: "I wish to heaven you may continue in the disposition to fix it in Albemarle. Short will establish himself there, and perhaps Madison may be tempted to do so. This will be society enough, and it will be the great sweetener of our lives. Without society, and a society to our taste, humans are never contented." This message, of course, recalls the language of the two earlier letters to Madison, except that to Monroe Jefferson did not stop after prophesying an idyllic community. He became emotionally involved. Monroe had married a short time before this, causing him to cancel plans to visit Jefferson in Europe. Jefferson appreciated his friend's sensibility. He must have been reminded of his own struggle between private and public obligations during Patty's lifetime. Congratulating the couple, he had offered Monroe more than standard praise: "Your own dispositions and the inherent comforts of that state [marriage] will insure you a great addition of happiness. Long may you live to enjoy it, and enjoy it in full measure. The interest I feel in every one connected with you will justify my presenting my earliest respects to the lady and of tendering the homage of my friendship." So, writing to reinforce the newlyweds' inclination to settle near Monticello, Jefferson incorporated into his vision for Monroe the prospect of that domestic tranquillity he himself had one enjoyed. He related his hope for news that "Mrs. Munroe will soon have on her hands domestic cares of the dearest kind, sufficient to fill her time and ensure her against the tedium vitae." He extolled the woman's place in the home at some length, pressing even further into his friend's affairs before concluding, "But I must not philosophize too much with her lest I give her too serious apprehensions of a friendship I shall impose on her."[12]

With Monroe, Jefferson dwelled constantly on emotional issues, knowing he could reach this friend with his Heart. After Monroe announced the birth of a daughter in July 1787 ("who tho' noisy, contributes greatly to our amusement"), Jefferson responded with a clear invocation of his own emotional history: "I sincerely take part with you in your domestic felicity. There is no other in this world worth living for. The loss of it alone can make us know it's full worth." These reflections caused him next to reiterate, "It would indeed be a most pleasing circumstance to me to see you settle in the neighborhood of Monticello, for thither all my views tend." [13]

Several years later, with the same project in mind, Jefferson enlisted Madison in his friendly advice to Monroe, who was then on his first diplomatic assignment in Paris: "Mr. Madison and myself examined your different situations for a house." Jefferson vowed to contribute fruit trees from his own nursery. Then, compulsively, he went on to offer suggestions on furnishings, before listing the wines Monroe should purchase in France. He recommended a particular bookseller, describing the man's good qualities: "I can assure you," Jefferson wrote energetically, "that after having run a severe gauntlet under the Paris book-sellers I rested at last on this old gentleman, whom I found in a long & intimate course of after dealings to be one of the most conscientiously honest men I ever had dealings with." Again, the Heart predominates. Later in the same letter, the tireless mentor returned in his thoughts to Monroe's projected resettlement, advising how to divide the "open grounds" of Ash Lawn, how to tend its fields, and what method of crop rotation to employ. He noted, "There are two or three objects which you should endeavour to enrich our country with. 1. The Alpine strawberry 2. The skylark 3. The *red* legged Partridge." Jefferson closed his long letter with another hint of the intense spirit in which he thought of Monroe: "Adieu. God Almighty bless you all." [14]

William Short can be placed in this ideal "partie quaree" by references in Jefferson's letters to others and on the basis of his words to Short during the same period in which he cultivated his friendships with Madison and Monroe. Jefferson purchased a 1,300-acre estate adjoining Monroe's lands, on Short's behalf in 1795. Jefferson and Short had probably first encountered one another through the Skipwiths, to whom both were related by marriage. In 1780, along with Monroe, Short studied the law under then Governor Jefferson, who was the same age that George Wythe had been when the legal scholar had tutored Jefferson and altered the course of his life. In 1781, while Patty lived, Short several times visited Jefferson at Monticello and was provided letters of introduction to leaders of the Congress in Philadelphia. To Madison, Jefferson wrote, "I chearfully add to what you may already have heard of him my testimony of his genius, learning and merit." The following year, Short shared in Jefferson's grief, losing his father soon after Patty's death." [15]

Much of the early Jefferson-Short correspondence is missing, but those letters which have been preserved show an uncommon bond. In one instance Short beamed when he received "a new and most pregnant Proof of your Friendship." Keeping Jefferson's secrets, he swore that he was able to remain "silent as the Grave to every Body but yourself." Before Jefferson and Short left American shores in 1784, Madison learned how much deeper Jefferson's conviction in Short's worth had grown: "His talents are great and his weight in our state must ere long become principal." Until Short determined to follow him to Europe, Jefferson entrusted this protégé with Peter Carr's guardianship, a responsibility which then fell to Madison.[16]

Though only Monroe in fact moved into Jefferson's neighborhood, the sense invoked by Jefferson's desire to bring them all together did not diminish. Jefferson found in these men the qualities of Heart and Head that he cherished, saw them as buttresses to his own public objectives, and expressed this readily in his correspondence.

Let us further examine the spirit underlying these extraordinary friendships. Without question, the most essential of Jefferson's mature relationships was with Madison. It is arguable that Jefferson would never have seen his republican ideals fine-tuned and translated into practical programs without the dynamic efforts and the calm and calculation of the legislative leader who was his chief collaborator and stalwart friend during the trying decade that followed Jefferson's return from France.

Jefferson and Madison subscribed to a common political philosophy, promoting liberal notions of individual liberty and a style of simple dignity. At the start of their friendship, Madison considered himself a learner in the presence of the more experienced Jefferson. Brant has credited Jefferson with introducing Madison to Enlightenment skepticism, "freeing his mind for exploration." Madison's years at Congress in Philadelphia — particularly 1782–83 — compelled this otherwise modest legislator to speak up and be heard. Merrill Peterson has written in a similar vein that for years the younger man was a "faithful lieutenant, undertaking assignments," who instinctively took over as promoter of their mutual causes. This was a role Jefferson — who would not thrust himself forward in representative bodies — happily yielded each time he despaired of active politicking and attempted to retreat to a life of farming, family, and study. Again in Peterson's words, "They were enough alike to work together [and] sufficiently different to complement each other."[17]

From an early point in their correspondence, Jefferson showed his high regard for Madison's mind, soliciting his views on policy before finalizing his own. Each conveyed his "cheer" in writing. "I shall cheerfully send you a line," wrote Madison, "as often as I have a subject for it." For his part Jefferson would "cheerfully communicate to you whatever could occur to me worth your notice." And, before closing: "I shall always be glad to hear from you." Before Patty Jefferson's slow wasting away in the middle months of 1782, the two friends still ended their letters with some variation of the formal "Your obedient, humble servant." Beginning in the months after Patty's death, and especially from the time they shared Philadelphia lodgings that winter, the closing became "Your sincere friend."[18]

Jefferson was a moralist. He made no more rigorous demand than to be sure he felt within his heart any literal expression of sincerity he committed to paper. To be "sincere," in Jefferson's vocabulary, meant to be pure in thought, free of doubt, close and affectionate. He did not use the term loosely. To elders or in deferential letters generally, when not signing off conventionally as "Your obedient, humble servant," Jefferson expressed "esteem" and "regard," but not "sincerity." When supportively urging Madison to seek "resources of happiness . . . within yourself" after having been jilted by Kitty Floyd, he conveyed confidence in Madison's strength and durability and expressed heartfelt support for his friend by declaring "sincere esteem." Other times, he might dash off a familiar "Adieu Adieu Yours affectionately." At the close of the American Revolution, Jefferson offered the retiring George Washington "individual tribute . . . for all you have suffered." He presumed that the general had received much "adulation" in letters from around the country and wanted his own sentiment to be separated from more common expression, "for such is become the prostitution of language that sincerity has no longer distinct terms in which to express her own truths." Just as he "sincerely" congratulated Monroe on his marriage, to Short, while traveling through the south of France, Jefferson signed one letter with "assurances of my perfect esteem & friendship to yourself" and another two weeks later with the even more extravagant "Be assured as to yourself that no person can more sincerely wish your prosperity and happiness, nor entertain warmer sentiments of esteem." The superlatives Jefferson applied in these instances suggested an unqualified commitment to friendship. His "sincerity" was more than an obligatory expression.[19]

Beyond his use of "sincere" in the closing of letters to true intimates, Jefferson joined the word with "sympathy" (in "My Head and My Heart"); with "friendly, liberal, learned, beloved by everybody" (writing to Madison in 1787 of a helpful French official); with "zeal" for the "inviolable preservation of our present federal constitution" in desiring to counter Federalist rumors and convince Elbridge Gerry in 1799 of his own political reasonableness; with "assurances of friendship" in desiring to "conciliate" a skeptical tribe of Indians. There were thus two related — though not identical — standards of sincerity: one in personal relations and another in public performance. Jefferson best described the limits of sincere display (in the wider public context) in a letter from France to Charles Bellini, friend and professor of modern languages at the College of William and Mary: "With respect to what are termed polite manners, without sacrificing too much the sincerity of language, I would wish [my] countrymen to adopt just so much of European politeness, as to be ready [to] make all those little sacrifices of self, which really render European manners amiable." Jefferson was sensitive here (as in the letter to Washington) to the "sincerity" that could be expressed in language without corrupting the word itself or debasing honest expression.[20]

It is interesting, in the context of nurturing friendships based on true sincerity, how Jefferson orchestrated the coming together of Madison and Monroe and, much later, had a role in patching up their differences. In 1784, before his departure for France, he encouraged the two to develop a relationship similar to that which he enjoyed with each of them separately. He wrote Madison that Monroe "wishes a correspondence with you; and I suppose his situation will render him an useful one to you. The scrupulousness of his honor will make you safe in the most confidential communications. A better man cannot be."[21]

Jefferson may have sensed the potential for competition between Madison and Monroe as early as 1787. To the former, whom he was describing around this time as his "most particular friend," he wrote candidly, in cipher, that Monroe was a man whose soul, turned "wrong side outwards," had "not a speck on it"; but at the same time he coupled Monroe with another acquaintance who had "one foible, an excessive inflammability of temper." As Jefferson had been urging his political protégés to settle in the neighborhood of Monticello, he could only imagine them in harmony. But not six months after Jefferson made his characterization, Monroe sent what must have been a disturbing letter across the Atlantic. Using cipher, the young legislator complained, "The governor [Edmund Randolph], I have reason to believe is unfriendly to me and hath shewn (If I am well inform'd) a disposition to thwart me; Madison, upon whose friendship I have calculated, whose views I have favoured, and with whom I have held the most confidential correspondence since you left the continent, is in strict league with him." In 1788 Madison and Monroe were set in opposition in the first congressional elections after adoption of the Constitution. Monroe had been cool to Madison's federalism, and Madison prevailed in a close contest.[22]

From the time of Jefferson's return from France and appointment as secretary of state, Monroe overcame his sensitivity and teamed successfully with Madison to oppose the policies of Alexander Hamilton. He had been elected senator from Virginia in 1790 and remained a very vocal campaigner in Jeffersonian causes throughout the turbulent decade. After having served as governor of Virginia (1799–1802) and as a negotiator on Jefferson's behalf in France and England (1803–7), Monroe owned a unique vantage point on America and the world, if a distanced perspective on internal politics by the time his mentor prepared to retire from public life. In 1808, the last year of Jefferson's presidency, Monroe found himself again at odds with Madison. The Monroe-Pinckney Treaty he had helped engineer in London fell far short of Jefferson's and Secretary of State Madison's expectations, and in this instance Jefferson did not sufficiently account for Monroe's sensitivity to criticism. When dissident Republicans courted Monroe, tensions increased. The president, quietly favoring Madison as his successor, was caught in the middle. As the two most renowned inheritors of his political legacy contested with one another, Jefferson tried to dissuade Monroe from being seduced by those who were acting to push him past Madison for reasons that Jefferson viewed as ill conceived.[23]

Jefferson's letters to Monroe during this period were reactive and meant to soothe. In February 1808 he began: "I see with infinite grief a contest arising between yourself and another, who have been very dear to each other, and equally so to me. . . . For independant of the dictates of public duty, which prescribe neutrality to me, my sincere friendship for you both will ensure it's sacred observance." In this letter Jefferson went so far as to state that "I have ever viewed Mr. Madison and yourself as two principal pillars of my happiness." The architectural metaphor for something solid and durable cannot be accidental. In

March he laid out the problem in more analytic terms: "I perceive that painful impressions have been made on your mind during your late mission, of which I had never entertained a suspicion. I must, therefore, examine the grounds, because explanations between reasonable men can never but do good." Personalizing Monroe's problem of perception, he showed his empathy by comparing the dynamic of his own position in 1784 as a first-time diplomat, "adjunct" to Franklin and Adams. After painstakingly demonstrating his support, the president found it necessary to reassert that political passions could not lessen his long regard for Monroe's character. He underscored the ongoing tension with a sea metaphor, symbolic, as always in Jefferson's correspondence, of the uncertainty and anxiety inherent in the subject under discussion: "Let us not, then, my dear friend, embark our happiness and our affections on the ocean of slander, of falsehood and of malice, on which our credulous friends are floating. If you have been made to believe that I ever did, said, or thought a thing unfriendly to your fame and feelings, you do me injury as causeless as it is afflicting to me. In the present contest in which you are concerned, I feel no passion, I take no part, I express no sentiment." Showing once again that nautical metaphors served him in writing about trials, afflictions, and uncertainties, Jefferson noted that he himself was nearing the "harbor" of retirement, while reminding the thin-skinned Monroe that his own "voyage" had been "so far favorable."[24]

As "sincere friendship" for both made Jefferson's neutrality in the conflict a "sacred observance" in the February letter, the March letter closed with a "sincere prayer," further expression of that religious quality long present in the friendship he bore for Monroe. Convinced by April that his words had had their intended effect, Jefferson optimistically sought to bury the matter: "Conscious that I have never felt a sentiment towards you that was not affectionate it is great relief to find that the doubts you have entertained on that subject are removed by an explanation of the circumstances which produced them."[25]

Monroe was snubbed by Madison that summer when he visited Monticello but avoided Ash Lawn. The retired Jefferson continued to take pains to patch up their differences, but three more years were needed before they finally reconciled, and Monroe became secretary of state. Once the friendship was restored, however, it remained on track for the rest of their lives. And so, in 1811, keenly aware of the effect of those years of disharmony, Jefferson wrote Monroe one more letter of sentiment: "I know that the dissolutions of personal friendship are among the most painful occurrences in human life. I have sincere esteem for all who have been affected by them."[26]

Jefferson had entered the stage of politics valuing the skills of sociability in accomplishing tasks large and small. By the time of his retirement, he had learned many times over that public-minded men — even those who had enjoyed long years allied with one another — could be torn apart by others' gossip and maneuverings and simple misunderstandings. Jefferson believed that his own estrangement from his two predecessors as president, George Washington and John Adams, was owing to these same causes.

Jefferson always gave deep thought to the language that he used to frame his appeals to the people he counted as friends. He understood Monroe to be, like himself, highly sensitive when his public reputation was at stake and yet willing to immerse himself in the rough-and-tumble world of politics (in which both, incidentally, proved themselves remarkably durable). Kindred spirits separated by a generation, Jefferson and Monroe compared both successes and bitter experiences. Jefferson's language toward Monroe was always richer in sensation than it was with Madison. For example, in an account of generally pedestrian commercial negotiations, Jefferson wrote Monroe of Great Britain: "The infatuation of that nation seems really preternatural. . . . If anything will open their eyes it will be an application to the avarice of their merchants. . . ." The English, he went on, were "deaf to every principle of common sense, insensible of the feelings of men." While equally strong in defending principle in his letters to Madison, Jefferson relied on words that expressed reason rather than sensation.[27]

Jefferson's appeals to each to visit him in Europe were the first that suggested this distinction. His words to Madison were businesslike, stressing money management over emotional value: "Do you not think the men, and arts of this country would be worth another summer. You can come in April, pass the months of May, June, July, August, and most of September here, and still be back to the commencement of real business in the Assembly following, which I would not have you absent from." He held out the prospect of great intellects and stimulating arts, assuring Madison, "You shall find with me a room, bed and plate, if you will do me the favor to become of the family." Carefully detailing the cost of passage, Paris theater, and appropriate attire, Jefferson concluded, "You will for that have purchased the knowledge of another

world." Even becoming part of Jefferson's "family" was construed rhetorically as a polite "favor" which lacked any apparent emotional content. To Monroe, on the other hand, Jefferson did not have to sell the
idea of Europe. He became animated instantly: "The pleasure of the
trip . . . will make you adore your own country, it's soil, it's climate, it's
equality, liberty, laws, people and manners. My god! How little do my
countrymen know what precious blessings they are in possession of,
and which no other people on earth enjoy. I confess I had no idea of
it myself."[28]

Jefferson and Madison readily indulged all issues that entered their
Heads. And as time passed, less and less artifice cluttered their substan-
tive letters. The extraordinary trust they were to enjoy over a lifetime
evolved through the mails most impressively during the nearly five
years Jefferson resided in Paris, when Madison took the lead in the
drafting and ratification of the federal Constitution. The correspondence flowed regularly, except from April until December 1786; during
the months of Jefferson's involvement with Maria Cosway, he did not
write Madison. Their many letters focused on political matters and contained uncensored musings about the particulars of bills before Congress. Jefferson the spirited liberal philosopher reflected his enthusiastic
immersion in European culture, and Madison the hardworking nation-
alist conveyed his own judgment on issues Jefferson cared about. Their
correspondence more than ever teemed with gossip about the men of
the new nation as well as those of the Old World. John Adams was
"vain, irritable and a bad calculator of the force and probable effect of"
motives. Diplomat William Carmichael's letters "shewed him vain and
more attentive to ceremony and etiquette than we suppose men of
sense should be." Banker William Bingham had "a rage for being presented to great men." Of the fawning David Franks, who "doubtless
will be asking some appointment," Jefferson wrote, "He is light, indiscreet, [ac]tive, honest, affectionate." Louis XVI was "irascible, rude and
very limited in his understanding." His queen, Marie Antoinette, was
"capricious . . . devoted to pleasure and expence." And Lafayette was
"a very valuable auxiliary to me. His zeal is unbounded. . . . He has a
great deal of sound genius. . . . His foible is a canine appetite for popularity and fame." These richly painted confidences served to maintain
the bond between Jefferson and Madison. At the end of that letter most
replete with gossip and characterizations, Jefferson assured Madison
there was more to come: "As particulars of this kind may be useful to

you in your present situation, I may hereafter continue the chapter. I know it is safely lodged in your discretion." If Jefferson could be of use to Madison from his listening post in Europe, Madison could test the waters for Jefferson back home. When the impending publication of *Notes on Virginia* threatened to expose Jefferson's more controversial views to conservative critics, Madison conferred with allies to try to minimize the damage. Jefferson went to great lengths to acquire books to Madison's taste and shipped curiosities like the pedometer and "phosphoretic matches" and mechanical inventions like the portable copying machine.[29]

In the fall of 1788 Jefferson mapped out a return trip from Europe, to reunite, if only briefly, with the man whose reputation he had helped to build among his cosmopolitan connections on the Continent (though, as it turned out, Madison would never leave America's shores). Jefferson was anticipating a spring-summer sabbatical in 1789, expecting to sail again for France. With this understanding he wrote: "I shall particularly hope for much profit and pleasure, by contriving to pass as much time as possible with you. Should you have a trip to Virginia in contemplation for that year, I hope you will time it so as that we may be there together. I will camp you at Monticello where if illy entertained otherwise, you shall not want that of books."[30] Books are, once again, an assured form of entertainment, an acceptable bribe, in Jefferson's mingling of wit and epistolary modesty. While the wording of this invitation still suggests that the tie between the two political thinkers was primarily of intellects, it also expresses a high level of mutual understanding and personal comfort. They would not have so freely gossiped without a complete trust in each other. They communicated with greater frankness but with less animation and less frequent personal flourishes than are present in Jefferson's more emotionally significant correspondence with Page and Monroe.

Jefferson always knew that he could not realize his larger vision by himself. His ideal of a neighborhood of sincere friends and like-minded republicans sprang from his optimism about the power inherent in human relationships—but also, just as plainly, from a sense of the presence of threats to the peace and happiness that friendship promised. Illustrative of Jefferson's sense of the dark forces governing human relationships is a letter he wrote Monroe from France in 1786, a time when presumably (and certainly compared to later times) Jefferson did not have reason to be concerned about opposition to his public position.

Monroe had declared his intent to leave government and attend to private affairs, and Jefferson, while sympathetic, could but mourn the loss of his eyes and ears in the Confederation Congress: "I feel too the want of a person there to whose discretion I can trust confidential communications, and on whose friendship I can rely against the unjust designs of malevolence. I have no reason to suppose I have enemies in Congress: yet it is too possible to be without that fear." Jefferson continued to see public life as inherently uncertain, ruled by human passions. Amid the bitter political disputes that rose during the 1790s, Jefferson, who preferred not to take up his own causes in public, relied on Monroe's active defense of him no less than he relied on Madison's. Whereas Madison plunged "Head"-first into the partisan battles of the day, Monroe reacted passionately and remained generally uncertain about his suitability for the turmoil of public disputation. In 1797, as vice president under John Adams, Jefferson volunteered career advice to his conflicted friend. "I do expect that your farm will not sufficiently employ your time to shield you from ennui," he assessed. "Your mind is active, & would suffer if unemployed. Perhaps it's energies could be more justifiably employed thus for your own comfort." These words could be unselfish, manipulative, or a projection onto Monroe of Jefferson's own conflict between rural retirement and political office. When Monroe resisted Jefferson's appeal to rejoin Congress, Jefferson related language "injurious" to Monroe that he had overheard, making it "absolutely necessary you should reappear on the public theatre."[31]

Monroe followed in Jefferson's footsteps all the way to the President's House but, as a more passion-prone figure than Jefferson, served as an arm of Jefferson's offense rather than an intellectual foil. Short, whom Jefferson at least once called "my adoptive son," remained in Paris after his patron's departure, having fallen in love with the French duchess. He chose diplomacy over a position back home (such as Jefferson might have preferred for him) and went on to build a fortune for himself, trading a political legacy for financial security.[32]

As in the case of Monroe, Jefferson had a hard time letting Short go. The trusted aide had observed Jefferson both during his wife's lifetime and during the emotion-filled weeks of his encounters with Maria Cosway. Jefferson knew intimate details of Short's affair with Rosalie. To this romantic young man, he could record his thoughts with exceptional warmth and ease. From Lyons in 1787 Jefferson had written in a tone reminiscent of his early letters to John Page: "So far all is well. No complaints, except against the weather-maker, who has pelted me with rain, hail, and snow, almost from the moment of my departure to my arrival here. Now and then a few gleamings of sunshine to chear me by the way. Such is this life: and such too will be the next, if there be another, and we may judge the future by the past."[33] To Short, as to Page, Jefferson could portray himself as a comic figure susceptible to larger forces; he could speculate carelessly about the course of life and the unknown possibilities for human beings after physical death.

In 1789, about to leave France for home, Jefferson recommended that Short stay in Paris, but only long enough for Jefferson to take care of business in Virginia, resettle his daughters there, consult with the new president, and sail back in the spring. After that, he wanted Short to calculate what was in his own best interest and reestablish himself in America. "Here my opinion will be against my own interest," wrote Jefferson in March. "For affection and the long habit of your society have rendered it necessary to me." If Short remained in Europe as a diplomat, Jefferson went on, the young man could expect "but a bare existence and a solitary existence too." Hinting at Short's amorous inclinations, he added that for one unmarried, living in a great city, "in the beginning it is pleasant enough; but take what course he will whether that of rambling, or of a fixed attachment, he will become miserable as he advances in years." Typically, Jefferson reminded Short of his firm conviction that "the happiness of your own country is more tranquil, more unmixed, more permanent." He urged this course upon Short selflessly, "with a bleeding heart: for nothing can be more dreary than my situation will be when you and my daughters shall all have left me." By June, however, Jefferson seemingly had come to terms with Short's decision not to follow his advice, expressing confidence that "his talents, his virtues, and his connections ensure him any thing he may desire. . . . nothing is more interesting to me than that he should do what is best for himself." Yet, as secretary of state in 1793, he would write his "adoptive son," newly appointed minister to the Netherlands, several strongly worded letters labeled "private" over and above the department's official correspondence. The young diplomat seemed to be drifting and required one more reining in. The now humorless, if forgiving, mentor noted at the end of one particular harangue: "I have written to you in the stile to which I have been always accustomed with you, and which perhaps it is time I should lay aside. But while old men are sensi-

ble enough of their own advance in years, they do not sufficiently recollect it in those whom they have seen young."[34] After this, the secretary
of state for all intents and purposes granted Short his independence
from the unequal relationship they had maintained for more than a
decade. The protégé turned sophisticate visited President Jefferson in
1802, returned to Europe, and did not come home for good until 1810,
after Jefferson had retired. He then chose to live in Philadelphia rather
than in Virginia.

Thus it was the resilient Madison, young father of the Constitution,
whom Jefferson in 1790 was already calling "the greatest man in the
world," who fast became his alter ego. Just as Madison had once
pressed Jefferson to accept the commission to Europe, he volunteered
to present George Washington's case in convincing a reluctant Jefferson
to become secretary of state. Congressman Madison then led what
shortly became the Jeffersonian faction through two Federalist administrations. As friends, Jefferson and Madison enjoyed an intimate tour
of upstate New York and New England in the spring of 1791, fishing
for bass and trout, eating strawberries — for the most part a relaxing
escape from political business and Jefferson's often debilitating tension headaches.[35]

Throughout the decade of the 1790s, Jefferson rested at Montpelier
when he rode the ten days from Philadelphia to Monticello. Madison,
particularly after his marriage to Dolley Todd in 1794, scheduled semi-
annual visits to Monticello (which included, from the end of that decade, visits to Monroe at Ash Lawn). Letters show the procession from
a cordial, grateful spirit to the intense desire to secure the triumph of
Jefferson's and Madison's common political creed. Each relied on the
other to fortify his defense of republican principles, contending with
what they saw as subversion of the natural rights of the mass of the
people by an arrogant elite. As this was, in their minds, a struggle to
counter not only cynicism but corruptibility, they suspected others' designs and communicated closely so as to prevent outsiders from in-
terfering in (or trying to corrupt) their personal relations.

Their close cooperation was most evident during the eight years of
Jefferson's presidency, when Madison assumed Jefferson's former station, serving as a tireless secretary of state. He was Jefferson's agent in
the personal embarrassments known as the Callender and Walker
affairs. He stood by Jefferson as the president endured repeated press
attacks and gave his pen to Jefferson's controversial decision to urge a

trade embargo in 1807. Ralph Ketcham has described the relationship of the president and his secretary of state as symbiotic: "Jefferson's colorful pen and personality, his genius for warm human relationships, and the passionate devotion he inspired among his followers made him, in the eyes of the public and of history, loom over his self-effacing friend, but in fact Jefferson's administration was very nearly as much Madison's as his."[36]

Samuel Whitcomb, a bookseller who boasted both men as customers, compared them in 1824. Madison, he wrote, appeared "less studied, brilliant and frank, but more natural, candid and profound." Jefferson possessed "more imagination and passion, quicker and richer conceptions."[37] This somewhat abstruse reflection may not greatly enrich our perception, but what remains most striking in their long friendship is the apparently untarnished confidence each had in the other. Eulogizing Jefferson on learning of his death, Madison recalled that their friendship had experienced no "interruption or diminution . . . for a single moment in a single instance." While this eulogy was appropriate, it does not tell the whole story. Jefferson and Madison did not always see eye to eye on important matters and even, in one crucial instance, sent contradictory instructions to negotiator Robert Livingston, who was in France in 1802, concerned with the issue that was to result in the Louisiana Purchase.[38] It was this divide that Madison was alluding to when he took account of Jefferson's tendency to react viscerally on sensitive public issues; he observed sympathetically that allowances "ought to be made for a habit in Mr. Jefferson as in others of great genius of expressing in strong and round terms, impressions of the moment."[39]

Of the two, Jefferson was perhaps the more socially graceful, and in their friendship the one more likely to take the initiative. Jefferson appreciated Madison's combination of modesty and resolve, admiring his "habit of self-possession, which placed at ready command the rich resources of his luminous and discriminating mind." He attributed Madison's rise to the very qualities he would have most appreciated hearing of his own life's work if he himself could have admitted to desiring public acclaim. This was to pursue his beliefs "in language pure, classical, and copious, soothing always the feelings of his adversaries by civilities and softness of expression."[40]

Certain incidents suggest that the selfless concern the two expressed in correspondence was not contrived. On one journey together in 1790, Jefferson and Madison vied with each other to pick up the greater share of expenses. Again, Madison felt obliged to refuse Jefferson's offer to reside together in a house Jefferson was renovating on Market Street, Philadelphia, because Madison knew that his friend would not allow him to pay a fair share of the rent. Then, in a series of exchanges during 1794–95, Jefferson privately proposed Madison for the highest office in the land, and his friend insisted that the more popular and distinguished former secretary of state, former minister to France, was the right man for the job. Jefferson's letters on the subject illustrate how he conceived virtue in friendship; he insisted to Madison that elevation to the presidency was "the only change of position I ever wished to see you make, and I expressed it with entire sincerity." Once again, "sincerity" meant something very particular to Jefferson, the unselfishness that follows from pure affection. He underscored that his sincere wish "was too pure, & unmixed with anything respecting myself personally."[41]

Madison, was in any case, Jefferson's greatest blessing. When caught in political struggle, Jefferson required a mature thinker with a practical persuasion to counteract his own occasionally rising passion. Monroe and Short, his other two oldest and closest political supporters, embodied Jefferson's desire to forge an alliance with the next generation of political leaders; but as dutifully as they served their patron, they could not equal Madison in the weight of their judgments, the consistency of their resolve, or the extent of their achievements.

Jefferson's close friendships that derived from the mentoring process centered (at least initially) on relationships of understood authority. The dual loss of his father at an early age and the lack of any male offspring who survived infancy may well have enhanced the value of the mentor relationship to Jefferson. Remarkably, the distinction between mentor and friend somehow dissolved, as what were formative procedures gradually grew into full-fledged friendships and political alliances based on an essential individual equality.[42] As a humanist he wished to pass on his ideas by cultivating young men of talent, virtue, and good sense. Once they were in his circle, Jefferson hoped to convince those most like family — Madison, Monroe, and Short — to settle near Monticello, and he wanted others to visit him there whenever possible. It is also worth noting that Jefferson protégé James Monroe followed a similar pattern himself. His father died when he, the eldest son, was in his teens; he reared daughters but no sons; and he became the patron of a nephew (also named James Monroe) whose character he helped to improve and who, like Peter Carr, never attained the stature his benefactor intended for him. Monroe, like Jefferson, made himself accessible to younger men of talent and emphasized self-improvement over the exercise of political influence to advance them.[43]

The overall picture, still, is one of some complexity. Jefferson battled with Monroe's tendency to become easily irritated, easily put off, the same way he battled with the spontaneous effusions of his own Heart when it wanted to thrust him into the heat of political conflict or fly from public to private life. The far less volatile Madison seemed more self-assured, rational and controlled, issue-oriented, like Jefferson's engaging Head. The enterprise of friendship, Jefferson's lifelong quest for neighborhood wherever he went, revolved around an expansiveness of ideas and intellect and containment of dangerous or unproductive passion.

JEFFERSON THE HARMONIZER: THE DEBT TO FRANKLIN

ATTESTING TO HIS sentiments for Thomas Jefferson at the end of a long and fruitful life, the "venerable and beloved" Benjamin Franklin, as Jefferson described him, handed his friend the last portion of his autobiography, dealing with negotiations in England designed to prevent war. Jefferson, as the recently appointed secretary of state, had left Monticello at the beginning of March 1790 and was stopping in Philadelphia en route to New York, where Washington's administration was assembling. At Franklin's bedside he indicated that he would return the precious manuscript after he had the chance to read it. Franklin, five weeks from death, said, "No, keep it." The last letter Franklin ever wrote was on April 8, to Jefferson, and discussed boundary matters on which the new secretary had sought information. Days later, Jefferson was eulogizing this American icon as "the ornament of our country."[44]

He had first met the celebrated statesman fifteen years earlier, at the Continental Congress in Philadelphia. In the spring of 1776, when Franklin was seventy, they were members of the committee of five instructed to prepare the Declaration of Independence. Jefferson was "unanimously pressed" to undertake the draft, and Franklin and Adams reviewed it before an eager Congress weighed it. As Jefferson, seated nervously beside Franklin, heard the heated debate over his language, the elder statesman entertained him with a vintage anecdote from his own life. It was about a hatter who had asked his friends to comment on the wording of a sign to go above his shop. By the time all had made their suggestions, nothing was left but the hatter's name and a simple picture.[45] It is not difficult to imagine the wise and experienced Franklin appreciating Jefferson's sensitivity and employing in his calm, comfortable manner the ready wit that long before had brought him wide popularity. Later that year the aging but ever-vital Philadelphian accepted a mission to France to secure a wartime alliance. He would remain in Paris until Jefferson arrived to succeed him.

Both men were devoted to self-improvement and had collected books from an early age. In this era before public libraries, Franklin distinguished himself as founder of the groundbreaking Library Company of Philadelphia, which enabled contributing members to use a collection larger than what each could acquire individually. Proud of his own cleverness and the personal growth it accorded, Franklin in his autobiography reflected with dignity on his humble beginnings, "the youngest son of the youngest son for five generations back." Jefferson similarly chose to open the memoir he prepared in his late years by smoothly belittling his Randolph genealogy: "They trace their pedigree far back in England and Scotland, to which let every one ascribe the faith and merit he chooses." Both Jefferson and Franklin went on to catalog their bold intellectual adventures, though Franklin, with perhaps less of a need to justify, made self-reformation a significant part of his narrative of self-improvement.[46]

Each lay emphasis on personal morality, equally bent on exhorting a younger generation to practice health-seeking frugality. Above all, they lived by strong convictions refined through study and experience. Describing how he questioned religion and found conviction, Franklin wrote, "I grew convinc'd that *truth, sincerity* and *integrity* in dealings between man and man were of the utmost importance to the felicity of life." Jefferson viewed sincerity as the foundation of friendship. Insisting (often claiming defensively) that he himself behaved personally in a way that was beyond reproach, he coupled the word *integrity* with *wisdom* and *discretion* in his letters and asserted that "integrity of views" was "the basis of esteem." To his youthful charge Peter Carr, Jefferson wrote in the manner of Franklin (shortly after he and Franklin had parted company in Paris) on the importance of a well-managed day. "Time now begins to be precious to you," ran Jefferson's version of the aphorism. "Every day you lose will retard your entrance on that public stage whereon you may begin to be useful to yourself." Nothing made a man dearer to his friends than "an honest heart." Pursue the interests of country, friends, and self "with the purest integrity, the most chaste honour." When uncertain about a pending choice, "ask yourself how you would act were all the world looking at you, and act accordingly. Encourage all your virtuous dispositions." The advice continued over several pages, shifting from reading to physical exercise, and closed, "Husband well your time, cherish your instructors, strive to make every body your friend."[47]

Both Franklin and Jefferson were sensitive to their public reputations and shied from too much self-exposure. Franklin spoke little and kept out of the controversy of congressional debate. He advocated prudence. Jefferson similarly judged the moral-philosophical nature of questions, but with a lawyer's gravity, unable to effect Franklin's humorous license. Reflecting the ready passions of his generation, Jefferson wrote as if fearing desperately for the consequences should his cause not prevail. As his reputation grew he eagerly sought allies and urged others to carry forth in legislative action what he himself was only comfortable initiating with his pen or in intimate groups.

Franklin and Jefferson were alike in the power they acquired through their individual styles. Though each was unique in his means of advancing his ideas, they were similarly adept at impressing their thought upon great numbers of people. Promotion of human knowledge lay at the core of both men's efforts. The disparity of their ages meant that while they knew one another, the elder was past the time of visualizing the future, and the younger was confined to profiting from a legacy, appreciating a charismatic presence, a flair for statesmanship. Franklin had great confidence in Jefferson and knew his worth. Jefferson revered Franklin as a man whose sparkling style could not be copied and whose capacity for friendship seemed unlimited.

In 1791, not quite a year after Benjamin Franklin was laid to rest, an admirer of the great man asked Jefferson what he had found most noteworthy in Franklin's character. Aside from the charming "bon mots," wrote Jefferson, and the doggedness with which he made trials and discoveries, Franklin was "a great and dear friend" who deserved "love and veneration." It was in this context that Jefferson next repeated the modest refrain he employed in Paris whenever a person asked, "Is it you, sir, who replace Dr. Franklin?" "No one can replace him, sir," Jefferson would remark. "I am only his successor."[48]

Jefferson admired Franklin as he did George Wythe, men whose distinctly different but equally desirable and practical qualities, he believed, could serve him in public life. He also admired John Adams but would not have desired to be like him in any discernible way. Indeed, though he spent as much time with Adams as with Franklin in Philadelphia in 1775–76 and in Europe in 1784–85, his relations with these two turned on a very different dynamic.

In the introduction to his edition of *The Adams-Jefferson Letters,* Lester J. Cappon expressed dismay that despite a "congenial" correspondence with Adams and a capacity for "easy-flowing conversation," Jefferson did not "reveal his character on more intimate terms." This is a fair characterization. Few could match John Adams's intensity in his candid (some would say gushing) revelation of deep affections and heated contentions in his letters. Jefferson understood Adams's eccentricity, his delicate temperament, and nevertheless esteemed him. This was a man who in 1774, one year before his first meeting with Jefferson, "suffered such torments in my mind . . . as have almost overpowered my constitution," and who yet determined to "be cool" amid "the mean-spirited, low-minded, fawning, obsequious scoundrels who have long hoped that my integrity would be an obstacle in my way" to success.[49]

The milder Jefferson was intent on working effectively with the intense Adams. He tried always to communicate on the level he considered most harmonizing. Often this occurred with classical allusions, by an appeal to the learned tastes the two shared. From the beginning, as the younger man, he both showed deference to the volatile senior statesman and assumed responsibility for maintaining equilibrium in their relationship. It was Jefferson who took the initiative, Merrill Peterson has recorded, reaching out to "a man whose republican heart beat in unison with his own." Yet Peterson has imagined how the Declaration of Independence would have read if Adams had written it: a less unifying document, in style "less elevated but perhaps more vigorous, less mannered and more natural, less trim and direct and more long-winded."[50] This assessment of their initially compatible philosophies but divergent styles suggests what the presentation of self can mean to statecraft.

Both men prized their reputations. Adams saw his life's struggle to be that of making himself understood. He believed he had been forced to withstand personal indignities in the course of becoming publicly known, and that he would only receive justice from history. Jefferson, on the other hand, thought it demeaning to voice too obvious a concern with public approbation. He remained apart from the heat of intense debates whenever possible, always gathering his energy. He mollified himself with the attention and the testimonials he received from his intimates.

It is not surprising that Jefferson's part in this correspondence should appear then to be on the whole cool and suppressive of emotion. Jefferson understood that it was not heat that Adams sought from him but a vibrant mind, ideas gleaned from ardent study. As much as Jefferson prized him for his genius, Adams's fire was close to the surface. The Virginian had to watch what he said, had to account for what Madison in 1788 called Adams's "extravagant self importance."[51] But circumstances drew them together when the genial Jefferson was newly arrived in Europe and his highly sensitive friend felt isolated.

At first formal, correct, and highly supportive of the legendary Dr. Franklin when he joined him in France in 1778, Adams grew suspicious and began to consider Franklin indolent when the two seemed to be working at cross-purposes. Quiet despondency led eventually to seething outrage. In 1782, when John Jay joined Franklin and Adams to negotiate the peace treaty acknowledging America's independence, Adams thought that he could cooperate with Jay, even though the latter was considered "family" by Franklin. The proud New Englander wrote in his diary with characteristic fervor: "F.s cunning will be to divide us. To this end he will insinuate, he will intrigue, he will maneuvre." By Jefferson's arrival two years later, Adams was feeling beaten by Franklin's patronizing attitude. The Virginian behaved in a manner that soothed Adams, who frequently needed to be soothed.[52] A comfortable bond grew between Adams and Jefferson, and they dined at each other's residences often. Jefferson was comfortable engaging intellects with Adams on such occasions and sought to convey an unselfish heart. Thus, on a personal level Paris was the high point of their association, consisting more of demonstrable actions than sentimental words.

Cappon called the record "half-satisfying," presumably because Jefferson was more guarded in his letter writing than Adams. However conscious Jefferson was of proper epistolary form and erudite presentation, there is yet a warmth to his letters, a sense of naturalness and a personal touch which is, for example, less apparent in his correspondence with another elder he deferred to, George Washington. Jefferson held back by choice, not because he was unable to express his feelings. His candid words to Madison in 1787 explain why did do so. Writing in cipher, Jefferson offered a revised assessment of Adams, acknowledging that it was Madison who "shook" the opinion of Adams which he had formed in 1775–76. He underscored that he had since seen "proofs which convicted him of a degree of vanity, and of a blindness to it, of which no germ had appeared in Congress. A 7-months' intimacy with him here and as many weeks in London have given me opportunities of studying him closely. He is vain, irritable and a bad calculator of the force and probable effect of the motives which govern men. This is all the ill which can possibly be said of him. . . . He is so amiable, that I pronounce you will love him if ever you become acquainted with him." It was typical of Jefferson to analyze the shortcomings in a man but, whenever possible, to conclude with an optimistic appraisal of the future.[53]

It is also consistent with Jefferson's character that as an industrious new diplomat, he mediated that first season in Paris between the easy-going Franklin and the jealous, combative Adams. The elder two were qualitative opposites. Jefferson remained a confidant of the independent octogenarian, who was surrounded by his French admirers; and he just as easily gravitated to the close family atmosphere of the Adamses. He took seventeen-year-old John Quincy Adams under his wing while behaving for all intents and purposes as Randall has portrayed him, a younger brother to John Adams. He was solicitous of Adams's opinion and equally modest about his own talents before Mrs. Adams, whom he had not met before and whom he considered a woman of "good sense and prudence." She no doubt was as solicitous of the gracious Virginian who had recently lost his wife.[54]

When the Adamses left for England in the spring of 1785, Jefferson wrote, "The departure of your family has left me in the dumps." Attesting to the warmth that existed, Abigail Adams called Jefferson "one of the choice ones of the earth." Protective of her husband, she expressed gratification that this "respected Friend" was "the only person with whom my Companion could associate with perfect freedom, and unreserve." The Adamses hung a Mather Brown portrait of their Virginia friend in their London home.[55]

In 1787, when Jefferson's nine-year-old daughter Maria sailed from Virginia, she stayed in London in the care of Abigail Adams for three weeks before being brought to Paris by Jefferson's trusted French servant. In that short time the girl became deeply attached to her caretaker. The "amiable lovely Child" talked of Mrs. Adams "often and much,"

Jefferson reported, having earlier offered "a thousand thanks" for their solicitude. John Adams himself wrote his friend: "I am extreamly sorry, that you could not come for your Daughter in Person, and that we are obliged to part with her so soon. In my Life I never saw a more charming Child." Abigail Adams, "loth to part with her," echoed these sentiments, declaring, "I never felt so attached to a child in my Life on so short an acquaintance." Maria received a letter of her own from Mrs. Adams, upon which "she flushed, she whitened, she flushed again, and in short was in such a flutter of joy that she could scarcely open it."[56]

Unhappily, the partisan debates of the 1790s caused a rift between the two principals who had earlier collaborated so well. The eagerness with which Abigail and John Adams had confided in Jefferson and the steady hand which he used in his coolheaded replies, gave way to a long, awkward silence. Jefferson clearly knew that the Adamses appreciated his reliability, his thoroughness. Comparing notes on commercial questions, they had communicated between Paris and London as patriots who saw eye to eye. Adams cautioned Jefferson, "We must not, my Friend, be the Bubbles of our own Liberal Sentiments." And Jefferson proposed a course, sent documents, and comfortably added, "Alter it or reject it as you please." Empathizing with the oft-embattled Adams, Jefferson admitted to Abigail Adams that "I do not love difficulties. I am fond of quiet, willing to do my duty, but irritable by slander and apt to be forced by it to abandon my post [a possible reference to the charges made in the wake of his governorship]. These are weaknesses from which reason and your counsels will preserve Mr. Adams." Jefferson regarded Adams as a fighter and thought of himself as one who, without strong backing, was less likely to persevere.[57]

Before the decade began that witnessed an end to their harmony, John Adams signed his letters, "I am with an affection that can never die, your Friend and Servant," and "With unabated respect, Esteem and Affection I am, dear Sir, your Friend and humble ser[van]t." Prior to leaving Paris, Jefferson congratulated Adams on his presumed election to the vice presidency: "No man on earth pays more cordial homage to your worth nor wishes more fervently your happiness. Tho' I detest the appearance even of flattery, I cannot always suppress the effusions of my heart."[58]

Jefferson no doubt appreciated the fact that he and Adams were sufficiently different in background and temperament to question whether they ought to be compatible. It was that very unlikelihood of their becoming close that caused Jefferson to rise to the challenge. Whatever else Adams was, he was intelligent and honest. Jefferson counted on that. Caught in the storm of public controversy, Vice President Adams and Secretary of State Jefferson were pulled apart by events in the news more than they consciously quarreled. Their personal misunderstanding began in Philadelphia in 1791 and enlarged year by year as the line forged by heated rhetoric between Federalists and Jeffersonian Republicans grew into an ever-widening gulf.

In 1790 Adams published his "Discourses on Davila," a series of newspaper essays evidencing his newfound comfort with the prospect of a titled aristocracy in America. The following spring Jefferson politely wrote a brief cover letter transmitting, at the behest of another, a borrowed copy of Thomas Paine's *The Rights of Man.* As one of the first copies of this pamphlet to arrive in Philadelphia, it was hastily reprinted by the brother of the man to whom Jefferson had been asked to address his note, prefaced with Jefferson's expression of pleasure that "something is at length to be publicly said against the political heresies which have sprung among us." The "political heresies" were those of Adams, admitted Jefferson in a letter to Washington, but any differences with Adams were friendly differences never meant to be aired publicly.[59]

A writer named "Publicola" began attacking *The Rights of Man.* Widely assumed from the style of the articles to be John Adams, the author was in fact young John Quincy Adams, writing without aid from his father. Jefferson refused to take personally the political barbs he read and wrote the elder Adams urgently in an attempt to clear the record and find common ground: "I hope, my dear Sir, that you will see me to have been an innocent *in effect* as I was in intention. I was brought before the public without my own consent, and from the first moment of seeing the effort of the real aggressor in this business to keep me before the public, I determined that nothing should induce me to put pen to paper in the controversy. The business is now over, and I hope it's effects are over, and that our friendship will never be suffered to be committed, whatever use others may think proper to make of our names."[60] This statement is key to understanding Jefferson's conception of friendship and affectionate ties in the republican style of politics. His words imply the capacity for calm reasoning amid public controversy. Knowing well their philosophic divergence and the emotional volatility of the New Englander, Jefferson relied on Adams's strong sense of honor and propriety to extinguish the fire generated by Paine's combustible pamphlet.

For a time this worked, or at least preserved a dialogue. In 1794, out of government for the first time since recovering from his wife's death more than a decade earlier, Jefferson wrote to Adams: "The difference of my present and past situation is such as to leave me nothing to regret but that my retirement has been postponed four years too long. . . . I return to farming with an ardour which I scarcely knew in my youth. . . . I put off answering my letters now, farmerlike, till a rainy day." He projected no future occasion for a return to politics and bade Adams to ignore past differences. Then Jefferson closed the letter by wishing the vice president "every degree of happiness to you both public and private." Adams replied with some testy comments on current politics but a half year later wrote a warmer note. The two continued to exchange friendly, politically neutral greetings. Adams forwarded a book on the French Revolution written by their mutual friend François d'Ivernois, for which the self-proclaimed farmer expressed thanks and complained disingenuously, "But it is on politics, a subject I never loved, and now hate."[61]

In the election of 1796, the first contested election in the new Republic, Adams bested Jefferson. Although by all accounts Jefferson was neither surprised nor dismayed by the results, their relationship cooled under the increasing strain of partisan differences. Indeed, politics so divided the nation by this time that nothing could have kept the two close. Adams endured a stormy presidency, attempting to assert his independence as Alexander Hamilton maneuvered to embarrass him and the Jeffersonians grew ever more fearful of "monocracy" and Federalist intrigue.[62]

Adams apparently took their political differences more personally than Jefferson. Upon wresting the presidency from Adams in 1800, Jefferson was "sensibly affected" when Adams "accosted me with these words: 'Well, I understand that you are to beat me in this contest.'" He responded by insisting that there was "no personal contest between you and me. Two systems of principles on the subject of government divide our fellow citizens into two parties. With one of these you concur, and I with the other." They only headed their respective tickets because they had been long on the "public stage" and their names were "more generally known." But were they "both to die to-day, to-morrow two other names would be in place of ours, without any change in the motion of the machinery." Adams accepted this explanation, reported Jefferson (soothing himself in the belief), but soon after fell prey to the "thousand calumnies" that Federalists "in bitterness of heart" carried to him.[63]

Jefferson did not blame the second president for the worst outrages of his term, and he certainly did not alter his personal feelings toward honest Adams. This becomes clearer in the tentative correspondence initiated by Abigail Adams in 1804, more than three years after the seemingly final estrangement of her husband and his successor. Responding to her letter of condolence after his daughter Maria's death, Jefferson invoked the word *friendship* six times in his two-page reply. He asserted that "one act of Mr. Adams's life, and one only, ever gave me a moment of personal displeasure." Hostile political appointments on the eve of Jefferson's presidency had given him cause for personal displeasure; but even these, Jefferson assured her, did not occupy his thoughts long. After "brooding" for "some little time," he promptly forgave his old comrade "cordially, and returned to the same state of esteem and respect." Professing his "sincere attachment" toward Mrs. Adams and feeling "relief from being unbosomed," Jefferson was clearly eager for the opportunity to employ his pen to set the record straight. It was painful, he declared finally, to know that politics had affected "private friendships" in such a manner. "The injury these [friendships] have sustained has been a heavy price to pay for what has never given me equal pleasure."[64]

Mrs. Adams echoed Jefferson's deeply held belief when she wrote him two months later: "Party hatred by its deadly poison blinds the Eyes and envenoms the heart. It is fatal to the integrity of the moral Character." Their common appreciation for a history of mutual esteem more meaningful than the years of partisanship should have served, it seems, to end the feud then and there. But somehow it did not, though Jefferson reassured Mrs. Adams that he had never performed any act with an "unkind intention" toward her husband. When the two men finally did renew their correspondence in 1812, Jefferson closed his first letter, "No circumstances . . . have suspended for one moment my sincere esteem for you; and I salute you now with unchanged affections and respect." He closed his second letter with "assurances of my sincere friendship and respect."[65] Jefferson and Adams, students of human nature who each over time had suffered for his humanity, now moved, letter by long letter, from happy reminiscences as "fellow laborers in the same cause" to the classics of their early education of which they had never tired, to biblical studies, Indians, morals, government—the human condition, in general.

Jefferson's eagerness to explain himself to Abigail Adams and his subsequent delight in formally mending fences with her husband require once again taking his sincerity at his word. Indeed, Jefferson had written one letter to Adams after the election of 1796 which on Madison's strong recommendation he did not send. It warned of "spies and sycophants" and "your arch-friend of New York" (Hamilton), while claiming for himself "no ambition to govern men." Jefferson would sleep more soundly "with the society of neighbors." As his "sincere wish," finally, he bade Adams "glory and happiness." In conferring with Madison, Jefferson explained that he had thought long and hard over this letter, having "deferred it under the despair of making him believe I could be sincere in it."[66] It was the credibility behind his expression of sincerity that had caused Jefferson such melancholy in contemplating the composition of a single letter, again suggesting strongly that the sincerity Jefferson invoked was used sparingly and never artificially contrived.

THE PHILADELPHIA CONNECTION

IN ADDITION TO conceiving his neighborhood of Virginia friends, his closest and most trusted allies, Jefferson required an emotional "neighborhood" when he took up office outside his native state. While in Philadelphia in 1775–76 and again in 1783, he met and befriended a number of the great intellects of young America, sharing with these men a love for science and philosophy. Jefferson carried on a long and fruitful dialogue with David Rittenhouse, Francis Hopkinson, Charles Thomson, Charles Willson Peale, and Benjamin Rush, all members of the American Philosophical Society founded by Benjamin Franklin in 1743, the year of Jefferson's birth, and revived by Charles Thomson in 1768. Jefferson resided in Philadelphia from 1790 to 1793 and 1797 to 1800 while assuming the duties of national office. He served as president of the society concurrent with his terms as vice president and president of the United States.

David Rittenhouse (1732–1796) was Jefferson's model of a great scientist. As an astronomer he created an orrery, a mechanical device which showed the positions and movements of heavenly bodies. On the occasion of an eclipse in 1778, Jefferson respectfully compared notes with Rittenhouse before addressing his further comments: "Writing to a philosopher, I may hope to be pardoned for intruding some thoughts of my own, tho' they relate to him personally." He expressed the opinion that Rittenhouse, like Franklin, should be freed from the responsibilities of government and permitted to give his genius to science full-time. "You should consider that the world has but one Ryttenhouse, and that it never had one before." In *Notes on Virginia* Jefferson called Rittenhouse "second to no astronomer living," a self-taught genius, and once again coupled him with Franklin: "As an artist he has exhibited as great a proof of mechanical genius as the world has ever produced." From France, Jefferson sent him news of Europeans' astronomical research and received updates on American inventions in return.[67]

Knowing Jefferson's opinion of Rittenhouse, John Page, an eager astronomical observer since their younger years, undertook a correspondence with the Philadelphian and eventually met him. Writing Jefferson in Paris, Page sang Rittenhouse's praises: "I had heard much of that Great Man . . . but I must confess, that I found him greatly superior to any Idea I had of him. For I found that he not only was a great and ingenious Mechanic, and profound Astronomer and Philosopher . . . but that his great and comprehensive Mind had taken a View of every Thing. His genius had penetrated as deep into the Secrets of the moral and political World, as into those of the natural." Showing deference to Rittenhouse's scientific gifts, Jefferson esteemed the entire household, where his daughter Martha took drawing lessons for a time. "Nothing could give me more pleasure," he wrote, "than your being much with that worthy family wherein you will see the best examples of rational life and learn to esteem and copy them."[68]

In 1793, as Secretary of State Jefferson was projecting retirement to Monticello, he sent Mrs. Rittenhouse a plaster bust of himself sculpted by Houdon in Paris, noting that the gift was a "useless" article among his "useless furniture" but nevertheless an expression of the "sincere affection of the giver." Rittenhouse, then serving as both director of the United States Mint and president of the American Philosophical Society, replied in the idiom in which Jefferson himself had long before become expert: "I feel most sensibly the misfortune of contracting so very few friendships in youth, which is certainly the proper season for

providing whatever will be necessary to us in old age . . . but I shall
ever remember with pleasure, whilst memory continues to perform its
office, that I have counted the name of Mr. Jefferson in the very short
list of my friends." In the character of a modest man, ignoring his accomplishments and titles, Rittenhouse was offering a testament to
friendship in classical terms, just as Jefferson did so often.[69]

Francis Hopkinson (1737–1791) was the son of an early intimate of
Franklin and himself a remarkable wit. A talented harpsichordist (in
Europe, Jefferson endeavored to promote an invention of Hopkinson's
meant to improve the tone of the instrument), he was a wordsmith,
too, the author of psalms, odes, and political satire. He was a signer of
the Declaration of Independence, chairman of the Navy Board during
the Revolution, designer of the seals of the American Philosophical Society and the state of New Jersey, and purportedly the designer of the
first American flag.[70]

Jefferson and Hopkinson appear to have been only passing acquaintances until 1783, when this good-natured friend offered to board the
young, motherless Martha Jefferson at his mother's home during the
confused period when Congress moved from Philadelphia to Princeton
to Annapolis. Hopkinson applied his literary wit to an early letter to
Jefferson, enclosing "for your Amusement a Christmas Gambol" and
"A Sample of Good Writing." In the latter effort Hopkinson fancified
words such as "ornament" (advocating that a word should illustrate
itself), wrote "condescend" at a slant, and lightly mocked the rules of
grammarians. The letter, addressed "Dear Friend," concluded: "I shall
be happy in corresponding with you if you give me any Encouragement. My Fancy suggests a Thousand whims which die for want of
Communication, nor would I communicate them but to one who has
Discernment to conceive my Humour and Candour with respect to my
Faults and Peculiarities. Such a Friend I believe you to be." Jefferson
answered from Annapolis that Hopkinson's composition, "a small en-
tremêt [sweet side dish] of philosophy," was relieving "amidst this eternal surfeit of politics." But relief was not the same as delight. Jefferson
examined the literary product of his elder, Hopkinson, with his Head
more than his Heart.[71]

Writing Monroe, Jefferson called this virtuoso "a man of genius,
gentility and great merit." Selecting news and stories he expected
would appeal to a man of Jefferson's taste, Hopkinson was sensitive
to his friend's lack of reliable information during his years in Europe.

Meanwhile, he continued to regale Jefferson with his own "off hand Performances," such as one he was proud to have published in a Philadelphia newspaper. This was a lampoon of an escalating public quarrel between two gentlemen, who upon discovering that "the Laugh of the Town was turned upon the Combatants" as a result of Hopkinson's ridicule, desisted in what otherwise might have ended in a mortal duel. Jefferson dutifully responded but demonstrated his preference to assist Hopkinson, as he did the other Philadelphians, in their scientific and philosophical enterprises.[72]

Charles Thomson (1729–1824) was best known during his lifetime as the tireless secretary of the Continental Congress, having served that body from 1774 to 1789. His life as a patriot and student of Enlightenment science reveals a success story reminiscent of Benjamin Franklin's prototypical experience. He left Northern Ireland at age ten with a widowed father who died during the voyage to America. On arrival, the young orphan was placed in a blacksmith's family but thirsted for knowledge and, through a chain of lucky circumstances, received a classical education in New London, Pennsylvania. After tutoring Latin and Greek, he moved to Philadelphia and met Franklin in 1750, perhaps the transforming moment in his life. Reviving the American Philosophical Society, he grouped its members by their interests: geography, mathematics, natural philosophy, and astronomy; medicine and anatomy; natural history and chemistry; mechanics and architecture; husbandry and "American Improvements." This society quickly became the embodiment of American intellectual ferment and secured Philadelphia's place as America's connecting point. Like Franklin, Thomson was a model of how an eighteenth-century American of moderate means could advance personally and organize for public purposes.[73]

Jefferson and Thomson met in 1766, when the Virginian first traveled to Philadelphia to be inoculated against smallpox. Though Thomson had been a leader of the Stamp Act resistance, he met Jefferson primarily on the plane of science and natural history studies. After both men were appointed "counsellors" of the American Philosophical Society in 1781, Jefferson suggested that Thomson examine his *Notes* in manuscript form, with an eye toward presenting the completed work to the membership. From this grew a fine collaboration, as Thomson's stimulating commentaries were appended to both the 1785 French and 1787 London editions of the *Notes*. Also in 1787, Thomson published his own *Notes on Farming*. He and Jefferson continued their intellectually

fruitful friendship through the 1790s, two distinguished men of learning who equally prized independence of thought, though Thomson
took no active role in the partisan political debate in which his friend
became embroiled.[74]

Charles Willson Peale (1741–1827) grew up an itinerant portrait
painter and studied for a short time in London with Benjamin West.
He fought bravely in the Revolutionary War, after which he became
more philosophically inclined, founding his natural history museum in
1784. Malone termed Peale a "zealous" friend; Daniel Boorstin has
called him "showman" of the Jeffersonian circle. Peale's 1791 portrait of
Jefferson as secretary of state reveals a comfortable yet dignified presence and suggests the artist's intimacy with his subject (see frontispiece). The artist chose to hang the portrait in his museum. The museum was removed to the American Philosophical Society for a period
of ten years, 1794 to 1804, until it outgrew that place. Jefferson, serving
as president of the society during much of that period, continuously
offered his moral support to Peale's ventures, urging him to exhume
mammoth bones. Jefferson then selected Peale to engrave the animals
discovered by Lewis and Clark. Their correspondence in later years was
deepened by the fact that it was Peale who held the American rights to
one of Jefferson's favorite inventions, the two-penned polygraph that
mechanically reproduced letters instantly. Once again conscious of the
idiom best understood by the recipients of his letters, Jefferson, in writing to Peale, expressed a closeness to nature (the Creator's art) and a
sense of release in escaping public controversy in favor of private pursuits.[75]

Benjamin Rush (1745–1813) was the only one of the Philadelphia
friends who was younger than Jefferson. A graduate of the College of
New Jersey (or Princeton), as was James Madison, he studied medicine
in Edinburgh and toured Europe while Jefferson was just entering the
practice of law. After returning home, Rush taught chemistry at the
College of Philadelphia and came to be known as a great physician. He
was a young man of great promise when he joined Jefferson in signing
the Declaration of Independence, a versatile thinker and writer who
delighted in probing the human mind and who related moral and physical health. Like Jefferson, he embraced the stormy publicist Thomas
Paine whose pioneering use of the English language helped create the
revolutionary ferment of 1776. Like Jefferson, he celebrated America's

innocence relative to Europe, and saw his nation as a generator of wisdom and human decency. He wrote, in sum, with republican optimism.

Jefferson made some of his most quotable declarations to this correspondent, as in his response to the opposition he was encountering from religious groups during the election year of 1800. Jefferson and Rush had been engaging in a friendly argument over the divinity of Jesus for perhaps three years. Rush was trying to convince his friend to identify the Christian faith with the republican Heart. Frustrated by clerical attacks, the embattled presidential candidate could assert without fear of censure from his friend, "I have sworn upon the altar of God, eternal hostility to every form of tyranny over the mind of man." Twenty-five years after their friendship began, Rush wrote nostalgically, "I shall always recollect with pleasure the many delightful hours we have spent together, from the day we first met on the banks of the Skuilkill [Schuylkill] in the year 1775." Both unbosomed themselves easily in their letters. In 1801, as Jefferson took office, Rush exulted over his friend's success: "Your character as a philosopher and friend of mankind predominates so much more in my mind over that of your new station. . . . You have opened a new era." He recalled Jefferson's sanguine prediction of a "resuscitation" (this from a medical doctor) of the "republican spirit," when many, including Rush, had been despairing. Rush signed the letter of congratulations, "your sincere and faithful friend."[76]

Rush's humanitarian persuasion was far from being an abstract philosophy. Upon Jefferson's retirement in 1809, Rush related to John Adams his "dream" that the second and third presidents had renewed their friendly correspondence. Over the next two years, he pressed both men in a cordial and spirited dialogue. Reading copies Jefferson had sent him of the abortive attempt at congenial correspondence with Abigail Adams in 1804, Rush was not dissuaded but persisted in helping the long silent friends envision their reconciliation. He finally cajoled from Adams the affirmation that "I have always loved him [Jefferson] as a friend" and shortly thereafter saw his friendly conspiracy succeed.[77]

It is appropriate, then, that Thomas Jefferson's most colorful comment on the powers of friendship over time was directed to Benjamin Rush in the midst of this drama. At sixty-eight, Jefferson told his distinguished Revolutionary comrade, "I find friendship to be like wine, raw when new, ripened with age, the true old man's milk and restorative cordial." This is vintage Jefferson, writing to one whose Heart he felt he understood, relying on the language of sensation. Since his return from France (where he had taken his slave James Hemings to learn the culinary arts), he had become renowned for entertaining generously. He relished fine wine as no other American of his day. Clearly he equated sustenance, nature's bounty artfully presented, with an appreciation for friendship that nourished the spirit and celebrated life. On learning of Rush's death little more than a year after the two former presidents had resumed their friendship, Jefferson wrote Adams, "And a better man than Rush could not have left us, more benevolent, more learned, of finer genius, or more honest."[78]

In July 1776, upon adoption of the Declaration of Independence by Congress, Jefferson, Franklin, and Adams were asked, as a committee of three, to design the Great Seal of the United States. Franklin, the inventive former printer, and Jefferson and Adams, well-read moral-philosophers, worked together on a symbol of national self-definition. They brought in a "drawer," Frenchman Pierre Eugène Du Simitière, to assist them, agreed on a heraldic design later abandoned, and the Latin motto *E Pluribus Unum,* which remained unchallenged. Any one of the four could have added the Roman numerals MDCCLXXVI and the all-seeing Eye of Providence in a triangle, which came to adorn the reverse of the seal as capstone of a pyramid. The discussions, according to Adams, focused on Greek and biblical imagery, with Jefferson supplying metaphors from nature. Four years later a new committee reworked the seal, inspired by the creative Francis Hopkinson. In 1782 Charles Thomson, secretary of the Continental Congress, introduced the American eagle to the design. That Jefferson's Philadelphia circle should have carried out the symbolic responsibility of perfecting the Great Seal over a six-year period illustrates again the union of creative friendship, classicism, and moral philosophy among a diverse Revolutionary elite seeking to express commonality of purpose.[79]

In communicating with the philosophical Philadelphians, Jefferson could satisfy his compulsion to air controversial ideas (while gathering new strength for public battles to come) and expect to receive temperate responses. He imagined an America of Rushes and Rittenhouses, an America distinguished by brilliant and inventive, forward-looking citizens. Jefferson needed these friendships to project his vision of a vigorous nation led by the learned, not bankers and other covetous manipulators but unselfish republicans applying their talents to national enterprise.

Jefferson's enthusiasm for the Philadelphians was by and large of his Head. The mature Jefferson tended toward restraint in his approach to friendship with males who were his senior in years. Francis Hopkinson was a man of both wit and intellect with whom he apparently preferred to relate almost exclusively on an intellectual level. Then, too, Jefferson carried on a long and thoughtful correspondence with Charles Thomson which never strayed from their shared scholarship. In awe of Rittenhouse, he took some time to warm up to what he considered a far superior scientific mind. Jefferson himself aspired to add to scientific knowledge through invention (in addition to collecting and analyzing artifacts of natural history). He designed and built a moldboard plow of least resistance, first tested in 1795 and perfected in 1805; and while he received an award for his invention from the Society of Agriculture in Paris, he may never have considered himself more than a tinkerer when comparing himself to Rittenhouse, from whom he had sought theoretical assurance with regard to the design in 1796.[80]

With Dr. Rush, Jefferson was, refreshingly, more fanciful. This may have been a function of their nearness in age, or, more likely, a matter of simple chemistry. How much his deference to elders softened in private meetings, we cannot be certain, though in one tension-filled letter John Adams recalled to Jefferson's mind that their private utterances concerning the nature of government had been "transient hints . . . jocular and Superficial."[81] At least with the testy Adams, Jefferson faced his friend head on; they related man to man. This begins to explain why their estrangement was so heartfelt, and the revival of their friendship so meaningful. Jefferson was by no means a humorless man or a rigid one, but he was careful to comport himself with an air of classical dignity.

THE SECOND MONTICELLO

FRIENDSHIP AND SOCIAL responsibility, of course, grew inseparable as Jefferson became worldly. On the other hand, he always required a retreat from the exposed life. By the time he returned from Paris in 1789, he had given great thought to reconstituting the peace, contentment, and rusticity — the classical model of rural retirement earlier drawn — of his Monticello idyll.

Patty's death in 1782 had radically changed the complexion of life at Monticello, precipitating his abandonment of the place he so closely identified with his marriage. Before Europe, the thought of surrounding himself with virtuous men of good minds gave him the hope of making his life worthwhile. Even before marriage, in his 1771 letter to Robert Skipwith, he had imagined a charmed circle. A dozen years later, mourning Patty, he eloquently urged Madison, Monroe, and Short to buy property near Monticello. When that ideal neighborhood did not materialize (although Monroe would later build Ash Lawn a few miles from Monticello and Madison's Montpelier plantation was but a day's ride north), in its place Jefferson focused on the enlargement of his own family.

Emotionally, the most important plan Jefferson formed after his re-establishment in Albemarle County during the winter of 1789–90 was the settlement of his daughters and first grandchildren at or near an improved Monticello. In February 1790, when Martha was seventeen, she married her third cousin Thomas Mann Randolph, of the Tuckahoe Randolphs. The wedding, held at Monticello, was one cause for Jefferson's lateness in joining Washington's cabinet. Young Randolph, twenty-two at the time of his marriage, was a man of education and European travel experience, who possessed an honest heart and, at least in later years, a fiery temper. Jefferson welcomed him to the family, saw that he took over the Edgehill plantation a few miles from Monticello, wrote to and confided in him often. Jefferson significantly referred to his son-in-law as "my inestimable friend to whom I can leave the care of every thing I love."[82] Maria, six years younger than her sister, was married in 1797 to her cousin John Wayles Eppes, whose mother Elizabeth was the half sister of Patty Jefferson. Learning of that match, Jefferson called it "an union of destiny" but added possessively, "I propose, as in the case of your sister, that we shall all live together as long as it is agreeable to you." Maria had lived at distant Eppington with her future husband from ages five to nine, until she was old enough to make the voyage to France. Despite the attachment she and Jack had to that place, Jefferson attempted to settle the couple on eight hundred acres near Shadwell, called Pantops.[83]

Life was bittersweet for Jefferson the widower, but after Europe, inspired by all he had seen and experienced, he was able to banish his sorrows sufficiently to think of bringing new progress to Monticello. From 1790 to 1793, while secretary of state, he made the arrangements for more than a decade of tearing down and rebuilding from the foundation up. Extensive work was done on the roof as he expanded the number of rooms. He established a nailery on the mountaintop in 1794, which did a flourishing local business. As the pace of work quickened, the presence of productive sounds no doubt made the reconstituted planter newly aware of the numbers of people dependent upon him. A roll taken in 1794 listed over a hundred slaves living on his Albemarle lands, which reflected sales of Negroes both during Jefferson's years in Europe and after his return. He experimented with wheat and studied agricultural science with tremendous enthusiasm, writing to accomplished planters like George Washington as well as European specialists. An Irish visitor offered an independent view of Monticello's surroundings in 1796: "The mists and vapours arising from the low grounds give a continual variety to the scene. The mountain whereon the house stands is thickly wooded on one side, and walks are carried round it, with different degrees of obliquity, running into each other. On the south side is the garden and a large vineyard, that produces an abundance of fine fruit." As enamored as he was with his return to wholesome agriculture, Jefferson probably did not see the field workers as often as he saw the Hemingses, house servants and skilled artisans, who presumably lived in the log cabins along Mulberry Row, within earshot of the master's house. The nearby nailery in particular gave Jefferson an opportunity to play with numbers, relating the usage of materials to labor efficiency. He reported to one correspondent that he was "delighted and occupied" with his imaginative world, having been robbed of his selfhood, to use Merrill Peterson's words, by long years of service to the nation.[84]

Away from public life Jefferson sounded more rhapsodic in his letter productions. He wrote as a private citizen to Maria Cosway: "I am become, for instance, a real farmer, measuring fields, following my ploughs, helping the haymakers, and never knowing a day which has not done something for futurity. How better this, than to be shut up in the four walls of an office, the sun ever excluded, the balmy breeze never felt, the evening closed with the barren consolation that the drudgery of the day is got through." Proposing fancifully that he, Mrs. Cosway, Angelica Church, and Mme de Corny might together retrace the route of his sentimental journey of 1787, Jefferson asserted (as if he might yet become free of concerns) that "whenever I think of you, I am hurried off on the wings of imagination into regions where fancy submits all things to our will."[85]

It was having friends and loved ones close at hand that stimulated his fancy and took his mind off the rigors of public life. From Philadelphia in 1790–93 Jefferson had written often of his desire to be with his family. "When I see you," he projected to daughter Martha, "it will be never to part again." He expressed his concern for what he sought to portray as no less pressing than affairs of state: "From Monticello you have every thing to write about which I have any care. How do my young chestnut trees? How comes on your garden? How fare the fruit blossoms &c. I sent to Mr. [Thomas Mann] Randolph, I think, some seed of the Bent-grass which is much extolled."[86] During his midcareer retirement, the years 1794–97, Jefferson (along with daughter Maria) cared for Martha's two young children, Anne Cary and Thomas Jefferson Randolph, while their parents were away for extended periods. He wrote of their health and their emotional development. But after three years away from the center of debate — except through the mails — he found his way back into politics and, upon becoming vice president in 1797, again took up missing his family, intensifying now the role of advice giver in his letters to them.

During one stay at Monticello as vice president, he wrote Martha at the Varina plantation of her husband's family. Professing "impatience" to know of her health, he supposed that she ought to see things as he did and return to her first home: "I have however so much confidence in the dose of health with which Monticello charges you in summer and autumn that I count on it's carrying you well through the winter. . . . The bloom of Monticello is chilled by my solitude." This last, potent, natural metaphor is an example of the graying, fifty-four-year-old Jefferson's heightened consciousness of the seasons of life as he himself aged. Knowing what her father liked to hear, Martha wrote the next spring: "Nothing makes me feel your absence so sensibly as the beauty of the season. . . . Monticello shines with a transcendent luxury of vegetation above the rest of the neighborhood." He immediately replied from Philadelphia that he yearned for home, "the only scene where, for me, the sweeter affections of life have any exercise."[87]

In 1771 Jefferson had struggled to import a pianoforte for his betrothed, for he believed that music added sweetness to domestic life. His friend the marquis de Chastellux had written in a philosophic letter,

"A harpsichord is a neighbor always at command, who answers all our questions and never speaks ill." In both men's estimation that instrument was a woman's proper amusement, companion to her home education. In the spring of 1798, the paternal Jefferson wrote to newlywed Maria, so similar in look and personality to her mother, about a harpsichord he had purchased for her. It was to be shipped from Philadelphia with "a box of trees" for Monticello, additional music and fruit to grace the scene. The harpsichord arrived in good condition except for a bit of broken molding, and Jefferson, still in the national capital, suggested to his younger daughter that once she had heard the tone of the instrument, she would find it "sweeter for a moderate room." Both Jefferson daughters played. To Martha he tended to write technically, of perpendicular strings and unyielding screws; to Maria he wrote fancifully of the joys of music. When yet another pianoforte arrived at Monticello in 1800, he told Maria, "It is the delight of the family, and all pronounce what your choice will be."[88]

Martha, the elder, was built of solid material. She was earnest and multifaceted like her father. Maria, on the other hand, was adorable but less durable. Jefferson treated his younger daughter with her feminine fragility in mind. When she wrote of her attendance at Cumberland of "the last melancholy rites paid to my Aunt Skipwith," he teased her in his prompt reply: "You are not aware of consequences of writing me a letter in so fair a hand, and one so easily read. It puts you in great danger of the office of private secretary at Monticello, which would sometimes be a laborious one." Two months later, in the letter informing her that her harpsichord had arrived, he told her, "I will convince you at Monticello whether I jested or was in earnest" in proposing secretarial chores, hinting coyly that "I shall perhaps be less scrupulous than you might wish."[89]

Jefferson would never have coddled the indomitable Martha in this manner. Indeed, he delivered to Martha all messages of importance, those which concerned the details of planning. His language was harsh and his imagery forceful. He wrote of his "impatience," grumbling that Philadelphia represented "every thing which can be disgusting," in contrast to Monticello and "my dear family, comprising every thing which is pleasurable to me in this world." To Martha he could describe his "agitation of mind," state that "my mind was fixed" and "purpose firmly declared," complain of being "assailed from all quarters," or write of his fear that a wrong choice might cause the public to suppose

"I had not tone of mind sufficient to meet slander." To Maria he was ever scrupulous to avoid too vexing a mention of conflict. He worried about her strength and acknowledged his treatment plainly: "To you I rather indulge the effusions of the heart which tenderly loves you, which builds it's happiness on your's, and feels in every other object but little interest." And she invariably responded in kind: "Suffer me dear Papa to tell you, how much above all others you are dear to me. That I feel more if possible every day how necessary your presence is to my happiness."[90]

Margaret Bayard Smith, the same age as Maria and a friend of both daughters, described the differences she perceived. Maria was "beautiful, simplicity and timidity personified when in company, but when alone with you of communicative and winning manners." Martha was homely, personable, sensible, "one of the most lovely women I have ever met with," certainly the more interesting of the sisters. Jefferson's tone with his two daughters showed that Martha was meant to be the instrument of judgment, the Head, of the family; she was encouraged less to feel than to be responsible and make things work. Maria pulled at his Heart; she was encouraged less to think than to evoke sympathy.[91]

In a rare use of strong imagery to Maria, Jefferson admitted in the year preceding the bitter presidential contest of 1800 that he was "environed here [Philadelphia] in scenes of constant torment, malice and obloquy. . . . I feel not that my existence is a blessing but when something recalls my mind to my family or farm. This was the effect of your letter." It was in preface to these comments that he drew from the image of Ossianic desolation "bright beams of the moon," by which Maria's words had broken through his darkness. Back at Monticello the following month, his letters to Maria (who was days away, at Eppington) became bright and filled with thoughts of new life. The peach and cherry trees were blossoming, asparagus was due, and nephews Peter and Samuel Carr each had produced sons. But then, when he was in Philadelphia again and learned that Maria was ill after losing her first child, he reminded her, amid anxious words, that "I know no happiness but when we are all together. . . . My attachments to the world and whatever it can offer are daily wearing off, but you are one of the links which hold to my existence, and can only break off with that. You have never by a word or a deed given me one moment's uneasiness."[92]

Jefferson used the phrase "our fireside" to symbolize the warmth of family and friendship. The "fireside" described a site both physical and psychic, where "jarring and jealousies" and "irregular passions" had no place. The "ineffable pleasures of my family society" brought the values of friendship into a structure that could not have existed until his children had grown.[93] The protective bosom of the family enlarged in importance through the decade of the 1790s, both as grandchildren were added and political strife deepened. The well-ordered dreamworld, in its second incarnation, became once again a haven for visiting friends, a fortress where political enemies could not reach the increasingly exposed party leader, and a hermitage of sorts where Jefferson could compose emotionally rich and revealing letters.

SELF-RESTRAINT, GREAT ENTERPRISE

JEFFERSON APPEARS TO have approached parenting not unlike the way he approached mentorship. He composed rigorous lesson plans for his daughters, that they should develop an enthusiasm for learning. He made sure that they were not lazy. But his words always remained encouraging. Success was measured according to standards of articulateness and conviviality; the Jefferson ladies were reared to be attractive partners to an accomplished mate. When Maria proved limited, her father did not evince any displeasure. The Heart still bound him to those who displayed goodness but by their nature could not achieve quite as much as he had initially set his sights on for them. The competent maintenance of a tranquil household in any case demanded more from the aesthetic sense and calm sensitivity (Heart). A letter to Maria when she was just entering her teens is comprehensive in this regard: "I love you dearly, am always thinking of you and place much of the happiness of my life in seeing you improved in knowledge, learned in all the domestic arts, useful to your friends and good to all. . . . Go on then my dear Maria in your reading, in attention to your music, in learning to manage the kitchen, the dairy, the garden, and other appendages of the houshold, in suffering nothing to ruffle your temper or interrupt the good humor which it is so easy and so important to render habitual."[94] Remaining unruffled by the affairs of the world — what no individual alone could change — and maintaining a consistent good humor loomed large in Jefferson's prescription for a stable and protected neighborhood.

Domesticity provided the model for social tranquillity, but to make sense of Jefferson's emotional history, we cannot stop there. What does it tell us that an eighteenth-century gentleman who possessed an insatiable curiosity for new knowledge cultivated a remarkable capacity to evoke emotions with his pen? Jefferson scoured the world for books and ideas. His friendships were the means by which he propelled himself along this path to greater knowledge. He began life on what seemed to him an Eden-like frontier landscape. Naturally inquisitive, committed to a superior education, he gradually discovered new and complex layers of society. It was through friendship that he envisioned a more secure path to the future, became caught up in momentous happenings, expressed himself eloquently, and over time built up a following. All human enterprise involves struggle, and all struggle, if it would satisfy the soul, must be emotional. He took the measure of his world, a world he believed he could improve; he built friendships and sustained them through letter writing, as he sought consensus among creative minds. Thomas Jefferson was made of contradictory elements: an enterprising spirit, but also a reticence about overcommitment and excessive self-exposure. As he saw more and more of the wider world, he tried to wall out the part that threatened him — the unreasoning dogmatist, the aggressively combative opponent — to preserve his mild inner order and delight in rural retirement that his family increasingly came to symbolize for him. Or, another way of putting it, he allowed only trusted friends within the protective walls he erected and enlisted these friends as sentinels, even attackers when he felt aggressive impulses toward others. In all this activity Jefferson maintained a clear conscience, relying on his own reconstitution of Franklinesque principles to order his life and the lives of those closest to him.

Jefferson was not an orator. He did not belong on a podium. He thrived in intimate settings. He was not meant for and did not serve in the United States Congress. He accomplished most in small committees or one on one. It was an age in which socially secure men dabbled in science, politics, and the arts. Friendship went hand in hand with public participation. Friendships among these generalists were, in a sense, easier to maintain than modern friendships, which tend to be based on specialized activity skills. Eighteenth-century friendships revolved most often around lifelong struggles, constructive tasks that required joint action, rather than mere entertainment. From early understandings grew profound commitment; from complementarity (joint concern), mutuality (common purposes).[95]

John Donne's dictum "No man is an island" applies particularly well to the age of Jefferson, to the community-conscious American Enlightenment, and to Jefferson's own ideal of developing friendship and good feelings among men. He required constant reassurance of the correctness of his basic tendency to trust, proof that the moral sense was active in human nature. Unable to ignore opportunities to advance his own political philosophy (indeed, often desperate to do so), he remained sensitive to the less altruistic instincts of men in political life and opposed whatever threatened his peace of mind. Intellectualizing, he judged, as did the eighteenth-century Scottish philosophers the earl of Shaftesbury and Francis Hutcheson, that even the pursuit of social virtue could lead through times of struggle and warfare.[96] He acted, then, not alone and spontaneously but through others and with caution. Familiar letter writing was a large component of this process; Jefferson could not give it up on any account. It was the medium that secured his belonging to the world and narrowed the gulf between himself and the thoughtful companionship he desired.

On another level, Jefferson proved his capacity for self-restriction in denying himself a second wife and forbidding any unmarried woman entry into his well-ordered dreamworld after Patty. Such a person, as Erik Erikson has written, often tends to overcompensate for his sexually repressive self-adjustment through "a great show of tireless initiative," assessing his personal worth on the basis of what he is doing and what he is going to do next. He overdoes, putting tremendous strain on himself, "with the engine racing, even at moments of rest."[97]

It was politics that most demonstrably upset the engine of Thomas Jefferson and caused him to suffer severe "periodical" (as he noted) tension headaches, lasting sometimes for weeks. Frequent collisions with political adversaries challenged body and spirit. He continued, despite it all, to conceive and promote what he believed was a realizable harmony for the nation over which he would finally preside for eight years, having first endured the strain of the less powerful but equally frustrating posts of secretary of state and vice president.

6   Obstructed Vision

ALTHOUGH POLITICS WAS the arena in which Jefferson achieved immortality, it was also an arena in which his vision of a virtuous republican community was constantly and gravely threatened. He was a national leader predisposed to relate political discourse to the values he ascribed to personal friendship and familial ties. He expected that other public men, educated to uphold similar values, would possess the strength to advance their views on government without assailing the private character of those with whom they disagreed. In this he was bound to be disappointed.

Friendship and fraternity propelled Jefferson, enabling him gradually to consolidate personal power. But there was also a boundary to the circle of friends, where a quality of comfort, fellowship, and predictability dissolved, where he drew the line between his "neighborhood" and those who, owing to character flaws he perceived, had to be excluded. This chapter examines how Jefferson construed a justification for expressing profound hostility, and how this was meant to preserve his moral principles. It also characterizes the tensions brought to bear when Jefferson the political leader — the prescriber of a civil, genteel republic who was somehow propelled into what he termed the "tumult of the world" — perceived a virulent opposition.

When he accepted Washington's offer to serve as secretary of state at the beginning of 1790, Jefferson had convinced himself that he would function as an executive, safely above any factional differences that might exist in the national legislature. Within a short time, however, he perceived a powerful body of elected representatives who had (in his mind) abandoned republican virtues in favor of self-aggrandizement and the establishment of an American aristocratic class. He came to associate their heresy with a consolidation of power and resources by Secretary of the Treasury Alexander Hamilton. Subsequent passage of the Jay Treaty in 1796, which surrendered important advantages to British commerce, was to Jefferson (retired to Monticello since January 1794) an astounding insult to the American people. Hoodwinking even President Washington, who praised this capitulation, the Hamiltonian Federalists were more plainly evidencing their desire to turn America into a state patterned on British-style corruption. Reaching cataclysmic conclusions, Jefferson convinced himself that his idealized republic was fast slipping away and returned to the tumult. In the process, as his letters show, he made language serve political partisanship.

He did not consider himself a partisan. To Jefferson, manipulation of language merely differentiated positive virtues from compromised values. To later generations, though, it also represented his means (if unconscious) of excluding individuals and groups from his circle. Adapting his sentimental vision of friendship and republicanism to an uncompromising political stance, Jefferson battled "tyranny" much as he had in his celebrated Declaration. After his election to the presidency in what he designated the "revolution of 1800," he insisted that the Republic was finally out of danger. He repeatedly expressed his trust in the inherent wisdom of the people, the guarantee that the apostate vision would never revive.

FOREST DEMOSTHENES

THE PROBLEM OF excluding people from Jefferson's genteel circle began a full decade before his encounter with Hamilton. Jefferson was not alone in cultivating a public image based on studied calm, candor, and conviviality. Outstanding figures like Franklin and Washington, with whose public styles Jefferson could identify, were silent on the floor during heated debates, adding their sensible voices only at the moment of decision. Men like the classically trained Richard Henry Lee and the ruder, charismatic Patrick Henry were accomplished orators who strove to persuade by the passion in their voices. All presented themselves as men of virtue and ability, but they made their reputations through varying means: Franklin and Jefferson through the scope of their interests and content of their writings, Washington through his sturdy military air and inspiring courage, Lee through his range of public activity and, along with Henry, the vigor of his calls for action.[1]

Jefferson had been moved by Patrick Henry's oratory before the Revolution. He looked up to the plain-dressed Hanover County storekeeper, seven years his elder, who represented the boldness of his own emerging generation. Jefferson recalled, "He appeared to me to speak as Homer wrote." Edmund Randolph, another lawyer in the shadow of Henry and through much of his political life a close ally of Jefferson, observed, "Mr. Jefferson drew copiously from the depths of the law, Mr. Henry from the recesses of the human heart."[2]

Henry was a common man with common sense, a leader by instinct. He was, in this sense, the opposite of Jefferson, who applied himself to books with an intensity none of his colleagues could match and judged men according to their mental exertions. Whereas Jefferson spent years perfecting his skills under George Wythe's tutelage, Henry was admitted to the bar on the basis of a cursory reading of the law. Jefferson later wrote that Henry was "the laziest man in reading I ever knew."[3]

Jefferson admired Henry at this time but would soon grow concerned over the personal faults he perceived. As Virginia's first governor (1776–79) and Jefferson's immediate predecessor, Henry was reputedly weak on the details of administration. His influence alarmed Jefferson during his own governorship, when it appeared that Henry was pulling the strings of those puppet legislators who criticized Jefferson's performance and impugned his courage while Virginia was under attack by Cornwallis in 1781. Though the effort to investigate Jefferson's actions fizzled for lack of concrete evidence, Jefferson felt no less abused. To his friend iron manufacturer Isaac Zane, he wrote by way of an appropriate metaphor that the instigator of the charges, George Nicholas, was merely "the tool worked with by another hand." This metaphor was succeeded by another telling image, as Jefferson compared the unnamed Henry to a whale under the sea, "discoverable enough by the turbulence of the water under which he moved."[4]

Beyond Jefferson's own misery, the trauma of wartime brought forth the prospect of giving Virginia's executive dictatorial powers, a suggestion inevitably associated with the confidence-inspiring name of George Washington, but in Jefferson's mind with Patrick Henry as well. Jefferson bristled at the thought, believing in the efficacy of conventions heralded by erudite men, the well-read and virtuous, who were not overawed by the charisma of a Henry and could focus instead, in war or peace, on promoting republican government by introducing humanistic laws. Only such activity, he felt, could mediate the natural passions of men and offset the hysteria of tense times. Indeed he was at work on his *Notes* at this time, in which he wrote strongly that "an elective despotism was not the government we fought for; but one . . . in which the powers" should be "divided and balanced."[5]

It was in this context that Jefferson distrusted Patrick Henry. The sincerity of this "forest Demosthenes" (a reference to Henry's modest, backwoods roots and a comparison to the greatest orator of ancient Greece) was open to question. Just as the orator had taken shortcuts to the Virginia bar, he was capable, to Jefferson's way of thinking, of abusing executive authority. What could immense popularity do to one with Henry's apparent lack of restraint? Might he have been manipulating the sentimental hearts of his countrymen, "bribing" the people with his calculated benevolence only in order to exploit them later? The same careful discernment that was required, for example, when Jefferson encountered beggars — some of whom were profligates merely preying on his sympathy, his moral sense, and the sensibility of the age — was required in judging the motives of self-styled protectors of the public good. By logical inference, Jefferson was advancing the suggestion that his own instincts, benevolence, and philanthropy, honed through intense study and careful reasoning, suited him for executive leadership. Only one like himself or the dignified George Washington could be proper symbols of republican rule, trustworthy men who could restrain their passions and ambitions in favor of the public interest.[6]

George Rogers Clark, who had led Americans against the British and their Indian allies throughout the Revolution and also was collecting specimens of natural history in frontier Kentucky, wrote a supportive Jefferson in 1782. The British had laid down their arms in the East, awaiting a negotiated peace, but they remained active in the West. With virtually no support, Clark was trying to administer the frontier according to instructions from the government in Richmond, and some of the state's leaders were either unaware of his predicament or complacent in asking more of Clark than he could deliver. Extemporizing, he waged war and managed the land as he saw fit.

He wrote to Jefferson of his disillusionment with the unnamed people who disapproved his "Quixotic Scheams." Though preoccupied at the time with his wife's final illness and death, Jefferson eagerly commiserated with the frontiersman: "I perceive by your letter you are not unapprised that your services to your country have not made due impression on every mind. That you have enemies you must not doubt, when you reflect that you have made yourself eminent. If you meant to escape malice you should have confined yourself within the sleepy line of regular duty. When you transgressed this and enterprized deeds which will hand down your name with honour to future times, you made yourself a mark for malice and envy to shoot at. Of these there is enough both in and out of office." Jefferson's words suggested on the one hand his sensitivity to the manner in which he had recently acquired in some circles the reputation of a less than courageous governor; on the other hand, they were also characteristically sympathetic in addressing a man he thought deserving, whose honesty and good intentions he appreciated, whose public virtue he applauded. But then the generality of his statement on malice in public life suddenly turned personal: "I was not a little surprized however to find one person hostile to you as far as he has personal courage to shew hostility to any man. Who he is you will probably have heard, or may know him by this description as being all tongue without either head or heart. In the variety of his crooked schemes however, his interests may probably veer about so as to put it in your power to be useful to him; in which case he certainly will be your friend again if you want him. That you may long continue a fit object for his enmity and for that of every person of his complexion in the state . . . is the earnest prayer of one who subscribes himself with great truth & sincerity. . . ." This assurance of "sincerity" is Jefferson's close of the letter. Casting doubt on Patrick Henry's "personal courage" (invoking the very charge leveled against Governor Jefferson) and describing him as "all tongue without either head or heart" constituted Jefferson's sharpest indictment of Henry as a man of limited character, intellect, and sensibility who spoke less from conviction than from private ambition. Calling Henry's projects "crooked" (connoting indirectness but not necessarily dishonesty) and noting that "his interests may probably veer about" likewise illustrate Jefferson's fear of Henry as a manipulator, a man without firm opinions, a man who possessed the dangerous gift of the cult leader, able to seduce any who could not perceive his true shallowness. Closing his letter "with great truth & sincerity," Jefferson underscored his own sense of the gravity of his warning to Clark.[7]

Though he did not possess the temperament to combat Henry directly, Jefferson sought to make common cause with others who would challenge his designs. This pattern emerged again in Jefferson's more critical contest with Alexander Hamilton, in which Jefferson denied private motives. His letter to Clark, though, seems to indicate a deepseated desire to avenge what Jefferson perceived as a personal wrong; it is especially significant that Jefferson felt motivated to damn Henry at this particular time, writing to Chastellux the same day that he had been "dead to the world" for months. To Madison the following spring, Jefferson wrote in cipher of Henry's unpredictability on the related issue of Virginia's handling of its western possessions: "Henry as usual is involved in mystery: should the popular tide run strongly in either direction, he will fall in with it." "Mystery" again connoted ethical uncertainty, equally suggestive of a personal and a public dimension.[8]

In 1784 Henry became governor again, as Jefferson embarked for Europe. That year he opposed Jefferson and Madison on the subject of religious freedom, a crusade so important to Jefferson that he eventually inscribed "Author of the Statute of Virginia for Religious Freedom" on his tombstone. Jefferson and Madison had also been working for a new Virginia constitution but realized that they had to postpone any legislative fight until Henry was out of the picture. Jefferson, from Paris, expressed his exasperation plainly: "While Mr. Henry lives another bad constitution would be formed and saddled for ever on us. What we have to do I think is devoutly to pray for his death, in the mean time to keep alive the idea that the present is but an ordinance and to prepare the minds of the young men."[9]

Jefferson believed that he could not silence his opposition except by outliving him or relying on a younger generation to advance past him. He felt that his own reasoned opinions could find best advantage by reaching eager and well-educated young minds, open to his and Madison's friendly persuasion. Jefferson judged Henry's causes, once patriotic, to have become impromptu personal struggles. He convinced himself that the self-centered orator inevitably would lose his power base, owing to a growing inability to relate to, let alone sway, the next generation. If Henry lacked substance, Jefferson calculated, he also lacked staying power. After telling Madison of his resolve to outlast Henry, he moved in the next paragraph to the subject of his desire for Madison, like Short and Monroe, to reside near Monticello, where they could more easily conceive and implement strategies to popularize their liberal causes, which Jefferson equated with disinterestedness or public spirit. Education remained his ideal (the most republican means) for publicly combating unrepublican ideas. And friendship remained the organizing principle for republicanization.

It is easy to see how, from 1781, Jefferson relegated Patrick Henry to the void beyond his circle of friendship and alliance. Writing the supportive Zane, he portrayed Henry as a plotter, an intriguer. Jefferson could, moreover, convince himself that his antagonist's lack of education and refinement contributed to such behavior. Henry's love of fame and his persistence as a power broker exasperated Jefferson, who assigned "malice and envy" solely to his enemy, absolving himself of sin. Writing Clark the next year, he inveighed against a "tongue without either head or heart," that is, an unprincipled person. To Madison, he further termed Henry a man of "mystery," unpredictable, and eventually projected eliminating him altogether. This emotional continuity (even escalation of emotion) over a period of a few years shows just how Jefferson distinguished friend and foe: one enlarged, the other narrowed the sense of community; the first was sincere, restrained, and respectful, the second insincere, unrestrained, and given to intrigue. And intrigue, for Jefferson, had to be met by a concerted effort to alert and continually educate the public, that is, by community vigilance.

Patrick Henry died in 1799, the year before Jefferson was elected president. In 1805 Jefferson was to call him "great," unique in his ability to touch the heartstrings of ordinary people. But if in retrospect, when Henry could not harm him, Jefferson remembered the good in the man, he did not by any means wish to deny history his less laudatory reflections. The president attempted to provide a realistic portrayal to William Wirt, Henry's adoring biographer. Noting first that "we acted in perfect concert until the year 1781," Jefferson elaborated. "I think he was the best humoured man in society I almost ever knew, and the greatest orator that ever lived. He had a consummate knoledge of the human heart, which direction the efforts of his eloquence enabled him to attain a great degree of popularity with the people at large never perhaps equalled. His judgement in other matters was inaccurate. In matters of law it was not worth a copper: he was avaritious & rotten hearted. His two great passions were the love of money & of fame: but when these came into competition the former predominated." If Jefferson first measured a person's worth by his or her Heart, then his characterization of Henry as "rotten hearted" is his final and telling indictment of an antagonist whose passion surpassed any virtuous qualities he might have possessed and who thus had distanced himself — Jefferson would have asserted his own passivity — from the circle of the sincere and reasonable (harmony-seeking) companions with whom Jefferson aimed to surround himself.[10]

Jefferson denied repeatedly any inclination of his own to invite controversy, terming his basic nature "too desirous of quiet to place myself in the way of contention."[11] Yet his manner of responding to personal hurt was to wield his pen as a weapon, to expose Patrick Henry as a deceptive manipulator unworthy of the public trust. Jefferson's desire to portray his enemy as power hungry shows that he himself understood power, and shows, too, that he was prepared to become what he in fact was, the most controversial of public men.

A Government of Character

To UNDERSTAND THE personal consequences Jefferson faced in the course of projecting his sentimental vision for America, it is necessary to characterize an atmosphere, to comment generally on notions of public discourse in the wake of the American Revolution. Politics in late eighteenth-century America was "little else but war conducted by the word," Thomas Gustafson has written. "A loquacious and some-times vicious people exercising their liberty of speech [became] victims of that liberty." From the time of the First Continental Congress in 1775 through the period of confederation, conventional wisdom held that mutual suspicions and jealousies — diversity of interests — would long remain a source of anxiety. Franklin and Adams had both expressed reservations about the viability of union.[12] After 1789 the formation of a national government and the expansion of the print medium brought cultural conflicts — and the reputations of political figures — into the open.

Joanne Freeman has written that "the fragile new republic was a gov-ernment of character striving to become a government of rules." Poli-tics came into focus at a primary level: taking the measure of a person's cultural refinement. Personal qualities and public sentiment were insep-arable. The widely read Hugh Blair, arbiter of rhetoric in this age, ex-plained that the "elevated sentiments and high examples which poetry, eloquence, and history are often bringing under our view naturally tend to nourish in our minds public spirit, the love of glory, contempt of external fortune, and the admiration of what is truly illustrious and great."[13] It is in this context that the eighteenth-century glorification of civic virtue makes most sense. As much as *virtue* meant placing the common good ahead of one's personal ambition, its polar opposite, *corruption,* foreshadowed the utter decay of society and complete politi-cal dissolution. Because these dramatic possibilities loomed before Americans, it took a special kind of citizen to be able to rise above all crudeness and self-aggrandizement in order to mirror the sublime principles for which the Revolution was fought and to serve the na-tion faithfully.[14]

The same individuals who sought to uphold a universal sense of personal honor through familiar letter writing sought public honor and celebrity by taking part in the implementation of the founding principles of the American Republic. No one considered these principles pliant. Philosophic disagreements over laws of nature and human governance remained entrenched in efforts ongoing since the American Revolution to define the ideal relationship between citizens and the federal authority. The two sides that emerged in the 1790s both predicted extreme results if their opponents should prevail: one side feared America would fall to tyranny; the other feared America was doomed to anarchy — the extreme of order, the extreme of chaos.

It was more than some abstract notion of success that hinged on the public reception of one's words and deeds. Reputation was all. The contemporary concept of honor could lead a statesman into a deadly duel with his accuser if he judged a political barb to be a personal insult. The pathways of gossip, accidents of speech, controversial pamphlets, any or all might take public discourse to new levels of anxiety and lead to embarrassing consequences for antagonists. Within such an experimental system as that provided by the new Constitution, men's natural proclivities led them to covert solutions. So-called reasonable, enlightened people found it easy, in this impressionable age, to believe in powerful conspiracies forming and developing among willful men. Underground communication networks gave definition to factions and personalized political disagreements. As William Plumer of New Hampshire noted in the middle of Washington's first term, "It is impossible to censure measures without condemning men." Those who ventured into political debate needed a wall of protection, a coterie of like-minded friends and trusted advisers, to consult with and disseminate the right kind of information to counter the opposition's slander. Jefferson was surely not the only public figure to thrive by forming a friendship network.[15]

Before becoming secretary of state, Jefferson had his own very pronounced ideas about the differences among the thirteen former colonies. His 1784 commercial notes for the American commissioners in Europe — Franklin, Adams, and Jay, who were negotiating on behalf of the Union as a whole — called attention to the "delicate point in America where a great party [individual states] are jealous of their separate independence."[16] Writing Chastellux in Paris in 1785, Jefferson defined northerners as "cool, sober, laborious" (industrious), but "chicaning" (practicing deceptions) and southerners as "fiery, Voluptuary" (gratifying their urges), "indolent," but "candid" by contrast. He found that the "character of the people" was so predictable as one traveled in a north-south direction that "without the aid of the quadrant [one] may always know his latitude." As the author of *Notes on Virginia* and a natural historian concerned with the effect of environment on the attributes of any organism, Jefferson was expressing a certain intellectual (if not cultural) prejudice. Yet it is possible that the average Virginian of his time was more restless and volatile than the average northerner and as a slave owner possessed of a stronger belief in his inherited social power. Cultural distance between North and South may be attributable as well to differing religious attitudes. Jefferson, again to Chastellux, found his neighbors to be "without attachment" to any religion "but that of the heart," while perceiving northerners "superstitious and hypocritical in their religion." These cultural tensions would demand delicate maneuvering if one was to attempt a cross-sectional political consensus.[17]

As a Virginia burgess and delegate to the Continental Congress, Jefferson, from early in his career, had faced difficult choices stemming from the nature of political debate. Dissimilar men had assumed the political stage, with varying ambitions for service and acclaim, and so the lawyer from Albemarle County had to contrive a means of expressing commitment that both suited his temperament and enabled the merits of his position to be voiced. He was, of course, entirely unnatural as a public speaker, unable to effect Patrick Henry's mastery of public oratory. With publication of the Declaration of Independence and the reform of Virginia laws that was begun later the same year, Jefferson's solution to the problem of self-promotion was to introduce measures using words and logic that compelled and to encourage others to elaborate on and debate these measures, but not to thrust himself forward. In his *Memoir* Jefferson wrote of the uneasy structure of the Confederation Congress in which he served during 1783–84. "Our body was little numerous, but very contentious. . . . A member, one of those afflicted with the morbid rage of debate, of an ardent mind, prompt imagination, and copious flow of words, who heard with impatience any logic which was not his own, . . . asked me how I could sit in silence."[18]

He equated the true American character with something akin to his own self-perception: "quiet," "loving peace," and "high-minded." As early as 1775 he expressed his desire to avoid hot-tempered debate when he wrote respectfully to Tory John Randolph (father of Edmund Randolph), who was returning to England, "There may be many people to whose tempers and dispositions Contention is pleasing, and who, therefore, wish a continuance of confusion, but to me it is of all states but one [war, presumably], the most horrid."[19]

Although Jefferson was in France while the Constitutional Convention met, his friends' reports showed him the range of interests that had to be accommodated and foretold the rough-and-tumble nature of politics to come.[20] In mid-1789, before Jefferson had left Paris, ill-tempered Senator Maclay of Pennsylvania wrote in his diary of the First Congress of the United States: "I came expecting every man to act the part of a god; that the most delicate honor, the most exalted wisdom, the most refined generosity, was to govern every act and be seen in every deed. What must my feelings be on finding rough and rude manners, glaring folly, and the basest selfishness apparent in almost every public transaction!" Maclay lost his Senate seat before the party system had time to harden, but his aggressive criticism of the behavior of public servants foreshadowed the rhetorical storm in which a host of passionate politicians would shortly be enveloped. Jefferson wrote David Humphreys as he prepared to return to the United States: "I know only the Americans of 1784. They tell me this is to be much a stranger to those of 1789."[21]

Politics, in sum, was very personal. Behind all the maneuvering, and keeping the self-sustaining circles of friendship and gossip intact, was a distinct sensitivity on the part of individual men toward others' assessments of personal character. Personal and public character were bound as closely as personal and political gossip. No matter who was momentarily under scrutiny, all political beings necessarily were led to reflect on their own qualities.[22]

"Alexander, the Amiable"

Jefferson was not one to ignore this delicate state of affairs. He may have believed that most Americans were republican at heart, but he harbored no illusions about human nature and the political process. In a sense, then, he was prepared for, but surely could not have anticipated, his monumental contest with Alexander Hamilton. Unlike Patrick Henry, Hamilton had both a seductive way with people and a strong education.

When they met as colleagues in 1790, Jefferson was impressed with the young secretary of the treasury, some fourteen years his junior. Jefferson already knew something of the New Yorker through Hamilton's sister-in-law, the communicative Angelica Schuyler Church. That lady remained quite taken with the talents and attentions of both men. She referred to Hamilton repeatedly as "dear Alexander, the amiable," when writing to her sister: "I love him very much and if you were as generous as the old Romans, you would lend him to me for a little while, but do not be jealous, my dear Eliza, since I am more solicitous to promote his laudable ambition, than any person in the world." In early 1783 Hamilton's activities in the Continental Congress were known to Jefferson through James Madison's letters, though Hamilton departed three months before Jefferson arrived there. In 1786 Jefferson read Chastellux's *Voyages,* wherein the author referred to meeting Hamilton and stated in a long biographical note that "there is no doubt that, with such talents and such knowledge, Mr. Hamilton must be in time of peace as in time of war one of the most highly regarded citizens in his new country." In 1788 Jefferson read *The Federalist,* which the skillful, energetic Hamilton had conceived in support of the unratified Constitution and placed before the public with the key collaboration of James Madison. Jefferson probably read unsentimental realism and neutrality rather than any hint of discord in Madison's factual description of the process: "Though carried on in concert, the writers are not mutually answerable for all the ideas of each other, there being seldom time for even a perusal of the pieces by any but the writer before they were wanted at the press." In 1790 there was every reason for Jefferson to be optimistic about his relationship with Alexander Hamilton.[23]

Hamilton was born illegitimate on the tiny island of Nevis in the British West Indies. His mother died when he was eleven, and his Scottish father had left home sometime before that. In his early teens the orphaned Hamilton clerked for a trader in nearby St. Croix, then succeeded to the business when his employer went to New York. He rose to the occasion and brought order and financial health to the firm, while reading Pope and Plutarch in his spare time. A powerful (if pompous and unoriginal) article on a hurricane which he wrote for the island newspaper brought Hamilton to the attention of the governor. After this, leading merchants underwrote the youth's passage to the American mainland. In 1772 Hamilton matriculated at King's College (later Columbia University) in New York City, where he debated. After Lexington and Concord he grabbed a musket and joined the resistance to the British presence off Manhattan's Battery. The erstwhile student of history, finance, and political economy was named an artillery captain in March 1776 and fought in several engagements. The following winter, encamped at Morristown, the cool and skillful Hamilton came to the attention of General Washington, who took him from a battlefield command and put his mind to work as a drafter of important military documents.[24]

Hamilton had tremendous personal charisma. A natural leader, well known among his peers as a ladies' man, he openly desired glory in battle. He was held in check by his commander, however, who increasingly needed his competent pen. Hamilton's resentment grew, and he began to behave peevishly in Washington's presence, even soliciting a letter from Lafayette on his behalf. Washington was not pleased. According to Dumas Malone, Hamilton suffered from a "lack of self-control and tendency to overreach himself," apparent during his wartime association with Washington and most likely continuing to shape their personal relations, though the magnanimous Washington did not cease to appreciate Hamilton's abilities. In any event, Hamilton took full advantage of his opportunities; through the circle of correspondence necessitated by military matters, he achieved intimacy with prominent families, including the upstate New York Schuylers, into which family he married in 1780.[25]

Hamilton biographer Nathan Schachner wrote, "To a clear head and logical mind Hamilton added a talent for phrasing, a bold but thoroughly controlled imagination, a rapid, fluent pen and a masculine and legible hand." Though no match for Jefferson as a familiar letter writer, Hamilton was also a man who valued friendship highly and expressed his affection with eagerness and satisfaction. South Carolinian John Laurens was his closest comrade on Washington's staff. In a conventional but appealing letter, Hamilton addressed his friend: "I wish, my dear Laurens, it were in my power, by actions, rather than words, to convince you that I love you. I shall tell you, that till you bid us adieu, I hardly knew the value you had taught my heart to set upon you. . . . You should not have taken advantage of my sensibility, to steal into my affections without my consent." In 1782, nearing war's end, the precocious lieutenant colonel wrote Laurens enthusiastically: "Quit your sword my friend, put on the *toga,* come to Congress. We know each other's sentiments, our views are the same; we have fought side by side

to make America free, let us hand in hand struggle to make her happy."
Unbeknownst to the writer, Laurens had just died in battle.[26]

Hamilton went on to represent New York in the Continental Congress and at the Constitutional Convention put forth bold propositions in favor of a strong national government. Supremely self-confident yet ready to disengage when his ideas were rejected by that body, he "swallowed his pride," as Schachner worded it, and reappeared in Philadelphia in time to embrace the compromise document. As secretary of the treasury, Hamilton hoped to witness the strengthening of a national identity among Americans (which explains his eager acceptance of a constitution that was, to him, less than ideal), while he acted to promote a political system less democratic and more aristocratic, with power concentrated in the monied and propertied class. The critical difference between Jefferson and Hamilton as they began serving the president in 1790 was, as Merrill Peterson has suggested, a matter of personal ambition: "Jefferson had traveled the road to fame; it still lay ahead for Hamilton."[27]

The only major development in American politics that Thomas Jefferson, in his own opinion, had failed to grasp during five years abroad was the waning of enthusiasm among the elite for the republican principles that the American Revolution had embodied for him. He arrived in the first national capital, New York, in March 1790. He recorded his disillusion with that city's society in the 1818 introduction to his *Anas,* a diarylike compilation of memoranda made while he was secretary of state: somehow, mourned the retrospective Jefferson, minds that he had formerly considered great were in 1790 open to the "apostacy" of an American monarchy.[28]

At first Jefferson gave Hamilton room to maneuver. The secretary of the treasury had unveiled a twofold program: to fund the national debt and to assume the wartime debt of the various states. America had borrowed heavily from France and the Netherlands and in addition owed its own soldiers their wages and its own merchants for supplies. Many of these domestic notes had been purchased at a discount from the original holders by wealthy speculators. Hamilton sought to alleviate the anxieties of the current noteholders by paying them face value plus interest, a reward for faith in the new government. All state debts were to be forgiven, in order to further national unity. And finally, Hamilton would establish a national bank under private direction.

These measures annoyed leading men in the southern states, who recognized that most of the government notes were held by northern speculators. The New England states also had the largest outstanding war debts and therefore the most to gain by assumption. And, most critical in Jefferson's perception, the "system" Hamilton "contrived" was, by its author's design, meant to corrupt members of Congress who "had feathered their nests with paper" before voting on measures that would enrich them personally. Neither did Hamilton identify with the lifestyles of southern oligarchs. And they resented an outsider who played off the fluctuations of the world credit market and idealized commercial competition. Jefferson wrote Washington ominously that North and South might become separate republics if the confidence-inspiring president refused a second term. This "incalculable evil," as Jefferson termed the prospect of disunion, could be related to the reluctance of many states to ratify the Constitution two years earlier. "Whenever Northern and Southern prejudices have come into conflict," he asserted, protective of his own section, "the latter have been sacrificed and the former soothed. . . . North and South will hang together," he insisted, "if they have you to hang on."[29]

Jefferson's premonition did not exaggerate conditions. Before their dispute crystallized, Hamilton had taken him aside one day in 1790 near the presidential mansion on Broadway. Predicting dissolution of the fragile Union if he could not realize the funding and assumption plan, he "walked me backwards and forwards before the President's door for half an hour," noted Jefferson. The two cabinet officers dined together the next day; subsequently, Jefferson and influential southern congressmen acceded to Hamilton's plan in return for the placement of a permanent national capital on the Potomac. As Jefferson explained to posterity in his *Anas,* only sometime after these meetings did he recognize Hamilton's seductive scheme for what it was, a "puzzle, to exclude public understanding and inquiry."[30]

In official communications the two sensitive cabinet officers maintained their composure, but matters of personal style continued to compound their increasingly personal differences. In a long and comprehensive letter, Hamilton wrote Federalist Virginian Edward Carrington of his profound discomfort in what he saw as Madison's defection. He insisted that Madison and he had been on excellent terms at the time of their collaboration on *The Federalist,* and that Madison had given every indication of subscribing to Hamilton's political philosophy. Insisting that he only accepted his post after having been persuaded first of Madison's "firm support" and "personal goodwill," Hamilton had experienced the loss of Madison's friendship upon Jefferson's arrival, "from the spirit of rivalship or some other cause." He could only suppose that Madison was either "seduced by the expectation of popularity" in Virginia or, more likely, by his "exalted opinion of the talents, knowledge and virtues of Mr. Jefferson," an outwardly mild man with "profound ambition & violent passions."[31]

Hamilton next complained to Washington: "I *know* I have been the object of uniform opposition from Mr. Jefferson, from the first moment of his coming to the City of New York. . . . I *know,* from the most authentic sources, that I have been the frequent subject of the most unkind whispers and insinuating from the same quarter. I have long seen a formed party in the Legislature, under his auspices, bent upon my subversion. . . . Nevertheless, I can truly say, that, except explanations to confidential friends, I never directly or indirectly retaliated or countenanced retaliation till very lately." Hamilton's perception that Jefferson's party was "bent upon my subversion" presents strong evidence of the joining of personal and political struggle that Senator Plumer noted. Washington himself failed to separate public from private criticism, using strong language on another occasion to tell Jefferson that newspaper articles which condemned administration measures were in fact directed at the president, despite the sweet words ("little sugar plums") that accompanied them.[32]

Republicans had been buoyed since 1791 by Philip Freneau's *National Gazette,* a newspaper set up to counter the already prominent Federalist newspaper, John Fenno's *Gazette of the United States.* The newspaper offensive of the summer of 1792, initiated against Jefferson by a pseudonymous Hamilton, drew the fire alternately of Edmund Randolph, James Monroe, and James Madison. Writing first as "An American," Hamilton charged Jefferson with malfeasance for hiring Freneau — whose views were critical of the administration — as a translator in the State Department and using government funds to support Freneau's newspaper. He further charged that Jefferson had been opposed to the main thrust of the Constitution and in subsequent pieces satirized Jefferson's political philosophy while portraying him as sly and morally lax. Publicly Jefferson was "the *promoter* of national disunion." More personally, and with brazen self-promotion, he stated that Jefferson "fears in Mr. Hamilton a formidable rival." And he mocked "plain

Thomas J——; wonderful humility on all occasions—the flimsy veil of inordinate ambition." In emotional language Monroe countered that the attack on the virtuous Jefferson was intended more than simply to "wound the fame of one deserving citizen." It aimed to subvert "that free and manly spirit of enquiry" which might expose the activities of the "friends of monarchy."[33]

In May 1792 Jefferson found himself speaking for a "public mind" no longer "confident and serene" when he warned Washington that a "corrupt squadron" was gaining control of the legislature, and that this sinister faction was preparing to throw out republican government and replace it with a monarchy. Its members would form "the most corrupt government on earth." With the newspaper war at fever pitch in August, the president requested "mutual forbearance" from his feuding cabinet officers.[34]

In September 1792, at precisely the same time as Hamilton was writing the president of Jefferson's "unkind whispers and insinuating," Jefferson was spelling out at great length his own perception of the problem.[35] With his emotion not well hidden, he identified himself with the president's "mortification" over "the internal dissentions which have taken place within our government, & their disagreeable effect on it's movements." Not assigning any human agency to dissensions taking place may have been Jefferson's way of projecting his own inactivity, that he saw himself, like the government itself, being acted upon. Protesting that "I am so desirous ever that you should know the whole truth, & believe no more than the truth," he went on to develop the case for his complete innocence. Having been "duped" by the secretary of the treasury and "made a tool for forwarding his [funding and assumption] schemes," Jefferson endured the "deepest regret" for a massive error in political judgment. He could recognize now that Hamilton's "system flowed from principles adverse to liberty, & was calculated to undermine and demolish the republic" by enriching legislators in return for their votes.

There was no subtlety in the images Jefferson presented, just as he saw no doubt that Hamilton's deliberate calculations, if unchecked, would "undermine and demolish the republic." Up to this point, Jefferson did not invoke Hamilton by name but by his official title. The letter was meant as an indictment of the man's political principles; nothing suggested that the secretary of the treasury had sought personal gain. If he was corrupting the legislature, subverting the Constitution through "cabals," it was only out of devotion to the British model. Jefferson strained to approach the issue as a lawyer, through dispassionate argument and observation. Given his talent for producing affecting prose, however, he inevitably sought to arouse a sympathetic response from his reader. He meant to strike a sensitive chord and soften up the president when he declared: "It has ever been my purpose to explain this to you, when, from being actors on the scene, we shall have become uninterested spectators only. . . . If it has been supposed that I have ever intrigued among the members of the legislature to defeat the plans of the Secretary of the Treasury, it is contrary to all truth." This is Jefferson at his most nimble, justifying himself and protesting his righteous nonaction while he moved to defeat his adversary.

His language intensified as he proceeded. Hamilton's men were "deserters from the rights and interests of the people." (Might General Washington react more dramatically to this war-begotten image of "deserters" from a noble cause?) Though embattled, indeed challenged to take up arms against his attacker, Jefferson presumed himself not to be exceeding the principled "mere expressions of dissent." Which of the two executives, he asked rhetorically, had continued to exhibit "purity, conscientious adherence" to his assigned office? At this point Jefferson finally referred to Hamilton by name.

By far the most scathing passages concerned Hamilton's deceptive tactics, his behavior — meant to be seen as cowardly — in attacking Jefferson pseudonymously in the press, "spelling my name & character at full length to the public while he conceals his own." Jefferson was clear to express his conviction that principled men ought not respond personally to unsigned attacks. To Edmund Randolph he wrote eight days later: "Though I see the pen of the Secretary of the Treasury plainly in the attack on me, yet since he has not chosen to put his name to it, I am not free to notice it as his. I have preserved through life a resolution . . . never to write in a public paper without subscribing my name, and to engage openly an adversary who does not let himself be seen. . . . Lying and scribbling must be free to those mean enough to deal in them, and in the dark."[36]

As to Hamilton's charges that Jefferson had opposed the Constitution, the defending attorney rose to counter forcefully. True, he had urged the addition of a bill of rights securing freedom of religion and the press (and was grateful that the country ultimately had seen fit to agree). Otherwise—offering copies of his correspondence on the subject as proof—he had written little about the document's imperfections. "I must tax you," he insisted to Washington, to peruse these letters and judge. Compare Hamilton, he went on, whose only objection to the Constitution was that it "wanted a king and house of lords."

As to the Freneau appointment, Jefferson expressed further astonishment to his chief executive. Again contrasting his actions with those of Hamilton, he observed that he had never "enquired what number of sons, relatives & friends of Senators, representatives, printers or other useful partizans Colo[nel] Hamilton has provided for among the hundred clerks in his department, the thousand excisemen, custom-house officers, loan officers, &c., &c. appointed by him, or at his nod, and spread over the Union." Having planted such suspicion of Hamilton's misdoings, Jefferson came to "protest in the presence of heaven, that I never did by myself or any other, directly or indirectly, say a syllable, nor attempt any kind of influence. I can further protest, in the same awful presence, that I never did by myself or any other, directly or indirectly, dictate or procure any one sentence or sentiment in *his* [Freneau's] *or any other gazette,* to which my name was not affixed or that of my office." The religious reference, the litany of repetition, was meant to magnify the rottenness of the charges.

The scrupulous Jefferson (as he would have himself known) wished to reveal his honest hurt, making his accuser appear—though he never termed him so—irrational. "Colo[nel] Hamilton can see no motive for any appointment but that of making a convenient partizan." But Washington, insisted his fellow Virginian, had to know better than to suspect Jefferson of these things. The secretary of state had only wished to elevate "men of genius." Hamilton, by his wrongful accusations as an "anonymous writer or paragraphist," had trampled on "the dignity, & even decency of government." Having thoroughly clarified his rival's misdeeds, Jefferson now stood back to enjoy the result of his work. "So much for the past," he breathed. "A word now of the future."

"When I came into office," he opened his conclusion, "it was with a resolution to retire from it as soon as I could with decency." He was intent on preserving a reputation for "decency," for exiting his letter, and his post, gracefully. The dire appeal of the previous pages was a matter of national decision, not one of the writer's self-defense. Jefferson now looked to his retirement "with the longing of a wave-worn mariner, who has at length the land in view." In spite of Hamilton's abandonment of republican principles, he himself would not veer from his honorable determination never to "intermeddle" with the legislature. Furthermore, when he did write publicly, Jefferson would do so properly, "subscribing my name to whatever I write, & using with freedom & truth the facts and names necessary to place a cause in it's just form before that tribunal [my country]."

Before closing the matter of Hamilton's "most false" charges, Jefferson could not keep from topping his effort with some powerful invective: "I will not suffer my retirement to be clouded by the slanders of a man whose history, from the moment at which history can stoop to notice him, is a tissue of machinations against the liberty of the country which has not only received and given him bread, but heaped it's honors on his head." He continued to see Hamilton's attack as both public and personal and his own as merely public. Yet, as in his reference to Patrick Henry in his letter to George Rogers Clark, Jefferson could not restrain himself from displaying a mean streak. Was he subtly thumbing his nose at upstart Hamilton's obscure birth? Jefferson was walking a fine line here, very much conscious of Washington's character, his noble bearing, his desire to distance himself from petty personal quarrels. Jefferson had to take care not to sacrifice his own long-nurtured sense of classical dignity or weaken the combined eloquence of an argument that incorporated both Heart and Head. In committing petulant words to paper, he must have known that the president would be unsympathetic to the message unless he could locate Hamilton's personal fault in the West Indian immigrant's ungratefulness to a nurturing country whose republican spirit was responsible for his promotion in its society.

Yet this was not enough. Jefferson again felt he had to contrast his own behavior, once more defend his honor. And he did so without forfeiting the offensive: "Though little known to the people of America, I believe that, as far as I am known, it is not as an enemy to the republic, nor an intriguer against it, nor a waster of it's revenue, nor prostitutor of it to the purposes of corruption, as the American [the pseudonymous Hamilton] represents me. . . . No cabals or intrigues of mine have produced those in the legislature." Jefferson used some variation of the word *intrigue* three times in the letter to Washington to deny any intriguing on his own part and to brand Hamilton.[37] The temper of the time had produced in Jefferson an equation of Hamilton's charges against him (which he had now turned on Hamilton) with the politically unhealthy atmosphere of Europe, which had occasioned his writing to Charles Bellini of the Old World's "intrigues . . . of ambition" that occupied "the great." This was not the kind of future Jefferson projected for his own country; indeed, he was relieved to contrast the European with American culture, in which happiness was enjoyed by "every class of people," a "tranquil permanent felicity with which domestic society in America blesses most of it's inhabitants."[38]

Facing what he had now come to perceive as a Federalist assault on the "tranquil permanent felicity" he envisioned himself preserving, Jefferson felt certain that he personally had done nothing to bring forth what he later described to Benjamin Rush as "the thousand calumnies which the federalists, in bitterness of heart . . . daily invented against me." Jefferson had convinced himself, as he hoped to convince President Washington, that he remained "perfectly passive" while others intrigued; he continued to regard himself a model of propriety who would never stoop to insult another man's honor, though he would on occasion confide in his intimates his disagreement over principle.[39]

Examining style a bit more closely, we can gain insight into Jefferson's manner of thinking by comparing this letter to Washington with his production of *Notes on Virginia*. His method, even in 1780–81, reveals a man who was driven to argue causes but who wished to believe that he could, by rhetorical stratagem, and to all but his friends, obscure the emotional intensity of his impulses, if not actually encode his program so that only his friends understood its prescriptive intent.

First, manipulating the twenty-three queries of Marbois, Jefferson shifted their order so as to suit his purpose. A conspicuous example is Query VI, in which he followed exhaustive factual descriptions of subterranean minerals and plant and animal life with an impassioned argument against Buffon's statement that American species are degenerative, that they suffer from the less active, less energetic operation of nature. Moving logically from quadrupeds to man himself (and expanding the scope of the query well beyond its factual purpose), Jefferson contested the notion that the Native American "savage" was "feeble," "timid and cowardly," with "no vivacity, no activity of mind." On the contrary, stated Jefferson, the Indian "meets death with more deliberation" than any other race on earth; "his friendships are strong and faithful to the uttermost extremity." Pages later, the author abruptly ended his defense and (logically, to him) returned to another dispassionately presented list, this one of species of birds in Virginia.

The *Notes,* as George Alan Davy has written, is far from being an encyclopedia, as others have portrayed it. It argues and proposes. It eagerly embraces controversy. But it does so within the structure of eighteenth-century philosophic argument, purporting to remove the author, taking nature as the basis for reasoning about society. Like Locke, it reasons by moving from sensation (perceptions of the external world) to judgment (based on self-evident comparisons). Jefferson took the noncontroversial, that is, what nature provides, and reasoned from that observable reality, before returning to the noncontroversial. In other words, he sandwiched his subjective argument between objective descriptions.[40]

Thus, in 1781, in the heat of the armed conflict occasioned by his Declaration, in the wake of his controversial flight from Tarleton's raiding party, and a full decade before his problems with Hamilton began, Jefferson defined himself as a thinker with bold purposes who could not help but take his pen into battle. His treatment of the controversy over the American Indian in Query VI can be effectively compared to his posture in the political battles of the 1790s. In his long letter to Washington in September 1792, he moved from observations about the legislature's impairment to judgments abut Hamilton's transgressions. He sought to disguise his own partisan objectives (and personal rancor) as best he could by constructing a logical argument that defeated Hamilton's position; it is similar in design to that which he employed against Buffon. He did not call Hamilton a traitor to the Republic — that would be too passionate a rush to judgment — but he wanted to leave that impression.

If President Washington did not find himself moved by Jefferson's logic, then, to Jefferson, there had to be something wrong with the president's perception of reality (Jefferson, in effect, later called it senility). Jefferson believed that when presented with facts, his correspondent would reason better and, if properly motivated, act to correct the situation, to promote justice and advance toward national (republican) harmony. This conviction is evident almost from the moment of Jefferson's entry into politics. In 1775, when he corresponded with Tory John Randolph on the eve of that gentleman's return to England, Jefferson was the familiar "apostle of reason." He expressed, as always, his yearning to "withdraw myself totally from the public stage and pass the rest of my days in domestic ease and tranquillity." Next he looked with "fondness" toward a reconciliation with the mother country, if only Great Britain could evidence a return to "wisdom." It was Randolph's task, Jefferson offered his virtuous elder, to "contribute towards expediting this good work." Advise the ministers of the crown that their officers in America had misrepresented the colonies' uniform opposition, describing ("for what purposes I cannot tell") a "small faction" of "cowards" ready to surrender at the appearance of an armed force. If Randolph could "undeceive" the British, who were "disjoined" from their colonies, he would be doing a "service to the whole empire."[41]

As personally reticent as he might have appeared (or effeminate, in Henry Adams's assessment), lacking the speaking voice of Patrick Henry or the battlefield courage of a Washington or Hamilton, Jefferson possessed nonetheless an instinctive combativeness which he at times attempted to sandwich between seemingly neutral expressions that were logically developed. He never denied the "meat" of his strong sentiments to his trusted friends or to the malleable future generation (he thought his *Notes* would be useful to the students at William and Mary); but he hoped that the "bread" of his sandwich would meet the eye of the remainder of his readership, those with whom he was not intimate, some of whom would be bent on criticism. He relied on form (the accepted structure of epistemological argument) to shield himself. He sought in this way to promote his convictions without calling undue attention to possible motives. He desired that his total "reality" could become palatable to all, that reason would permit acceptance first of his method of observation and eventually lead to acceptance of his sentimental assumptions.

Surely he knew that the combative and sentimentally dissimilar Hamilton would never be swayed. Jefferson respected Hamilton's intellect, though he regarded it as somehow perverted by un-American values. Thus he felt the need to remind Washington of Hamilton's West Indian roots. He further charged that owing to a strong ego, Hamilton was prone to public intrigue, though this implied less about the man's private character than it had when he attributed the same intent to Patrick Henry. To the "slanders" and "machinations" for which Hamilton was responsible, Jefferson contrasted his own directness. He was attempting to convince the president that his mildness was genuine, that it suggested a conciliatory soul within. Hamilton, on the other hand, lacked the humility to be a model of republican good — to be a Jeffersonian friend — as indeed there had to be qualities beyond mere political agreement to comprise Jeffersonian friendship.

Because he held himself morally blameless, Jefferson was able to maintain the self-possession that allowed him to continue his friendly correspondence with Angelica Church in London, despite the heat of his dispute with her brother-in-law. First he conversed warmly about his French friends and responded incredulously to her news that Maria Cosway had entered a convent in Italy, "her mind entirely placed on a world to come." He complained only of "dry and oppressive scenes of business," contrasting the tranquillity of Monticello, "for which alone my heart was made." Later, when unwilling to compete any longer for the president's ear, he wrote Mrs. Church, "I am then to be liberated from the hated occupations of politics, and to remain in the bosom of my family, my farm, and my books." He did not mention Hamilton or suggest reasons for his displeasure with political life, for that would have been unnecessary as well as unwelcome. He only hinted at his need for a defense in stating that Philadelphians "must love misery indeed who would rather at the sight of an honest man feel the torment of hatred & aversion than the benign spasms of benevolence & esteem." The cruelest Jefferson could be on the matter of personal honor was in venting his spleen to Madison in the fall of 1793, after Hamilton's newspaper attacks had subsided. When Hamilton took ill during an outbreak of yellow fever, Jefferson wrote, "A man as timid as he is on the water, as timid on horseback, as timid in sickness, would be a phaenomenon if the courage of which he has the reputation in military occasions were genuine."[42]

Jefferson could no longer tolerate the intensity of his rivalry with the New Yorker and soon after resigned from the cabinet. By then the battle lines were clearly drawn between oppositionists, taking Jefferson as their principal, and the administration party.

"A Willingness to Let Others Act"

Convincing Washington of his integrity and sound reasoning was not Jefferson's only problem, but it certainly helped to crystallize in Jefferson's mind the grand scale of that conflict he perceived between his expansive world of friendship and the intrigue of a pretentious, self-perpetuating, monied elite who would systematically deny plain and honest Americans the exercise of their constitutional sovereignty. With Hamilton's success, the vigor of republican America would be replaced by a lethargic order. It was moral character as much as the constitutional apparatus that would suffer.

Anglo-French war had broken out early in 1793. America was officially neutral. Hamilton referred to divisions already present in American politics in 1792 when in his long letter to Edward Carrington he complained that Jefferson and Madison were men of "unsound and dangerous" views with "a womanish attachment to France and a womanish resentment against Great Britain."[43] In contrast to the Jeffersonians, who saw benefits to the young nation remaining agricultural and self-sufficient and pressing for reciprocity in trade, Hamilton believed that America's financial health was contingent on emulating, not discriminating against, Britain's commercial empire. Acquiescence to its maritime superiority was essential to increasing Anglo-American trade, establishing American credit, and concentrating private capital in the hands of entrepreneurs.[44]

The emerging parties, Federalist and Republican, contested over what position to adopt toward events in Europe. Diplomatic problems intensified. Because England was seizing American ships, President Washington dispatched John Jay to London in the spring of 1794, a short time after Jefferson had retired to Monticello. Jay was a Hamiltonian stalwart who preferred accommodation with the powerful British to alliance with revolutionary France. The treaty he negotiated, approved by Washington and passed by the Federalist-led Congress in 1796, renounced discriminatory tariffs for ten years and did nothing to relieve the impressment of American sailors by the British navy. Incensed Republicans saw America cowering before British might, still a cog in the British mercantile machine.[45]

Jefferson's relationship with Washington, like his relationship with John Adams, tested the strength of long-held friendship in the face of potent public issues. However, the procession of the Jefferson-Washington relationship from one of deference to mutual admiration to dire misunderstanding is an anomalous one; it ended at the death of Washington, leaving the appearance of friendship sacrificed to partisanship, before Jefferson could vindicate himself as he was to do with Adams.

Jefferson first encountered Washington in Williamsburg in 1769. The two Virginians corresponded (officially, for the most part) during the Revolutionary War and while Jefferson was in France, but to that point experienced nothing of the intimacy Hamilton and the general had shared. In his privately recorded notes of cabinet meetings incorporated into the *Anas,* Jefferson nonetheless expressed a confidence in his ability to read Washington's thoughts. He knew Washington as he was, a cordial man of pronounced integrity, an often austere presence, of modest intellectual talents, only occasionally unreserved in conversation. "His heart was not warm in its affections," Jefferson wrote, "but he exactly calculated every man's value and gave him a solid esteem proportioned to it."[46]

Washington sought from Jefferson "frankness and the fullest latitude of a friend," and Jefferson obliged him each time Washington wrote him for advice on handling questions of private ethics in public affairs. In 1784, when Washington was pondering the position he should take toward the Society of the Cincinnati, Jefferson was most candid, urging the retired general to "stand on ground separated from" that hereditary order of demobilized army officers formed at the end of the war. Jefferson was wary of the passions engendered in such an institution, whose proud members were as conscious of their preeminence as they were disdainful of notions of human equality. Hereditary societies, he wrote further, tended to reserve "privilege and prerogative" to themselves, while oppressing the natural rights of the people. Glory-seeking alarmed Jefferson, who knew the general was too virtuous to capitalize crudely on his tremendous popularity.[47]

Impressed with Jefferson's reasoning, Washington continued to address sensitive questions to him, writing the next year that "I have accustomed myself to communicate matters of difficulty to you, and have met forgiveness for it."[48] It was not just Jefferson's cosmopolitan connections and diplomatic experience but his character and their common stance on public morality and dignified behavior that led the president to appoint his fellow Virginian to his administration. And it was Washington's desire to draw equally upon the intellects of his two talented, strong-willed cabinet officers that caused him to believe he did not have to choose between their incompatible principles.

Washington presided over his administration with calm self-assurance. By Jefferson's estimation his "passions were naturally strong; but his reason, generally stronger." Mediating the Jefferson-Hamilton feud, he had accepted both men's advice and made each feel important. But after resolving to leave office in 1793, Jefferson came to view Washington as an unfortunate pawn: "His memory was already sensibly impaired by age, the firm tone of mind for which he had been remarkable was beginning to relax, it's energy was abated; a listlessness of labor, a desire for tranquillity had crept on him, and a willingness to let others act and even think for him." It was easier for Jefferson to point to Washington's limitations than to accept the premise that the president had carefully weighed their contesting positions and still did not agree with Jefferson's view of Hamilton.[49]

In spite of himself, the letter-writing Jefferson consistently invited controversy when moved to speak his mind to his correspondents. As he had not anticipated in 1791 that a single phrase carelessly introducing Paine's pamphlet to a stranger would produce a stormy season in politics and injure his relations with John Adams, neither did he suspect five years later that a paragraph to Philip Mazzei in Italy would set in motion a series of events that would embitter his esteemed friend George Washington.

In the spring of 1796, planter Jefferson, retired to Monticello, gave Mazzei a detailed report on his former neighbor's financial interests in America. Then, after asking the Florentine literally to "put a few seeds in every letter you may write to me," he casually described Congress's final deliberations on the treaty brought back by Jay, already approved by Washington: "In place of that noble love of liberty, & republican government which carried us triumphantly thro' the war, an Anglican monarchical, & aristocratical party has sprung up. . . . the whole landed interest is republican, and so is the great mass of talents. Against us are the Executive, the Judiciary. . . . It would give you a fever were I to name to you the apostates who have gone over to these heresies, men who were Samsons in the field & Solomons in the council, but who have had their heads shorn by the harlot England." An overeager Mazzei turned over this part of the letter to a Florentine newspaper, and it was published; the Italian text was then translated in a French newspaper, before finding its way back to the Federalist press in America. Noah Webster called the letter treasonable. Jefferson, after consultation with Madison and Monroe, elected not to comment on it, though the several translations had marred some of its original meaning. Adding to the confusion, around the time that the Mazzei letter was made public Jefferson's nephew Peter Carr apparently took it upon himself to write a sympathetic note to Washington, under a pseudonym. The Albemarle county clerk, a Federalist, gave Washington the identity of the writer and convinced the former president that Carr's deception was part of a scheme being concocted by Jefferson. Washington subsequently told his own nephew, Bushrod Washington, that he believed Jefferson to be capable of shabby tricks. Washington and Jefferson did not communicate at any point after this, and the former president took to the grave whatever sense of outrage he might have felt, leaving only the obscure suggestion that he took the Mazzei letter to be a personal indictment.[50]

Five years into his own retirement, Jefferson tried to reclaim Washington through fantasy. Though the general had become subject to the "wiles" of "federal monarchists," persuaded by Jefferson's enemies that Jefferson would lead America "infallibly to licentiousness and anarchy," and though he had often expressed to Jefferson his belief that republican government was merely on trial in America, Washington might yet have been made to see the truth. Once the letter to Mazzei was published, "I never saw him afterwards," wrote Jefferson, "or these malignant insinuations should have been dissipated before his just judgment, as mists before the sun." Jefferson, in his own last years, explained the Mazzei letter, clarifying to Martin Van Buren that by "Samsons" and "Solomons" he had meant merely the members of the Society of the Cincinnati, whose motives he had denounced to Washington directly. Jefferson weakly assumed that Washington had understood this.[51]

Another indication of the complexity of maintaining personal friendship amid political struggle was the loss to Jefferson of the trust and goodwill of John Trumbull, his dear friend in Paris and courier of his letters to Maria Cosway. The Connecticut painter was a Federalist who was revolted by the social disruptions of the French Revolution. And as a devout Congregationalist, he had ample reason to doubt that at this time religion played a very important role in Jefferson's life. Their differences had not amounted to much before the divisive 1790s, as Trumbull acknowledged; "I revered him," the painter wrote, but "a coldness gradually succeeded." In 1793 Jefferson invited Trumbull to dinner at his Philadelphia residence. Virginian William Branch Giles was present, a leader in the congressional movement to investigate Hamilton's alleged financial improprieties. Giles and Trumbull recently had had a falling out over a woman in whose presence, according to Trumbull's account, he had made young Giles to appear "ridiculous." Trumbull was "scarcely seated," when Giles began to lampoon the puritanical character of New England Christians. When dinner was served, Giles "renewed his attack with increased asperity." Jefferson smiled approvingly at Giles. The only man present to come to Trumbull's defense was David Salisbury Franks, a Jew. Trumbull recorded that, still troubled, he sought Jefferson's ear, but the previously attentive host made no attempt to stifle the skeptic Giles, who continued to portray the

Christian faith as "a miserable delusion." Finally, Trumbull felt obliged to walk out, and he remained distant from Jefferson from then on.[52]

THE FURTHER ANXIETIES OF LETTER WRITING AND PUBLISHING

BY 1798, DURING the Adams presidency, Jefferson had witnessed a further drift from republican values. Most noteworthy was the suspension of diplomatic relations with France and passage of the nefarious Alien and Sedition Acts, legislation designed to crush any and all criticism of the administration. A person found guilty of seditious speech or printed libel against the government or who threatened "danger to the character, person, or property of any government office holder" could be fined or sent to prison. Any encroachment on freedom of speech or the press was an audacious assault on the quintessential Jeffersonian principle. The implacable Virginian, now vice president, responded. He covertly teamed with alter ego Madison to write the Kentucky and Virginia Resolutions, likening the Alien and Sedition Acts to the Stamp Act in the usurpation of rights by a tyrannical government and announcing the states' power to ensure that their citizens' constitutional liberties remained inviolate.[53]

Once the legislatures passed the resolutions, Jefferson, recalling past missteps, took particular care in the composition of letters to all acquaintances. To former Virginia congressman Alexander White, he wrote, "So many persons have of late found an interest or passion gratified by imputing to me sayings and writings which I never said or wrote, or by endeavoring to draw me into the newspapers to harass me personally, that I have found it necessary for my quiet & my other pursuits to leave them in full possession of the field, and not take the trouble of contradicting them in private conversation." To Thaddeus Kosciusko, the Polish patriot who had once fought for American independence and was now attempting from exile in France to liberate his own homeland, Jefferson pronounced, "On politics I must write sparingly, lest it should fall into the hands of persons who do not love either you or me." To his unqualified ally, arch-republican John Taylor of Caroline, he flatly acknowledged fearing to write "fully & freely" owing to "infidelities of the post office and the circumstances of the times." His "dispositions" were "against mysteries [recall the criticism of Patrick Henry], innuendoes, & half-confidences. I know not which mortifies me most, that I should fear to write what I think, or my country bear such a state of things."[54]

To the sympathetic but controversial Elbridge Gerry of Massachusetts, a fond admirer of both Jefferson and Adams, he realized that it was worth taking the chance of committing his potentially explosive thoughts. Gerry, a signer of the Declaration of Independence, obeyed his conscience issue by issue rather than align at once with a party. He had supported the Hamiltonian financial system but abhorred factionalism in American politics and would find eventually that he had to choose the Republican side. Jefferson revealed his anxiety in addressing Gerry so forthrightly: "When I sat down to answer your letter, but two things presented themselves; either to say nothing or everything; for half confidences are not in my character. I could not hesitate which was due to you. I have unbosomed myself fully; & it will certainly be highly gratifying if I receive like confidence from you. For even if we differ in principle more than I believe we do, you & I know too well the texture of the human mind, & the slipperiness of human reason, to consider differences of opinion otherwise than differences of form or feature. Integrity of views more than their soundness, is the basis of esteem."[55]

Jefferson counted on Gerry to agree that differing political views need not strain a relationship. This was essentially the language of friendship Jefferson had pursued in his letters to Adams during the same decade (if somewhat more precariously in that case). But Jefferson wanted to build a relationship with Gerry that was publicly more useful than that with Adams, whose politics had strayed too far from his own. After Gerry's Federalist colleagues had given up, he persisted in negotiation with the testy French during the XYZ affair. Three French officials had demanded money as a precondition to talks, causing the other American envoys, John Marshall and Charles Cotesworth Pinckney, to sail for home. Gerry appeared to have salvaged the Franco-American relationship, much to the gratification of Vice President Jefferson, and allowed President Adams to avert war. Jefferson now looked to extend areas of agreement with Gerry, cautiously restating opinions that his political enemies had intentionally distorted: "I was a sincere well-wisher to the success of the French revolution, and still wish it may end in the establishment of a free & well-ordered republic. . . . The first object of my heart is my own country. In that is embarked my family, my fortune, & my own existence. I have not one farthing of interest, nor one fibre of attachment out[side] of it, nor a single motive of preference of any one nation to another." It required all his political know-how, diplomatic skills, and intellectual optimism to disavow any part in the machinations and proclaim his aversion to the turbulence that racked political life during the closing years of the eighteenth century. It was not he, the letter subtly inferred, who suffered the "slipperiness of human reason."[56]

By the election year of 1800, the time for republican ascendancy — Jefferson's time — had come. "A little patience," he had urged John Taylor of Caroline, "and we shall see the reign of witches pass over, their spells dissolved, and the people recovering their true sight." The bitterness of public life had intensified the images in Jefferson's letters to political allies; the harmonizer he wished he could be often had to yield to the heat of the moment.[57]

In his conciliatory first inaugural address, Jefferson did not speak of witches but asked humbly for all Americans' "indulgence." He attempted to convey genuineness, to hint at conciliation. "We have called by different names brethren of the same principle," he declared, speaking to those who feared anarchic results from Jefferson's democracy. "We are all republicans — we are all federalists." He pronounced a time of healing and encouraged the airing of diverse opinions in an environment of calm reason.

But was Thomas Jefferson the right person to mediate the controversy the Federalists accused him of having produced himself? Jefferson was not naive. His inaugural appeal was a statement of Jeffersonian optimism about the republican future, rather than an expression of the president's near view of politics. It is revealing that in the speech the new president allowed for his natural human fallibility, saying, "I shall often go wrong through defect of judgment." He was at the same time silently inferring that he would not go wrong through any defect of Heart.

Jefferson may have bested the witches, but he had far to go to douse the flames of party passion. At the conclusion of four years in office he would unreservedly write the once-imprudent Mazzei that "there remains a phalanx of old tories and monarchists, more envenomed, as all their hopes become more desperate. Every word of mine which they can get hold of, however innocent, however orthodox even, is twisted, tormented, perverted, and like the words of holy writ, are made to mean everything but what they were intended to mean." "Twisted, tormented, perverted": words describing the physical as well as mental anguish Jefferson came to feel in office. Words, what he prized in the expression of human sentiment, could be transmuted into a kind of poison. Writing Mazzei, he was still mourning his daughter Maria, whose death three months earlier had crushed him. And just four days before this letter, the funeral of the slain Alexander Hamilton had taken place. Jefferson did not write of the sensational duel, but such a sudden event which shed a tragic light on human fallibility must have touched him in some way. He was convinced that his enemies alone, a "phalanx" besieging him, were responsible for the current state of politics. He held himself blameless, later in his second term writing William Short that "I never did them [the Federalists] an act of injustice nor failed in any duty to them imposed by my office."[58] It was a lonely and anxious time for the president, who was often reminded that words had come to mean "everything but what they were intended to mean." He turned with disgust from the press. "Nothing can now be believed which is seen in a newspaper," Jefferson railed. "Truth itself becomes suspicious by being put into that polluted vehicle."[59]

It pained Jefferson that he was misunderstood. The criticism of his behavior as governor in 1781 had been short-lived (if profoundly disquieting), and no one had called for anything more than an "investigation." Hamilton's innuendos in 1792 had hurt, but Jefferson's friends rallied to his cause, doing as much as Jefferson could have hoped to present Hamilton as irritable, unsparing, and unrestrained — what his ego had made him. James Thomson Callender, however, represented a darker and more personal kind of trouble for the president.

A political refugee from Scotland, Callender was a journalist found guilty of sedition in 1800 because of a pamphlet unfriendly to President Adams. *The Prospect before Us* referred to Adams as a "hoary headed incendiary" and compared the incumbent, a man who had "deserted and reversed all his principles," to candidate Jefferson, "whose life is unspotted by crime." When Federalist judge Samuel Chase expressly came to Richmond to make an example of the loose-tongued Callender, Virginia Republicans led by John Taylor of Caroline and William Branch Giles fought the inevitable; but the journalist was convicted. Before this election year, Jefferson was pleased with Callender's writing and approvingly sent the ragged writer small sums of money. He did not, however, wish to become any closer to a man whom most readers would soon recognize as a bitter, ranting mercenary.[60]

Fueled by what Merrill Peterson has called a "self-induced hysteria" resulting from the humiliating loss of the presidency, Federalist critics charged that Jefferson planned to unleash Jacobin-style terror in America. In the quest to prove Jefferson vile and debauched, they had painted him during the campaign as anti-Christian, but they now received their greatest blessing from the un-Federalist Callender, who was released from jail as Jefferson took office and sought from his onetime benefactor a patronage job in the Richmond post office. When Jefferson did not comply with Callender's demand, the journalist began placing slanderous stories about Jefferson's previous collusion with him in the Federalist *Richmond Recorder.* The stories kept building until in 1802 one declared, "It is well known that the man *whom it delighteth the people to honor,* keeps, and for many years past has kept, as his concubine, one of his own slaves." He alleged that Sally Hemings, the "African Venus," had borne Jefferson several children, including one named Tom who was said to resemble the president very much. (Callender himself had never visited Monticello.) The heavy-drinking journalist drowned in the James River the following year, a possible suicide, yet the allegations he made public brought the waning Federalists the revenge they had long sought.[61]

There was precedent for sensational accusations such as these. Five years earlier, Alexander Hamilton had been obliged to divulge that in 1791—at the time of his escalating quarrel with Jefferson—he had had an affair with Maria Reynolds, the semiliterate wife of an inconsequential man named James Reynolds. It was a rather sordid matter, apparently instigated by the husband himself in order to blackmail the lustful treasury secretary. The Republicans did not reveal their knowledge of Hamilton's infidelity until 1797 when John Beckley, clerk of the House of Representatives and the Republicans' eyes and ears, may have leaked the information to Callender. Out of office but still wielding power, Hamilton confessed to his private transgressions in order to save his honor as a public man. In his published pamphlet on the affair, he wrote that he was guilty of nothing but "an irregular and indelicate amour." But the ever-vindictive Callender did not let the matter rest, promptly calling the letters Hamilton had released (as part of his defense) forgeries designed to obscure the true facts of his betrayal of the public trust.[62]

As the responsibilities of the Treasury and State Departments overlapped in certain areas during the first administration, so the Hamilton and Jefferson scandals, though years apart, were tied by the common thread of James Callender. Yet the two accused were as different in personal style as two men could be. As a twenty-two-year-old soldier, Hamilton had given his friend Laurens, en route to the Carolinas, instructions to scour the South for a "chaste and shapely" companion for Hamilton. Should Laurens encounter such a lady, he went on, "it will be necessary for you to give an account of the lover — his *size,* make, quality of mind and *body,* achievements, expectations, fortunes, &c. . . . mind you do justice to the length of my nose [the same innuendo employed by Sterne] and don't forget, that I [balance of sentence censored, presumably by a protective descendant]." Compare the sheepish Jefferson, unable at a comparable time in his life to speak plainly in the company of his first love interest, Rebecca Burwell, later so sanctifying of home life with his wife, Patty, and so conflicted over his feelings for the married Maria Cosway.[63]

Indeed, unlike Hamilton, whose reputation as a womanizer had remained on the lips of his comrades, the widower Jefferson had never before been suspected of such improper behavior. Callender's scandalous "revelation" dramatically changed that. The publicity-craving writer capitalized on his latest success — the Sally Hemings story — with the more palpable charge that Jefferson had once made indecent overtures to Betsy Walker, wife of John Walker, his lifelong Albemarle neighbor and his classmate at both James Maury's school and the College of William and Mary.[64]

With his alleged misconduct creating a stir, the president was placed in a difficult position. He preferred simply to ignore the Hemings story, while prepared to acknowledge the truth of the Walker incident, a lapse of judgment committed without premeditation as a bachelor thirty-five years earlier. A statement later made to George Logan seems to indicate Jefferson's mature judgment with regard to the unpleasant challenges he had faced: "As to federal slanders, I never wished them to be answered, but by the tenor of my life. . . . The man who fears no truths has nothing to fear from lies." Jefferson had, in his words, "offered love to a handsome lady" while her husband was gone from home. This was the only one of his enemies' allegations, he asserted, which was founded in truth.[65] Walker had lost to Jefferson's ally Monroe in his 1790 Senate bid and now courted the Federalists. Why else, posed Jefferson's friend Page (also a friend of Walker), would the old incident have been publicized? Discreetly attempting to clear the air with the offended husband, Jefferson insisted in a private communication that Mrs. Walker had refused his advances. Wishing to preserve her virtuous reputation and patch up differences with the politically hostile Walker, the chief executive did his best to deny the hungry press more fodder for their politically inspired exposés.[66] This was in character. Jefferson surely felt he was responding in a manner superior to Hamilton's, and the crime, in any case, may have been no more than a kiss. He could not stop those who did not know his private conduct from assuming what they wanted. However, as far as the self-respecting president was concerned, the vulgarity of the miscegenation charge rendered it undeserving of a direct reply.

As to actual evidence in the matter of Sally Hemings, nothing fully satisfies. Thomas Jefferson Randolph told biographer Henry Randall in the years before the Civil War that his grandfather had given no reason for any of the family to suspect intimacy with Sally Hemings. She "was treated and dressed just like the rest" of the Monticello servants. Randolph confided to Randall that, in fact, Peter Carr was the culprit. Randolph's sister Ellen, however, fingered Peter's younger brother Samuel. Either explanation is plausible, insofar as Jefferson's Account Books show that both nephews were either present at Monticello or having transactions with Jefferson during specific periods that correspond to Sally's conceptions. Peter was three years older than Sally and had grown up as a favorite on his uncle's estate; Jefferson was thirty years older and preoccupied with reputation. On the other hand, there is the response of Martha Jefferson Randolph, who as mistress of Monticello could hardly have ignored the paternity of her house servant's children. She wished for her sons to be able to refute the rumors for the sake of history and, before her death in 1836, gathered two of them in order to make some calculations concerning her father's whereabouts at the time Sally Hemings had conceived the male child who most resembled Jefferson. Unless Martha still felt obliged to protect the Carr family, the question remains why she chose this method to acquit her father. Trying to prove what did not occur, after all, could never be as satisfying to history as proving what did.[67]

The evidence against Jefferson is largely provided by the testimony of Madison Hemings, Sally's son who was born in 1805, when Jefferson was sixty-two. Madison told an Ohio newspaper in 1873 that his mother had informed him that Thomas Jefferson was his father, and that Sally first carried a child of Jefferson when she returned from France in 1789. Presumably, Madison believed these statements to be true. But it is also possible that his claim was contrived—by his mother or himself—to provide to an otherwise undistinguished biracial carpenter a measure of social respect. Would not his life have been made more charmed by being known as the son of Thomas Jefferson than the more obscure Peter or Samuel Carr? Also, there is no record of Sally having given birth until 1795.[68]

In any case, the callous work of James Thomson Callender set in motion giddy and often malicious satire during Jefferson's lifetime. Knowing what we do about Jefferson's Heart and Head, that the first made him generous and the second ruled his actions, it seems highly unlikely that because light-skinned Sally Hemings bore light-skinned children at Monticello, they necessarily were fathered by Monticello's master. Moreover, Jefferson would have been uncharacteristically imprudent to be responsible for giving Sally Hemings the two children that she bore in the years after the charges surfaced, while he remained president.[69]

"High Time to Make Him Known"

CALLENDER WAS NOT long on the scene, but the same cannot be said for John Marshall. Appointed chief justice of the Supreme Court by John Adams on the eve of Jefferson's inauguration, he served in that highly visible post without interruption until nine years after Jefferson's death. Like Jefferson, he was of Randolph ancestry, a man of stature. But to his distant cousin Thomas Jefferson, Marshall was a malignancy on the body politic, a bitter political antagonist who baldly used his position for partisan purposes and posed a powerful challenge to Jefferson's presidency.

A Virginian, rusticated in his manners, Marshall was, atypically, a champion of the Hamiltonians. Not insignificantly, he was also the son-in-law of Rebecca Burwell (now Ambler), who had once spurned a romancing Thomas Jefferson. He was not well read, preferring business to political philosophy. His passion was land speculation. As a prominent figure in Virginia state politics from the end of the Revolutionary War through the passage of the Jay Treaty, he attracted a following; but at the last, supporting a treaty which, to Jefferson, none but Hamilton, writing under a pseudonym, could declare favorable,[70] he drew fire from Republicans. Jefferson wrote Madison acidly: "Though Marshall will be able to embarras the republican party in the assembly a good deal, yet upon the whole, his having gone into it will be of service. He has been hitherto able to do more mischief acting under the mask of Republicanism than he will be able to do after throwing it plainly off. His lax lounging manners have made him popular with the bulk of the people of Richmond, & a profound hypocrisy with many thinking men of our country. But having come forth in the plentitude of his English principles the latter will see that it is high time to make him known."[71]

Marshall entirely abandoned the Virginia Republican persuasion when in 1798 he became the Federalists' hero as the principled, un-ruffled negotiator who stood up to undiplomatic French behavior during the XYZ affair. Marshall sailed home and suddenly found himself a celebrity, drawing Philadelphia crowds. As a witness to the event, Jefferson reported to Madison: "M was received here with the utmost eclat. The Secretary of State [arch-Federalist Timothy Pickering] & many carriages, with all the city cavalry, went to Frankfort to meet him, and on his arrival here in the evening the bells rung till late in the night, & immense crowds were collected to see & make part of the shew, which was circuitously paraded through the streets before he was set down at the city tavern."[72] Supported by Patrick Henry, a late convert to the Federalist cause, Marshall was promptly elected to Congress and then became secretary of state in the last year of Adams's presidency. Within his own party he was considered a moderate. But to Jefferson he was a cause for alarm, because, like the seductive Henry, he possessed winning ways, a popular appeal, and represented competition for the plain-talking Republicans.

After Jefferson's election and the triumph of the Republican party, the Federalists succeeded in naming Marshall chief justice of the Supreme Court to avert the loss of all three branches of the government. For the next thirty-four years, Marshall asserted the power of the national government over the rights of the states, opposing almost every principle Jefferson stood for.

Immediately after administering the oath of office to Jefferson at his inauguration, Marshall unburdened himself to Charles Cotesworth Pinckney, combining sarcasm and disgust: "The new order of things begins." Fearing a government under "democratic guidance" (intending "democratic" to mean fostering a "mobocracy"), the disgruntled Marshall wrote: "The democrats are divided into speculative theorists & absolute terrorists: With the latter I am not disposed to class Mr. Jefferson. If he arranges himself with them it is not difficult to forsee that much calamity is in store for our country — if he does not they will soon become his enemies & calumniators."[73]

Classifying his distant cousin as a "speculative theorist," Marshall had no sympathy for airy philosophy and might even have welcomed a situation in which Jefferson was trampled by the more radical of his own party, thus facilitating the rise to power of "honest men who have honorable feelings," as he termed his fellow Federalists. Becoming "disgusted" and "gloomy" after a year and a half of the Jefferson presidency, the chief justice wrote again to Pinckney, this time with a morsel of hoped-for revenge. Jefferson had backed the return to America of the ever-controversial Thomas Paine, seen lately as the vilifier of George Washington (for having failed to rescue Paine from a French jail). "It is whisper[e]d among those who affect to know a great deal," wrote Marshall, "that a certain eminent personage [Jefferson] is already fatigued almost beyond bearing with a great democratic & religious writer. . . . I cannot help feeling some gratification at this. I wish such deeds would always bring their own reward."[74] In plain language, Marshall thought Jefferson deceptive, immoral, and power-hungry; Jefferson thought Marshall politically dangerous and personally vindictive.

What was personal and what was public? Both men's words suggest that their conflict was more personal than the conflict with Hamilton, perhaps more politically motivated than that with Henry, and at least as intense as either. In 1795, to Madison, Jefferson had reacted to Marshall's "mischief," to his "mask," his "hypocrisy," his "English principles." He was seductive, like both of Jefferson's earlier enemies. Jefferson could feel disdain, at least at first, toward Marshall's crass concern for material success; but the conflict finally rested on suspicion and on a shared natural distaste, one for the other.

Jefferson's first-term vice president was Aaron Burr of New York, regarded by both his political foes and allies as an unpredictable character. He was tied with Jefferson in the presidential contest of 1800 when the ballots were counted, although clearly intended by Republicans to fall just shy of Jefferson's total and take the second position. For a few tense months, Burr waited, and Jefferson wondered whether the Federalists would "debauch" the New York Republican by securing him the presidency in return for favors.[75]

Like Hamilton, his wartime comrade at the battle of Harlem Heights in the summer of 1776, Burr was an emotional man in search of personal glory and political power. Out of jealousy or a merely personal distaste, Hamilton resented Burr, who, as he gained a New York following, ingratiated himself with the Republican leadership and defeated Philip Schuyler, Hamilton's father-in-law, in the senatorial contest of 1791. Burr let Jefferson know (according to the *Anas*) that he had long been fascinated with Jefferson's "company and conversation." But in office he showed that he would support the Federalist cause if by doing so he could advance himself past Jefferson. Removed from the Republican ticket in 1804, he lost his bid for the governorship of New York despite his flirtation with the Federalists. When Hamilton spread the word that the ambitious Burr was of bad character and too dangerous to support, Burr issued a challenge by letter, resulting in the senseless duel in which one nemesis of Jefferson martyred another.

Although he never commented on Hamilton's sudden demise, Jefferson did write of the other man to trusted Republican William Branch Giles: "Against Burr, personally, I never had one hostile sentiment. I never indeed thought him an honest, frank-dealing man, but considered him as a crooked gun, or other perverted machine, whose aim or shot you could never be sure of. Still, while he possessed the confidence of the nation, I thought it my duty to respect in him their confidence, and to treat him as if he deserved it." It is difficult to accept at face value Jefferson's protest that he "never had one hostile sentiment." Also, one cannot help but note the loaded metaphor Jefferson chose: the "crooked gun" had taken sure aim on the morning of July 11, 1804, in Weehauken, New Jersey.[76]

Fleeing prosecution for the murder, Burr went west and concocted a plot by which an army of American frontiersmen, supported by British funds, would attack Spanish possessions and set up an independent country under Burr. In his subsequent trial for treason, Burr found an unlikely champion in Chief Justice Marshall. Though clearly guilty, the former vice president was twice acquitted of the charges on the basis of insufficient evidence, a result assured by Marshall's orchestration of the process. The chief justice determined that Burr would face trial in Richmond, where Marshall presided over the federal district, and where many of the leading citizens were unfriendly to the president. He further directed that a subpoena be issued to Jefferson, and when the president complied with written demands but would not appear in person due to his presidential duties, Marshall indicated that such a response was not satisfactory. For his part, Jefferson made his feelings widely known, coaching the prosecution, collecting information, corresponding with witnesses, and reveling in newspaper criticisms of the chief justice, all seemingly injudicious actions for a president to take. But it seemed as always clear to Jefferson that Marshall's goal was to undermine his administration.[77]

Jefferson made every effort to deflect charges of partisan pressure, or intrigue, from himself. When he wanted to chip at Marshall, he generally worked through the aggressive William Branch Giles, who served first as a member of the House and then as a member of the Senate. Giles termed Marshall less than dignified in setting out to make the court "supreme over all other departments of the Government." An unfriendly contemporary remarked that Giles, speaking in the Senate chamber, had "attacked Chief Justice Marshall with insidious warmth." Giles was a crucial mouthpiece for Jefferson, his agent on Capitol Hill. He was, like Monroe, a man whose combative temperament lent itself to instigating legislative battles on Jefferson's behalf, while returning political intelligence to his seemingly uninvolved "handler."[78]

During Jefferson's second term, while heading the court, Marshall completed his five-volume biography of George Washington, offering an anti-Republican interpretation of the 1790s. This was another severe slap at Jefferson, who struggled for years afterward to enlist political allies in producing a Republicanized history of the period that Marshall had so misrepresented. His consternation was such that, in an 1815 letter to John Adams, who had appointed Marshall chief justice, Jefferson described Marshall's history as a "party diatribe."[79] Jefferson remained troubled by Marshall's work and eventually compiled the *Anas* for public consumption in order to prompt what he regarded as a balanced and dignified insider's history, one which would tip the scale back in favor of the Republican interpretation of the first two administrations. As in the conflict with Hamilton, Jefferson was desperate to expose Marshall as a man who falsified facts, if not a man of faulty understanding.

He did not succeed in seeing history retold in his own lifetime, though not for a lack of trying. It was in the promotion of a "proper" history that Jefferson corresponded in 1814 with Dr. Walter Jones. Born in 1745, Jones had graduated from the College of William and Mary and received a medical education in Edinburgh. He was a congressman with Republican leanings who had served intermittently both before and after the election of 1800, a Virginian who wrote Jefferson informally and to whom Jefferson felt he could in turn write freely.[80]

Dr. Jones was as embittered as Jefferson that political parties had "assumed the character of personal Factions . . . *particular sets* of *men*. Language the most gross, brutal, and unsparing . . . invade, like the plagues of Egypt, our innermost dwellings." He was immersed in writing a sympathetic account of Washington in the early days of federalism, before its "corruption." In this nostalgic enterprise he hoped for supporting material from Jefferson, who happily obliged. Unnerved by federalism's persistent refusal to die, the retired sage of Monticello was intent on recovering Washington from the old "monocrats" and "Anglomen" who still claimed him. Jones held out this hope.[81]

Deploring, along with his correspondent, the "putrid state" of journalism, "the malignity, the vulgarity, and mendacious spirit of those who write" for newspapers, Jefferson decried "party spirit." As in his 1799 letter to Gerry, he claimed to yearn for a style of public discussion "the tone of which renders difference of opinion even amiable." He wanted the history of his times to be recorded in "dispassionate" words, which in his judgment it had yet to be, and he placed all the blame for this state of affairs on the stubborn pessimism of his libelous opposition.[82]

Jefferson was so intent on disseminating his unadulterated "truth" — and hopeful of results — that upon discovering in his copy of the letter to Jones a single sentence left out, he wrote a quick note eight days later, containing the added sentence and the assertion that his "conscience" required him to instruct Jones to moisten and "stick it close under the 14th line [so] it will stand in it's place." Having received the one-sentence enclosure and in possession of Jefferson's full characterization of Washington, Jones replied, "If you mean to prepare any memoir for Publication, as is generally supposed by your friends, I hope this character will have a place in them."[83] Jones seems to have missed the point, missed what was expected of him. Jefferson's preference was for others to promote his cause. Jones could have done only so much, in any case, for the tidewater Republican died the next year.

In 1818 Jefferson bound his scraps of "opinions" dating from 1791 into three volumes, creating the *Anas.* He was distant now, he claimed in its pages, from the passions of the Washington administration. He was able to offer "a calm revisal" of those times, having removed all of the records he now understood to be "incorrect or doubtful, or merely personal or private," leaving what future historians could draw upon for a balanced account to contest Marshall's partisan work. The chief justice had grossly misused Washington's papers that had been "confided" to him, so much so that the *Life of Washington* not only would have been distasteful to its subject but had brought on the "suicide" of Washington's cause.[84]

An openly solicitous eight-page letter to Supreme Court justice William Johnson on the eve of Jefferson's eightieth birthday in 1823 begged for a "history of parties." Jefferson had appointed the Charleston, South Carolina, native to the court in 1804 (where he would serve until 1834). Their correspondence had been building for several months. In a letter of twenty-one pages and another of ten, Johnson had mourned to Jefferson that the "whole remains of the Federal party are in Arms against me," and Jefferson had urged the competent jurist to expand his political writings. Johnson countered, "But what inducement, my dear Sir, can I have to proceed with that undertaking?" Jefferson replied: "We have been too careless of our future reputation, while our tories will omit nothing to place us in the wrong. Besides the five-volumed libel [Marshall's] which represents us as struggling for office, and not at all to prevent our government from being administered into a monarchy, the life of Hamilton is in the hands of a man who, to the bitterness of the priest, adds to the rancor of the fiercest federalism." Federalist diatribes were yet building, Jefferson continued. John Adams's papers would inevitably "descend" to John Quincy Adams, "whose pen, you know, is pointed, and his prejudices not in our favor. And doubtless other things are in preparation, unknown to us." Johnson, like Dr. Jones before him, had wanted Jefferson to tell his side firsthand: "We have looked up to you as our common Father," he said on behalf of all true republicans. "We have hoped for a rich Legacy of History from your Pen." Jefferson, reticent about partaking in controversy as an author, wanted to shift the burden. Who better than Justice Johnson to undo the damage begun by Justice Marshall? Yet, in the end, all Johnson would say was, "I will pursue it [the history of parties] Leisurely."[85]

WARRIOR OF WORDS

THE WORDS HE left behind were ultimately all that Jefferson had to promote his American vision. Friendship was reciprocated through letter-borne conversation and meaningfully codified in the Ciceronian form, heightened by appeal to reason and justice. This is how Jefferson and the Jeffersonians separated virtuous republicans from their less en-

lightened, selfish-minded opponents, men who were driven by repug-
nant principles. Jefferson believed that every good-hearted citizen could
be educated to his brand of republicanism. Patrick Henry (though no
aristocrat) could not, because his powerful oratory and emotive words
were merely decorative; the speaker lacked substance, was gravely defi-
cient in moral principle. John Marshall and Aaron Burr could not either, because they, too, were rotten-hearted, self-promoting, and deceptive.[86] Once they proved themselves beyond salvage, such men were
systematically excluded from Jefferson's circle. Indeed, the genteel, generous Jefferson was capable of an uncompromising, rancorous energy.

Behind all expressions of classical grandeur in Jefferson's world lay
the bitter, personal, quintessentially American brand of political gossip.
To combat an organized opposition, Jefferson, his familiar lieutenants
Madison and Monroe, and more recent recruits like William Branch
Giles, dramatically supported by partisan newspapers and quietly sustained by the luminaries of the American Philosophical Society, constantly bolstered each other's efforts. When separated, as they frequently were by long congressional recesses and the exigencies of
plantation management, they maintained regular correspondence. As
much as possible, they reached out to sympathetic supporters and took
the pulse of the country before planning their next moves.

Despite the persistence of self-interest in government and the cultural distinctiveness of America's various parts, Jefferson remained convinced throughout his life that the cultivated moral sense was active in
public as well as private affairs and that the better instincts of humanity
would ultimately prevail—certainly in America if not elsewhere. This
was what the Republic meant to him. England had grown insensitive
and tyrannical, had contracted that official blindness which made many
of its ruling elite tragically unable to apprehend the eloquence of American Revolutionary logic and the spirit inherent in "We the People." On
the other hand, the enlightened community of liberal nobles with
whom Jefferson had communed in Paris provided him with a European
counterpart to his own abiding optimism.

Yet it would appear that a perception of conspiracy led Jefferson and
his closest friends to decisions which were based, to a greater extent
than Jefferson would admit, on passions. Certainly he had a passion for
making history "right." From the beginning he wrote to influence. He
identified and disseminated damning information about Patrick Henry's character. More obviously, once his feud with Hamilton began, he

collected evidence week by week (his anas), recording others' statements and his own reflections as carefully as he noted how the wind blew or when peas came to the table each spring. He was prepared to go to great lengths to pass on his perception of public affairs, convincing himself and his close allies that there existed a mountain of evidence for Hamilton's offenses. The cocky Hamilton did not disguise his intentions and made it relatively easy for Jefferson to catalog his heresies. The compulsive Jefferson, lifelong collector of data, became so committed to obtaining Hamilton's self-incriminating statements that he recorded every bit of gossip he could. Tench Coxe, Hamilton's former colleague at Treasury, related in 1798 that just before leaving office, Hamilton had come clean: "'I avow myself a monarchist; I have no objection to a trial being made of this thing of a republic, but,' &c." In 1800 a merchant passed to Jefferson more damning gossip about Hamilton, that at a recent dinner in New York, he had ignored a toast to President John Adams, but stood and insisted on "three cheers" in toasting King George III.[87] Jefferson wrote it all down.

Later, desirous of doing all he could to expose the Federalist corruption of history, Jefferson found it useful to come to terms with the Hamilton phenomenon. More than a decade after the New Yorker's death, he coolly reflected on his chief adversary. He had distanced himself from the newspaper slanders of 1792. He had seemingly set aside his hatred for the man who had attacked his character in public without putting forth his own name. Jefferson recollected: "Hamilton was, indeed, of a singular character. Of acute understanding, disinterested, honest, and honorable in all private transactions, amiable in society, and duly valuing virtue in private life, yet so bewitched and perverted by the British example as to be under thorough conviction that corruption was essential to the government of a nation."[88]

Jefferson's aim at this late date was to depersonalize their struggle, as he had previously attempted (less convincingly) in the lengthy appeal to Washington in September 1792. Depersonalizing conflict gave Jefferson the edge, or so he thought, when offering a new generation his preferred interpretation of history. The "virtue in private life" he granted Hamilton referred to a sense of personal honor. He did not believe his antagonist corrupt in the management of his financial affairs and excluded marital infidelity from his measure of private virtue. All that now revolted Jefferson was Hamilton's political perversion. As if to underscore his newfound comfort with his old adversary, Jefferson placed a bust of Hamilton opposite his own in the main entrance hall of Monticello and remarked to visitors "with a pensive smile" that the two remained "opposed in death as in life."[89]

Jefferson became so caught up in cataloging others' activities that he generally failed to note how subjective his interpretations were, how he himself might have contributed, for example, to the growing divisions in Washington's cabinet. Both he and Hamilton had iron principles, but Jefferson appears the more extreme in his fear of the other's designs. When Republican victory was certain in the election of 1800, Hamilton expressed his preference for Jefferson over the cruder and more conniving Aaron Burr. This does not make Hamilton reasonable or prove that, despite all the rhetoric, he considered Jefferson a moderate (it may merely indicate how deeply he despised Burr); but it suggests that, politically, he could conceive abiding with Jefferson as president. It seems hardly likely that Jefferson could have been so magnanimous toward Hamilton, whose politics, he insisted, prefigured the wholesale collapse of republican government.

Hamilton was at least as loose with his words as Jefferson, but he never conspired to replace the Republic with a monarchy. In 1792, after Washington (acting on Jefferson's charges) had craftily solicited from him a plan for allaying republican fears of a return to monarchism, Hamilton had written Vice President Adams, "Were ever Men more ingenious to torment themselves with phantoms?"[90] In a society accustomed to a stable social hierarchy, Federalists' social conservatism would not inevitably produce a fixed aristocracy either. Hamilton simply felt that his understanding of political economy was superior to Jefferson's, that Britain's commercial position in the world was a worthy model of emulation, that consolidation of capital in America would do more to nurture the economy than dispersing wealth across a wide agrarian landscape according to the ideal of the Jeffersonians. But to Jefferson, Hamilton's theory, shared with others in political life, was the equivalent of conspiracy.

Deploying the language that he and others had invoked to declare independence from Britain's tyrannical authority, Jefferson depicted Hamiltonianism as a homegrown version of British corruption. He might have overstated (even for his time) the dangers to the Republic. Moreover, he neglected to consider that Hamilton may have had just cause to sense that a whisper campaign against him had been initiated by his mild-mannered colleague. Similarly, Jefferson was, or pretended to be, unaware that to those outside his circle he might have seemed crafty or visionary, causing his rather uncompromising pronounce-ments (or those made by Madison and Monroe which were ascribed to him) to sound more democratic to the Federalists than they actually were. His 1792 letter to Thomas Paine is hard to interpret as anything but a call for further troublemaking: "Go on then in doing with your pen what in other times was done with the sword: shew that reforma-tion is more practicable [recalling that this word, to Jefferson, conjured the resolutions of reasonable men] by operating on the mind than on the body of a man." Jefferson, of course, would not have seen this as troublemaking. He was convinced — and, arguably, remained con-vinced — that his case was so compelling that even "violent," "person-ally bitter" Federalists (as he wrote his daughter in 1801) could in time be "tamed."[91]

He clung to his concept of republican virtue, believing, whether it was Patrick Henry's mirage, or Hamilton's perverse machine, or Burr's abortive conspiracy, that the people were essentially uncorrupt and could always be educated to distinguish between good and bad choices. Jefferson wrote in 1804, "The firmness with which the people have withstood the late abuses of the press, the discernment they have mani-fested between truth and falsehood, show that they may safely be trusted to hear everything true and false, and to form a correct judg-ment between them." It was, above all, this ideal of the people's wis-dom that gave the Republic its vitality. Similarly, upon election to the presidency of the American Philosophical Society in 1797, Jefferson had expressed "an ardent desire to see knowledge so disseminated through the mass of mankind, that it may at length reach even the extremes of society, beggars and kings." The people were competent, as he later asserted with respect to the Burr trial, to pass final judgment on "both the offender & judges." Identifying with the popular voice, Jefferson essentially declared that voice indivisible.[92]

Spurred by his brother's request that he compose poetry, Cicero had expressed frustration and at the same time knowledge of himself when he wrote from his villa: "I withdraw myself, it is true, from all public cares, and devote myself to literature; and yet, I will divulge to you what, on my oath, I especially wished to keep hidden from you. It is agony to me, my dearest brother, sheer agony, to think that there is no constitution, no administration of justice, and that during the period of my life when my proper influence in the Senate should have been at its zenith, I am either distracted by my forensic labours, or fortified only by my literary pursuits at home, while that aspiration to which I had been passionately devoted from my very boyhood, '*Far to excel, and alone to be leader of others*,' has completely vanished." Jefferson's epistolary record is less clear. Perhaps he lacked Cicero's pride and ambition; perhaps not. If he privately yearned to be an executive, he kept such desires well hidden. On his election to the vice presidency in 1796, narrowly losing the presidency to Adams, he wrote Madison, "Pride does not enter into the estimate; for I think with the Romans that the general of today should be a soldier of tomorrow if necessary." Jefferson protested (though his words are a bit convoluted) that he did not desire the presidency at this point, that "it was impossible that a more solid unwillingness settled on full calculation, could have existed in any man's mind, short of the degree of absolute refusal." But as his frustrations mounted after 1797, when his political enemies were in the ascendant, he could not turn away again as he had in 1793. He accepted his historic fate, pushing back another decade his final retirement from public cares and his return to literature.[93]

Jefferson's lifelong problem, his inability to steer clear of controversy, crystallizes in a 1789 letter to Francis Hopkinson. "I never had an opinion in politics or religion which I was too afraid to own," he proclaimed, as he prepared to return from Europe. "A costive reserve on these subjects might have procured me more esteem from some people, but less from myself." Refusing to compromise himself, Jefferson went on to protest that he did not intend his honest expression to ruffle others: "My great wish is to go on in a strict but silent performance of my duty: to avoid attracting notice and to keep my name out of the newspapers, because I find the pain of a little censure, even when it is unfounded [likely a reference to the criticisms of his conduct as governor in 1781], is more acute than the pleasure of much praise."[94]

His observable calm hid his private remorse. Falling prey to the powerful implications of his own language, Jefferson ultimately felt that no one could rescue the principles of '76 as effectively as he himself. At first, from his position as vice president ("the only office in the world about which I am unable to decide in my own mind whether I had rather have it or not have it"), he rationalized to his correspondents, as he had during three years of midcareer retirement, that he would be content for others to guide the country back to the republican standard. He seemed for a time incapable of acknowledging what he must have known about his own impulses; he told the truth when, quitting Washington's cabinet a few years earlier, he had informed Madison bluntly that he remained "committed singly in desperate & eternal contest against a host who are systematically undermining the public liberty & prosperity." Indeed, as president, he explained to his daughter how dissatisfied he had been when he tried to remove himself from the world during the retirement years of 1794–96. Like Cicero, while standing on the sidelines, he had mourned the lack of a counterforce, of a dynamic capable of preventing what was, in his mind, abuse in government.[95]

To define a mission as Jefferson did required a strong sense of one's superior knowledge of rightness, almost of revealed Truth. It made it plausible for his critical contemporaries to see Jefferson as a secretly ambitious destroyer of order and for posterity to condemn him as stubborn and clannish. The obstructed vision of this chapter's title refers to two notions at once: Jefferson came up against obstructions to his liberal humanist vision for America; and the obstructed vision was in fact his own shortsightedness. He refused to seek compromise and made a drastic equation of basic policy differences (notably Hamilton's purported Anglophilia) with the complete overthrow of the recently established national government. In preparing his papers for history, he claimed he could be objective, as he consistently assigned blame to sources outside himself. But there was a battle for the American mind in progress. The world had not known a republic on the scale Americans were attempting, and its success was by no means assured. So, was Jefferson justified? He was, but only if excused for not recognizing in himself the bitter partisan.

He defined his strategy with greatest clarity during the course of his estrangement from the Adamses, when he had occasion to write Abigail Adams: "With those who think amiss of me, I have learnt to be perfectly indifferent: but where I know a mind to be ingenuous [i.e., open, generous], and to need only truth to set it to rights, I cannot be as passive." He was convinced that the qualities which built and sustained friendships could carry over into public discourse, that personal honor, unquestioned sincerity, and affability were republican attributes. Thus he invested his Heart in shaping his political world, despite his knowledge that it was a place of contentiousness, plots, and secrecy.[96]

Benjamin Franklin, like Jefferson a man of friendships, once wrote that the reputation he most coveted was that of a doer of good. Yet to his daughter Sally, in a less exalted moment, Franklin also acknowledged, "I have many enemies, all indeed on the public account (for I cannot recollect that I have in a private capacity given just cause of offence to any one whatever), yet they are enemies, and very bitter ones." Jefferson understood that he could not sway all those who disputed his political beliefs. Just as the pragmatic Franklin had recognized the ubiquity of public contest, Jefferson, in retirement, wrote John Adams that "men of energy of character must have enemies: because there are two sides to every question." What he could not accept, though, was that he in any way warranted personal enmity. He saw himself again like Franklin, whose enemies were all on the "public account," who claimed sensitivity enough not to have given cause for personal offense.[97]

Jefferson should not have been as surprised as he made out. He went further than Franklin in prompting reactions, detested those who he believed threatened him, and retained a firm belief that virtuous, reasoning citizens, including a good number who called themselves Federalists, ought and would take the path that he prophesied for his nation. His path was the inevitable path of human progress, Jefferson insisted, the path first charted when Americans listened to their Hearts instead of their Heads, took on a more powerful British adversary, and won the right to test their capacity for enlightened self-rule. Jefferson's message was personal and personalized his politics. It made him a hero to the many who believed and a devil to those who were convinced that the mild, benevolent, thoughtful man he presented hid an anarchic experimenter, that Jefferson was a dissembler.

There is no question but that Jefferson was hurt by the personalization of political disagreement. At the end of his presidency, he could still charge with considerable spite, that his enemies "had not the liberality to distinguish between political and social opposition; who transferred at once to the person, the hatred they bore to his political opinions." Of the "political sect, who wished to transform [the government] ultimately into the shape of their darling model, the English," he reiterated, "they have concentrated all their hatred on me, till they have really persuaded themselves, that I am the sole source of all their imaginary evils." At the end of his life, it was much the same, his enemies having "created an imaginary being clothed with odious attributes, to whom they had given his name."[98]

Jefferson pushed himself. His "periodical head-ach," first documented in 1764, marred his otherwise energetic presidential efforts.

There were times when, his mind oppressed with pain, he repaired to a darkened room for days, shutting out his natural ally, the sun, losing valuable time for business and letter writing, waiting until relief came finally, naturally. These tension headaches ceased after he retired to Monticello in 1809. Other than occasional bouts with diarrhea during his first term (on which subject he wrote Dr. Benjamin Rush) and rheumatism after 1808, Jefferson's health remained good. He ate and drank in moderation, favoring light wines. Beyond such concerns with his health, he was, as he later wrote John Adams, alarmed by the prospect that he might live too long, that is, suffer a slow deterioration of the mind or long-term physical impairment. None of these fears was ever realized. He remained lucid and rode his horse daily up until the year he died. Daniel Webster found Jefferson, at eighty-one, full of "health, vivacity, and spirit."[99]

He had been long conflicted about politics. His mind could not leave it alone. His sensitive Heart wished a psychic victory over regressive Federalism, and his unmartial body just as instinctively wished visceral release. Political struggle was debilitating and, in a certain sense, a life-and-death contest to him. French commercial expert Pierre Samuel Du Pont de Nemours, whom Jefferson had known only in an official capacity in Paris, became a faithful correspondent after emigrating to America just before Jefferson became president. In advance of the election of 1800, upon receiving proof of the falsehood of a rumor that Jefferson had taken ill and died, Du Pont wrote poignantly that "I believed I had lost the greatest man on this continent . . . the one who by his similarity to our principles gives me the hope of the firmest sort of friendship so necessary to one living far from his native land." Jefferson answered stylishly, "I am much in debt to my enemies for proving, by their recitals of my death, that I have friends."[100]

It was a sardonic response but one hinting at the strength and ultimate confidence that allowed Jefferson to carry on. He let Head and Heart contend, and he suffered at each twist and turn. But no force overcame his inner drive. His vision had been nurtured over the years through an intense love of reading, of contemplating and expressively writing, and had been fortified by a network of sturdy, sympathetic, and giving friends. All of this, combined, protected his life. He sensed how hard it was for him to die.

7 Retirement, Religion, and Romantic Death

NEVER ABLE TO be explicit about the optimum length of his stay in any public office, Jefferson had projected his retirement from Washington's cabinet in a letter to James Madison in mid-1793: "To my fellow-citizens the debt of service has been fully & faithfully paid. . . . If the public then has no claim on me, & my friends nothing to justify; the decision will rest on my own feelings alone. . . . The motion of my blood no longer keeps time with the tumult of the world. It leads me to seek for happiness in the lap and love of my family, in the society of my neighbors & my books, in the wholesome occupations of my farm & my affairs, in an interest or affection in every bud that opens, in every breath that blows around me, in an entire freedom of rest or motion, of thought of incogitancy, owing account to myself alone of my hours & actions." These were not the phrases of a cunning politician but a man of sensibility exhausted by the trails of office, seeking "wholesome occupations" in order to refashion himself as a gentleman farmer, to restore his relationship to the productive land. A further characterization of his state of mind came the following year. "I would not give up my own retirement for the empire of the universe," Jefferson proclaimed, once again to Madison.[1]

Thirteen years later, nearing the end of his second term as president, Jefferson's manner of expression was less poetic and more resigned. To seventy-four-year-old John Dickinson, who had tried in the Continental Congress to temper a bold, young Jefferson's words on the eve of independence, the run-down chief executive wrote from Washington of his "tedium": "I am tired of an office where I can do no more good than many others, who would be glad to be employed in it. To myself, personally, it brings nothing but unceasing drudgery & daily loss of friends. . . . My only consolation is in the belief that my fellow citizens at large give me credit for good intentions."[2] The president's fatigue was more than rhetorical, and he was indeed in need of consolation.

AFTER MARIA

IT WAS, PERHAPS more than any other single event, the death of his daughter Maria at the end of his first term that had drained Jefferson and impelled him toward retirement. This fragile and attractive young woman who had, as her father told her the year he was elected president, "never by a word or deed given . . . a moment's uneasiness," endured three pregnancies in less than five years. Her second child, Francis, survived and would be the only one of the three to reach adulthood. In February 1804, when Francis was two and a half, she gave birth to a daughter, also named Maria Jefferson Eppes. Jefferson learned in Washington of the successful delivery and wrote Maria a rejoicing letter, anticipating a March reunion at Monticello. But when March arrived, she was gravely ill. Before his departure for home, he wrote Martha, by now the mother of six healthy young ones, "Tell my dear Maria to be of good chear, and to be ready to mount on horseback with us." But Maria continued to fade. Carried the four miles from Martha and Thomas Mann Randolph's Edgehill estate to be at Monticello near her father's side, twenty-five-year-old Maria died on the morning of April 17. Her body was "covered with white cloth over which had been strewed a profusion of flowers." Jefferson was left alone for a time, after which he asked for Martha, who found him uncharacteristically clutching a Bible.[3]

After three weeks elapsed, he returned to Washington and wrote to his surviving daughter, the "single thread" on which his life now hung, as he mourned to John Page. His three-day journey had worn him down terribly. He regretted having nothing to tell Martha beyond "this long chapter about myself." She answered with reassurance that "no appology can be necessary for writing lengthily to me about your self. I hope you are not yet to learn that no subject on earth *is* or *ever can be* so dear and interesting to me. . . . It is truly the happiness of my life to think that I can dedicate the remainder of it to promote yours. It is a subject however upon which I ought never to write for no pen on earth can do justice to the feelings of my heart." Her letters were far more than rhetorical exercises; Jefferson's dutiful Martha served without complaint and soothed her father's aches with unfaltering devotion.[4]

Firm in his conviction that peace and satisfaction became less elusive only when he placed himself near his loved ones, Jefferson continued to think of keeping the family close. He reminded Maria's husband,

Jack Eppes, that the nearby estate at Pantops would someday belong to little Francis. Lamenting that Jack had not stayed at Monticello longer after burying Maria, he wrote, "While I live, both of the children will be to me the dearest of all pledges: and I should consider it as increasing our misfortune, should we have the less of your society."[5]

Maria's death was unbearable, but it merely reconfirmed what had been branded into Jefferson's breast over a lifetime. "I have been happy and cheerful," he wrote in 1784. "I have had many causes of gratitude to heaven, but I have also experienced it's rigours. I have known what it is to lose every species of connection which is dear to the human heart: friends, brethern, parents, children." His Heart had spoken again two years later to Maria Cosway, when it mingled tears with another who grieved. "The world abounds indeed with misery," he declared then. Jefferson protested often of having grown "tired of a life of contention." He wished to be among his remaining family "where I know nothing but love and delight." He knew how to free himself from public duties, finally, but the age of science and reason would never discover a remedy for the disquieting persistence of pain and loss. Jefferson was long convinced of this and remained tormented.[6]

Despite Jefferson's emphasis on developing a Head in his firstborn, the sturdy Martha inherited a sensitive Heart as well. Her reports on the grandchildren's health crises were a constant source of alarm, though she tried to rely on their spirits (and in one known instance bleeding) to ensure recovery. When Jefferson's seven-year-old granddaughter Ellen, stricken with a potentially deadly dysentery, was suffering "agonies indescribable" in 1803, Martha noted with some relief her active mind, which "even the most acute bodily pain was never capable of subduing." Yet the experience caused Martha herself to suffer "so much from fatigue and anxiety since my return home that I have not had spirits to write to My Dearest Father." Jefferson likewise expressed anxiety when he learned of outbreaks of influenza and measles, or when he undertook detailed arrangements for smallpox inoculations. Only months after Maria's death, Jefferson began to fear for Martha. Of one of her rare illnesses, he wrote: "It has filled me with anxiety respecting you, and this is increased by your not having communicated it to me. Because in endeavoring to spare my feelings on your real situation it gives me the pain of fearing everything imaginable; even that the statement of your recovery may not be exact." He had faced so many such trials that he demanded complete clinical details.[7]

Typically, when Jefferson traveled to and from Monticello, he straightforwardly announced that he had arrived "without accident." This notification was more than a formality. One could regularly expect to encounter problems with roads, horses, or wet weather, bringing on illness. Indeed, before his presidency ended, Jefferson would become troubled by rheumatic muscles and joints, occasioning pain in travel.[8]

The tenor of his correspondence with the family had always centered on issues of physical and emotional health. He was profoundly conscious of all that produced ill humors and was exacting in his prescriptions for restoring or maintaining balance. He and Martha constantly wrote to one another of "health" and "spirits," "heart" and "suffering," "ills" and "derangements," and the desire to be with each other, free from interruptions by "crowds" of well-wishers or political voices. Typical, too, was what Jefferson wrote to Maria as she entered her last pregnancy: "Have good spirits and know that courage is essential to triumph in your case as in that of the souldier. Keep us all therefore in heart by being so yourself." This time, all of Jefferson's urging proved useless, and he was left heart-stricken. Despite his custom of command, when his emotions were engaged, when his soul was stirred, he was no "souldier" himself.[9]

Resilient Martha, ever the reliable correspondent, balanced her responsibilities at Edgehill with her attachment to Monticello. When her father was anticipating his final removal to private life in 1809, she readied the house for him. Life as they had known it was to change. As early as January 1808, this self-sacrificing daughter received word that she would have to prepare herself for a less lavish lifestyle. Long absent, Jefferson had been unable to devote adequate attention to his plantation. He had anticipated being able to count on the profitability of Edgehill, but Thomas Mann Randolph's loose command of his own affairs had dashed that hope. The retiring president wrote his daughter, "I have now the gloomy prospect of retiring from office loaded with serious debts, which will materially affect the tranquility of my retirement." Knowing that her husband had been obliged to support his own sisters during these recent trying times, Martha vowed to teach her children moderation. She blamed herself. "It cuts me to the heart," she sighed, "to think how much it will cost you in retirement to raise what I so wantonly squandered in going to live with you, My Dear Father. It was never my intention to burthen you with the maintenance of our large family."[10]

She wrote her tenderest letters in the last months before Jefferson returned home for good. Feeling a "sacred duty" to see that the "evening" of her father's life passed in "serene and unclouded tranquility," she divulged, "As the *period* [end] of your labours draws near My heart beats with an inexpressible anxiety and impatience." He in turn expressed "but a single uneasiness. I am afraid that the enforcing the observance of the necessary economies in the internal administration of the house will give you more trouble than I wish you to have to encounter." Pointing to the ease afforded by their "good and capable servants," he reassured her that her happiness remained paramount in his mind. "My own personal wants will be almost nothing beyond those of a chum [essentially, a lodger] of the family." She could not help writing once more the week before his arrival. "*Your* comfort My Dearest Father" must be the only thing taking precedence over economy. "I can bear any thing but the idea of seeing you harrassed in your old age by debts or deprived of those comforts which long habit has rendered necessary to you. . . . We shall be happy if you are so." Monticello overseer Edmund Bacon described the tireless Martha during the early period of Jefferson's retirement as "always in a happy mood. She had her father's pleasant smile and was nearly always humming some tune." The overseer marveled at her industriousness in household affairs and her reading and writing. "She used to sit in Mr. Jefferson's room a great deal and sew, or read and talk, as he would be busy about something else."[11]

The familiar presence of disease and death, constantly conveyed in letters, had made Jefferson's life away from Monticello particularly fretful. Having been conditioned to accept this slow vehicle for unpleasant news over so many years, Jefferson no doubt brought to his retirement a mixture of profound relief in being close to his loved ones and a lingering fear of loss. Martha was only thirty-eight in 1810, when her nineteen-year-old daughter Anne, two years married, gave birth to a son. From Monticello, Jefferson wrote the new mother, to whom he had imparted his horticultural interest, "The flowers come forth like the belles of the day, have their short reign of beauty and splendor, and retire like them to the more interesting office of reproducing their like." His reference to transient beauty and the perishability of nature, while in praise of "the more interesting office" of reproducing life, metaphorically linked his delight in the growth of things with his consciousness of the sorrows attending life. He would live to bury Anne.[12]

In the last years of his presidency, Jefferson had begun to turn his thoughts more and more to the grandchildren, "the dear little objects of our natural love," as he described them to Martha. Anne had kept him apprised of the flourishing of nature and the yield of the garden, while the second oldest, his namesake, Thomas Jefferson Randolph, was at school in Philadelphia and in the care of the president's old friend, painter Charles Willson Peale. Jefferson Randolph was, according to his mother, a teenager whose "judgement when not under the influence of passion is as good as can be expected at his age but he is indolent impatient of reproof and *at times* irritable." These were not Jefferson but Randolph qualities, she insisted. Two years earlier, as a member of Congress, temperamental Thomas Mann Randolph had insulted his cousin, former Jeffersonian leader turned agitator John Randolph of Roanoke, in the House of Representatives, an event that nearly ended in a duel. Jefferson had been so concerned over his son-in-law's behavior that he sent a troubled letter to him by way of an Albemarle neighbor, so as to keep Martha at least temporarily in the dark. In it he appealed to reason and prudence, writing of the dueling prospect, "The least expression of passion on the one side draws forth a little more on the other, and ends at last in the most barbarous of appeals."[13]

But Martha, more than anyone else, knew her husband's foibles. Alerting her father to the presence of the Randolph temperament in young Jefferson Randolph, she was greatly pleased by the grandfather's attentiveness and desire to improve him through study. On the eve of the decision to send her son to Philadelphia, Martha herself pressed him to employ his time at home reading French, mathematics, history, and geography. To present him to good company, the president gave his grandson letters to deliver to such notables as Dr. Benjamin Rush, an advice giver to rival Jefferson. Concurring that science offered a secure future for the youth, Jefferson warned against all controversy occasioned by mixing with "the ill-tempered and rude men in society who have taken up a passion for politics." Thinking, no doubt, of the Randolph genes, he pursued this cautionary tone further: "Be a listener only, keep within yourself, and endeavor to establish with yourself the habit of silence, especially in politics. In the fevered state of our country, no good can ever result from any attempt to set one of these fiery zealots to rights either in fact or principle. They are determined as to the facts they will believe, and the opinions on which they will act. Get by them, therefore as you would an angry bull: it is not for a man of sense to dispute the road with such an animal." The grandson replied with ready emotion, "Although I never speak on the subject [politics] myself, yet when I hear these vile pensioners and Miscreants expressing Tory sentiments and abusing you, it is with difficulty I can restrain myself."[14]

Jefferson Randolph remained in Philadelphia some months longer, requesting funds from his grandfather so that he could join him at the inauguration of James Madison in March 1809. Thereafter, this devoted, if not always diligent, young man followed a course of study in Richmond, but he did not possess the intellectual powers to follow in his grandfather's footsteps and attend the College of William and Mary, as hoped. He became increasingly involved in the management of Jefferson's farms and eventually executor of his grandfather's estate.[15]

Ellen Wayles Randolph, the next oldest, was perhaps the most spirited and most dutiful of all the president's correspondents. In 1806, at age ten, she engaged Jefferson in a contest to see who could write more often, while professing a mature understanding of his epistolary burden. He followed up: "I believe it is true that you have written me 2. letters to my one to you. Whether this proceeds from your having more industry or less to do than myself I will not say." A year later, sensitive to her concerns, Jefferson predicted that the upcoming congressional campaign would cause him to become "an unpunctual correspondent." She was accustomed to the demands of his office when she subsequently wrote, "This is the second letter I have written to My dear grandpapa without recieving an answer but as I know the reason I will continue to write until you have leisure to answer my letters." She told preciously of a pet bantam: "He had got so tame that he would fly up in my lap and eat out of my hand. All the children were sorry at his death." At last able to reply, Jefferson made light of his "paiment in full of my debt." He refrained from news of politics because "you would not care a fig about that." The following spring he offered further guidance in raising bantams, writing her even while under the torture of a "periodical head-ach." He was "glad to learn" of her dedication and lovingly coupled their hobbies: "Our birds and flowers are well and send their love to yours."[16]

Ellen regaled him with increasingly long letters during his last year in office. He was delighted with what he termed her "small news," being "more than surfeited" by "great news" from his other correspondents. He encouraged her writing habit: "In order that your letters may not be shortened by a bad pen of which you complain, I have got a pen for you which will be always good, never wearing or needing to be mended." Later, an adult Ellen recalled childhood at Monticello, writing that her grandfather "talked with us freely, affectionately; never lost an opportunity of giving a pleasure or a good lesson. . . . Our smaller follies he treated with good-humored raillery, our graver ones with kind and serious admonition." Her sister Virginia, who married Nicholas P. Trist (grandson of Eliza House Trist), wrote of a vital presence: "Cheerfulness, love, benevolence, wisdom, seemed to animate his whole form. His face beamed with them. You [Nicholas] remember how active was his step, how lively and even playful were his manners."[17]

After having sought to become, with each in turn, the correspondent of his grandchildren, Jefferson enjoyed the regular company of this growing brood, already ten at his retirement. He saw Maria's son, Francis Eppes, less but urged the boy often to visit his Monticello cousins, flattering the young hunter on one occasion that his visit would make all happy, "only deprecated by the partridges and snow birds against which you may commence hostilities."[18] Whatever anxieties he harbored over matters of health, his immersion in gardening and physical exercise and interaction with robust and responsive youth clearly livened his retirement years and fueled him with that spirit he had always wished to exhibit: optimism about the future.

As "sage of Monticello," Jefferson did not withdraw entirely to a hermitage but generously entertained old friends, European intellectuals, and a new generation of American statesmen, even as his financial woes mounted. He had begun building his second or summer home at Poplar Forest in 1806, on Bedford County property some ninety miles to the southwest, a three-day ride from Albemarle. When completed, Poplar Forest would become another architectural delight, a structure based on the octagon, and a somewhat rustic escape from the busier and more cluttered Monticello.[19] Jefferson journeyed here two to three times each year after 1810, often taking along his granddaughters. He enjoyed spoiling the girls with gifts of watches, musical instruments, furniture, and pretty clothes. Cornelia Jefferson Randolph, born in 1799, produced architectural drawings for her grandfather, a hobby which no doubt amused him.[20]

He indulged easily in nostalgic thought. Writing to James Maury, an early classmate and son of his Albemarle classics teacher, Jefferson described the tranquillity of his retirement. Mourning the passing of old friends, he wished that Maury, removed to England, might come back and help restore something of the comforting past. "We would beguile our lingering hours," wrote Jefferson, "with talking over our youthful exploits, our hunts on Peter's mountain, with a long train of *et cetera* in addition, and feel, by recollection at least, a momentary flash of youth. Reviewing the course of a long and sufficiently successful life, I find no portion of it happier than those were."[21]

While reading and writing on issues of political significance, Jefferson gave up his active role and allowed the initiative to pass to younger men. Life at Monticello and Poplar Forest offered sufficient stimulation, physical, intellectual, and emotional. The former president would remain occupied with mastering his mountaintop to the end of his days, planting seeds and watching them grow. He described his new philosophy simply: "Something pursued with ardor is necessary to guard us from *tedium vitae,* and the active pursuits lessen most our sense of the infirmities of age." During Margaret Bayard Smith's 1809 visit, he accompanied his guest on "a charming walk round the edge of the lawn and showed us the spots from which the house appeared to most advantage." He had flower beds laid out around the lawn and under windows and encouraged his grandchildren to learn the scientific names of each root and bulb. He rose each day before the sun, dressed plainly but neatly, answered his correspondence before breakfast, and at nine or so went for a ride on his horse. He was, according to overseer Bacon, "passionately fond of a good horse." The sum total of these pursuits—allowing that Jefferson still could not rest easy about his political or financial legacy—was peace of mind. "Tranquillity," he wrote in 1813, "is the *summum bonum* of a Septagenaire." His doctor reported that Jefferson's intellectual powers were "unshaken" even in his eighty-second year, his physical condition such that he could "exercise on foot with all the activity of one twenty or thirty years younger."[22]

Having devoted himself to Monticello and then to Poplar Forest, Jefferson energetically promoted and proceeded to design and oversee construction of one more architectural marvel: the University of Virginia. He concerned himself with every detail, from the selection of professors and framing of the curriculum to note taking at board meetings. Whatever he built he viewed as a site for learning and repose, formed in concert with nature. To future Harvard professor George

Ticknor, whose visit to Monticello in 1814 led to a fruitful correspondence, he wrote of his efforts to convince the state legislature that such an institution was essential, astonished that politicians might not yet "possess information enough to perceive the important truth, that knoledge is power, that knoledge is safety, and that knoledge is happiness." To Maria Cosway, recently widowed and now an educator herself at the Catholic College of Dame Inglesi in Lodi, Italy, he wrote: "The sympathies of our earlier days harmonize, it seems, in age also. You retire to your college at Lodi and nourish the natural benevolence of your excellent heart by communicating your own virtues to the young of your sex. . . . I am laying the foundation of an University in my native state. . . . I have preferred the plan of an academical village rather than that of a single massive structure." He detailed its architectural plan, its classical pavilions whose construction he supervised, and added: "It is within view, too, of *Monticello* so it's a most splendid object, and a constant gratification to my sight."[23] How apt that his final contribution to his country, his last passionate project, was an "academical village" to be enjoyed by promising minds, and properly situated where the patriarch could readily spy it from his mountain.

"Let Us Seek *DEATH*"

In retirement, as Jefferson reassessed his life, he gave much thought to the prospect of eternal rest. With seven decades and more to reflect upon, he had few pressing goals and little fear of death. He dwelled contentedly on ancient assessments of the human condition. When entertaining thoughts of mortality in his third decade, however, he had been a learner, filled with imagination. In his 1771 pocket account book, during what Henry Randall presumed were "the cogitations of unfilled hours on the circuit," attorney Jefferson jotted a note to himself about the "Burying place" he intended to arrange on his mountaintop. He would choose a site that was absent of sound and make sure there was "'no mark of any human shape that had been there, unless the skeleton of some poor wretch, who sought that place out to despair and die in.' Let it be among antient and venerable oaks; interspace some gloomy evergreens." Half the area was intended for Jefferson's family, the rest for "strangers, servants, &c."[24]

Fully sixty of Jefferson's Commonplace Book entries in the 1760s and early 1770s concerned death. He copied Herodotus in Greek: "The

Egyptians were the first to teach that the human soul is immortal, and at death of the body it enters into some other living thing then coming to birth." He copied Cicero in Latin: "What satisfaction can there be in living, when day and night we have to reflect that at this or that moment we must die?" From Milton's *Paradise Lost* he reproduced a number of passages, such as: "Let us seek *Death:* — or, he not found, supply / With our own Hands his Office on ourselves" and "But have I now seen Death? is this the Way / I must return to native Dust? O Sight / Of terror, foul, & ugly to behold, / Horrid to think, how horrible to feel."[25]

William Sherlock (1641–1707) was the only clerical authority whose works Jefferson recommended along with Sterne (under the heading "Religion") in his 1771 letter to Robert Skipwith. Sherlock's 1689 *A Practical Discourse concerning Death* had gone through more than twenty editions by the time Jefferson acquired his copy. It announced that "when we die, we do not fall into Nothing, or into profound Sleep . . . but we only change our place, and our Dwelling." Asserting that God's "design for Happiness" ensures that heaven must be "a better place" than earth, Sherlock added that in that "new and unknown State of Life," all becomes "immutable and unchangeable." Once "stripp'd of Flesh and Blood," we die "once and for all, and must never live again, as we do now in this World." Like Sterne, Sherlock recognized bodily pleasures, "natural Appetites"; men are "made for the enjoyment of sense." He commented as well that "it is fit before Men go out of this World, that they should recover the possession of themselves, and grown a little more acquainted and intimate with themselves, [should endeavor] . . . to make their peace with God and their own Consciences." Through such words and images, we can appreciate Jefferson's curiosity; here he is in early adulthood, exploring questions of ultimate importance to the management of everyday life, pondering the inevitability of death without subscribing to any particular system of belief or expecting to reach any quick determination.[26]

Jefferson could also describe death coldly and scientifically — especially odd in this one instance because his young daughters were with him — writing in 1789 to William Short from Le Havre, while en route to America: "On our return [from a fruitless errand] we came on the body of a man who had at that moment shot himself. His pistol had dropped at his feet, and himself fallen backward without ever moving. The shot had completely separated his whole face from the forehead to the chin and so turn it to atoms that it could not be known. The center of the head was entirely laid bare — This is the only kind of news I have for you."[27] Death was so matter-of-fact in this period that announcements were appended to letters, sometimes without comment, other times with clinical descriptions. The ages of decedents seemed less traumatic to report than the degree of suffering attending their demise. Jefferson himself, though sensitive to the "joy of grief" in Ossian, recorded the deaths of his mother, his children, and his wife in his Account Book in the eighteenth-century fashion, without any suggestion of the emotion he was feeling at the time; diaries that yielded to the temptation to record deathbed scenes in tear-filled detail were to be the mark of his grandchildren's generation.[28] As the Revolutionary generation slowly, inexorably, faded from the scene, he unceremoniously marked off their deaths one by one. He kept a mental record of the signers of the Declaration of Independence and, as their numbers dwindled, charted what remained of the old.[29]

Jefferson the grandfather returned to reading ancient history and philosophy. As his varied correspondence and dedication to the University of Virginia show, he remained fixed on understanding and promoting the humanist spirit and the ideals, ever sacred to him, of the American Revolution. Past, present, and future coalesced. Human happiness, individual assertiveness, the progress of civilization, beauty and sublimity in the natural world, all occupied his thought. His correspondence with John Adams, resumed in 1812, flourished in these years and frequently mingled classical lessons with commentaries on the human condition.

In an exchange in 1816, Adams queried Jefferson whether he would want to live his seventy-three years over again. Answering in the affirmative, Jefferson judged, "It is a good world on the whole . . . framed on a principle of benevolence, and more pleasure than pain dealt out to us." Recurring to a sea metaphor, he continued: "I steer my bark with Hope in the head, leaving Fear astern. My hopes indeed sometimes fail; but not oftener than the forebodings of the gloomy. There are, I acknoledge, even in the happiest life, some terrible convulsions. . . . I have often wondered for what good end the sensations of Grief could be intended." As a man who had suffered many losses of loved ones, he could not find any positive value in the pain associated with living. This view led him to anticipate his own death as an event of release.[30]

Adams was stimulated by Jefferson's well-rounded answer and philosophized: "What is human life? A Vapour, a Fog, a Dew, a Clould a Blossom a flower, a Rose a blade of Grass, a glass Bubble, a Tale told by an Idiot . . . an eternal succession of which would terrify me, almost as must as Annihilation." Projecting Jefferson's reaction to this statement, Adams could not wait to add that he himself would prefer "the risque of Annihilation" upon physical death to living another life. From here, though, he mused about materialist philosophers d'Alembert and Voltaire, who in the end could not face death with the same courage that they had displayed in challenging religious faith. Of Jefferson's seafaring optimism, Adams concurred, "I admire your Navigation and should like to sail with you, either in your Bark or in my own, along side of yours; Hope with her gay Ensigns displayed at the Prow; fear with her Hobgoblins behind the Stern." He concluded that "the Maker of the Universe, the Cause of all Things, whether We call it, *Fate* or *Chance* or God has inspired this Hope. If it is a *Fraud,* We shall never know it."[31]

To all this, Jefferson directly responded: "There is a ripeness of time for death . . . when it is reasonable we should drop off, and make room for another growth. . . . I assure you I am ripe for leaving all, this year, this day, this hour." He closed this letter with an ironic sentiment, coming as it did from the pen of an ardent classicist: "I like the dreams of the future better than the history of the past. So good night. I will dream on."[32]

Both Adams and Jefferson had, at this point, ten years of life yet allotted to them.

JEFFERSON'S JESUS

JEFFERSON HAD LONG kept his religion a mystery, or at least placed his emphasis on religious freedom in republican society. This had served to make political enemies of most of the clergy, a hatred he welcomed. "The *genus irritabile vatum,*" Jefferson proudly reported, "are up in arms against me."[33] To him the New England Congregationalists and Episcopalians had been encouraged by the politically repressive Alien and Sedition Acts to anticipate legislation that would next curtail religious freedom and, each believed, establish their sect as the proper American religion. During the late 1790s, while this debate simmered, Jefferson enjoyed a lively dialogue on matters of religion with Benjamin

Rush. Rush believed in religious freedom according to Jefferson's pre-scription, adding that republicanism and Christianity were the symbi-otic match that history had been awaiting.[34]

As president, Jefferson's interest in religion expanded, but he would not allow himself to be drawn beyond the merely earthbound lessons that Christianity bore to him. This he clarified to Rush, who believed strictly in Jesus's divinity. "To the corruptions of Christianity I am in-deed opposed," wrote the president, "but not to the genuine precepts of Jesus himself. I am a Christian, in the only sense which he wished any one to be." What Jefferson found in Jesus was "every *human* excel-lence."[35] His theology more closely corresponded with that of the Uni-tarian Joseph Priestley, whom Jefferson had come to know as vice pres-ident.

Jefferson and Priestley became tied both by political and theological interests. In England, Priestley had expressed pro-French sentiments in 1790, the year after the French Revolution broke out. Mobs burned down his church. As a refugee from England in 1794, he arrived in Philadelphia, to the delight of the American Philosophical Society. In its letter of commendation to the clergyman-chemist who had discov-ered oxygen in 1774, the society made Priestley "an illustrious member" of its body and welcomed the "talents and virtues" of this "enlightened republican," urging him to seek American citizenship. Jefferson was sensitive to Priestley's problems of being an alien and pro-French amid the hysteria that surrounded the Alien and Sedition Acts. He wrote, "How deeply have I been chagrined and mortified at the persecutions which fanaticism and monarchy have excited against you, even here!"[36]

Jefferson and Priestley corresponded amiably and philosophically. The latter's *History of the Corruptions of Christianity* (1782) had stressed the simplicity of early Christian practices and morals and rejected the later complex forms of worship. Jefferson translated Priestley's sense of "corruption" more cynically as theories conceived by a clerical caste ever bent on maintaining power by confusing people and compelling submission. Priestley believed in divine revelation through the Bible, that Jesus was a human with a divine role; Jefferson, who did not read Priestley's book until sometime in the 1790s, believed that Jesus was a sublime teacher but only human, whose great contribution was in rendering benevolent the wrathful God of the Jews. Jefferson pasted together his own collage of the Gospels that made sense to him, titled "The Philosophy of Jesus," in 1804. He went on to prepare a more elaborate, rationalistic version, "The Life and Morals of Jesus," in response to his 1813–16 exchanges with Adams and others.[37]

Jefferson stated his position on personal faith and clerical narrow-mindedness most plainly in a letter to Margaret Bayard Smith: "I have ever thought religion a concern purely between our god and our consciences, for which we are accountable to him, and not to the priests. I never told of my religion, nor scrutinised that of another. . . . But this does not satisfy the priesthood. They must have a positive, a declared assent to all their interested absurdities. My opinion is that there would never have been an infidel, if there had never been a priest." Similarly, in a letter to the Quaker Dr. George Logan a few months later: "The sum of all religion as expressed by it's best preacher, 'fear god and love thy neighbor' contains no mystery, needs no explanation. But this wont do. It gives no scope to make dupes; priests could not live by it."[38]

When someone was inadvertently left to peruse a letter Jefferson wrote to old, absentminded Charles Thomson relating to his rediscovery of the moral Jesus, an eager Christian heard about its contents and wrote Jefferson to congratulate him on his apparent conversion to belief in the divinity of Jesus. Quite in character, when Jefferson wrote to Thomson next, he informed him that whatever he felt about his religion was "known to my god and myself alone. It's evidence before the world is to be sought in my life." Why, he reasoned, should people believe alike any more than they should look alike?[39]

To Adams, he elaborated. He hoped the day would come when "the dawn of reason and freedom of thought in these United States" would render the "artificial scaffolding" of "the mystical generation" of the divine Jesus a "fable" no less credible than "the generation of Minerva in the brain of Jupiter." Once the "primitive and genuine doctrines" of Jesus as a spiritual man, a "venerated reformer" of religion, took hold again, the original structure of Christianity would be recovered and truth made less obscure.[40]

Production of "The Philosophy of Jesus" and "The Life and Morals of Jesus" put sentiment above scholarship and aided Jefferson in defining his own brand of Christian morality. He did not care to interpret the Bible. Though he was convinced that the universe could not have been created and maintained but by an intelligence, a "superintending power" capable of "design" and "consummate skill," he did not articulate what heaven meant to him, if anything. This is not to suggest that because Jefferson's most prominent position with respect to religion was in separating it from politics and promoting tolerance, he was indifferent to what faith meant to the individual. He, like other leading thinkers of the Enlightenment, adopted the approach that religion (as any other moral sentiment) should originate from active thought; it was not "a matter of mere receptivity," a strange, supernatural power which struck a person and produced conviction. Religion was the opposite of dogma.[41]

The power of reason alone could draw Thomas Jefferson to the infinite, as he himself once suggested to his nephew Peter Carr: "Fix reason firmly in her seat, and call to her tribunal every fact, every opinion. Question with boldness even the existence of a god; because, if there be one, he must more approve the homage of reason, than that of blindfolded fear." Then, after introducing his nephew to the historical Livy, Tacitus, and Bible and "a personage called Jesus," he concluded with an open mind: "If you find reason to believe there is a god, a consciousness that you are acting under his eye, and that he approves you, will be a vast additional incitement. If that there be a future state, the hope of a happy existence in that increases the appetite to deserve it; if that Jesus was also a god, you will be comforted by a belief of his aid and love."[42]

The Greek inscription that Jefferson had carved onto Patty's tombstone in 1782, this most poignant symbol of his love and loss, was in the voice of the deceased, who yet remembered ("even in the house of Hades") the one left behind. It was Jefferson's fantasy, then, if not belief, that the deceased could somehow retain thoughts of the surviving loved one. A fascination with mortality and the question of an afterlife returned again to his thoughts, at least briefly, in 1801, as he wrote the Reverend Isaac Story from the President's House: "The laws of nature have witheld from us the means of physical knowledge of the country of spirits and revelation has, for reasons unknown to us, chosen to leave us in the dark as we were. When I was young I was fond of speculations which seemed to promise some insight into that hidden country, but . . . I have for very many years ceased to read or think concerning them." It is possible to infer from Jefferson's words that having put away Sherlock and his Commonplace Book, he hoped still for a "hidden country" which contained sensation; but this was merely his hope. He could convince himself only of a passage to a kind of peace. At the age of seventy-five, he wrote Adams of his hoped-for heaven, a place where after slipping from "our sorrows and suffering bodies," we "ascend in essence to an ecstatic meeting with the friends we have loved and lost and whom we shall still love and never lose again." But in what "essence," he did not suggest. Five years later he phrased similar thoughts to the same correspondent with the help of a political metaphor, awaiting "with more readiness than reluctance" the next world and the reconvening of Congress "with our antient Colleagues," who would award Jefferson and his friend Adams "the seal of approbation" for their earthly activities, a "Well done, good and faithful servants."[43]

Physical deterioration made these notions more and more welcome. To Adams in 1814 he employed the metaphor of the human body as a time-conscious machine: "But our machines have now been running for 70. or 80. years, and we must expect that, worn as they are, here a pivot, there a wheel, now a pinion, next a spring, will be giving way: and however we may tinker them up for awhile, all will at length surcease motion." Nine more years passed, and the theme of disintegration was repeated often in their correspondence. Still wearing down but not yet worn out, Jefferson at eighty told the now eighty-nine-year-old Adams that "while writing to you, I lose the sense of these things [physical impairments], in the recollection of antient times, when youth and health made happiness out of every thing." They were left, he suggested, seeking ways "to get rid of our heavy hours until the friendly hand of death shall rid us of all at once." And Adams signed off his reply, "J.A. In the 89 year of his age still too fat to last much longer."[44]

Having endured the deaths of so many over the years, Jefferson was ever conscious of life's inevitable processes, but he reacted to the grief that the living faced much more than he worried about mortality itself. Jefferson's most enduring statement about his own life and memory can be found in his arrangement of the Monticello graveyard. Margaret Bayard Smith described the scene as one of intense solitude: "A rude stone wall encloses a small square, left in a state of nature, full of forest trees and rocks and wild plants." Jefferson had placed horizontal slabs above the coffins of his wife and daughter, in parallel positions; between them his own central marker would point up. The obelisk, of his own design, symbolizes Jefferson's reaching from the mountaintop to the sky, an upward movement, future-directed, decidedly hopeful. It seems of more than passing significance that Jefferson's mother, who died in 1776, lies well off to the side of this planned configuration, remote from the family circle, while boyhood friend Dabney Carr (d.

1773) and Jefferson's sister Martha (d. 1811), Carr's widow, lie much closer.[45]

His 1820 letter to Maria Cosway, reporting yet again on his "stiffened" wrist, dislocated in Paris so many years before, was a nostalgic exercise filled with funerary images yet suggestive of unknown possibilities. He mourned "our former coterie — dead, diseased, and dispersed. But *'tout ce qui est différé n'est pas perdu.'* [all that is postponed is not lost] says the French proverb, and the religion you so sincerely profess tells us that we shall meet again." Allowing that he was ready to be the next to pass on, Jefferson asserted, "For after one's friends are all gone before them, and our faculties leaving us too, one by one, why wish to linger in mere vegetation, as a solitary trunk in a desolate field, from which all its former companions have disappeared." Believing this might be his parting letter to her (it was not), he closed by wishing her health and happiness, as "the last and warmest wishes of an unchangeable friend."[46]

THE FIFTIETH FOURTH

IN FEBRUARY 1826 Jefferson wrote his thirty-three-year-old grandson, Thomas Jefferson Randolph, that though he had suffered in life less "affliction" than most men and had "no complaint against the world which has sufficiently honored me," he would leave his daughter Martha, "the cherished companion of my early life, and nurse of my age, and her children," in financial ruin. To alleviate debt he had sold his vast personal library to the Library of Congress in 1815, but the combination of loans, drought, and a note imprudently endorsed so that friend Wilson Cary Nicholas could borrow from the bank ensured that Jefferson could not fulfill his obligations. "I should not care were life to end with the line I am writing, were it not that I may be of some avail to the family." Three days after this tormented letter, Jefferson wrote again to his grandson, but briefly: "Bad news, my dear Jefferson, as to your sister Anne. She expired about half an hour ago. I have been so ill for several days that I could not go to see her till this morning, and found her speechless and insensible. . . . Heaven seems to be overwhelming us with every form of misfortune, and I expect your next will give me the *coup de grâce.*" Anne, the eldest grandchild, was thirty-five when she gave birth prematurely and never recovered. Hers had been a bittersweet life, a beloved first grandchild, so closely attended in her emotional and educational development. But she had married Charles Bankhead, an abusive alcoholic, who on one occasion stabbed Anne's brother Jefferson in the hip and arm during a scuffle in Charlottesville. Anne remained with this dangerous and unpredictable man, though her grandfather believed that he deserved to be incarcerated. His doctor recorded that at the moment Jefferson accepted his granddaughter's fate, "it is impossible to imagine more poignant distress than was exhibited by him. He shed tears, and abandoned himself to every evidence of intense grief."[47]

He was weakened by diarrhea, which had once during his presidency caused him to solicit Dr. Rush for a remedy. In March 1826 he composed his will, giving the Pantops estate to Maria's surviving son, Francis Eppes, gold watches to his other grandchildren, and a "gold-mounted walking staff of animal horn, as a token of the cordial and affectionate friendship," to James Madison. He also gave freedom to "my good servants," carpenter John Hemings, glazier Burwell (who often accompanied his master on journeys), and blacksmith Joe Fossett, with the necessary tools to succeed at their trades; and to the first he apprenticed Madison and Eston Hemings, each to be freed at the age of twenty-one. To grandson Jefferson Randolph, Jefferson confided all his correspondence files, separated into two collections: family letters and others. (Letters received were filed alphabetically, copies of letters sent filed chronologically.) It is not precisely known when Jefferson designed the obelisk to mark his grave ("to be of coarse stone"), but the paper on which the directions for his monument were written contained, folded up inside, the scrap on which he had conceived Patty's tombstone inscription.[48]

Facing the final bleak prospect in his life, losing Monticello, Jefferson was slowly giving way. In April, Martha Jefferson Randolph wrote her daughter Ellen: "To my father the shock was as we foresaw dreadful. He said he had lived too long, that his death would be an advantage to the family." Grandson Jefferson Randolph had assured him that, on the contrary, his death would be "a calamity of *frightful* magnitude, that his life was as necessary to the *interests* of his grandchildren and [Martha herself], as it was precious to our hearts." Martha vowed to do her utmost to retain "undisturbed possession of Monticello during his precious life."[49]

In the last weeks Jefferson Randolph listened to his grandfather speak of the inevitable. "I am like an old watch," said the dying Jefferson, "with a pinion worn here, and a wheel there, until it can go no longer." On June 29 Virginia writer Henry Lee stopped by. "My emotions at approaching *Jefferson's dying bed,* I cannot describe," he later wrote. "There he was extended, feeble, prostrate; but the fine and clear expression of his countenance not all obscured. At the first glance he recognized me, and his hand and voice at once saluted me. The energy of his grasp, and the spirit of his conversation, were such as to make me hope he would yet rally." But Jefferson Randolph knew better. His grandfather's mind recurred to scenes of the Revolution. Thoughts of the new University of Virginia led its dying rector to suppose that James Madison, whose wisdom and virtues he once more touted, would succeed him in that position. He interviewed each of the grandchildren who were present, urging them one last time to practice virtue. Emerging suddenly from a sleep, Jefferson at one point imagined that he had heard the name of the Reverend Frederick Hatch, a local minister. "I have no objection to see him, as a kind and good neighbor," he told his grandson, the closest Jefferson came to desiring solace from a man of religion.[50]

Jefferson Randolph was with Dr. Robley Dunglison at his grandfather's bedside near the end, as the patriarch passed in and out of consciousness, asking whether it was yet the Fourth of July. Shortly before, Randolph had sent down a note to his wife, at the nearby Tufton estate: "My poor grandfather . . . his countenance & breathing . . . he refused last night to take anything and is evidently anxious for death, and we are looking on in momentary hope of seeing him relieved." Then, on July 2: "After passing a very good night; this morning my dear grandfather began to give unequivocal indication of approaching dissolution. He sank rapidly for some time and has since remained stationary, nearly sensible, occasionally, we look from hour to hour to a close to the scene. My mother perfectly conscious of his situation, I hope will bear it. I wish you could come up, with none but Virginia and Mary [two of the other grandchildren] with her. I think your presence might be serviceable."[51]

Thomas Jefferson had his wish granted to survive until Tuesday, July 4, 1826, fiftieth anniversary of the Declaration of Independence. He died just after noon, and John Adams followed him a few hours later. Jefferson had directed his daughter on July 2 to a drawer in which he had placed a final message for her. He titled his poem "A death-bed Adieu. Th:J. to MR."

Life's visions are vanished, it's dreams are no more.
Dear friends of the bosom, why bathed in tears?
I go to my fathers; I welcome the shore,
which crowns all my hopes, or which buries my cares.
Then farewell my dear, my lov'd daughter, Adieu!
The last pang of life is in parting from you!
Two Seraphs await me, long shrouded in death:
I will bear them your love on my last parting breath

Pasted at the bottom of the piece of paper is a printed line in Latin: "Heu! quanto minus est cum reliquis versari quam tui meminisse." [Alas! How much less a thing it is to abide with those who remain than to remember you.] The motto, perhaps cut from a newspaper, derived from a memorial urn inscription on the farm of the English poet William Shenstone. It was presumably Martha (in conjunction with son-in-law Nicholas Trist) who appended this clipping to the adieu, in effect a reply to her late father.[52]

The sentiment Jefferson chose at the end of his life resembles the passage from Sterne that he and Patty had shared on her deathbed. Indeed, the "Two Seraphs" who awaited him were his departed wife and younger daughter. Just as the days and hours had once flown by like clouds of a windy day for Patty, never to return, now, for her husband, life offered no further dreams. As a public man and as a family man he was at heart fulfilled with all he had accomplished, with nothing left to grieve but separation from his daughter Martha, the remaining link to his constructive beginnings and to the years he had spent with Patty.

The Grieving Optimist

UNLIKE HAMILTON AND Burr and the many like them, Thomas Jefferson did not live for politics above all else. He regarded friendship, especially old friendship, as something above the fray, bigger than political ambition, to be prized for its sturdiness in an imperfect world where human weakness was always evident, where disease ravaged communities and stole loved ones without warning. It is hard to exaggerate the powerlessness that was constantly reinforced by the proximity and imminence of death. The tone of John Page's 1788 letter to Jefferson, then in Paris, underscores this reality. After relating "the long Indisposition, and at length the Death, of my beloved Wife" at the opening of his letter, he closed it several pages later by bringing his friend up-to-date on other losses. John Paradise (recently introduced to Page via a letter from Jefferson) had "lately received a severe Shock by the Account of his Daughter's Death in England. Mr. Paradise was a great Relief to Mr. Wyth[e] who had lost his Lady. Mentioning Mr. Wyth[e]'s loss reminds me of the many Husbands who have been bereaved of their Wives in the Course of a Year. Mr. Harrison of Brandon, his Namesake of Richmond, R. Bolling of Petersburg, Mr. Carter of Nomony, and St. Ge[orge]. Tucker mourn with Mr. Wyth[e] and myself our similar Fate."[53] The young Jefferson experienced the poignancy of friendship and love with the loss of his wife and the deaths of his father as a young teen, a favorite sister at twenty-two, and his best friend Dabney Carr just as he turned thirty. That "virtuous suffering" Hugh Blair extolled in his dissertation on Ossian went far in providing Jefferson with a lifelong appreciation for affectionate ties among friends. The "joy of grief" was useful in identifying those wrenching feelings which were shared by many, in understanding (if not banishing) pain, and in achieving eventual catharsis. By acknowledging his vulnerability in letters, Jefferson indulged his feelings of anguish without becoming absorbed in self-pity. He honed his ability to perceive others' hopes and forebodings at the same time as he discerned (if he could not overcome) his own fears.

Letter writing was the chief means of shortening time and distance. As Jefferson opened one letter to Eliza House Trist, "Unable to converse with my friends in person, I am happy when I do it in black and white." Later on the same page: "The happiest moments it [my heart] knows are those in which it is pouring forth it's affections to a few esteemed characters. I will pray you to write me often. I wish to know that you enjoy health and that you are happy."[54] Jefferson wrote in search of health and happiness, his own and those he cared for. To John Page he combined striking images of friendship and loss: "When you and I look back on the country over which we have passed, what a field of slaughter does it exhibit! Where are all the friends who entered it with us, under all the inspiring energies of health and hope?" To James Madison he was artful in his praise of the new Constitution: "It is a good canvas, on which some strokes only want retouching," the addition of a bill of rights. To Madison, too, he vented his frustration, as in the accident of his opening the *Rights of Man* controversy: "I tell [Adams] freely that he is a heretic, but certainly never meant to step into a

public newspaper with that in my mouth."[55] Having something unde-
sirable "in my mouth" can be construed in terms of the health crises
that so often occasioned an eighteenth-century familiar letter; this time
the cause of Jefferson's indisposition was the word that was physically
debilitating and needed, somehow, to be removed. On both an intellectual and emotional level, from both Head and Heart, Jefferson thus
recognized an enduring need for a network of correspondents to sustain his vital energy and to serve as outlets for him when faced with
problems. He always seemed to have an Eliza Trist when he felt sentimental, or a John Page when he wished to indulge in nostalgic thought,
or a James Madison when he was compelled to state a position or find
his way out of a controversy.

Politics is the obvious example of his failure to find uncontentious
growth and harmony. But in private life, too, Jefferson was systematically frustrated in his pursuit of perfect love and productive nature that
would not wither and die. Paradoxically, his pursuit of happiness derived at once from expansiveness and containment, from self-
cultivation and self-restraint, from the idea of virtue and actual slave
labor. The grieving optimist shared fanciful and even delicate words
with women, but not (as much as late twentieth-century voyeurs would
prefer) his physical passion and desire to rekindle love.

Here, the thematic contradiction of expansiveness and containment
in Jefferson's life becomes more self-evident. Physical intimacy with a
woman represents the continuance of being beyond the self, thoroughly sharing the chemical components of the self with another. The
self is nakedly displayed and then in a sense dispossessed; it is similar
to giving oneself to God, a force and influence beyond the command
of the ego. Jefferson had great reluctance to engage in this form of self-
dispossession.

He once wrote to Angelica Church that public affairs need not "agi-
tate" her. "The tender breasts of young ladies were not formed for political convulsion," he asserted, "and the French ladies miscalculate much
of their own happiness when they wander from the true field of their
influence into that of politicks."[56] Because women offered him turmoil
and distress — made him feel, above all, vulnerable — he was only comfortable thinking of a woman relegated to that place in society where,
no matter what her talents, she could not interfere with the male re-
gime.[57] Men were charged with striving to calm the political waters,
women with ensuring domestic calm; the two roles were distinct. A

wife (as he often reminded his daughters) should be deferential, should sacrifice when necessary, so that all within her circle would love her. She was qualified to read and teach "moral tales" and only that poetry which was "useful for forming style and taste." She should avoid "the inordinate passion prevalent for novels. . . . When this poison infects the mind, it destroys its tone and revolts it against wholesome reading." The result is "a bloated imagination, sickly judgment."[58]

Some have speculated that this desire for control over the potentially explosive passions of women can be traced to Jefferson's unsatisfying relationship with his mother, who is scarcely mentioned in his memoir. When Peter Jefferson died in 1757, she inherited a life interest in the Shadwell estate and thereby exercised control over her son's "patriarchal resources," to use Kenneth Lockridge's expression.[59] Jefferson went on to mold his eldest daughter, Martha, into a strong and reliable woman who was always wise and always knew her place. As an eleven-year-old staying in Philadelphia while Jefferson attended Congress in Annapolis, she had received a stern reminder from her father, a widower of one year: "I have placed my happiness on seeing you good and accomplished, and no distress which this world can now bring on me could equal that of your disappointing my hopes."[60] Once the women of his family submitted to his standards, and comfortable in having them thus bound and protected (that is, shorn of power), he was indulgent rather than impatient with any "natural" feminine weaknesses he observed. With his daughter Maria and, it seems safe to presume, his wife Patty, he indulged and protected, expecting then that he could thereby rationalize his public activity.

The curious part of this calculus, though, is Jefferson's conflict over the allotment of time between the private desires and responsibilities that his Heart embraced and the public participation that others (and his Head, and sometimes even his Heart) came to expect of him. He needed to be needed, to be considered by his family a reliable provider of physical sustenance and emotional support, to be considered by his country a beacon of republican hopefulness. He professed to desire the removal of the second obligation, but public expectations long remained a usable rationale; he admitted that he was miserable when out of public life from 1794 to 1796. He thrived on what he hated — what his pronounced preference for bookish detachment dictated against, but what his drive for success commanded him to engage in — political combat.

If Jefferson did not outwardly slight himself for the selfishness of private pursuits, he demanded moral consistency beyond the capacity of "ordinary" people. What he referred to as "unalloyed pleasure" eluded him until he was able to put public life to rest. The man most renowned in American history for the pursuit of happiness could not pursue happiness without feeling stress. The fatherless Jefferson, projecting manly self-sufficiency, apparently tried to repress his own need for love by offering it, in a fashion, to others in need. This would explain his tender regard for women who were willing to receive consolation when left by their husbands (emotionally, if not actually) to fend for themselves.

The widow Martha Wayles Skelton, Eliza House Trist, and Maria Cosway all fit this profile. After his loss of the first, who needed him and whom he could not save from months of suffering before death, he repeated the act of saving through consolation, though without sustaining the intense feelings Patty had awakened in him. In this, Jefferson again resembled Sterne, who had fallen in love with his wife while she was suffering from consumption and "courted her with a sentimental gallantry." Jefferson upheld the myth by writing fantasy into his letters, imagining bringing unfulfilled women to Monticello for inspiration, if not resuscitation. As Sterne's biographer has written, "The essential of sentimental love as Sterne reinvented it [and Jefferson perpetuated it] was to *jouer des sentiments,* to toss them back and forth, to give and receive expressions of sympathy."[61]

But for Jefferson himself? He could not, alas, delight in love. His Head planned his 1787 spring tour of southern France in effect to overcome the expressive Heart, to flee the allure of Maria Cosway by providing tasks for Jefferson's pen and presenting objects to divert or replace his feelings for the woman of his imagination. He tried the same strategy on his romancing protégé William Short, whom he urged to take a similar journey in 1788–89 rather than dwell upon his feelings for the married duchess.[62] (Curiously, while Sterne traveled to evade Death, Jefferson traveled to evade Love.) Perhaps Jefferson knew no more pure delight than escape into a foreign world of the imagination, Homer's Greece. It was a distant, heroic, poetic life. The lifelong appeal of Ossian and Jefferson's refusal to confront the fraud of its contemporary author suggest again that the creative reach of Jefferson's pen is the best guide to an understanding of his inner conflict.

Love for family was certainly no illusion. But it was a linchpin which held together a precarious state of existence. The mountaintop was meant by its developer to be a sturdy overlook, a rich source of natural inspiration. When Patty died, she proved to her husband how fragile his dreams in fact were. He literally lost consciousness — fainted for several minutes — and could not regain his self-possession for weeks. The devastating loss equated with a loss of balance at Monticello, a loss of power for Thomas Jefferson, a loss of control over life. For once his books, his thoughts, could not so easily carry him forward.

As a result, this already self-contained man became ever more afraid of his own passion. He searched for peace and safety. To look for a solution through God was pointless for one who refused to countenance mysticism; all mystical experience was, for Jefferson, the same as forfeiting control. When he allowed himself to feel for a woman again, he never lost control; nor was he as pained when he consciously tempered his feelings. The lovely Maria Cosway plainly stimulated him, but he successfully commanded self-restraint. Indeed, though she appears to have possessed a passion to have others love her, this was not necessarily accompanied by physical passion. Her life was marked by flight from the symbols of physical love. She bore Richard Cosway a daughter nine years after having married him, and only months after Jefferson left Paris. But she stayed for more than two years in Italy — away from her husband and daughter — before returning to England, where the little girl died at the age of six. Tellingly, while Mrs. Cosway grieved in solitude, Mr. Cosway "romanced with his usual veracity." It is generally believed that Maria Cosway suffered from depression, both before and after her acquaintance with Jefferson in Paris. There seems little doubt that hers was a loveless marriage, and that she was most relieved from the stresses of life when she found the safety and repose of a convent.[63] If she ever entertained the thought of reviving herself through such a life as the romancing Virginian offered, surely, in the end, he would not have allowed it to be. It is hard to imagine a permanent place on Jefferson's mountain for a woman of discord — married or not — a woman who could not settle easily into domestic activity, who liked the sound of church bells.

Jefferson, at the end of his life, may have allowed himself to acknowledge his need for a woman, the one most faithful, his daughter, whom he called the "nurse of my age." If his reason weakened at all at this late stage, it was in his becoming a prisoner to nostalgic feeling. Reason, after all, can function as an aid to the imagination. Did the balance finally tip in favor of the latter? Was he indulging in a rhetorical experiment for others, a technique to charm his grandchildren, when he claimed almost to hear the "sweet voice" of his sister Jane, who died young, carried by "some sacred air" in church? Might he, as a founding father, have come back to the creative principle — of life and liberation — in his late images of death? Did death come to his mind as the life-giving sun that "gilded" his mountaintop? Did it take the form of the spirits that had taunted him in the poetry he read as a young man? Or was death, for Jefferson, the one prophesiable pathway to knowledge of the infinite sea he sometimes conjured in letters? (His "deathbed Adieu" to Martha, at the end of the voyage of life, was to carry him to the welcome "shore" of his fathers.) It is fancy, it is pure speculation to ask these questions, to suggest that such thoughts crossed Jefferson's mind, for he did not share thoughts so carelessly or in such romantic imagery with the correspondents of his late years.

Conclusion

By the time of America's independence, letter writing had become many things. It was a political necessity for those who wished to achieve united action, a social form for elites seeking to maintain and expand valuable connections, but, most affectingly, a personal form to carry news to friends and loved ones, to announce births, marriages, deaths, journeys, and changes of heart.

For Jefferson letter writing was a medium for creative experiments of the mind, which served as an emotional release during personal crises. He was, as one commentator has written, "a farmer of the word who cultivated not just a style of grace but a habit of turning words over in his mind."[1] He was a letter writer whose naturalness of manner was comparable to that of the eminent wits of Augustan England known for their conversational prowess; he showed, like them, an impressive variety of attitudes and tones. But he was not the unconventional letter writer that Laurence Sterne was. Sterne treated familiar correspondence as a word game or, at times, a private joke in which he applied a similar kind of that "illogical association" which pervaded his fiction.[2] Unlike Sterne, Jefferson found no humor at all in the melancholy details of his own life. He could borrow from Sterne the license to be informal and imaginative, confining himself, though, to expressions his gallant Heart / erudite Head could defend with a clear conscience. As aggressively as Sterne used words without undue fear of personal recrimination from unsympathetic readers, Jefferson was sensitive to the damage his freely spun words could do to him even when addressed to those sympathetic to his personal and political causes. His pen provoked him; line by line he might seem desirous of revealing, but, ever on the verge, he checked himself in anticipation of the undesired consequences of self-exposure.

Malvin R. Zirker, Jr., has written of Samuel Richardson that he "found in letters a way to *create* for himself an emotional life otherwise unavailable to him." The fiction he composed in letters as "an artistic medium for representing real life" enabled him to develop "otherwise dormant aspects of his own personality, [and to tap] emotional resources probably largely unavailable to him in direct confrontation with other personalities."[3] The generally reserved Jefferson had too tight a

273

grip on his public obligations to confuse any airiness in his familiar letters—for example, metaphorically taking flight—with the substance of his daily life; but he, too, appears to have developed dormant aspects of his personality through the emotional release occasioned by letter writing. It is that quality which this book has consistently emphasized.

Jefferson's conventionality did not detract from the freshness and power of his message. Convention cannot entirely cancel invention, just as rigidly defined principles of conduct did not confine his imagination. As Patricia Spacks has written of eighteenth-century life and literature, the imagination led people to "remarkable freedoms of action and narration beneath the accepted concealments of convention." Imagination, Spacks has shown, brings triumph to Robinson Crusoe, who achieves self-mastery on his island by imagining it; Richardson's Pamela, obsessed with the importance of her own writing, takes her inner fantasies and, through sheer determination to live out a moral drama, does so; Tristram Shandy obtains what he seeks from his world of the imagination, writing a story and winning a kind of control over his unconventional reality. The imagination produces for eighteenth-century fictional characters a more stable self and a more powerful self.[4] Jefferson, though not a creator of fiction, brought his imagination to writing and friendship; he mediated between self and society and found the great values of his own life. In the process, because of the values his public writings express, he was nationally hailed for having captured a spirit many shared but few could as ably articulate. It was a liberal and effective use of words, not rigid conformity, that distinguished him in his time.

Bruce Redford has observed that at its most successful "epistolary discourse accomplishes something even more inventive [than creating a context]: it fashions a distinctive world at once internally consistent, vital, and self-supporting." Bernard Bailyn has termed Jefferson's writing remarkable not for having introduced anything radically new but for having raised prose to a higher power without departing from eighteenth-century conventions.[5] Jefferson's craft allowed his natural judgment and reasoning, invention, and versatility to coexist. In the act of writing, whether a public or private document, he found fortitude and inspiration: an inner meaning which was, for this generally unreligious man, something just short of salvation.

There is no question that Jefferson knew the familiar letter as intimate conversation, in addition to an instrument of Ciceronian ethos, and knew its emotive power well. Amid the bitter struggle that preceded the election of 1800, he wrote from Philadelphia to his elder daughter Martha, then twenty-seven and the mother of four, in Virginia: "I ought oftener, my dear Martha, to receive your letters, for the very great pleasure they give me, and especially when they express your affections for me. For though I cannot doubt them, yet they are among those truths which tho' not doubted we love to hear repeated. Here too they serve like gleams of light, to chear a dreary scene where envy, hatred, malice, revenge, and all the worse passions of men are marshalled to make one another as miserable as possible. I turn from this with pleasure to contrast it with your fire side, where the single evening I passed at it was worth more than ages here." This was more than merely a reinforcement of thoughts he had conveyed to her in 1784 when he chastised his child tenderly from the Continental Congress: "Your long silence had induced me almost to suspect you had forgotten me and the more so as I had desired you to write to me every week." Only the most cynical would consider Jefferson's words formal or calculating in associating Martha with "gleams of light" or doubt that he honestly ached inside as the object of constant political attacks. His hyperbolic evaluation of the "single evening" with his daughter and the "ages" of political misery in Philadelphia may be conventional writing, but this does not dilute the emotion-laden message he intended to convey.[6]

Back in 1784, he had taken leave of Congress and had carried eleven-year-old Martha to France with him. He was obliged at that time to leave Maria with her maternal aunt. A year passed before he and Martha were secure in Paris, and Jefferson began to wrestle with the problem of exposing his six-year-old to an ocean voyage. He confronted his dilemma in letters. To Elizabeth Wayles Eppes: "No event in your life has put it into your power to conceive how I feel when I reflect that such a child, and so dear to me, is to cross the ocean, is to be exposed to all the sufferings and risks, great and small, to which a situation on board a ship exposes every one. I drop my pen at the thought — but she must come." Jefferson, figuratively dropping his pen, presented his reader an image of a man who regularly brought his Heart to his writing desk. Indeed, one month earlier he had written of his "present anxiety" over Maria to Eliza House Trist: "My wishes are fixed, but my resolution is wavering."[7]

Different letters, of course, expressed different intentions. Those designed to enlarge civic activity, to influence, were more self-conscious and less emotionally revealing. Jefferson's personal letters, lacking the overt posturing of documents that he might have expected to circulate, retained a spontaneous spirit and effusive expression. It was only as a former president constantly solicited for advice or assistance that Jefferson began to "suffer . . . under the persecution of letters." In his seventies he complained to Adams of "drudging at the writing table." To Dr. Benjamin Waterhouse he explained the lack of "epistolary industry" as an "aversion [that] has been growing on me for a considerable time," now, at seventy-five, "almost insuperable." But even in the final decade of his life, he became animated in putting forth freewheeling ideas about creative word usage, which he had culled from a lifetime of writing. Again to Adams: "Dictionaries are but the depositories of words already legitimated by usage. Society is the work-shop in which new ones are elaborated. When an individual uses a new word, if ill-formed it is rejected by society, if wellformed, adopted, and, after due time, laid up in the depository of dictionaries. And if, in this process of sound neologisation, our transatlantic brethren shall not choose to accompany us, we may furnish, after the Ionians, a second example of a colonial dialect improving on it's primitive." He replied to a grammarian whose book he had received that he was "no friend to purism." Because English had proliferated "from the latitude of London into every climate of the globe," the language could never be bound to the strictures of Johnson's *Dictionary*. English would contribute to the expansion of knowledge "by encouraging and welcoming new compositions of its elements."[8]

This was the optimistic and sweet-sounding Jefferson speaking. The politically canny Jefferson employed language according to the necessity he perceived. In post-Revolutionary America, defining words for the public accorded power and thus sustained political controversy. Both parties of the 1790s were equally bent on mastering the human passions when, for example, they interpreted the word *liberty*. Notions of security and justice were implicit in the meaning of "liberty," which ultimately hinged on the question of who in society deserved how much of a political voice. Madison, Hamilton, and Jay's *Federalist* correlated the body politic and the human mind, interpreting the meaning without fully defining the boundaries of "virtue" or "reason." The founding fathers could always be certain that "passion" and "self-interest" were undeniably present in all human beings, but what choice constituted "wisdom"? Who should govern the Republic?⁹

Federalists believed in a national honor which could only be preserved through the establishment of a reasonable order led by an elite corps of public-spirited men, a "natural aristocracy." They feared anarchy disguised as "democracy." The Jeffersonian Republicans feared the corrupt tendencies of "natural aristocrats" who would claim too much power and divorce themselves from the interests of the people.¹⁰ "Liberty" could mean either "security" under prudent Federalists, trustees of the public good, or the abstract "voice of the people," a more inclusive body of citizens whom Republicans presumed to claim for themselves. Given the possible range of meaning that words had, their prejudiced use could have dire consequences, signaling a Republican fear of the excess of security and order—the tyranny of a self-perpetuating ruling class—or a Federalist fear of the excess of freedom—chaos and mob rule. This sensitivity reflected a common belief that the American people were susceptible to the misrepresentation of words. In such an environment Jefferson, self-described "friend to neology," sought to reinvent "republican" as "Republican." He could not be swayed from his belief that the Federalists had corrupted the literal principles of 1776 and had become themselves the "British party." In expanding the American language, he was knowingly or unknowingly responsible for exaggerating party conflict. We might say that he "corrupted" language owing to an excessive fear that policy (capitulation to British power) was the same as, or would lead inexorably to, abandonment of the Constitution. He hoped that as the American people adopted the sense he brought to critical words, they would accept his interpretation of political affairs.

High Federalists did not respond to Jeffersonian idiom because they had their own. They did not understand Jefferson as a moderate man who would seek to preserve order and harmony in government as he did in his private pursuits. They overreacted to what seemed obscure in his language and translated it into an advocacy of Revolutionary French terror. They suspected everything he did, every statement he issued. The popular press, in particular, exacerbated the differences inherent in Republican and Federalist use of language. Even after Jefferson's death, upon his grandson's publication of his memoir and four volumes of letters, the opposition picked apart his language and presented the case for a self-promoting, history-mangling Jefferson who had opposed the federal Constitution but "with an adroitness that marked all his movements as the head of a party, soon devised the more captivating [than Anti-Federalist] title of republican for his adherents to adopt as their watchword and countersign."[11]

Clearly, Jefferson felt that his personality was conducive to reasonable, frank discussion among reasonable men. Ironically, both he and Hamilton were alike in their self-assessments, convinced that reason was theirs. They never thought themselves facile in their reasoning. Jefferson judged (and presumed everyone else would judge) Hamilton to be combative in nature. Hamilton's realism caused him to appeal to the self-interest of his colleagues in government; the spirit of making money would eventually make America great. Jefferson's optimism urged the removal of strict social distinctions, extolled government by consent, the broadening of citizens' rights, and the careful scrutiny of public officials on the basis of their disinterestedness and benevolence: the values of 1776.[12]

To Jefferson, American alone was not effete, was fresh, unsullied by institutionalized rivalries of the kind that made Europe an incestuous, bloody battleground. Hamilton, he presumed, would have America return to that dysfunctional family. Jefferson despaired of Europe. He had witnessed firsthand the opening scenes of the French Revolution, decried the tyranny of Bonaparte, and believed that bloodbaths would have to precede republicanization.[13] Aside from the fast-vanishing philosophes, the muted voices of brave and enlightened intellectuals like the pro-American Condorcet, the Old World was socially degenerative, spiritually stunted. In contrast, Peter Jefferson had been a surveyor in largely untrodden frontier. The inherited view of boundaries, physical and sensory, provided his son with strong conviction; he knew what he wanted his Republic to become. It was already diverse and would remain so. Acquisition of the vast Louisiana territory from France during Jefferson's first term and then the Lewis and Clark expedition supported the vision of a peacefully expanding, liberty-loving agrarian nation. America's vigor and natural genius, Jefferson insisted, were best applied to the manly exploitation of productive land rather than to the sterile love of making paper profits.[14]

Why, then, could Jefferson not find a place in his boundless, productive America for emancipated blacks? It is interesting that in *Notes on Virginia*, assuming among his select readership a wide familiarity with

Tristram Shandy, Jefferson chose to demonstrate black inferiority by belittling the just published epistles of Ignatius Sancho, a correspondent of Sterne. Sancho, who identified with the "honest corporal" (Sterne's character Trim) and was "touch'd" to the heart by the *Sermons,* nonetheless, in Jefferson's estimation, lost proper epistolary force "when he affects a Shandean fabrication of words." His letters did "more honour to the heart than the head." His imagination was "extravagant" without the accompaniment of "sober reasoning." Though Sterne met and befriended the slave-born writer in London and addressed him as "good-hearted Sancho," Jefferson took this man as an example of a letter writer who had failed to find the proper balance between sentiment and reason. Jefferson was, in an odd way, covetous of his Sterne. Surely he would not have criticized Sterne himself for an excess of imagination, but in deploring Sancho's lack of taste (or, crudely, the lack of a reasoning Head), Jefferson was implying that cultural refinement as he knew it — self-restraint — was the prerequisite of superior letter writing, a fuller appreciation of Sterne, and, ultimately, complete and equal participation in the America he dreamed about.[15]

In disparaging the inherent capacity of the black to rise to a level warranting social equality, Jefferson merely selected the knowledge of his day that comported with empirical reason. He considered that his was a scientific or philosophic and not an emotional response to the race issue. He did not consciously feel anything beyond the compassion required for a naturally superior white man with eighteenth-century values, or sensibility. Jefferson, of course, did not anticipate a twentieth-century sensibility. He was, then, not tormented enough by racial injustice to risk his political career on this issue. Slavery, in the abstract, was an evil; Jefferson wrote Edward Coles in 1814 that an abolitionist movement would "do honor to both the head and heart of the writer [Jefferson himself]."[16] But he did not extend the argument, did not feel a pressing moral requirement to free his own slaves. His logic was augmented, no doubt, by economic pragmatism and the real possibility that he was providing for people who might not survive without so dutiful a master. His only choice (as he understood it, and until southern society was ready to abandon the institution) was between being a just slave owner and an unjust one. Perhaps the most accurate comment on this subject was that of John Quincy Adams, who stated, "Mr. Jefferson had not the spirit of martyrdom."[17]

Jefferson did not feel any pronounced desire to be liberated from the social constraints of the Virginia planter, instead to be the most learned, the most cosmopolitan, the most honorable one he could be, in accordance with the Virginia planters' group self-definition. But there is still more to be ascertained by studying his attitude on the delicate topic of race. In his mind blacks lacked judgment and lived their lives with excess passion. They therefore ought not to be allowed to assimilate with whites, to interbreed. Jefferson wrote in his *Notes* that among other reasons why the races should be separate, "the real distinctions which nature has made [will] produce convulsions which will probably never end but in the extermination of the one or the other race." While the "fine mixtures" of white and Indian comported with natural beauty, the mixing of black and white did not. Blacks were, observably, externally and internally, different. Their secretions produced a "strong and disagreeable odour." Their bravery likely proceeded "from a want of forethought." And significantly, they were "more ardent after their female: but love seems with them to be more an eager desire than a tender delicate mixture of sentiment and sensation. Their griefs are transient. . . . In general, their existence appears to participate more of sensation than reflection."[18] Once again, the sensibility he cultivated in familiar letter writing symbolized Jefferson's self-defining effort to elevate his thoughts, which only a rejection of the coarser instincts (most easily accomplished by disparaging African-Americans) could achieve for him.

To Jefferson there was nothing immoral in sexual desire if it was expressed in an appropriate context. That does not mean he fell (the directional metaphor is one he himself might have considered) into Maria Cosway's arms in the promiscuous atmosphere of Paris. Intellectual passion and the power of his imagination seem to have brought him to the verge of satisfying his physical needs, but the power of his conscience likely constrained him from realizing his private fantasy. Or, if he did indeed succumb to a few moments of unrestrained passion, the consciousness of these acts must have riddled him with guilt, as he returned to a friendship marked by controlled passion.

The married woman allowed him to express tenderness, to remain in touch with sexual energy that he could never entirely suppress. But to succumb to temptation, to physical passion, would have been to fail to remain in possession of the self he cultivated, the moral voice that lectured the younger generation—Peter Carr, John Banister, Jr., and Thomas Jefferson Randolph—on the value of self-control.[19] He would have been acting akin to the judgment-lacking black, whom he considered an inferior human. Entirely aside from his "scientific" denial of blacks' social and intellectual parity with whites, on a moral level he could not have allowed himself to submit to the self-degrading passion some suggest he felt in the presence of a mulatto half sister to his wife on his plantation. If he had not the compulsion to remarry in his forties (to seek a morally acceptable solution to those physical needs of which Maria Cosway's challenge reminded him), then he surely had not the mind to seek such selfish pleasure with one who labored for him.

Jefferson's denial of common attributes among the African and European races was a measure of self-protection, because he feared excess of passion in himself. He was relieved when someone like Madison restrained the "natural effusions" of his creative compulsion to challenge social orthodoxy unrealistically, to become a "visionary" philosopher. But most often, his own Head asserted itself and checked his Heart's desire for intimacy or excess by calling up self-restraining reason. He employed the written word to create meaning and secure order, to justify his politics, to declare salvation for himself. By refusing to submit to his passions, he maintained himself as an ultimately didactic model of integrity.

One then must wonder how a man so devoutly seeking self-consistency and judging others in accordance with his own struggle to moderate his passions could compose words so seemingly spontaneous and so resonating. Three-quarters of a century ago, Carl Becker tackled this problem. "Felicity of expression," he wrote, "certainly Jefferson had that; but one wonders whether he did not perhaps have too much of it." To this historian Jefferson's "placidity, the complacent optimism of his sentiments and ideas," bordered on the "fatuous." Crediting him with candor and humanity, a sensitive nature, and "a mind finely tempered," Becker still yearned to see repeated the homeliness of Franklin, the profound passion he sensed just under the surface in Washington. Jefferson gave forth light but no heat. Why couldn't he lose his temper? Why wouldn't Jefferson bear his soul?[20]

This book has tried to get to the bottom of Becker's plaint, and that of so many capable historians since who have found Jefferson to be inscrutable. The explanation for Jefferson's behavior resides in his lifelong pursuit of friendship and moderation. He bore the responsibilities of a firstborn son without a father to guide him through adolescence, with a mother who apparently did not convey great warmth. He developed a need to see things through. He soaked up the written word, found moral-philosophical grounding, responded to both Enlightenment skepticism and optimism, and pursued a steady course to ensure his place first among the Virginia gentry and then among the cosmopolites. Social success was his first priority in life, though once he had achieved it, he began to feel more profoundly both the torment of contention in public affairs and the corresponding absence of the company of loved ones.

With this practical persuasion—the drive to be successful—came also an appreciation for aesthetics. His imagination took him places that were at the edges of controversy, most notably into the world of Sterne. But Jefferson had early found that life contained enough natural turmoil and produced enough human anxieties, that he wished to avoid intentionally adding to controversy and uncertainty. Though throughout his political career he plainly failed in the attempt to keep key relationships from becoming overheated (and minimized his personal role in this failure), he never failed to embrace republican manners. Reason was meant to lead. At his best Jefferson combined prudence and art. It was politics, principally, that was not conducive to the ideal of gentility, politics that undercut his vision of the harmonious order he maintained on a small scale at Monticello and wished to enlarge by establishing a neighborhood of trusted friends.

Champion of the American Enlightenment, he was not a philosopher, though he had a philosophic mind.[21] He did not paint as Peale did, did not compose clever and satirical bits as Hopkinson did, did not master the universe as Rittenhouse did, did not have medical skills or publish his social views as prodigiously as Rush. He was a competent but far from exceptional violinist. He was a tinkerer who, with the help of his son-in-law, improved on the design of a plow. He was not a genius so much as the quintessential overachiever, the most wide-ranging of all men, the ultimate adapter. If he could not do all of what his philosophic friends could do, that is, invent systems, he could nonetheless absorb himself in detail, converse knowledgeably, and derive inspiration. He understood and appreciated natural history, pure mathematics, art, and literature. That he was yet remarkable and had a creative spark is immediately evident in the house he built for himself and was forever improving.

For Jefferson friendship was a moral and philosophical condition which could only falter if bound too closely with politics, ruptured by public disagreement. He had the happy example of Madison and Monroe, whose breach through his intercession and simply over the course of time repaired itself. He had the unhappy example of George Washington and himself; distanced in the 1790s as a result of Jefferson's feud with Alexander Hamilton and finally estranged in 1797 after the indiscreet publication of the letter to Mazzei, Washington turned his back on Jefferson and died bitter. This was profoundly ironic, for Jefferson had, if not forecast, at least anticipated the possibility of such unhappiness when he wrote cautiously of friendship and politics to Washington years earlier, in 1784: "The way to make friends quarrel is to pit them in disputation under the public eye. An experience of near twenty years has taught me that few friendships stand this test."[22]

But then, there was also the example of his friendship with John Adams, broken by politics and the dramatic election of 1800 only to blossom into a rich correspondence during the last fourteen years of the two men's long lives. The harmonizing side of Jefferson again came through here. As much as he wished to see Marshall's version of history repudiated, he also strove for personal comfort in inducing Adams and himself to appreciate each other's genius, rather than dredging up old antagonisms which would create new misgivings. Jefferson claimed not to have the stomach for thrashing out the details of what he had really intended when he wrote letters on political subjects critical of Adams, letters which were leaked to the newspapers during emotion-filled political contests. He explained: "The renewal of these old discussions, my friend, would be equally useless and irksome. To the volumes then written on these subjects, human ingenuity can add nothing new: and the rather, as lapse of time has obliterated many of the facts. . . . My mind has been long fixed to bow to the judgment of the world, who will judge me by my acts, and will never take counsel from me as to what that judgment shall be."[23]

For his part Adams persisted in an irascible but friendly way of critiquing all kinds of political mischief, past and present. Before turning to questions of religion, he said, "You and I ought not to die, before We have explained ourselves to each other." Jefferson, from this point, moved inexorably into the philosophical, seeking his own peace, understanding, and deliverance. When, in their final years, the political enemies of presidential candidate John Quincy Adams sought once more to publicize damning letters of John Adams, Jefferson forewarned his ancient friend and avowed that no such "outrage" could again "draw a curtain of separation" between them. The "circumstances of the times . . . and the partiality of our friends" had once placed them "in a state of apparent opposition, which some might suppose to be personal also," but they were now well past permitting such "hideous phantoms" to infect their minds. Jefferson, speaking now for both of them, realized that it was human nature to see "false colours under which passion sometimes dresses the actions and motives of others," and yet these were passions which subsided "with time and reflection, dissipating, like mists before the rising sun, and restoring to us the sight of all things in their true shape and colours."[24]

Despite his lingering private bitterness over Federalist harangues, Jefferson dispassionately reported in 1811 to Destutt de Tracy, the living political philosopher he most admired in the world, that the system devised in 1787 indeed worked, that "the tranquil and steady tenor of our single executive, during a course of twenty-two years of the most tempestuous times, . . . gives a rational hope that this important problem is at length solved." In the 1790s, he went on, "the President heard with calmness the opinions and reasons of each, decided the course to be pursued, and kept the government steadily in it, unaffected by the agitation." And in Jefferson's own cabinet "there never arose . . . an instance of an unpleasant thought or word between the members." It was through "conversing and reasoning, so as to modify each other's ideas," that this harmony ensued.[25]

In the history of Cicero's accomplishments that Lucceius was being enjoined to write, the subject himself communicated his preference for the personal over a strict chronology of events. Cicero was convinced that "the uncertain and varied fortunes of a statesman who frequently rises to prominence give scope for surprise, suspense, delight, annoyance, hope, fear." Jefferson, though he tried always to sound mild, reasonable, and accommodating, would hardly have welcomed a history devoted to his consistency and inconsistency as an emotional man. He had been disappointed in Marshall's Washington, of course, as well as Wirt's unrealistic Patrick Henry. He must have anticipated what in fact occurred, that his own life would be chronicled by unremitting antagonists and nostalgic republicans. There were so many Jeffersons to seek in his voluminous writings that he could be adopted by such disparate causes as secession and union, the American Communist party, and Franklin Roosevelt's New Deal. William Jennings Bryan, called the last Jeffersonian, paid an ironic homage at Monticello just before traveling to Dayton, Tennessee, to defend revealed religion against scientific evolution in the celebrated Scopes trial.[26]

Recognizing Jefferson's mutability, historians frequently ask, "Which Jefferson are we talking about?" A story Henry Randall heard firsthand illustrates the point. At Ford's tavern, where the retired Jefferson sometimes stopped while traveling between Monticello and Poplar Forest, a clergyman entered into conversation with a "respectable looking stranger." They first discussed "mechanical operations," which led the clergyman to believe he was talking to an engineer. Then they moved on to agriculture, and he changed his mind: the stranger was a "large farmer." Taking up religion, he next became convinced that he was with a fellow clergyman, though of what persuasion he could not be certain. At ten o'clock the men retired, and in the morning the clergyman asked the landlord who it was that he had conversed with the evening before. When assured that the stranger was Thomas Jefferson, the clergyman was astounded. "I tell you that was neither an atheist nor irreligious man — one of juster sentiments I never met with." Jefferson drew vigorously on a sociable foundation, wide experience, and book learning. He emphasized different interests at different times and appeared amenable to all persuasions but those of religious bigots and unrelenting political enemies.[27]

In this assessment Jefferson seems most like Benjamin Franklin. Yet if the disarming Franklin (judging from his autobiography) was able to confess his pride in the course of charting the good he had been responsible for producing, Jefferson found himself blameless in all things, examining circumstances before self. Generational differences may figure in this comparison. Jefferson was more closely scrutinized, given the greater political sophistication and skepticism of the public he served while he held office. Embracing the power of the written word to support public and private purposes, he was as vivid a writer as his distinguished predecessor, and like Franklin he possessed qualities that charmed the ladies; but he could never be so easily excused for self-conscious calculation in the construction of a self through writing in the way the autobiographical Franklin could. Less able to acknowledge his own cunning, Jefferson was forced to be self-protective; thus he proves ultimately less warmhearted in his self-effacement than Franklin was in his self-promotion.

But Thomas Jefferson remains a standout among the leaders of the American Revolutionary generation who saw themselves and their readers as "mutual participants in an intellectual fraternity, the 'republic of letters.'" They were a young and supple branch of the Enlightenment tree of learning, emotionally charged, contentious friends of varying backgrounds who cultivated a modern political philosophy based on reason and concepts of science, while incorporating classicism into their everyday sense of self. Having imbibed, as a significant part of their collective education, Greek ideas of friendship and poetry and Roman lessons of friendship and epistolography, they communicated with the language and perceived values of a distant past close to their hearts. Resisting the dogmas of church and an oppressive state, they adopted the terms and imagery of Greece and Rome to establish their autonomy, articulate their hopes for humankind, and pronounce wit and sociability among themselves. Jefferson's self-identification as an Epicurean in an 1819 letter to William Short, as a man seeking tranquillity through an ordering of the soul, emerges from this ethos. But whereas the ancient humanists had relied on oratory to create and enlarge a community of mind, the eighteenth century witnessed the ascendancy of its "new" intellectual style through the printed word.[28]

How do we look beyond the apparent stiffness and conventional obscuring of emotion in eighteenth-century language? The answer, as these pages have sought to provide, lies in searching for those clues in language which lead us from the Head to the Heart. While this kind of expression becomes more fully revealed during the romantic age, it is present in preromantic images in the eighteenth century. Jefferson's response to Ossian and to the self-revelation implicit in Sterne, his adoration of uncontained nature, his manipulation of political language, all reveal Heart.

The eighteenth century was rooted in an ordering of life, in mastering the disorder in nature. Such efforts were supported by the physical sciences, by models of mechanical rationality, lists compiled confidently and with unprecedented precision. Much of Jefferson's writing, of course, bears this out. As secretary of state he proposed systematizing coinage and measures of length for the new Republic. As president, while preoccupied with matters of gravity for the nation's future, he assiduously charted the earliest and latest appearance of thirty-seven varieties of vegetables in the Washington market over eight consecutive years.[29] Throughout his life he kept account books filled with seemingly inconsequential payments and instructions to his servants. And, of course, he maintained for forty-three years a massive index of all correspondence he sent and received.

What was hidden (or perhaps we should say repressed), in spite of the rash of inquiry and exploration that undergirded eighteenth-century thought, was a quality of spontaneity in human affairs, what today we more or less describe as the "inner life." This analysis of Jefferson, accordingly, has contended not that Jefferson rebelled against convention, but that he was part of the transition from neoclassical to romantic, from visible to inner life. Indeed, as one scholar has written, classical and romantic are "the systolic and diastolic of the human heart in history," representing alternately the need for order, for synthesis, and for a greater spiritual sustenance.[30]

In her study of social values in Jefferson's Virginia, Jan Lewis has emphasized the pretransition state of mind. She has examined the lives of gentlemen farmers through account books that detail their personal routines and patterns of planting. These journals, which concern the writers' involvement with social inferiors on a daily basis, emphasize external events and are dispassionately presented even when recording sexual activities or the punishments meted out to slaves. Virginians of the mid-eighteenth century, Lewis has concluded, were not exploring human motivations. They were not yet living in a psychological realm or probing the recesses of the heart. This was to become a nineteenth-century trademark, evidenced in the self-expansive expressions of a new generation of diaries. Eighteenth-century Virginians had "neither the taste nor the skill for self-examination."[31]

This apt characterization is not meant to limit Jefferson, whose life and letters must be seen as a guidepost to cultural transition. We must do full justice to his inner drive, to his sense of the world and his place in it. He resisted the imposition of past dogmas, combining Heart and intellect to reform laws he found oppressive (excepting his failure to improve the prospects of men and women held in bondage). He sought a path to the undiscovered truth of existence and the soul, one that was not closed to intellectual exploration by biblical or other convention. He blended his respect for Newtonian physics with a reverence for nature and a belief in the natural goodness of humanity, in order to derive a religious perspective that he could live with comfortably in his later years. An arranger of nature as landscape architect and gardener, Jefferson did more than imitate the external appearance of nature; he imitated the creative organizing spirit of nature, building a bridge between the real and ideal. Internal processes and not just taxonomy inspired these efforts. In sum, while ordering his activities in eighteenth-century fashion, he desired to be creative, to project his thoughtful inner energy outward in spirited words and vivid images.[32]

The change in emphasis from classification to imagination loomed during the last quarter of the eighteenth century and first quarter of the nineteenth. Jefferson, reared in the neoclassical, experienced the anxiety of changing times, though it is extremely difficult to date when or postulate just how the romantic transformation entered and affected American life. It must suffice to state that life was beginning to occupy an internal space from which it could be readily drawn out, from which it could and would shortly be willed out. The difference between the eighteenth-century neoclassical mind and the modern mind must be said to be a matter of will, and Jefferson should be seen as a transitional figure in this process of liberating thought.

John Dewey would have us see the age of Jefferson as the opening of individual consciousness, a new dawn of indefinite but still perfectible visions of human progress. He called Jefferson "the first modern to state in human terms the principles of democracy."[33] If Dewey was correct in elevating Jefferson's thinking to this moral height, then we ought to relate America's romantic self-conception to Thomas Jefferson himself. In Jefferson's ideal for America, the pursuit of happiness crystallized in a man's mind when he became conscious that moral sentiment stood behind his conduct of daily affairs. He could restrain his baser passions and his self-interest. He could enlighten others. He could, in politics, theoretically overcome the "spirit of party" by exhibiting his respect for the diversity of opinions, trusting that the popular course would ultimately lead to good effects.[34]

Jefferson never ceased believing in this virtue, in the benevolence and expansiveness by which he defined the American character. He never lost hope. He apotheosized the distinct temper of Virginia plantation society in the age of Enlightenment, adoring the Republic that he saw radiating from Monticello, a society at once parochial and world-transforming. His conviction is most plainly evidenced by the effusive tone of his letters of Adams in their late years. But how different would his reflections have been had the Jeffersonians not triumphed in national politics? Jefferson, after all, saw no possible compromise with the Federalist party. He was convinced that his opponents were a narrow-minded and conspiratorial clique, representative only of those selfish and privileged elements who favored the establishment of an American aristocratic class. Adams broke with Hamilton, whom he also regarded as conspiratorial, and in his retirement years deplored Federalists who sought shelter "under the Wings of the British Navy."[35] This must have strengthened Jefferson's already firm resolve, ever projecting the Republicanization of political life. Jefferson saw only his own politics as a reliable echo of the popular voice. His belief in the singularity of America's choice, while founded in an optimism about the American people's future, can be construed as evidence that he was a Revolutionary pedant as contentious as Adams, constantly trying to justify his image of society, impatient with the real diversity of his country. It can only seem ironic to more recent generations that he represented a social order led by men whose humanitarian outlook was sustained by a slave economy.

The larger contradictions in Jefferson's life seem clearer when we consider that the person who wrote of the pursuit of happiness left to his family stable values and constructions never ceasing, but an estate that was hopelessly in debt. As a last-ditch effort to deliver the dying patriarch from these financial woes in 1826, the Virginia legislature sponsored a lottery to dispose of a considerable portion of his property, an idea conceived by Jefferson and put forward by his grandson. It achieved some results but not enough nor in time for Jefferson to see. Ironically, a contribution of $500 was made by Philadelphia millionaire William Short, whom Jefferson had years earlier showered with paternal advice on how to make his fortune.[36] In the end Monticello itself was sold in 1831 and fell into disrepair. Jefferson's last months were spent in contemplation of the fate of Monticello and the other properties bequeathed by his father nearly seventy years before.

The tendency is to describe the end of Jefferson's life and the beginnings of modernity, underscoring his limitations, the conflicts he could not tackle that remained unresolved at his death. On the other hand, it is instructive that Thomas Jefferson Randolph lived by his grandfather's principles with less fear of the public and private consequences. He championed emancipation in the Virginia legislature five years after his grandfather's death, in the wake of Nat Turner's slave revolt. In the course of his campaign, Randolph berated those "false Jeffersonians" whose statements of principles reflected Jefferson's "literal words and little of his spirit and meaning." If not the intellectual equal of his namesake—indeed, he was not at all creative with words—Jefferson Randolph vigorously put forward the best Jefferson he knew.[37]

Thomas Jefferson himself was uncertain about the good that the politicians of his latter days could accomplish, but he believed in the future in spite of them. "When I contemplate the immense advances in science," he wrote, "and discoveries in the arts which have been made within the period of my life, I look forward with confidence to equal advances by the present generation, and have no doubt that they will consequently be as much wiser than we have been as we than our fathers were."[38]

Jefferson made the autonomous individual the centerpiece of his conception of law and human rights, demanding that moral responsibility begin with the self. He saw life, in part, as a struggle between self-mastery and self-deception. His politics were the politics of consent, his idea of family that of a marriage based on love and devotion and development of the moral sense in offspring. Cultivation of sensibility, sanctification of life, appreciation for the sublimity of nature as a further nourishment of the soul: here was Jefferson's pursuit of happiness, co-existing and contending with the intense reality of frequent early death.

Jefferson expressed with unmatched eloquence the secular source of individual morality to offset what he saw as the persistence of clerical bigotry and false righteousness. A man is his temper. He becomes virtuous by discovering the softness of his inward nature, by drawing wisdom from his introspective moments, by finding in his Heart his sympathy toward humanity, and by acquiring nobility in taste. Jefferson sought peace of mind in this fashion. He was a man who thereby made himself beloved—and at the same time sought to undermine, with unusual ferocity, those he despised. Controversial as he was in his lifetime, he no doubt felt the goodness of his harmonious intent.

If we judge by intent, then Thomas Jefferson remained true to his conscience. Yet we must be careful not to liberate him from his world, the world of the late eighteenth century. We cannot ask him to anticipate log cabin presidents. The Jefferson who responded to the sentimental spirit of Ossian did not bring forth Walt Whitman's "Song of Myself," no matter how Jeffersonian we might want the latter poet's transcendent democracy to appear. The Jefferson who was absorbed in the consciousness of Sterne did not foresee the language of Sigmund Freud. The slave-owning liberal could never have brought to mind—no matter how we might wish to imagine him persuaded by—the message of Reverend Martin Luther King. We should not expect his disengagement from the moral space he occupied.

The way Thomas Jefferson would have wanted his private story to end is with a definition of his humanism, the part of Jefferson shared by his durable public persona and his energetic, if tormented, inner self. He believed in a free mind. He was a liberal in the particular sense that John Dewey gave to the word in 1940: "Liberalism is humble and persistent, and yet it is strong and positive in its faith that the intercourse of free minds will always bring to light an increasing measure of truth."[39] And so it is that Jefferson's optimism endures in the minds of Americans and others who continue to search for happiness.

Notes

ABBREVIATIONS

Adams-Jefferson Letters   *The Adams-Jefferson Letters: The Complete Correspondence between Thomas Jefferson and Abigail and John Adams.* Ed. Lester J. Cappon. 1959; rept. Chapel Hill, N.C., 1987.

Anas   *The Complete Anas of Thomas Jefferson.* Ed. Franklin B. Sawvel. New York, 1903.

Boyd   *The Papers of Thomas Jefferson.* Ed. Julian P. Boyd et al. 25 vols. to date. Princeton, N.J., 1950—.

Domestic Life   Sarah N. Randolph. *The Domestic Life of Thomas Jefferson.* 1871; rept. Charlottesville, Va., 1978.

Family Letters   *The Family Letters of Thomas Jefferson.* Ed. Edwin Morris Betts and James Adam Bear, Jr. Columbia, Mo., 1966.

Ford   *The Writings of Thomas Jefferson.* Ed. Paul Leicester Ford. 10 vols. New York, 1892–99.

L&B   *The Writings of Thomas Jefferson.* Ed. Andrew A. Lipscomb and Albert Ellery Bergh. 20 vols. Washington, D.C., 1905.

Malone   Malone, Dumas. *Jefferson and His Time.* 6 vols. Boston, 1948–81.

Memoir   *Memoir, Correspondence, and Miscellanies, from the Papers of Thomas Jefferson.* Ed. Thomas Jefferson Randolph. 4 vols. Charlottesville, Va., 1829.

Notes   *Notes on the State of Virginia.* Ed. William Peden. Chapel Hill, N.C., 1954.

Randall   Henry S. Randall. *The Life of Thomas Jefferson.* 3 vols. New York, 1858.

INTRODUCTION

1. John Dewey, "Presenting Thomas Jefferson," *John Dewey: The Later Works, 1925–1953,* ed. Jo Ann Boydston, 14 (Carbondale, Ill., 1988):204, 223.

2. Malone's Foreword to Karl Lehmann, *Thomas Jefferson, American Humanist* (New York, 1947; rpt. Charlottesville, Va., 1985); Malone 1:xii, xviii; Merrill Peterson, *John Adams and Thomas Jefferson: A Revolutionary Dialogue* (New York, 1976), 7; Peterson, *Thomas Jefferson and the New Nation* (New York, 1970), viii; Wilson Carey McWilliams, *The Idea of Fraternity in America* (Berkeley, Calif., 1973), 208; Bernard Bailyn, "Boyd's Jefferson: Notes for a Sketch," *New England Quarterly* 33 (1960): 382. See also James A. Bear, Jr., ed., *Jefferson at Monticello* (Charlottesville, Va., 1967), xi.

3. For examinations of the private Jefferson, see Fawn M. Brodie, *Thomas Jeffer-*

son: An Intimate History (New York, 1974); Page Smith, *Jefferson: A Revealing Biography* (New York, 1976); Winthrop D. Jordan, *White over Black: American Attitudes toward the Negro, 1550–1812* (Chapel Hill, N.C., 1968), 464–67; John Chester Miller, *The Wolf by the Ears: Thomas Jefferson and Slavery* (New York, 1977), chap. 20; Virginius Dabney, *The Jefferson Scandals* (New York, 1981); Elizabeth Langhorne, *Monticello: A Family Story* (Chapel Hill, N.C., 1989); Scot A. French and Edward L. Ayers, "The Strange Career of Thomas Jefferson: Race and Slavery in American Memory, 1943–1993," in Peter S. Onuf, ed., *Jeffersonian Legacies* (Charlottesville, Va., 1993), 418–56; and Douglas L. Wilson, "Thomas Jefferson and the Character Issue," *Atlantic Monthly* 270, no. 5 (Nov. 1992): 57–74.

4. Charles A. Miller, *Jefferson and Nature: An Interpretation* (Baltimore, 1988); Jay Fliegelman, *Declaring Independence: Jefferson, Natural Language, and the Culture of Performance* (Stanford, Calif., 1993). See also Peter S. Onuf, "The Scholars' Jefferson," *William and Mary Quarterly* 50 (1993): 671–99.

5. See Fliegelman, *Declaring Independence*, 31–37.

6. Walter J. Ong, *The Presence of the Word: Some Prolegomena for Cultural and Religious History* (New Haven, Conn., 1967), 6, 65–69; Eleanor Davidson Berman, *Thomas Jefferson among the Arts: An Essay in Early American Esthetics* (New York, 1947), 229.

7. *Jefferson's Literary Commonplace Book*. ed. Douglas L. Wilson (Princeton, N.J., 1989); Jefferson's Summary Journal of Letters is in the Library of Congress, photocopy available in the Manuscripts Division, University of Virginia Library. For part of the period covered by the SJL, Jefferson also maintained an alphabetical index of his correspondents and brief subject headings to enable him to recall matters addressed. See also John Catanzariti, "Thomas Jefferson, Correspondent," *Proceedings of the Massachusetts Historical Society* 102 (1990): 1–20.

8. Bruce Redford, *The Converse of the Pen: Acts of Intimacy in the Eighteenth-Century Familiar Letter* (Chicago, 1986), 10; TJ to Thomas Jefferson Randolph, Apr. 16, 1810, *Family Letters,* 397; Bear, *Jefferson at Monticello,* 12.

9. TJ to Maria Jefferson Eppes, Jan. 1, 1799, *Family Letters,* 170; to Madison, Feb. 20, 1784, Boyd 6:550.

10. TJ to Madison, Jan. 1, 1797, Ford 7:98.

11. TJ to Lafayette, Feb. 14, 1815, Lafayette to TJ, Oct. 10, 1815, *The Letters of Lafayette and Jefferson,* ed. Gilbert Chinard (Baltimore, 1929), 367–73, 376.

12. Eliza House Trist to TJ, Dec. 8 (?), 1783, Boyd 6:375.

13. TJ to Charles W. Peale, Aug. 20, 1811, L&B 13:78.

14. TJ to John Adams, Aug. 15, 1820, *Adams-Jefferson Letters,* 566–67.

1. THE WELL-ORDERED DREAMWORLD

1. Jack McLaughlin, *Jefferson and Monticello: The Biography of a Builder* (New York, 1988), 7.

2. Malone 1:13–14; Randall 1:2. According to the Julian calendar (in use before 1752) Thomas Jefferson's birth date was Apr. 2, 1743, "Old Style" (O.S.).

3. Malone 1:27–32.

4. Charles Wilder Watts, "Colonial Albemarle: The Social and Economic His-

tory of a Piedmont Virginia County, 1727–1775" (M.A. thesis, Univ. of Virginia, 1948); TJ to Adams, Oct. 28, 1813, *Adams-Jefferson Letters,* 389. See also Rhys Isaac, *The Transformation of Virginia, 1740–1790* (Chapel Hill, N.C., 1982), 68–70, 120.

5. TJ to Madison, July 24, 1797, Ford 7:157; Margaret Bayard Smith, *The First Forty Years of Washington Society,* ed. Gaillard Hunt (New York, 1906), 233.

6. Watts, "Colonial Albemarle"; William Minor Dabney, "Jefferson's Albemarle: History of Albemarle County, Virginia, 1727–1819" (Ph.D. diss., Univ. of Virginia, 1951), esp. 32–33, 153–59; John Hammond Moore, *Albemarle: Jefferson's County, 1727–1976* (Charlottesville, Va., 1976), 23–28; Malone 1:29.

7. *Virginia Will Records* (Baltimore, 1982), 6; Moore, *Albemarle,* 23, 40–41; Watts, "Colonial Albemarle."

8. Randall 1:12; TJ to John Adams, June 11, 1812, *Adams-Jefferson Letters,* 307. See also *Notes,* 62–63 and app. 4.

9. Isaac, *Transformation of Virginia,* 34–39; Gordon S. Wood, *The Radicalism of the American Revolution* (New York, 1992), 30–41; Jack P. Greene, *Landon Carter: An Inquiry into the Personal Values and Social Imperatives of the Eighteenth-Century Virginia Gentry* (Charlottesville, Va., 1965); Greene, "The Intellectual Reconstruction of Virginia in the Age of Jefferson," in Onuf, *Jeffersonian Legacies,* 225–53; Greene, "Society, Ideology, and Politics: An Analysis of the Political Culture of Mid-Eighteenth-Century Virginia," in Richard M. Jellison, ed., *Society, Freedom, and Conscience: The American Revolution in Virginia, Massachusetts, and New York* (New York, 1976), 14–76; Hunter Dickinson Farish, ed., *Journal and Letters of Philip Vickers Fithian, 1773–1774: A Plantation Tutor of the Old Dominion* (Williamsburg, Va., 1957).

10. T. H. Breen, *Tobacco Culture: The Mentality of the Great Tidewater Planters on the Eve of the Revolution* (Princeton, N.J., 1985). On the effects of tobacco culture, see TJ to Alexander Donald, July 28, 1787, Boyd 11:633.

11. Farish, *Journal and Letters of Fithian,* journal entry of Dec. 13, 1773, and letter of Dec. 1, 1773.

12. TJ to Thomas Jefferson Randolph, Nov. 24, 1808, *Family Letters, 362–63.*

13. TJ to John Harvie, Jan. 14, 1760, Boyd 1:3.

14. Malone 1:99.

15. Frank L. Dewey, *Thomas Jefferson, Lawyer* (Charlottesville, Va., 1986), chaps. 3 and 4.

16. Randall 1:47; Malone 1:129–33; Peterson, *Thomas Jefferson and the New Nation,* 33.

17. See McLaughlin, *Jefferson and Monticello,* esp. p. 15.

18. From *Life, Letters, and Journals of George Ticknor,* in Merrill D. Peterson, ed., *Visitors to Monticello* (Charlottesville, Va., 1989), 61.

19. *Notes,* 153. See also TJ to Madison, Feb. 20, 1785, Boyd 8:535.

20. TJ to Maria Cosway, Oct. 12, 1786, Boyd 10:445.

21. McLaughlin, *Jefferson and Monticello,* 35, 54.

22. Ibid., 58–62; John Dos Passos, *The Head and Heart of Thomas Jefferson* (Garden City, N.Y., 1954), 153–55.

23. Lehmann, *Thomas Jefferson, American Humanist,* 61; *The Letters of Pliny the Consul,* trans. William Melmoth (London, 1757), 2.17.105–15.

24. *Letters of Pliny the Consul,* 2.17.105–15; Robert Castell, *Villas of the Ancients* (1728; rept. New York, 1982); McLaughlin, *Jefferson and Monticello,* 156–57.

25. *Letters of Pliny the Consul* 5. 6.254–76. Jefferson similarly extolled Monticello's view and temperatures in *Notes,* 76.

26. TJ to Hamilton, July 1806, in *The Garden and Farm Books of Thomas Jefferson,* ed. Robert C. Baron (Golden, Colo., 1987), 191.

27. Lehmann, *Thomas Jefferson, American Humanist,* 170; Rudolf Wittkower, *Palladio and Palladianism* (New York, 1974), 181. See also Ernst Cassirer, *The Philosophy of the Enlightenment* (Princeton, N.J., 1951), 38.

28. Berman, *Thomas Jefferson among the Arts,* chap. 7.

29. Randall 1:11; Isaac, "The First Monticello," in Onuf, *Jeffersonian Legacies,* 79–80; Account Book entries for June–Oct. 1771 (Jefferson's Account Books were copied, indexed, and bound for reference by James A. Bear, Jr., and are in the University of Virginia Library; a formal edition is in production); Malone 1:114, 163, 391; Isaac, "Memoirs of a Monticello Slave," in Bear, *Jefferson at Monticello;* Lucia C. Stanton, "'Those Who Labor for My Happiness': Thomas Jefferson and His Slaves," in Onuf, *Jeffersonian Legacies,* 147–80; *Notes,* 139.

30. Daniel J. Boorstin, *The Lost World of Thomas Jefferson* (Chicago, 1948), 27–56; Charles B. Sanford, *The Religious Life of Thomas Jefferson* (Charlottesville, Va., 1984), 86–88, 94–96. See also Paul K. Conkin, "The Religious Pilgrimage of Thomas Jefferson," in Onuf, *Jeffersonian Legacies,* 19–49.

31. Cassirer, *Philosophy of the Enlightenment,* 57.

32. See Malone 3:221–42; McLaughlin, *Jefferson and Monticello,* chap. 8.

33. Rhys Isaac, "First Monticello," 87–88; undated Account Book entry of 1770.

34. TJ to Ogilvie, Feb. 20, 1771, Boyd 1:63.

35. S. Drummond to TJ, Mar. 12, 1771, ibid., 65–66.

36. TJ to T. Adams, June 1, 1771, ibid., 71–72.

37. Randall 1:64; *Domestic Life,* 44.

38. Robert Skipwith to TJ, July 17, 1771, Massachusetts Historical Society (on microfilm) and Boyd 1:74–75; TJ to Skipwith, Aug. 3, 1771, Boyd 1:76–81; Fliegelman, *Declaring Independence,* 58, 60–61.

39. See, for example, David Hume, *An Inquiry concerning Human Understanding,* ed. Charles W. Hendel (Indianapolis, 1955), sec. 10, 125.

40. TJ to Skipwith, Aug. 3, 1771, Boyd 1:78.

41. The "new Rowanty" has been presented vaguely by previous scholars as a fanciful name for Monticello. In their exchange of letters, Jefferson and Skipwith made sport of this name, indicating its familiarity to each. There exists a Rowanty Creek, tributary of the Nottaway River, near the boundary of Dinwiddie and Prince George counties. Just across the James River was the Charles City County home of John Wayles, where Jefferson and Skipwith had met. In a Prince George County deposition taken in 1707 concerning boundaries, a longtime resident stated, "The Nottoway Indians lived some at Rowantee and some at Tonnatorah." See "The Indians of Southern Virginia, 1650–1711," *Virginia Magazine of History and Biography* 7 (1900):341. Jefferson mentioned the Nottaway tribe in *Notes,* 93, 97; for Skipwith's landholdings, see *Virginia Tax Records* (Baltimore, 1983), 50. Editor Julian

Boyd offered an obscure explanation for Rowanty in *The Papers of Thomas Jefferson*
1:81, associating the term with the "Accadian Olympos" of the third milennium
B.C. The eighteenth century, however, was unaware of the myth to which Boyd
referred; it was introduced in A. H. Sayce, *The Ancient Empires of the East* (New
York, 1892), 91–107.

42. Marie Kimball, *Jefferson: The Road to Glory, 1743–1776* (New York, 1943),
162–63.

43. Randall 1:63; *Domestic Life,* 337; Skipwith to TJ, Sept. 20, 1771, Boyd 1:84.

44. *Memoir* 1:3; Malone 1:157–58, 432–33. Jefferson's Account Book indicates
that he was at the Forest on May 9 and July 22–24.

45. Account Book, Jan. 2 and 3, 1772; "Reminiscences of Th. J. by MR," bound
volume of Martha Jefferson Randolph's writings, inside cover titled "Select Peices
from Different Authors," in the Edgehill Randolph Papers, University of Virginia
Library.

46. Account Books, 1772–73; *Garden and Farm Books of Thomas Jefferson;* Barbara
McEwan, *Thomas Jefferson: Farmer* (Jefferson, N.C., 1991), esp. 67, 150–51; Paul Wil-
stach, *Jefferson and Monticello* (Garden City, N.Y., 1925), 38–40.

47. Johnson to James Macpherson, Jan. 20, 1775, in *Samuel Johnson: Rasselas,
Poems, and Selected Prose,* ed. Bertrand H. Bronson (New York, 1952), 20; *Diary of
John Quincy Adams,* vol. 1, *November 1779–March 1786,* ed. Robert J. Taylor et al.
(Cambridge, Mass., 1981), 254–55.

48. *Jefferson's Literary Commonplace Book,* 214–15, 150n, 172; E. Millicent Sowerby, *Catalogue of the Library of Thomas Jefferson,* 5 vols. (Washington, D.C., 1952–59),
1:47; TJ to Maria Jefferson Eppes, Feb. 7, 1799, *Family Letters,* 173.

49. This inscribed volume, which Jefferson probably purchased in France, remains in the Monticello collection. Jefferson made new purchases of Ossianic poetry in 1802 and again in 1807 (Sowerby, *Catalogue of the Library of Thomas Jefferson*
4:464).

50. Marquis de Chastellux, *Travels in North America in the Years 1780, 1781, and
1782,* 2 vols., trans. and ed., Howard C. Rice, Jr. (Chapel Hill, N.C., 1963), 2:389–95;
Peterson, *Visitors to Monticello,* 10–13; Randall 1:373–75.

51. John Dwyer, "The Melancholy Savage: Text and Context in the Poems of
Ossian," in Howard Gaskill, ed., *Ossian Revisited* (Edinburgh, 1991), 164–206. See
also Louis I. Bredvold, *The Natural History of Sensibility* (Detroit, 1962), esp. chap.
3, "The Exaltation of Unhappiness."

52. Hugh Blair, "Critical Dissertation on the Poems of Ossian," in James Macpherson, trans., *The Poems of Ossian* (London, 1807), esp. 102–11, 128–29.

53. Ibid., 47, 49.

54. Marshall Brown, *Preromanticism* (Stanford, Calif., 1991), 82–83.

55. Dwyer, "Melancholy Savage," 169.

56. See Fiona J. Stafford, *The Sublime Savage: A Study of James Macpherson and
the Poems of Ossian* (Edinburgh, 1988), esp. chap. 4 and 9; James McKillop, *Fionn
mac Cumhaill: Celtic Myth in English Literature* (Syracuse, N.Y., 1986). 89–90.

57. TJ to Madison, Nov. 26, 1782, Boyd 6:207. See also TJ to Chastellux, June
7, 1785, ibid., 8:186.

58. TJ to Maria Cosway, Oct. 12, 1786, ibid., 10:447.

59. Philip P. Wiens, ed., *Dictionary of the History of Ideas* (New York, 1973), 4:333–37; McLaughlin, *Jefferson and Monticello,* 34–35.

60. Hugh Blair, *Lectures on Rhetoric and Belles Lettres* (1783; rept. Philadelphia, 1833), lecture 3, 32–37.

61. Ibid., lecture 4, 48.

62. TJ to Charles Macpherson, Feb. 25, 1773, Boyd 1:96; James Macpherson, trans., *The Works of Ossian, the Son of Fingal,* vol. 3 (Paris, 1783) (this is the volume preserved in the collection at Monticello); Paul J. Degatano, "'The Source of Daily and Exalted Pleasure': Jefferson Reads the Poems of Ossian," in Gaskill, *Ossian Revisited,* 105; *Jefferson's Literary Commonplace Book,* 145.

63. Blair, *Lectures,* lecture 3, 32.

64. Thomas McFarland, *Romantic Cruxes: The English Essayists and the Spirit of the Age* (Oxford, 1987), 3; Henry Steele Commager, *Jefferson, Nationalism, and the Enlightenment* (New York, 1975), 135.

65. Roderick Nash, *Wilderness and the American Mind* (New Haven, 1982), 48–50; Miller, *Jefferson and Nature,* 100–106. The dichotomy of terms comes from Edmund Burke's *A Philosophical Enquiry into the Origin of Our Ideas of the Sublime and Beautiful* (1757). See also Garry Wills, *Inventing America: Jefferson's Declaration of Independence* (New York, 1978), 259–72.

66. *Notes,* 24, 25. The word *convulsion,* as a fear-inspiring phenomenon, also connotes the sublime. See Samuel H. Monk, "The Sublime: Burke's *Enquiry,*" in Harold Bloom, ed., *Romanticism and Consciousness: Essays in Criticism* (New York, 1970), 24–41.

67. Randall 1:375; TJ to Trumbull, Feb. 20, 1791, Boyd 19:298; TJ to Martha Randolph, Aug. 18, 1817, *Family Letters,* 418; Malone 6:294.

68. Peterson, *Visitors to Monticello,* 75; *Notes,* 80–81; Nash, *Wilderness and the American Mind,* 57.

69. Account Book entries of Nov. 4, 1772, Apr. 5, 1780; TJ to Abigail Adams, June 21, 1785, *Adams-Jefferson Letters,* 35; TJ to Martha, June 10, 1793, *Family Letters,* 120; Smith, *First Forty Years of Washington Society,* 385.

70. Account Book, undated 1771 entry.

71. TJ to Baron de Geismar, Sept. 6, 1785, Boyd 8:500; *Notes,* 164–65.

72. Henry Nash Smith, *Virgin Land: The American West as Symbol and Myth* (Cambridge, Mass., 1978), 53–56; the eighteenth-century antecedents of American primitivist sensibility are explored in Lois Whitney, *Primitivism and the Idea of Progress* (Baltimore, 1934).

2. Sensitivity and Sterne

1. Malone 1:162–63; *Memoir* 1:3.

2. Dating of the entry is made on the basis of handwriting analysis in *Jefferson's Literary Commonplace Book,* 201, 206.

3. See Max Byrd, *Tristram Shandy* (London, 1985), 72–75 and chap. 4.

4. Laurence Sterne, *The Life and Opinions of Tristram Shandy, Gentleman* (New York, 1945), 1:6, 2:12.

5. Edward D. Bloom and Lillian D. Bloom, "'This Fragment of Life': From Process to Mortality," in Valerie Grosvenor Meyer, ed., *Laurence Sterne: Riddles and Mysteries* (London, 1984), 57.

6. See Arthur H. Cash, *Laurence Sterne: The Early and Middle Years* (London, 1975), 196–201; Cash, *Laurence Sterne: The Later Years* (London, 1986), 74; Introduction to John Locke, *An Essay concerning Human Understanding,* ed. John W. Yolton (London, 1961).

7. "Introduction to *A Sentimental Journey,*" in Laurence Sterne, *A Sentimental Journey through France and Italy by Mr. Yorick with "The Journal to Eliza" and "A Political Romance,"* ed. Ian Jack (New York, 1968).

8. See, for example, Sterne to Eliza Draper, June 17, 1767, ibid., 166.

9. TJ to Peter Carr, Aug. 10, 1787, Boyd 12:15. No doubt Jefferson also had in mind Sterne's *Sermons.*

10. Sterne, *Tristram Shandy* 2:9. See Byrd, *Tristram Shandy,* 15, on Sterne's parody of Henry Fielding's use of the author's voice.

11. See Byrd, *Tristram Shandy,* 111; editor's "Introduction," Meyer, *Laurence Sterne: Riddles and Mysteries.*

12. Sterne, *Tristram Shandy* 2:11. See Bruce Stovel, "Tristram Shandy and the Art of Gossip," in Meyer, *Laurence Sterne: Riddles and Mysteries,* 122–23.

13. Sterne, *Tristram Shandy* 3:28. See Frank Brady, "Tristram Shandy: Sexuality, Morality, and Sensibility," *Eighteenth-Century Studies* 4 (1970): 41–56.

14. See Jacques Berthoud, "Shandeism and Sexuality," and Alan B. Howes, "Laurence Sterne, Rabelais, and Cervantes: The Two Kinds of Laughter in Tristram Shandy," in Meyer, *Laurence Sterne: Riddles and Mysteries.*

15. Elizabeth W. Harries, *The Unfinished Manner: Essays on the Fragment in the Later Eighteenth Century* (Charlottesville, Va., 1994), esp. chaps. 2 and 4. Next to Sterne, Cervantes was the most popular novelist among Virginians of Jefferson's day. See Joseph F. Kett and Patricia A. McClung, "Book Culture in Post-Revolutionary Virginia," *Proceedings of the American Antiquarian Society* 94 (1984): 97–147.

16. See Jonathan Lamb, "Sterne's Use of Montaigne," *Comparative Literature* 32 (1980): 1–41; Cash, *Laurence Sterne: The Early and Middle Years,* 206.

17. See Howard Anderson, "Tristram Shandy and the Reader's Imagination," *PMLA* 86 (1971): 966–73.

18. Brown, *Preromanticism,* 274.

19. Sterne, *Tristram Shandy* 5:3. See William Holtz, *Image and Immortality: A Study of Tristram Shandy* (Providence, R.I., 1970), 138–43.

20. *Domestic Life,* 39.

21. See TJ to Maria Cosway, Apr. 24, 1788, Boyd 13:104. However, Jefferson protégé William Short laughed privately at the way Jefferson would "blush like a boy" at some of what the French said (Short to TJ, March 2, 1789, ibid., 14:608–9). See also Randall 1:421n.

22. *Jefferson's Literary Commonplace Book,* 62. The passage in Sterne is longer (editor Douglas L. Wilson compares the two), contains oblique references, and mentions a character drawn from Sterne's own life.

23. *Memoir* 1:42.

24. Melvyn New, "Laurence Sterne," in Martin Battestin, ed., *The Dictionary of Literary Biography* 39 (Detroit, 1985): 491.

25. Ibid., 487, 495.

26. Laurence Sterne, "The Abuses of Conscience Considered," *The Sermons of Mr. Yorick* 2 (Oxford, 1927): 67–68. This sermon was one of which the anticlerical Voltaire approved (Cash, *Laurence Sterne: The Early and Middle Years*, 234).

27. Catherine Glyn Davies, *Conscience as Consciousness: The Idea of Self-Awareness in French Philosophical Writing from Descartes to Diderot* (Oxford, 1990), 3.

28. Johnson, *A Dictionary of the English Language* (London, 1783); Richard Steele, *The Conscious Lovers*, ed. Shirley Strum Kenny (Lincoln, Nebr., 1968), 5.3. See also Elizabeth Hedrick, "Locke's Theory of Language and Johnson's Dictionary," *Eighteenth-Century Studies* 20 (1987): 422–44.

29. TJ to Peter Carr, Aug. 10, 1787, Boyd 12:15–16. See also *Notes*, 93; TJ to John Adams, Oct. 14, 1816, *Adams-Jefferson Letters*, 492. For the notion of a "moral sense" shared by all men, see Wills, *Inventing America*, chap. 13; Bredvold, *Natural History of Sensibility*, chap. 1, "The Ethics of Feeling"; Cassirer, *Philosophy of the Enlightenment*, 321; Lee Quinby, "Thomas Jefferson: The Virtue of Aesthetics and the Aesthetics of Virtue," *American Historical Review* 87 (1982): 337–56.

30. TJ to Adams, Oct. 12, 1813, *Adams-Jefferson Letters*, 385; Roger Grimsley, "Jean-Jacques Rousseau: Philosopher of Nature," in S. C. Brown, ed., *Philosophers of the Enlightenment* (Atlantic Highlands, N.J., 1979), 193–94; Davies, *Conscience as Consciousness*, 6.

31. Richard E. Aquila, "The Cartesian and a Certain 'Poetic' Notion of Consciousness," *Journal of the History of Ideas* 49 (1988): 543–62; Davies, *Conscience as Consciousness*, 63–64.

32. Frederick Garber, *The Autonomy of the Self from Richardson to Huysmans* (Princeton, N.J., 1982), 65–66; Martin C. Battestin, *The Providence of Wit: Aspects of Form in Augustan Literature and the Arts* (Charlottesville, Va., 1989), 243–44.

33. Locke, *An Essay concerning Human Understanding*, 2.27; Davies, *Conscience as Consciousness*, 31–32, 64–69. On Sterne and Diderot, see Cash, *Laurence Sterne: The Later Years*, 138–39.

34. Byrd, *Tristram Shandy*, 49; Whitney, *Primitivism and the Idea of Progress*, 101; Jay Fliegelman, *Prodigals and Pilgrims: The American Revolution against Patriarchal Authority* (New York, 1982), 63.

35. Patricia Spacks, *Imagining a Self: Autobiography and Novel in Eighteenth-Century England* (Cambridge Mass., 1976), 153.

36. Stephen Greenblatt, *Renaissance Self-Fashioning: From More to Shakespeare* (Chicago, 1980), 2–3.

37. Fliegelman, *Declaring Independence*, 115–17.

38. Laurence Sterne, *The Sermons of Mr. Yorick* 1:37–48.

39. Ibid., 81–90, 93–100.

40. Ibid., 3.

41. Locke, *An Essay concerning Human Understanding* 2.11.

42. See Robert DeMaria, Jr., *Johnson's Dictionary and the Language of Learning* (Chapel Hill, N.C., 1986), 98–102.

43. Sterne, *Tristram Shandy* 2:12.

44. TJ to Maria Cosway, Oct. 12, 1786, to John Page, Dec. 25, 1762, Boyd 10:451, 1:5.

45. TJ to John Banister, Jr., Oct. 15, 1785, Boyd 8:637.

46. Entries of the late 1750s and early 1760s (and app. B) in *Jefferson's Literary Commonplace Book;* TJ to Francis Wayles Eppes, Jan. 19, 1821, *Family Letters,* 438, cited in ibid., 157. The "periods" in "periods of just measure" is as defined in rhetoric and means full sentences. For Bolingbroke, see Lance Banning, *The Jeffersonian Persuasion: Evolution of a Party Ideology* (Ithaca, N.Y., 1978), 57–62, 66–67, and Adrienne Koch, *The Philosophy of Thomas Jefferson* (Gloucester, Mass., 1957), 9–14.

47. "A Summary View," Boyd 1:134; Malone, however, doubted that the impact of *A Summary View* was as pronounced in England as Jefferson himself asserted in late life (Malone 1:189–90).

48. Boyd 1:121–35; Peterson, *Thomas Jefferson and the New Nation,* 73–77; William L. Hedges, "Telling Off the King: Jefferson's Summary View as American Fantasy," *Early American Literature* 22 (1987): 166–73.

49. For Jefferson's careful writing and rewriting, see Malone 1:205–6.

50. TJ to F. Eppes, Oct. 24, Nov. 7, 21, 1775, Boyd 1:249, 252, 264.

51. Account Book, May 7, 14, 20, June 3, 1776.

52. For various analyses of Jefferson's Declaration, see Carl Becker, *The Declaration of Independence* (1922; rept. New York, 1970), stressing Locke's influence; Wills, *Inventing America,* downplaying Locke in favor of the Scottish philosophers; Boyd 1:299–328, 413–33, providing chronology and documentation; Elizabeth M. Renker, "'Declaration-Men' and the Rhetoric of Self-Presentation," *Early American Literature* 24 (1989), 120–31.

53. Account Book, July 4, 1776.

54. TJ to John Page, Oct. 31, 1775, Boyd 1:251.

55. On Apr. 29, 1779, Jefferson sold his pianoforte to Hessian prisoner General Riedesel for £100 (Account Book).

56. *Memoir* 1:40–41.

57. TJ to Page, July 30, Aug. 5, 1776, Boyd 1:482, 486.

58. Martha Jefferson Randolph's "Reminiscences of Th. J. by MR," Edgehill Randolph Papers, printed in *Domestic Life,* 63; TJ to Elizabeth Wayles Eppes, Oct. 3(?), 1782, Boyd 1:198.

59. Boyd 1:196; *Jefferson's Literary Commonplace Book,* 184. Editor Douglas L. Wilson explained that the punctuation is the same as Jefferson's in the Commonplace Book, slightly different from what Sterne published; see also *Domestic Life,* 430–31.

60. Randall 1:384. The relic, nearly illegible now, is in the possession of the James Monroe Museum, Fredericksburg,Va.

61. *Domestic Life,* 64; Lehmann, *Thomas Jefferson: American Humanist,* 54.

62. TJ to Monroe, Dec. 18, 1786, Boyd 10:612.

63. TJ to Elizabeth Wayles Eppes, Oct. 3(?), 1782, to Chastellux, Nov. 26, 1782, Boyd 6:198–99, 203.

64. Edmund Pendleton to TJ, Aug. 10, 1776, Boyd 1:489; Wood, *Radicalism of the American Revolution,* 206.

65. TJ to Chastellux, Nov. 26, 1782, Boyd 1:203; Peterson, *Thomas Jefferson and the New Nation,* 247.

66. Madison to TJ, Apr. 22, 1783, TJ to Madison, Aug. 31, 1783, Boyd 6:262, 335–336; Ralph Ketcham, *James Madison: A Biography* (New York, 1971), 109–11.

67. TJ to Eliza House Trist, Dec. 11, 1783(?), Boyd 6:382–83. Mrs. Trist learned in Mississippi of her husband's death and recalled Jefferson's poignant letter "wherein you compared my then situation to heaven in comparison to those who was cut off from all hope . . . commiserating the pang your heart must have felt. . . . I have thought of your sufferings when I was allmost sinking under my own" (Trist to TJ, Dec. 25, 1784, Boyd 7:583).

68. Charles Thomson explained that the eagle in the 1782 design of the Great Seal of the United States denoted America's reliance on virtue (U.S. Dept. of State, *The Great Seal of the United States* [Washington, D.C., 1980]).

69. TJ to Abigail Adams, June 21, 1785, *Adams-Jefferson Letters,* 35; TJ to Maria Cosway, Dec. 24, 1786, Boyd 10:627.

70. Battestin, *Providence of Wit,* 249.

71. William Dunlap, *The Father: or American Shandy-ism* (New York, 1789); Sterne, *Tristram Shandy* 2:12.

72. The subscriber list for the first American edition of Sterne's *Works,* published in Philadelphia in 1774, contained several hundred names from across the colonies. I thank Jay Fliegelman for bringing these rare volumes to my attention.

3. THE SENSATIONS OF EUROPE

1. *Domestic Life,* 73; Account Book entries of July 5–26, 1784; TJ to Monroe, Nov. 11, 1784, Boyd 7:508; Martha Jefferson to Eliza House Trist, (Aug.?) 1786, Edgehill Randolph Papers.

2. Dos Passos, *Head and Heart of Thomas Jefferson,* 255; Howard C. Rice, Jr., *Thomas Jefferson's Paris* (Princeton, N.J., 1976), 14–19.

3. Malone 2:7–8, 21–25; Rice, *Thomas Jefferson's Paris,* 37–42. The convent was home to as many Protestant as Catholic girls (see TJ to James Maury, Dec. 24, 1786, Boyd 10:628).

4. News of Lucy's illness and death reached Jefferson in painful installments (see Francis Eppes to TJ, Sept. 16, Oct. 24, 1784, Dr. James Currie to TJ, Nov. 20, 1784, TJ to Eppes, Feb. 5, 1785, Boyd 7:441–42, 538–39, 635–36). John Quincy Adams noted in his diary on Jan. 29, 1785, that Jefferson "looks much afflicted. The last letters, brought him news of the death of one of his daughters: he has a great deal of sensibility" (*Diary of John Quincy Adams* 1:218).

5. TJ to Madison, Dec. 8, 1784, to Monroe, Dec. 10, 1784, Jan. 14, Mar. 18, 1785, Boyd 7:559, 564, 7:607, 8:43.

6. Malone 2:33; Carl Van Doren, *Benjamin Franklin* (New York, 1938), 635–48; Rice, *Thomas Jefferson's Paris,* 91–92.

7. "Reminiscences of Th. J. by MR," in Edgehill Randolph Papers.

8. Malone 1:364, 294–97; Philip Mazzei, *Philip Mazzei: My Life and Wanderings,* trans. S. Eugene Scalia, ed. Margharita Marchione (Morristown, N.J., 1980), esp.

226–27. See also TJ to Richard Henry Lee, Apr. 21, 1779, to Geismar, Mar. 3, 1785, Boyd 2:255, 8:10.

9. Mazzei, *Philip Mazzei,* esp. 19, 204, 283, 326; Plan of Philip Mazzei's Company, 1774, Mazzei to TJ, Oct. 26, 1785, Boyd 1:156–58, 8:675–78.

10. Mazzei to TJ, ca. July 1784, Crèvecoeur to TJ, July 15, 1784, Boyd 7:386, 376.

11. TJ to Franklin, Aug. 14, 1786, to Humphreys, Aug. 14, 1786, ibid., 10:247–48, 251; to Abigail Adams, June 21, 1785, Aug. 9, 1786, *Adams-Jefferson Letters,* 33–34, 149.

12. See Dena Goodman, "Enlightenment Salons: The Convergence of Female and Philosophic Ambitions," *Eighteenth-Century Studies* 22 (1989): 329–50.

13. Alan Charles Kors, *D'Holbach's Coterie: An Enlightenment in Paris* (Princeton, N.J., 1976), 92–93.

14. Claude-Anne Lopez, *Mon Cher Papa: Franklin and the Ladies of Paris* (New Haven, 1966), 248, 252–57; TJ to Abigail Adams, June 21, 1785, *Adams-Jefferson Letters,* 35.

15. Condorcet to TJ, Sept. 12, 1789, Boyd 15:419. See also TJ to Maria Cosway, Oct. 12, 1786, ibid., 10:452.

16. TJ to Mme de Tessé, Jan. 30, 1803, in Gilbert Chinard, *Trois amitiés françaises de Jefferson* (Paris, 1927), 123; ibid., 67–69, 153.

17. TJ to Chastellux, [Oct. 1786], Boyd 10:498–99 and note; Kors, *D'Holbach's Coterie,* 129–33.

18. See Malone 2:98–103.

19. Ibid., 1:373–89; TJ to Chastellux, Jan. 16, 1784, Sept. 2, 1785, Chastellux to TJ, June 2, 1785, Boyd 6:467, 7:467–70, 174; *Notes,* xi–xx.

20. Thomas Schlereth, *The Cosmopolitan Ideal in Enlightenment Thought* (Notre Dame, Ind., 1977), 47–53, 126–33.

21. Helen Duprey Bullock, *My Head and My Heart: A Little History of Thomas Jefferson and Maria Cosway* (New York, 1945), 13–16.

22. Ibid., 47–51.

23. Ibid., 26.

24. Malone 2:73; Account Book, Sept. 4–Nov. 15, 1786, entries. Note, however, that Martha Jefferson Randolph said that her father was returning from one of his "rambles" with an unnamed male companion when, "earnestly engaged in conversation," he fell and dislocated the wrist ("Reminiscences of Th. J. by MR," in the Edgehill Randolph Papers).

25. TJ to William S. Smith, Oct. 22, 1786, Boyd 10:478.

26. Malone 2:76; *Jefferson Himself: The Personal Narrative of a Many-Sided American,* ed. Bernard Mayo (Charlottesville, Va., 1942), 128.

27. TJ to Maria Cosway, Oct. 12, 1786, Boyd 10:443–53; Rice, *Thomas Jefferson's Paris,* 4 (illus.).

28. John Trumbull, *The Autobiography of Colonel John Trumbull,* ed. Theodore Sizer (New Haven, 1953), 111–12; G. S. Rousseau, "The Sorrows of Priapus: Anticlericalism, Homosocial Desire, and Richard Payne Knight," in Rousseau and Roy Porter, eds., *Sexual Underworlds of the Enlightenment* (Chapel Hill, N.C., 1988), 101–53; d'Hancarville to TJ, Feb. 25, 1787, Maria Cosway to TJ, Dec. 1, 1787, Boyd 11:182, 12:387; Bullock, *My Head and My Heart,* 80.

29. Jefferson tended to write long paragraphs. A space left on a line indicates an intended break in his thoughts. Boyd's editing does not always take account of these spaces, which are apparent in the original letter in the Jefferson Papers, Library of Congress.

30. *Memoir,* 40; TJ to Monroe, May 20, 1782, to G. K. van Hogendorp, May 4, 1784, Boyd 6:184–85, 7:208.

31. TJ to Eliza Trist, Aug. 18, 1785, Boyd 8:403–5.

32. TJ to Page, May 25, 1766, ibid., 1:19; *Domestic Life,* 321–22.

33. Sea metaphors were employed during the Renaissance, as well. See Francesco Petrarca, *Letters on Familiar Matters (Rerum familiarium libri),* trans. Aldo S. Bernardo, 3 (Baltimore, 1985): 1.1.8–9.

34. George Anson, *A Voyage round the World in the Years MDCCXL, I, II, III, IV* (London, 1748); TJ to Eliza Trist, Dec. 15, 1786, Boyd 10:600.

35. TJ to Francis Eppes, Aug. 30, 1785, Boyd 8:451; "Reminiscences of Th. J. by MR," in Edgehill Randolph Papers; TJ to Tucker, Sept. 10, 1793, to Mazzei, Apr. 24, 1796, Ford 6:425, 7:75–76. See also Miller, *Jefferson and Nature,* 114–15.

36. Jefferson originally wrote "we ride, placid, above" but then altered the text, crossing out "placid" and adding the euphonic "serene and sublime."

37. TJ to Eliza House Trist, Dec. 15, 1786, Boyd 10:600; to Gallatin, Apr. 24, 1811, L&B 13:45.

38. TJ to Abigail Adams, Sept. 25, 1785, *Adams-Jefferson Letters,* 69–70; to Du Pont, Mar. 2, 1809, to Priestley, Jan. 27, 1800, L&B 12:259, 9:147.

39. Edmund Burke, *A Philosophical Enquiry into the Origin of Our Ideas of the Sublime and Beautiful* (1757), ed. James T. Boulton (Notre Dame, Ind., 1958), 34–37, 45–46.

40. TJ to G. K. van Hogendorp, May 14, 1784, Boyd 7:208–9.

41. Dr. Johnson's 1783 *Dictionary* defines *visionary* with the identical image: "affected by phantoms."

42. Possibly, Patty Jefferson was beside Jefferson in the phaeton when he overlooked the "poor, wearied souldier"; Randall (3:233) quoted an "intimate friend of Mr. Jefferson" discussing what appears to be the same episode.

43. "The Monk, Calais," and "The Snuff Box," in Laurence Sterne, *A Sentimental Journey through France and Italy* (London, 1967), 31, 43–44.

44. TJ to Skipwith, Aug. 3, 1771, Boyd 1:77. There has long been controversy over whether Sterne indeed took this incident from his own experience.

45. Martha Jefferson to Eliza House Trist, [Aug.?] 1786, in Edgehill Randolph Papers; TJ to Madison, Oct. 28, 1785, Boyd 8:681.

46. Sterne to Mrs. James, Nov. 12, 1767, in *Letters of Laurence Sterne* (Oxford, 1927), 174.

47. See for example, Peterson, *Thomas Jefferson and the New Nation,* 348–49. Bullock reprinted the letter but does not editorialize. Malone (2:75–78) downplayed its emotional content and kept reminding the reader of Jefferson's seriousness.

48. Maria Cosway to TJ, Oct. 30, 1786, and subsequent, all undated letters, in Massachusetts Historical Society collection (microfilm), dated by Boyd (see Boyd 10:494–95 for translation of the Oct. 30 letter); Trumbull to TJ, Oct. 9, 1786,

Jefferson Papers, Library of Congress; TJ to Thomas Jefferson Randolph, Apr. 16, 1810, *Family Letters,* 397.

49. Maria Cosway to TJ, Nov. 17, 27, 1786, Boyd 10:538–39, 552; TJ to Maria Cosway, Nov. 19, 1786, letterpress copy in Thomas Jefferson Papers, Manuscripts Division, University of Virginia Library, and Boyd 10:542–43.

50. TJ to Maria Cosway, Nov. 29, 1786, Boyd 10:555.

51. See Bullock, *My Head and My Heart,* ix.

52. TJ to Maria Cosway, Dec. 24, 1786, letterpress copy in Thomas Jefferson Papers, Manuscripts Division, University of Virginia Library, and Boyd 10:627. Compare the aging Benjamin Franklin's flirtatious phrase in a letter to young Madame Brisson: "If I had wings I should have flown to you, and I think I should sometimes scratch at the window of your bedchamber" (Van Doren, *Benjamin Franklin,* 644).

53. TJ to Thomas Lee Shippen, Sept. 29, 1788, Boyd 13:643.

54. TJ to William Short, Apr. 7, 12, May 21, 1787, Boyd 11:280–81, 287, 372; TJ to Martha Jefferson, May 21, 1787, *Family Letters,* 41. See also Edward Dumbauld, *Thomas Jefferson, American Tourist* (Norman, Okla., 1946), esp. chap. 5; Malone 2:112–26; Jefferson's memoranda, emphasizing his investigations into wine and agriculture, Boyd 11:415–64.

55. TJ to John Stockdale, Jan. 28, 1787, Boyd 11:85; Sowerby, *Catalogue of the Library of Thomas Jefferson* 4:446.

56. Sterne, *A Sentimental Journey,* 34–35.

57. TJ to Mme de Tott, Apr. 5, 1787, Boyd 11:271, 273 n.6; Sterne, *A Sentimental Journey,* 28.

58. TJ to Lafayette, Apr. 11, 1787, Boyd 11:283–85; Sterne, *A Sentimental Journey,* 142.

59. TJ to Maria Cosway, July 27, 1788, Boyd 13:423–24; Sterne, *Tristram Shandy,* vol. 7; *A Sentimental Journey,* 137–40; Abigail Adams to TJ, Feb. 11, 1786, *Adams-Jefferson Letters,* 119. See also John Adams to Abigail Adams, Mar. 16, 1777, in *Familiar Letters of John Adams and His Wife Abigail Adams, during the Revolution,* ed. Charles Francis Adams (New York, 1876), 251.

60. Sterne, *A Sentimental Journey,* 96–99.

61. Ibid., 89–91.

62. Sterne to Eliza Draper, Apr. 15, June 3, 1767, in *Journal to Eliza,* 136, 157–58.

63. TJ to Maria Cosway, Apr. 24, 1788, Boyd 13:104.

64. See Berthould, "Shandeism and Sexuality," 24–38.

65. Spacks, *Imagining a Self,* 130.

66. Sterne, *Tristram Shandy* 3:35, 2:5; TJ to Mme de Tessé, Mar. 20, 1787, Boyd 11:226–28.

67. Winthrop Jordan has attributed to Jefferson only a "dim awareness" of a sexual struggle during his years in Europe (*White over Black,* 462). Bernard Bailyn has associated Jefferson's flirtation with Maria Cosway with his overall flirtation with the "careless, semi-bohemian, café society world of the Anglo-French artistic set" ("Boyd's Jefferson," 391–92).

68. Paul-Gabriel Boucé, "Imagination, Pregnant Women, and Monsters, in

Eighteenth-Century England and France," in Rousseau and Porter, *Sexual Underworlds of the Enlightenment,* 86–100; Malone 2:19.

69. Spacks, *Imagining a Self,* 88–90. For incipient changes in male perceptions of female roles and stirrings of female independence, see Linda K. Kerber, *Women of the Republic: Intellect and Ideology in Revolutionary America* (New York, 1986).

70. TJ to Trumbull, Feb. 23, 1787, to Maria Cosway, July 1, 1787, Boyd 11:181, 519–20.

71. Maria Cosway to TJ, July 9, 1787, TJ to Trumbull, July 17, 1787, ibid., 12:567–68, 595.

72. Bullock, *My Head and My Heart,* 77–80.

73. TJ to Trumbull, Nov. 13, 1787, Boyd 12:358.

74. Maria Cosway to TJ, Dec. 25, 1787, ibid., 459.

75. TJ to Angelica Schuyler Church, Feb. 17, 1788, ibid., 600–601.

76. Maria Cosway to TJ, Mar. 6, June 23, Aug. 19, 1788, TJ to Maria Cosway, July 30, 1788, ibid., 12:645, 13:288, 525, 435.

77. Angelica Church to TJ, July 21, 1788, TJ to Angelica Church, Aug. 17, 1788, ibid., 13:391, 521; "The Case of Delicacy," in Sterne, *A Sentimental Journey.*

78. Maria Cosway to TJ, Apr. 29, 1788, Boyd 13:115.

79. TJ to Mme de Tott, Apr. 5, 1787, ibid., 11:270–71. For this familiar convention, see TJ to John Page, Dec. 25, 1762, ibid., 1:5.

80. Sterne, *Journal to Eliza,* Apr. 28 [1767]; Sterne, *Tristram Shandy* 7:28.

81. Sterne, *Journal to Eliza,* June 17 [1767].

82. Cash, *Laurence Sterne: The Later Years,* 274.

83. TJ to Maria Cosway, May 21, 1789, to Gilmer, Aug. 12, 1787, Boyd 15:143, 12:26.

84. TJ to Alexander Donald, Feb. 7, 1788, ibid., 12:572.

85. TJ to Maury, Aug. 19, 1785, to Thomson, Nov. 11, 1784, ibid., 8:409–10, 7:519.

86. TJ to John Banister, Jr., Oct. 15, 1785, ibid., 8:636–37.

87. TJ to Madison, Jan. 30, 1787, ibid., 11:95.

88. TJ to Anne Bingham, Feb. 7, 1787, ibid., 122–23.

89. Anne Bingham to TJ, June 1, 1787, ibid., 392–93.

90. TJ to Randolph Jefferson, Jan. 11, 1789, ibid., 14:434; Peterson, *Thomas Jefferson and the New Nation,* 387.

91. TJ to Bellini, Sept. 30, 1785, Boyd 8:568–69; to Adams, Oct. 28, 1813, *Adams-Jefferson Letters,* 391.

92. Short to TJ, Mar. 2, 1789, Boyd 14:608–9.

93. Maria Cosway to TJ, Feb. 6, 1789, ibid., 526; Francis Bacon, "On Travel," in *The Wisdom of the Ancients and Miscellaneous Essays* (New York, 1932), 67.

4. LETTER WRITING AND FRIENDSHIP

1. Adams to Robert Treat Paine, Dec. 6, 1759, cited in Richard D. Brown, *Knowledge Is Power: The Diffusion of Information in Early America, 1700–1865* (New York, 1989), 90; letter of July 7, 1776, *Familiar Letters of John Adams and His Wife Abigail Adams, during the Revolution,* 195–96.

2. Brown, *Knowledge Is Power,* 91–101. See also, Boorstin, *Lost World of Thomas*

Jefferson 219–21; Peter Gay, *The Enlightenment: An Interpretation,* 2 vols. (New York, 1966–69), 1:41–44; Kenneth Cmiel *Democratic Eloquence: The Fight over Popular Speech in Nineteenth-Century America* (New York, 1990), 14ff.

3. *Notes,* 147. See also TJ to Priestley, Jan. 27, 1800, L&B 9:146; Randall 3:346.

4. See, for example, TJ to Short, Mar. 29, 1787, Boyd 11:254–55.

5. Lehmann, *Thomas Jefferson, American Humanist,* 33; Boyd 6:591 map.

6. Lehmann, *Thomas Jefferson, American Humanist,* 60; TJ to John Adams, Dec. 10, 1819, July 5, 1814, *Adams-Jefferson Letters,* 549, 433. See also James M. May, *Trials of Character: The Eloquence of Ciceronian Ethos* (Chapel Hill, N.C., 1988); Gay, *The Enlightenment: An Interpretation* 1:105–9.

7. *Cicero's Epistles to Atticus,* trans. William Guthrie, 3 vols. (London, 1806), 2.10, 1:124, 3.5, 1:174–75.

8. See Peterson, *Thomas Jefferson and the New Nation,* 235–39.

9. TJ to Monroe, May 20, 1782, Boyd 6:184–86.

10. *Cicero's Epistles to Atticus* 3.23, 1:157–58, 3.24, 1:159, 10.42, 3:78, 10.14, 3:26–27; Cicero to Quintus, 54 B.C., *The Letters to His Brother Quintus . . . (Epistulae ad Quintum Fratrem),* trans. W. Glynn Williams et al. (Cambridge, Mass., 1972), 579. See also James J. Murphy, *Rhetoric in the Middle Ages: A History of Rhetorical Theory from Saint Augustine to the Renaissance* (Berkeley, Calif., 1979), 194–95.

11. *Cicero: Laelius, On Friendship, The Dream of Scipio,* ed. J. G. F. Powell (Warminster, Eng., 1990), 23.82, 65.

12. *Cicero's Epistles to Atticus* 1:viii–ix.

13. Ibid., xiii, xvi.

14. John Adams, for one, coupled Cicero and Pliny as the two ancients whose letters conveyed a full range of sensations "in as much simplicity, ease, freedom, and familiarity as language is capable of." See letter of July 7, 1776, *Familiar Letters of John Adams and His Wife Abigail Adams, during the Revolution,* 196.

15. *Letters of Pliny the Consul* 2.13.96–97; TJ to Madison, Jan. 30, 1787, Boyd 11:97. See also TJ to Washington and to ?, Apr. 18, 1877, ibid., 2:12–13.

16. TJ to Thomas McKean, Sept. 30, 1781, Boyd 6:123. See also Ezra Stiles to TJ, May 28, 1792, ibid., 23:550–51.

17. Murphy, *Rhetoric in the Middle Ages,* chap. 5.

18. Petrarca, *Letters on Familiar Matters (Rerum familiarium libri)* 1.1.6–7, 18.8.56–59.

19. John F. Tinkler, "Renaissance Humanism and the genera eloquentiae," *Rhetorica* 5 (1987): 279–309.

20. See TJ to his daughter Martha, May 21, 1787, in *Family Letters,* 41; to Maria Cosway, Apr. 24, 1788, Boyd 13:104. Note also Laurence Sterne's avowed desire to "pay a sentimental visit" to Petrarch's tomb, in Sterne to Lydia Sterne, Feb. 23, 1767, in *Letters of Laurence Sterne,* 132.

21. See Tinkler, "Renaissance Humanism and the genera eloquentiae." See also Wood, *Radicalism of the American Revolution,* 99–104.

22. TJ to William B. Giles, Apr. 27, 1795, Ford 7:12. See also TJ to Alexander Donald, Feb. 7, 1788, Boyd 12:572; Gisela Tauber, "Reconstruction in Psychoanalytic Biography: Understanding Thomas Jefferson," *Journal of Psychohistory* 7 (1979): 189–207.

23. See May, *Trials of Character,* esp. 5–9, 162–66. See also Fliegelman, *Declaring Independence,* 105.

24. See TJ to Edmund Randolph, Feb. 3, 1794, to Story, Dec. 5, 1801, L&B 9:280, 10:299; to Mann Page, Aug. 30, 1795, Ford 7:24. See also Gilbert Chinard, *Thomas Jefferson, The Apostle of Americanism* (Boston, 1939), 130. Jefferson owned two editions, 1659 and 1669 (Sowerby, *Catalogue of the Library of Thomas Jefferson* 2:45–46).

25. Jeffrey Martin Green, "Montaigne's Critique of Cicero," *Journal of the History of Ideas* 36 (1975): 599.

26. "Of Books," in *The Complete Essays of Montaigne,* trans. Donald Frame (Stanford, Calif., 1958).

27. Graham Good, *The Observing Self: Rediscovering the Essay* (London, 1988), 28–29; Lehmann, *Thomas Jefferson, American Humanist* 113, 119; TJ to Priestley, Jan. 27, 1800, L&B 10:148.

28. "Of Friendship," in *Complete Essays of Montaigne,* 137.

29. George M. Logan, "The Relation of Montaigne to Renaissance Humanism," *Journal of the History of Ideas* 36 (1975): 613–32; Johnson, *Dictionary* (1783).

30. Gay, *The Enlightenment: An Interpretation* 2:58–65.

31. Richardson to Sophia Westcomb, 1746(?), cited in Redford, *Converse of the Pen,* 1; TJ to Robert Skipwith, Aug. 3, 1771, Boyd 1:79; Fliegelman, *Declaring Independence,* 58. See also Fliegelman, *Prodigals and Pilgrims,* 100–101.

32. Malvin R. Zirker, Jr., "Richardson's Correspondence: The Personal Letter as Private Experience," in Howard Anderson et al., eds., *The Familiar Letter in the Eighteenth Century* (Lawrence, Kans., 1966), 74–78.

33. See DeMaria, *Johnson's* Dictionary *and the Language of Learning.*

34. Johnson to Mrs. Thrale, cited in Philip B. Daghlian, "Dr. Johnson in His Letters: The Public Guise of Private Matter," in Anderson, *Familiar Letter in the Eighteenth Century,* 120; Johnson to Mrs. Thrale, Oct. 27, 1777, in *Samuel Johnson: Rasselas, Poems, and Selected Prose,* 23; Redford, *Converse of the Pen,* 3, citing Boswell's *Life of Johnson.*

35. See Goodman, "Enlightenment Salons."

36. McFarland, *Romantic Cruxes,* chap. 1. See also George Lakoff and Mark Johnson, *Metaphors We Live By* (Chicago, 1980), 190–91.

37. Good, *Observing Self,* 48, 53; TJ to Benjamin Rush, Jan. 16, 1811, Ford 9:296.

38. TJ to John Minor, Aug. 30, 1814, Randall 1:53–57, copying a letter he sent nearly fifty years earlier to Bernard Moore, and to John Garland Jefferson, Apr. 14, 1793, L&B 19:104. See also Madison to TJ, Feb. 11, 20, 1784, Boyd 6:537–38, 544; Cmiel, *Democratic Eloquence,* 34–35, 40.

39. Blair, *Lectures,* lecture 1, 12, lecture 2, 16–19.

40. Ibid., 20.

41. Miller, *Jefferson and Nature,* 27; Lehmann, *Thomas Jefferson, American Humanist,* 143–44.

42. Blair, *Lectures,* lecture 13, 134–42; TJ to Edward Everett, Feb. 24, 1823, L&B 15:414.

43. "Thoughts on English Prosody," L&B 18:415–51. See also Fliegelman, *Declaring Independence,* 4–15.

44. L&B 18:447–48; Blair, *Lectures,* lecture 38, 431–32, lecture 42, 470.

45. Lehmann, *Thomas Jefferson, American Humanist,* 151; TJ to George Hammond, Feb. 16, 1793, to John Page, Aug. 20, 1785, Boyd 25:207, 8:418.

46. Blair, *Lectures,* lecture 6, 58b.

47. Ibid., lecture 36, 414.

48. Melmoth, preface to *Letters of Pliny the Consul*; W. S. Lewis and John Riely, eds., *Horace Walpole's Miscellaneous Correspondence* 3 (New Haven, 1980): 97–98, 100.

49. Bolingbroke and Alexander Pope to Jonathan Swift, Apr. 9, 1730, in *The Correspondence of Jonathan Swift,* cited in Keith Stewart, "Towards Defining an Aesthetic for the Familiar Letter in Eighteenth-Century England," *Prose Studies* 5 (1982): 185.

50. As an inveterate collector and cataloguer of correspondence, Jefferson was self-conscious about the historical value his letters, posthumously published, would possess. Still he termed his letters "secret" and "sacred" and wrote with conviction and little inhibition "in the warmth and freshness of fact and feeling" so that letters would "carry internal evidence that what they breathe is genuine" (TJ to Adams, Aug. 10, 1815, *Adams-Jefferson Letters,* 453; TJ to William Johnson, Mar. 4, 1823, Ford 10:248).

51. TJ to Logan, May 19, 1816, Ford 10:26.

52. See Roy Porter and Sylvana Tomaselli, eds., *The Dialectics of Friendship* (London, 1989); Robert R. Bell, *Worlds of Friendship* (Beverly Hills, Calif., 1981); Lawrence A. Blum, *Friendship, Altruism, and Morality* (London, 1980); Valerian J. Derlega and Barbara A. Winstead, eds., *Friendship and Social Interaction* (New York, 1986); Erik H. Erikson, *Identity and the Life Cycle* (New York, 1980); McWilliams, *Idea of Fraternity in America;* in Jefferson's day the word *friendship* also could denote a relationship based not on equality but on dependency. See Wood, *Radicalism of the American Revolution,* 58; see also Alan Taylor, "From Fathers to Friends of the People: Political Personas in the Early Republic," *Journal of the Early Republic* 11 (1991): 465–92.

53. Randall 1:24; *Memoir* 1:2.

54. Ibid. See also TJ to Small, May 7, 1775, Boyd 1:165–66, written before Jefferson learned of Small's death a few months earlier.

55. Lehmann, *Thomas Jefferson, American Humanist,* 40–42; Fliegelman, *Prodigals and Pilgrims,* 47; TJ to Wythe, Sept. 16, 1787, Boyd 12:129; to John Saunderson, Aug. 31, 1820, *Memoir* 1:91–94; Benjamin Rush, *The Autobiography of Benjamin Rush: His "Travels through Life" Together with His Commonplace Book for 1789–1813,* ed. George W. Corner (Princeton, N.J., 1948), 151.

56. "Reminiscences of Th. J. by MR," in Edgehill Randolph Papers; Smith, *First Forty Years of Washington Society,* 75; Joyce Blackburn, *George Wythe of Williamsburg* (New York, 1975), 41–43; William Clarkin, *Serene Patriot: A Life of George Wythe* (Albany, 1970), 40; Malone 1:104. See also TJ to Priestley, Jan. 27, 1800, L&B 9:146–47.

57. See Daniel J. Levinson, *The Seasons of a Man's Life* (New York, 1978), esp. 97–101, 253; Wood, *Radicalism of the American Revolution,* 74–77.

58. Erickson, *Identity and the Life Cycle,* 157–58; Amos Handel, "Formative En-

counters in Early Adulthood: Mentoring Relationships in a Writer's Autobiographical Reconstruction of His Past Self," *Human Development* 33 (1990): 289–303; Dennis O. Vidoni et al., "The Mentor-Protégé Relationship in a University Setting," *College Student Journal* 22 (1988): 404–7.

59. Roy F. Baumeister and Dianne M. Tice, "How Adolescence Became the Struggle for Self: A Historical Transformation of Psychological Development," in Jerry Suls and Anthony G. Greenwald, eds., *Psychological Perspectives on the Self* 3 (Hillsdale, N.J., 1986): 183–201; Malone 1:80–81. See also Fliegelman, *Prodigals and Pilgrims,* esp. 18–20; Harold Hellenbrand, *The Unfinished Revolution: Education and Politics in the Thought of Thomas Jefferson* (Newark, Del., 1990), chap. 1.

60. *Memoir* 1:3; Randall 1:38–40, citing Jefferson's Aug. 14, 1814, letter to William Wirt, Henry's biographer.

61. See Boyd's explanatory note, 1:384–86. See also George Wythe to TJ, July 27, 1776, ibid., 476–77. Bills are detailed in ibid., 2:305ff.

62. Malone 1:126–27, 5:139; Smith, *First Forty Years of Washington Society,* 73.

63. TJ to Thomas Jefferson Randolph, Nov. 24, 1808, *Family Letters,* 362–63. For Jefferson's later comments on Peyton Randolph, see TJ to Joseph Delaplaine, July 26, 1816, Ford 10:58.

64. Hume, *An Inquiry concerning Human Understanding,* 61.

65. John Page's "Memoir," a letter to Skelton Jones, Aug. 1808, *Virginia Historical Register* 3 (1850): 142–51.

66. TJ to Page, Dec. 25, 1762, Boyd 1:5–6.

67. TJ to Page, Jan. 20, 1762, ibid., 7–8.

68. TJ to Page, July 15, 1763, ibid., 10–11.

69. TJ to Page, Jan. 23, 1764, ibid., 15.

70. TJ to Page, May 25, 1766, Feb. 21, 1770, ibid., 18–19, 34–36. See Sterne, *Tristram Shandy* 1:5.

71. Blair, *Lectures,* lecture 16, 169–70.

72. TJ to Page, Feb. 21, 1770, Boyd 1:34–36.

73. Page to TJ, Nov. 11, 1775, Apr. 6, July 20, 1776, ibid., 259, 287, 470.

74. Page to TJ, June 2, 1779, TJ to Page, June 3, 1779, ibid., 2:278, 279.

75. Page to TJ, Apr. 28, 1785, TJ to Page, Aug. 20, 1785, ibid., 8:117, 417.

76. Page to TJ, Aug. 23, 1785, ibid., 428–29.

77. TJ to James Madison, Dec. 8, 1784, to Page, May 4, 1786, ibid., 7:558, 9:444–46. Boyd noted that "out" should be read with the sense of "outside."

78. TJ to William Hamilton, Apr. 22, 1800, Ford 7:441.

79. Randall 2:103; *Annals of the Congress of the United States,* 4th Cong., 1st sess. (Washington, D.C., 1849), 1097–98; TJ to Page, Jan. 1, 1798, Ford 7:185.

80. TJ to Page, Feb. 20, 1802, Ford 9:351.

81. Page to TJ, May 25, 1804, Jefferson Papers, Library of Congress; TJ to Page, June 25, 1804, in *Domestic Life,* 302–4. That the phrase "under all the inspiring energies . . ." is an insertion is apparent only in the original letter in the Library of Congress (see fig. 10).

82. TJ to Page, Sept. 6, 1808, Page to TJ, Aug. 6, 1805, Sept. 13, 1808, Jefferson Papers, Library of Congress; Malone 5:658.

83. Randall 1:82; TJ to Page, Feb. 21, 1770, Boyd 1:36.

84. *Memoir* 1:4; Randall 1:83.

85. TJ to James Madison, May 8, 1784, to Thomas Stone, Mar. 16, 1782, Boyd 7:233, 6:168.

86. TJ to Peter Carr, Aug. 19, 1785, Boyd 8:406; to Thomas Jefferson Randolph, Nov. 24, 1808, *Family Letters*, 363–65.

87. TJ to Rush, Jan. 3, 1808, L&B 11:413. By "science," Jefferson meant any kind of knowledge which was built on demonstrable principles. In today's terms, this encompassed both liberal arts and the physical sciences.

88. Smith, *Forty Years in Washington Society*, 6–7; Bear, *Jefferson at Monticello*, 71. See also letter of Apr. 3, 1790, in *New Letters of Abigail Adams, 1788–1801*, ed. Stewart Mitchell (Boston, 1947), 44.

89. Hogendorp Papers, cited in Boyd 7:82n; TJ to Hogendorp, May 4, 1784, ibid., 209.

90. Alexander Donald to TJ, Nov. 12, 1787, ibid., 12:348. See also TJ to Maury, Dec. 24, 1786, ibid., 10:628.

91. Henry Adams, *History of the United States of America during the Administration of Thomas Jefferson*, 2 vols. (1889; rept. New York, 1930), 1:144.

92. TJ to Monroe, Dec. 18, 1786, Boyd 10:612; Jan Lewis, "'The Blessings of Domestic Society': Thomas Jefferson's Family and the Transformation of American Politics," in Onuf, *Jeffersonian Legacies*, 139.

93. Howard Anderson and Irvin Ehrenpreis, "The Familiar Letter in the Eighteenth Century: Some Generalizations," in Anderson, *Familiar Letter in the Eighteenth Century*, 276–82; TJ to John D. Burke, June 21, 1801, Ford 8:65; to Eliza House Trist, Dec. 11, 1783 (?), to Page, May 4, 1786, Boyd 6:382–83, 9:444–46; to Priestley, Jan. 27, 1800, L&B 9:147.

94. TJ to Washington, May 23, 1792, Ford 7:341–49; Stanley Elkins and Eric McKitrick, *The Age of Federalism* (New York, 1993), 48–50.

95. McWilliams, *Idea of Fraternity in America*, 208, 210.

5. Friends, Neighborhood, and the Family Fireside

1. Randall 1:20–21, 49–51; Chinard, *Thomas Jefferson: Apostle of Americanism*, 37.

2. Randall 1:33.

3. Ibid., 1:45, 50, 3:312.

4. William Maclay, *The Journal of William Maclay* (1890; rept. New York, 1965), 265–66.

5. Ibid., 302.

6. Irving Brant, *James Madison*, 6 vols. (Indianapolis, 1941), 1:273–77; Ketcham, *James Madison*, 81 and chaps. 6 and 7. See also Malone 1:396–401, 406; Charles B. Sanford, *Thomas Jefferson and His Library* (Hamden, Conn., 1977).

7. TJ to Madison, Feb. 20, 1784, Boyd 6:550.

8. TJ to Washington, Mar. 13, 1784, ibid., 7:25–26; to Du Pont, Jan. 18, 1802, *Correspondence between Thomas Jefferson and Pierre Samuel du Pont de Nemours, 1798–1817*, ed. Dumas Malone (Boston, 1930), 40.

9. TJ to Madison, Dec. 8, 1784, Boyd 7:558–59.

10. For some differences of opinion between Madison and Jefferson, significant but neither of lasting consequence nor personally disruptive, see Merrill Peterson, *Jefferson and Madison and the Making of Constitutions* (Charlottesville, Va., 1987), 8–12; Drew R. McCoy, *The Last of the Fathers: James Madison and the Republican Legacy* (Cambridge, 1989), 44–60.

11. Harry Ammon, *James Monroe: The Quest for National Identity* (New York, 1971), chaps. 1 and 2; Malone 1:324–25; Peterson, *Thomas Jefferson and the New Nation,* 196.

12. TJ to Monroe, July 9, Dec. 18, 1786, Boyd 10:114–15, 612–13. See also Monroe to TJ, May 11, 1786, ibid., 9:511.

13. Monroe to TJ, July 27, 1787, TJ to Monroe, Aug. 9, 1788, ibid., 11:630, 13:490.

14. TJ to Monroe, May 26, 1795, Ford 7:16–21.

15. Malone 6:508; TJ to Madison, Sept. 30, 1781, Boyd 6:122; George Green Shackelford, *Jefferson's Adoptive Son: The Life of William Short, 1759–1848* (Lexington, Ky., 1993), 8.

16. Short to TJ, May 8, 1784, TJ to Madison, Feb. 11, 1784, Boyd 7:236, 6:548.

17. Brant, *James Madison* 1:277; Peterson, *Thomas Jefferson and the New Nation,* 266; Peterson, *Jefferson and Madison and the Making of Constitutions,* 1.

18. Madison to TJ, Jan. 15, 1782, TJ to Madison, Mar. 24, 1782, Boyd 6: 149, 171. See also Madison to TJ, Nov. 18, 1781, Jan. 15, Mar. 18, Apr. 16, 1782, Feb. 11, May 13, 1783, ibid., 132, 149, 170, 177, 235, 269, and TJ to Madison, Mar. 24, Nov. 26, 1782, Jan. 31, June 1, 1783, ibid., 171, 207, 226, 274.

19. TJ to Madison, Aug. 31, 1783, Mar. 16, 1784, to Washington, Jan. 22, 1783, to Short, Mar. 15, 29, 1787, ibid., 6:336, 7:31, 6:222, 11:215, 255. During this period Jefferson did on occasion express "perfect esteem" to others (including one who was not his intimate: French physicist Jean Baptiste Le Roy, Nov. 13, 1786, ibid., 10:530). However, only to Short did he join "perfect" to "friendship" in a single phrase. Short, in turn, wrote to Jefferson on Mar. 12 (the letter crossed in the mail with Jefferson's of Mar. 15), signing off, "None of [your friends] can be half so much attached to you either by the ties of affection or gratitude as Your friend & servant" (ibid., 11:210).

20. TJ to Maria Cosway, Oct. 12, 1786, to Madison, Jan. 30, 1787, to Bellini, Sept. 30, 1785, ibid., 10:447, 8:569, 11:96; to Gerry, Jan. 26, 1799, Ford 7:335; to Gov. William H. Harrison, Feb. 27, 1803, L&B 10:372.

21. TJ to Madison, May 8, 1784, Boyd 7:234.

22. TJ to Madison, Feb. 5, 1787, Monroe to TJ, July 27, 1787, ibid., 11:97, 631.

23. Peterson, *Thomas Jefferson and the New Nation,* 829–31; Malone 5:413–14.

24. TJ to Monroe, Feb. 18, 1808, Ford 9:177–78; to Monroe, Mar. 10, 1808, L&B 12:3–8.

25. Ibid.; TJ to Monroe, Apr. 11, 1808, Ford 9:181.

26. Ammon, *James Monroe,* chap. 15; Malone 5:549–53; Ketcham, *James Madison,* 437–38, 467, 485; TJ to Monroe, May 5, 1811, Ford 9:323.

27. TJ to Monroe, Nov. 11, 1784, Boyd 7:509.

28. TJ to Madison, Dec. 8, 1784, to Monroe, June 17, 1785, ibid., 7:559, 8:233.

29. TJ to Madison, Jan. 30, June 20, 1787, ibid., 11:94, 481–82; Adrienne Koch, *Jefferson and Madison: The Great Collaboration* (New York, 1950), chaps. 2 and 3.

30. TJ to Madison, Nov. 18, 1788, Boyd 14:189–90.

31. TJ to Monroe, Dec. 18, 1786, ibid., 10:612; to Monroe, Feb. 8, Mar. 8, 21, 1798, Ford 7:198, 216, 257–59. See also Monroe to TJ, Apr. 10, 1788, Boyd 13:49.

32. TJ to John Trumbull, June 1, 1789, Boyd 15:164; Shackelford, *Jefferson's Adoptive Son*, chaps. 9, 14.

33. TJ to Short, Mar. 15, 1787, Boyd 11:214.

34. TJ to Short, Mar. 24, 1789, to John Trumbull, June 1, 1789, ibid., 14:695–97, 15:163–64; to Short, Jan. 3, 1793, Ford 6:156. See also TJ to Jay, Nov. 19, 1788, Boyd 14:215.

35. Rush, *Autobiography*, 181; Madison to Washington, Jan. 4, 1790, *The Papers of James Madison*, ed. Charles F. Hobson et al. 12 (Charlottesville, Va., 1979): 467; TJ to his daughter Martha, May 31, June 23, 1791, *Family Letters*, 84–85. For a critical viewpoint, see Elkins and McKitrick, *Age of Federalism*, 241–42.

36. Malone 5:484, 487; Brant, *James Madison* 4:402; Ketcham, *James Madison*, 412.

37. Cited in Ketcham, *James Madison*, 630.

38. Madison to Nicholas Trist, July 6, 1826, in Randall 3:550; Malone 4:254–55. I am indebted to John Stagg, editor of *The Papers of James Madison*, for shedding light on the preliminaries to the Louisiana Purchase.

39. Madison to Nicholas Trist, May 1832, cited in Malone 3:268.

40. *Memoir* 1:33–34.

41. Ketcham, *James Madison*, 317–18, 388; Malone 2:324; TJ to Madison, Dec. 28, 1794, Apr. 27, 1795, Ford 6:519, 7:8–9; Koch, *Jefferson and Madison*, 162–66.

42. See Fliegelman's exposition of the Lockean-Scottish Common Sense consensus on rearing children in *Prodigals and Pilgrims*, chap. 2.

43. Daniel Preston, "James Monroe and Personal Patronage in Jeffersonian Virginia," Society for Historians of the Early American Republic, July 1993.

44. *Memoir*, 1:88; TJ to Ferdinand Grand, Apr. 23, 1790, Boyd 16:369.

45. TJ to Madison, Aug. 30, 1823, in Randall 1:165; Van Doren, *Benjamin Franklin*, 550; TJ to Robert Walsh, Dec. 4, 1818, Ford 10:120.

46. Benjamin Franklin, *The Autobiography of Benjamin Franklin* (New York, 1962), 17; *Memoir* 1:1. See also Herbert Leibowitz, *Fabricating Lives: Explorations in American Autobiography* (New York, 1989), chap. 2.

47. Franklin, *Autobiography*, 61–62; TJ to Caesar Rodney, Feb. 10, 1810, to John Melish, Jan. 13, 1813, to Elbridge Gerry, Jan. 26, 1799, Ford 9:272, 9:376, 7:335; to Carr, Aug. 19, 1785, Boyd 8:405–8.

48. TJ to Rev. William Smith, Feb. 19, 1791, Boyd 19:112–13.

49. *Adams-Jefferson Letters*, xxxiii; John Adams to Abigail Adams, July 1, 1774, *Familiar Letters of John Adams and His Wife Abigail Adams, during the Revolution*, 6–7.

50. Peterson, *Thomas Jefferson and the New Nation*, 165; Peterson, *John Adams and Thomas Jeferson*, 15.

51. Madison to TJ, Oct. 17, 1788, Boyd 14:17.

52. John Ferling, "John Adams, Diplomat," *William and Mary Quarterly* 51 (1994):227–52; Peter Shaw, *The Character of John Adams* (Chapel Hill, N.C., 1976),

chaps. 6 and 7 and esp. 167–68; William Cabell Bruce, *Benjamin Franklin Self-Revealed,* 2 vols. (New York, 1917), 1:350–51.

53. TJ to Madison, Jan. 20, 1787, Boyd 11:94–95. See also TJ to Madison, July 29, 1789, ibid., 15:315–16.

54. Randall 1:423–424; TJ to Benjamin Rush, Jan. 16, 1811, Ford 9:296.

55. TJ to Adams, May 25, 1785, Abigail Adams to TJ, June 6, 1785, July 23, 1786, *Adams-Jefferson Letters,* 23, 28, 145; Malone 2:13–14.

56. TJ to Abigail Adams, July 1, Oct. 4, 1787; Abigail Adams to TJ, July 6, Sept. 10, 1787; John Adams to TJ, July 10, 1787; *Adams-Jefferson Letters,* 179, 201, 183, 197, 187.

57. John Adams to TJ, Sept. 4, 1785, TJ to Abigail Adams, Sept. 25, 1785, ibid., 61, 70.

58. Adams to TJ, Jan. 2, Mar. 1, 1789; TJ to Adams, May 10, 1789, ibid., 234, 237, 239.

59. TJ to Jonathan B. Smith, Apr. 26, 1791, to Washington, May 8, 1791, to Adams, July 17, 1791, Boyd 20: 290, 291, 302. In general, see ibid., 268–74. For Adams's reply, see Adams to TJ, July 29, 1791, ibid., 305.

60. TJ to Adams, Aug. 30, 1791, ibid., 311.

61. TJ to Adams, Apr. 25, 1794, Feb. 6, 1795, Feb. 28, 1796; Adams to TJ, May 1, Nov. 21, 1794, *Adams-Jefferson Letters,* 254, 258–60, 255–58.

62. See Elkins and McKitrick, *Age of Federalism,* 539–40 and chap. 13.

63. TJ to Benjamin Rush, Jan. 16, 1811, Ford 9:296–97.

64. TJ to Abigail Adams, June 13, 1804, *Adams-Jefferson Letters,* 269–71.

65. Abigail Adams to TJ, Aug. 18, 1804; TJ to Abigail Adams, July 22, 1804; to John Adams, Jan 21, 23, 1812, ibid., 277, 276, 292–93.

66. TJ to Adams, Dec. 28, 1796, ibid., 262–63; to Madison, Jan. 1, 1797, Ford 7:95–97.

67. TJ to Rittenhouse, July 19, 1778, Nov. 11, 1784; to Francis Hopkinson, Jan. 13, 1785; Rittenhouse to TJ, Apr. 14, 1787, Boyd 2:202–3, 7:516–17, 602, 11:293; *Notes,* 64.

68. Page to TJ, Apr. 28, 1785, Boyd 8:117–18; TJ to Martha Jefferson, Jan. 15, 1784, *Family Letters,* 23.

69. TJ to Rittenhouse, Jan. 7, 1793; Rittenhouse to TJ, Jan. 11, 1793, Boyd 25:31, 46.

70. George Everett Hastings, *The Life and Works of Francis Hopkinson* (New York, 1926), esp. 217, 243–44.

71. Hopkinson to TJ, Jan. 4, 1784, TJ to Hopkinson, Feb. 18, 1784, Boyd 6:443–46, 542.

72. TJ to Monroe, May 21, 1784, Hopkinson to TJ, Nov. 8, 1786, Boyd 7:281, 10:512.

73. Boyd Stanley Schlenther, *Charles Thomson: A Patriot's Pursuit* (Newark, Del., 1990); J. Edwin Hendricks, *Charles Thomson and the Making of a New Nation* (Rutherford, N.J., 1979); Boorstin, *Lost World of Thomas Jefferson,* 10–11.

74. Dumbauld, *Thomas Jefferson, American Tourist,* 48; TJ to Thomson, Dec. 20, 1781, Boyd 6:142; Schlenther, *Charles Thomson.*

75. Malone 4:178, 419, 5:26; Boorstin, *Lost World of Thomas Jefferson*, 19–21; Miller, *Jefferson and Nature*, 124–25; TJ to Peale, Aug. 20, 1811, L&B 13:79. See also Fliegelman, *Prodigals and Pilgrims*, 213.

76. TJ to Rush, Sept. 23, 1800, L&B 10:175; Rush to TJ, Oct. 6, 1800, Mar. 12, 1801, *Letters of Benjamin Rush*, ed. L. H. Butterfield, 2 vols. (Princeton, N.J., 1951), 2:826, 831–33.

77. Rush to Adams, Oct. 17, 1809, *Letters of Benjamin Rush* 2:1021–22; *Adams-Jefferson Letters*, 284–86.

78. TJ to Rush, Aug. 17, 1811, Ford 9:329; TJ to Adams, May 27, 1813, *Adams-Jefferson Letters*, 323.

79. U.S. Dept. of State, *Great Seal of the United States*. See also John Adams to Abigail Adams, Aug. 14, 1776, *Familiar Letters of John Adams and His Wife Abigail Adams, during the Revolution*, 210–11.

80. See McEwan, *Thomas Jefferson: Farmer*, chap. 5.

81. Adams to TJ, July 29, 1791, Boyd 20:306.

82. TJ to Martha, June 8, 1797, *Family Letters*, 146; William H. Gaines, Jr., *Thomas Mann Randolph, Jefferson's Son-in-Law* (Kingsport, Tenn., 1966).

83. TJ to Maria, June 4, 1797, *Family Letters*, 148; Malone 3:239.

84. *Garden and Farm Books of Thomas Jefferson*, 236–48; Stanton, "Those Who Labor for My Happiness," 150–51; Isaac Weld, Jr., *Travels through the States of North America* (London, 1799), in Peterson, *Visitors to Monticello*, 19; TJ to William Branch Giles, Apr. 27, 1795, Ford 7:12; Peterson, *Thomas Jefferson and the New Nation*, 518–19.

85. TJ to Maria Cosway, Sept. 8, 1795, in Bullock, *My Head and My Heart*, 142–43.

86. TJ to Martha, May 12, Mar. 24, 1793, *Family Letters*, 117, 114.

87. TJ to Martha, Mar. 27, 1797, May 17, 1798; Martha to TJ, May 12, 1798, ibid., 142, 161, 160.

88. Chastellux to Rev. James Madison, Jan. 1783, *Travels in North America*, 529–31, 543 (letter added as appendix to 1786 edition on Jefferson's advice); TJ to Martha, Apr. 5, 1798, Feb. 11, 1800; Martha to TJ, May 12, 1798; TJ to Maria, June 6, 1798, July 4, 1800, *Family Letters*, 159–60, 183–84, 160, 165–66, 189.

89. Maria to TJ, Mar. 20, 1798; TJ to Maria, April 1, June 6, 1798, *Family Letters*, 157–58, 166.

90. TJ to Martha, May 31, 1798, Jan. 26, 1793; TJ to Maria, Jan. 1, 1799; Maria to TJ, Jan. 21, 1799, ibid., 164, 110, 170, 171.

91. Smith, *First Forty Years of Washington Society*, 34.

92. TJ to Maria, Feb. 7, Apr. 13, 1799, Feb. 12, 1800, *Family Letters*, 173–74, 177, 185.

93. TJ to Martha, June 8, 1797, ibid., 146.

94. TJ to Maria, May 30, 1791, ibid., 83–84.

95. Mark Snyder and Dave Smith, "Personality and Friendship: The Friendship Worlds of Self-Monitoring," in Derlega and Winstead, *Friendship and Social Interaction*, 63–64. See also Daniel Perlman and Beverley Fehr, "Theories of Friendship: The Analysis of Interpersonal Attraction," ibid., 19–22.

96. See Quinby, "Thomas Jefferson: The Virtue of Aesthetics and the Aesthetics of Virtue."

97. Erikson, *Identity and the Life Cycle*, 85.

6. OBSTRUCTED VISION

1. *Memoir* 1:47; Thomas Gustafson, *Representative Words: Politics, Literature, and the American Language, 1776–1865* (Cambridge, 1992), 231–33. See also Fliegelman, *Declaring Independence*, 103–7; TJ to Adams, Aug. 22, 1813, *Adams-Jefferson Letters*, 369.

2. *Memoir* 1:3; Randolph cited in Malone 1:121.

3. *Memoir* 1:7.

4. TJ to Zane, Dec. 24, 1781, Boyd 6:143.

5. Malone 1:361. See also *Notes*, 120.

6. For the seductive villain type, see Fliegelman, *Prodigals and Pilgrims*, 232–33.

7. Clark to TJ, Feb. 20, 1782; TJ to Clark, Nov. 26, 1782, Boyd 6: 159–60, 204–5.

8. TJ to Madison, May 7, 1783, ibid., 266.

9. TJ to Madison, Dec. 8, 1784, ibid., 583.

10. TJ to Wirt, Aug. 4, 1805, Jefferson Papers, Library of Congress.

11. TJ to Thomas Ritchie, Dec. 25, 1820, Ford 10:171.

12. Gustafson, *Representative Words*, 20; Jack P. Greene, *Peripheries and Center: Constitutional Development in the Extended Polities of the British Empire and the United States, 1607–1788* (New York, 1986), 157–61.

13. Joanne Freeman, "Slander, Poison, Whispers, and Fame: Jefferson's *Anas* and Political Gossip in the Early Republic" (M.A. thesis, Univ. of Virginia, 1993), 7; Blair, *Lectures*, lecture 1, 15.

14. See, esp., Bernard Bailyn, *The Ideological Origins of the American Revolution* (Cambridge, Mass., 1967); Banning, *Jeffersonian Persuasion*, chap. 2; Gordon S. Wood, *The Creation of the American Republic, 1776–1787* (Chapel Hill, 1969), esp. 34–43, 67–75.

15. Plumer to Jeremiah Smith, Dec. 10, 1791, Plumer Papers, Library of Congress, cited in Freeman, "Slander, Poison, Whispers, and Fame," 7. See also Robert A. Ferguson, "Mysterious Obligation': Jefferson's Notes on the State of Virginia," *American Literature* 52 (1980):404–6; Gordon S. Wood, "Conspiracy and the Paranoid Style: Causality and Deceit in the Eighteenth Century," *William and Mary Quarterly* 39 (1982):401–41.

16. Boyd 7:478.

17. TJ to Chastellux, Sept. 2, 1785, ibid., 8:468. See also TJ to Trist, Dec. 15, 1786, ibid., 10:600; Adams, *History of the United States during the Administration of Thomas Jefferson* 1:137–38, 145–48.

18. *Memoir* 1:47.

19. TJ to Madison, June 9, 1793, to Robert Livingston, April 18, 1802, Ford 6:291, 8:144–45; to John Randolph, Aug. 25, 1775, Boyd 1:241.

20. Notably, see Edward Carrington to TJ, Oct. 23, 1787, Boyd 12:252–57. See also Madison to TJ, Oct. 24, 1787, ibid., 270–84.

21. *Journal of William Maclay*, Aug. 29, 1789, 140; TJ to Humphreys, Mar. 18, 1789, Boyd 14:679.

22. See "Slander, Poison, Whispers, and Fame"; Elkins and McKitrick, *Age of Federalism*, 78.

23. Nathan Schachner, *Alexander Hamilton* (New York, 1946), 1–15; Angelica Church to Elizabeth Hamilton, June 5, 1793, Feb. 4, July 30, 1794, in Allan McLane Hamilton, *The Intimate Life of Alexander Hamilton* (New York, 1910), 66, 258–59; Madison to TJ, Apr. 22, 1783, Aug. 10, 1788, Boyd 6:262–63, 13:498–99; Chastellux, *Travels in North America* 1:343–44.

24. Schachner, *Alexander Hamilton*, chaps. 3–5.

25. Ibid., 120–23; Broadus Mitchell, *Alexander Hamilton: The Revolutionary Years* (New York, 1970), chap. 11; Malone 2:271.

26. Schachner, *Alexander Hamilton*, 62; Hamilton to Laurens, Apr. 1779, Aug. 15, 1782, *The Papers of Alexander Hamilton*, ed. Harold C. Syrett, et al., 27 vols. (New York, 1961–87), 2:34–35, 3:145.

27. Schachner, *Alexander Hamilton*, 204; Peterson, *Thomas Jefferson and the New Nation*, 397.

28. *Anas*, 30.

29. Ibid., 54–55; Forrest McDonald, *Alexander Hamilton: A Biography* (New York, 1979), chap. 8 and 212–13; Malone 2:339; TJ to Washington, May 23, 1792, Boyd 23:538–39.

30. *Anas*, 30–35. See also Jacob E. Cooke, "The Compromise of 1790," *William and Mary Quarterly* 27 (1970):523–45; exchange between Cooke and Kenneth Bowling, "Dinner at Jefferson's: A Note on Jacob E. Cooke's 'The Compromise of 1790,'" ibid., 28 (1971):629–48; further notes by Norman K. Risjord, ibid., 33 (1976):309–14; Elkins and McKitrick, *Age of Federalism*, 155–60.

31. Hamilton to Carrington, May 26, 1792, *Papers of Alexander Hamilton* 11:426–45.

32. Hamilton to Washington, Sept. 9, 1792, ibid., 12:348; *Anas* 84.

33. *Gazette of the United States*, Aug. 4, Sept. 22, Nov. 24, 1792, in Philip M. Marsh, ed., *Monroe's Defense of Jefferson and Freneau against Hamilton* (Oxford, Ohio, 1948).

34. TJ to Washington, May 23, 1792; Washington to TJ, Aug. 23, 1792, Boyd 23:535–38, 24:317.

35. TJ to Washington, Sept. 9, 1792, Ford 6:101–9 (quoted in the next several paragraphs).

36. TJ to Edmund Randolph, Sept. 17, 1792, ibid., 112.

37. For other instances of "intrigue," see TJ to Peter Carr, Aug. 19, 1785, to John Banister, Jr., Oct. 15, 1785, to John Jay, May 9, 1789, Boyd 8:406, 636, 15:112; to John Adams, July 11, 1786, Nov. 13, 1787, *Adams-Jefferson Letters*, 142, 212.

38. TJ to Bellini, Sept. 30, 1785, Boyd 8:568–69.

39. TJ to Rush, Jan. 16, 1811, Ford 9:297–99.

40. George Alan Davy, "Argumentation and Unified Structure in *Notes on the State of Virginia*," *Eighteenth-Century Studies* 26 (1993):581–93.

41. TJ to John Randolph, Aug. 25, 1775, Boyd 1:241–42.

42. Angelica Church to TJ, Aug. 19, 1793, in Bullock, *My Head and My Heart,* 138; TJ to Angelica Church, Oct. 1792, June 7, 1793; to Madison, Sept. 8, 1793, Ford 6:115–16, 289–90, 419.

43. Hamilton to Carrington, May 26, 1792, *Papers of Alexander Hamilton* 11:440. See also TJ to Short, Jan. 3, Mar. 23, 1793, Ford 6:153–56, 207.

44. See Drew R. McCoy, *The Elusive Republic: Political Economy in Jeffersonian America* (New York, 1980), chap. 6.

45. See TJ to Mann Page, Aug. 30, 1795, Ford 7:25. Cf. Elkins and McKitrick, *Age of Federalism,* chap. 9.

46. TJ to Dr. Walter Jones, Jan. 2, 1814, L&B 14:49.

47. Washington to TJ, Apr. 8, 1784, TJ to Washington, Apr. 16, 1784, Boyd 7:88, 105–8.

48. Washington to TJ, Feb. 25, 1785, ibid., 8:5.

49. *Anas,* 24, 40. See also TJ to Dr. Walter Jones, Jan. 2, 1814, L&B 14:46–52.

50. TJ to Mazzei, Apr. 24, 1796, Ford 7:72–78. See also Malone 3:302–10; Elizabeth Dabney Coleman, "Peter Carr of Carr's-Brook (1770–1815)," *Papers of the Albemarle County Historical Society* 4 (1943–44):16–17.

51. TJ to Dr. Walter Jones, Jan. 2, 1814, L&B 14:48–52; to Van Buren, June 29, 1824, Ford 10:325–35. It is hard to accept Jefferson's explanation in full, as "Solomons in the council" suggests Washington above all.

52. *Autobiography of Colonel John Trumbull,* 173–75.

53. James Morton Smith, *Freedom's Fetters: The Alien and Sedition Laws and American Civil Liberties* (Ithaca, N.Y., 1956), chap. 6.

54. TJ to White, Sept. 10, 1797, to Taylor, Nov. 26, 1798, Ford 7:174, 309; to Kosciusko, Dec. 21, 1799, L&B 10:115.

55. TJ to Gerry, Jan. 26, 1799, Ford 7:335; George Athan Billias, *Elbridge Gerry* (New York, 1976).

56. TJ to Gerry, Jan. 26, 1799, Ford 7:325–26.

57. TJ to Taylor, June 1, 1798, ibid., 265.

58. TJ to Mazzei, July 18, 1804, L&B 11:38; to Short, May 19, 1807, Ford 9:51. For a reference to Hamilton's "mercenary phalanx," see *Anas,* 35.

59. TJ to John Norvell (a young Kentuckian), June 14, 1807, Ford 9:73.

60. Smith, *Freedom's Fetters,* chap. 15; Account Book entries from June 1797–June 1798, May 28, 1801. See also Michael Durey, *"With the Hammer of Truth": James Thomson Callender and America's Early National Heroes* (Charlottesville, Va., 1990), 104–6.

61. Peterson, *Thomas Jefferson and the New Nation,* 635–37, 707–8; Malone 4:207–14.

62. Schachner, *Alexander Hamilton,* 364–69; "Reynolds Pamphlet," *Papers of Alexander Hamilton* 21:238–67.

63. Hamilton to Laurens, Apr. 1779, *Papers of Alexander Hamilton* 2:37–38. Moreover, Hamilton had used deception shamelessly during his affair with Maria Reynolds, contriving to keep his wife and children in Albany while he remained in Philadelphia. See Hamilton to Elizabeth Hamilton, Aug. 2, 21, 1791, ibid., 9:6–7, 87; Madison to TJ, Oct. 20, 1797, cited ibid., 12:139.

64. See Malone 1:153–55, 447.

65. TJ to Logan, June 20, 1816, Ford 10:27; to Robert Smith, July 1, 1805, cited in Malone 1:448.

66. Malone 4:217–23. See also ibid., 1:451.

67. James Parton, *Life of Thomas Jefferson* (Boston, 1874), 568–70; Account Books, 1795, 1798, 1800, 1802, 1803. For biographical information about Peter Carr, see Coleman, "Peter Carr of Carr's-Brook."

68. Malone 4:494–98. See also *Garden and Farm Books of Thomas Jefferson*, 236, 246, 248.

69. Examples abound of Fawn Brodie's distortions of eighteenth-century language in the course of her crusade to link Jefferson and Sally Hemings romantically. Jefferson's use of "ardour" and "appetite" in letters possessed, for this author, the "unmistakable flavor of sexuality." Misinterpreting Jefferson's letter to Maria Cosway regarding Sterne and noses, she made reference to the unpictured Sally's ostensibly African nose. And Martha Jefferson's 1790 marriage allegedly reflected the daughter's "disillusionment and rage" toward her father for taking up with Sally who, even at age fifteen, was to have "represented all that had been alluring and forbidden in the world of [Jefferson's] childhood." See Brodie, *Thomas Jefferson,* 298–99, 323–26, 384–87.

70. See TJ to Monroe, Mar. 2, 1796, Ford 7:58.

71. TJ to Madison, Nov. 26, 1795, ibid., 37.

72. TJ to Madison, June 21, 1798, ibid., 273.

73. Marshall to C. C. Pinckney, Mar. 4, 1801, *The Papers of John Marshall,* ed. Charles F. Hobson, 6:89 (Chapel Hill, N.C., 1990).

74. Marshall to C. C. Pinckney, Nov. 21, 1802, ibid., 125–26; Malone 3:307, 4:192–98.

75. TJ to Maria Jefferson Eppes, Jan. 4, 1801, *Family Letters,* 190.

76. TJ to William B. Giles, Apr. 20, 1807, Ford 9:46.

77. Albert J. Beveridge, *The Life of John Marshall,* 4 vols. (Boston, 1916–19), 3:343–469; Chinard, *Thomas Jefferson: Apostle of Americanism,* 431–39; Malone 5:291–355, esp. 304–6. See also TJ to Giles, Apr. 20, 1807, to Lafayette July 14, 1807, to Du Pont de Nemours, July 14, 1807, Ford 9:46, 111, 113.

78. Malone 4:465–83; Dice Robins Anderson, *William Branch Giles: A Study in the Politics of Virginia and the Nation from 1790 to 1830* (Menasha, Wis., 1914), 117, 119; James Sterling Young, *The Washington Community, 1800–1828* (New York, 1966), 128–30, 163–65.

79. TJ to Adams, Aug. 10, 1815, *Adams-Jefferson Letters,* 453.

80. See Jones to TJ, Mar. 15, 1801, Nov. 25, 1813, TJ to Jones, Mar. 31, 1801, Jefferson Papers, Library of Congress.

81. Jones to TJ, Nov. 25, 1813, ibid.

82. TJ to Jones, Jan. 2, 1814, L&B 14:46–47.

83. TJ to Jones, Jan. 10, 1814, Jones to TJ, Feb. 16, 1814, Jefferson Papers, Library of Congress.

84. *Anas,* 23–25.

85. Johnson to TJ, Dec. 10, 1822, Apr. 11, 1823, Jefferson Papers, Library of Congress; TJ to Johnson, Mar. 4, 1823, Ford 10:247.

86. On erstwhile Republican Aaron Burr, see Monroe to Madison, Aug. 5, 1795, *Papers of James Madison* 16:44.

87. *Anas,* 187, 200.

88. Ibid., 37. See also TJ to John Melish, Jan. 13, 1813, Ford 9:374.

89. Randall 3:336.

90. Hamilton to Adams, Aug. 16, 1792, *Papers of Alexander Hamilton* 12:209.

91. TJ to Paine, June 19, 1792, Ford 6:88; to Martha, Jan. 16, 1801, *Family Letters,* 191.

92. TJ to Judge John Tyler, June 28, 1804, L&B 11:33–34; Malone 3:340–41; TJ to Giles, Apr. 20, 1807, Ford 9:46. See also Alfred H. Kelly, "American Political Leadership: The Optimistic Ethical World View and the Jeffersonian Synthesis," in the Library of Congress Symposium on the American Revolution, *Leadership in the American Revolution* (Washington, D.C., 1974), 7–39; Ralph Lerner, *The Thinking Revolutionary: Principal and Practice in the New Republic* (Ithaca, N.Y., 1987), 32–37; Michael Lienesch, "Thomas Jefferson and the American Democratic Experience: The Origins of the Partisan Press, Popular Political Parties, and Public Opinion," in Onuf, *Jeffersonian Legacies,* 316–39.

93. Cicero to Quintus, 54 B.C., *Letters to His Brother Quintus* 3.5,6; TJ to Madison, Jan. 1, 1797, Ford 7:98.

94. TJ to Hopkinson, Mar. 13, 1789, Boyd 14:651.

95. TJ to Madison, Jan. 1, 1797, June 9, 1793, Ford 7:97, 6:292; TJ to Maria Jefferson Eppes, Mar. 3, 1802, *Family Letters,* 219.

96. TJ to Abigail Adams, Sept. 11, 1804, *Adams-Jefferson Letters,* 278.

97. Bruce, *Benjamin Franklin Self-Revealed* 1:4, 340; TJ to Adams, May 5, 1817, *Adams-Jefferson Letters,* 513.

98. TJ to Richard M. Johnson, Mar. 10, 1808, L&B 12:9–10; comment as repeated by Thomas Jefferson Randolph, *Domestic Life,* 428.

99. Catanzariti, "Thomas Jefferson, Correspondent," 14–15; Malone 4:185–89; Jefferson to Adams, June 1, 1822, *Adams-Jefferson Letters,* 577–79; Peterson, *Visitors to Monticello,* 97–98.

100. Du Pont to TJ, July 6, 1800, TJ to Du Pont, July 26, 1800, in *Correspondence between Thomas Jefferson and Pierre Samuel du Pont de Nemours,* 17–18.

7. Retirement, Religion, and Romantic Death

1. TJ to Madison, June 9, 1793, Dec. 28, 1794, Ford 6:290–91, 519.

2. TJ to Dickinson, Jan. 13, 1807, Ford 9:10.

3. TJ to Maria, Feb. 26, 1804, to Martha, Mar. 8, 1804, *Family Letters,* 258–59; as described by one of Jefferson's granddaughters (presumably Ellen Wayles Randolph Coolidge), in Randall 3:101–2.

4. TJ to Martha, May 14, 1804, Martha to TJ, May 31, 1804, *Family Letters,* 259–60.

5. TJ to John W. Eppes, June 4, 1804, in Randall 3:99.

6. TJ to Hogendorp, May 4, 1784, to Maria Cosway, Oct. 12, 1786, Boyd 7:208, 10:449; to Martha, Nov. 23, 1807, *Family Letters,* 315.

7. Martha to TJ, Jan. 16, 1793, July 10, 1802, July 12, 1803, TJ to Martha, Apr. 9,

1797, Jan 21, 1805, Nov. 23, 1807, to Anne Cary Randolph, Nov. 1, 1807, *Family Letters,* 109, 233, 246–47, 143, 266, 315, 313.

8. TJ to Ellen Wayles Randolph, Oct. 25, 1808, to Martha, Nov. 1, 1808, Martha to TJ, Oct. 27, 1808, ibid., 354–56; TJ to Benjamin Rush, Aug. 11, 1811, Ford 9:328.

9. Martha to TJ, Jan. 31, 1801, TJ to Martha, Feb. 5, 1801, to Maria, Nov. 27, 1803, *Family Letters,* 192–93, 195, 249–50.

10. TJ to Martha, Jan. 5, 1808, Martha to TJ, Jan. 16, 1808, ibid., 319, 322.

11. Martha to TJ, Feb. 17, Mar. 2, 1809, TJ to Martha, Feb. 27, 1809, ibid., 382, 385–87; Bear, *Jefferson at Monticello,* 84.

12. TJ to Anne Randolph Bankhead, May 26, 1811, *Family Letters,* 400.

13. TJ to Martha, Feb. 5, 1801, Martha to TJ, Nov. 18, 1808, ibid., 196, 360; Malone 5:130–31. John Randolph of Roanoke (1773–1833) took to opposing President Jefferson after 1805 and lived to serve as both senator and congressman through the late 1820s. He fought a duel in 1826 with Henry Clay, in which neither of the duelists was hurt.

14. Anne Cary Randolph to TJ, Mar. 4, 1808, TJ to Thomas Jefferson Randolph, Nov. 24, 1808, Jan. 3, 1809, T. J. Randolph to TJ, Dec. 3, 1808, *Family Letters,* 331, 364, 376, 367.

15. Joseph Carroll Vance, "Thomas Jefferson Randolph" (Ph.D. diss., Univ. of Virginia, 1957).

16. Ellen Randolph to TJ, Dec. 19, 27, 1806, Nov. 11, 1807, TJ to Ellen, Feb. 4, Oct. 19, Dec. 8, 1807, Mar. 14, 29, 1808, *Family Letters,* 294–95, 312–17, 333–34, 338.

17. TJ to Ellen, Mar. 14, 1808, ibid., 333; *Domestic Life,* 344; Virginia to Nicholas Trist, May 26, 1839, cited in Randall 3:349.

18. TJ to F. W. Eppes, Sept. 6, 1811, *Family Letters,* 402.

19. See Randall 3:331; *Domestic Life,* 402–3. See also TJ to Martha, Nov. 4, 1815, *Family Letters,* 411–12.

20. Malone 6:298.

21. TJ to Jaury, Apr. 25, 1812, Ford 9:350–51.

22. TJ to John Garland Jefferson, Jan. 25, 1810, Ford 9:271; Smith, *First Forty Years of Washington Society,* 74–75; *Domestic Life,* 341; Bear, *Jefferson at Monticello,* 60, 72–74; TJ to John Melish, Jan. 13, 1813, Ford 9:377; Dr. Dunglison's memoranda, in *Domestic Life,* 394. See also Randall 3:505–6; Peterson, *Visitors to Monticello,* 97–99.

23. Malone 6:233–82, 365–425; TJ to Ticknor, Nov. 25, 1817, Ford 10:96; to Maria Cosway, Oct. 24, 1822, in Bullock, *My Head and My Heart,* 179, 182.

24. Randall 1:60.

25. *Jefferson's Literary Commonplace Book,* 23–24n, 56, 99.

26. William Sherlock, *A Practical Discourse concerning Death* (London, 1735), 3, 57–58, 65–67, 126. See also Sowerby, *Catalogue of the Library of Thomas Jefferson* 2:151. Jefferson also recommended Sherlock's 1692 *A Practical Discourse concerning a Future Judgment* to Skipwith.

27. TJ to Short, Oct. 7, 1789, Boyd 15:509.

28. See Jan Lewis, *The Pursuit of Happiness: Family and Values in Jefferson's Virginia* (Cambridge, 1983), chap. 3.

29. See TJ to Adams, Jan. 21, 1812, *Adams-Jefferson Letters,* 292.

30. TJ to Adams, Apr. 8, 1816, ibid., 467.

31. Adams to TJ, May 3, 1816, ibid., 469–71.

32. TJ to Adams, Aug. 1, 1816, ibid., 484–85.

33. TJ to Rush, Sept. 23, 1800, L&B 10:175. The Latin phrase, literally "the excit-able order of prophets," is taken from the epistles of Horace; the word *irritabile* connotes a system of belief not rooted in reason.

34. See Introduction by Eugene R. Sheridan, in *Jefferson's Extracts from the Gospels,* ed. Dickinson W. Adams (Princeton, N.J., 1983).

35. TJ to Rush, Apr. 21, 1803, ibid., 331.

36. American Philosophical Society to Priestley, June 20, 1794, TJ to Priestley, Jan. 18, 1800, in *The Theological and Miscellaneous Works of Joseph Priestley,* vol. 1, *Life and Correspondence (1787–1804),* ed. John Towill Rutt (New York, 1972), 261, 435.

37. Malone 4:203–4; Conkin, "Religious Pilgrimage of Thomas Jefferson."

38. TJ to Smith, Aug. 6, 1816, *Jefferson's Extracts from the Gospels,* 376; TJ to Logan, Nov. 12, 1816, Ford 10:68.

39. TJ to Thomson, Jan. 29, 1817, *Jefferson's Extracts from the Gospels,* 384.

40. TJ to Adams, Apr. 11, 1823, *Adams-Jefferson Letters,* 594.

41. Ibid., 592; Sanford, *Religious Life of Thomas Jefferson,* chap. 9; Cassirer, *Philosophy of the Enlightenment,* 164–65.

42. TJ to Carr, Aug. 10, 1787, Boyd 12:15–17.

43. TJ to Rev. Isaac Story, Dec. 5, 1801, L&B 10:299; TJ to Adams, Nov. 13, 1818, Apr. 11, 1823, *Adams-Jefferson Letters,* 529, 594. Upon the death of George Wythe in 1806, Jefferson similarly wrote that he had hoped to spend time in retirement with "my antient master, my earliest & best friend," but "this may yet be the enjoyment of another state of being" (Malone 5:137). And to Abigail Adams in 1817: "Our next meeting must then be in the country to which [the years] have flown, a country, for us, not now very distant. For this journey we will need neither gold nor silver in our purse, nor scrip, nor coats, nor staves" (TJ to Abigail Adams, Jan. 11, 1817, *Adams-Jefferson Letters,* 504).

44. TJ to Adams, July 5, 1814, Oct. 12, 1823, ibid., 430–31, 599; Adams to TJ, Nov. 10, 1823, ibid., 602.

45. Smith, *First Forty Years of Washington Society,* 230. See also Jack G. Voller, "The Textuality of Death: Notes on the Reading of Cemeteries," *Journal of American Culture* 14 (1991): 1–9.

46. TJ to M. Cosway, Dec. 27, 1820, in Bullock, *My Head and My Heart,* 176–77.

47. TJ to T. J. Randolph, Feb. 1826, *Family Letters,* 469–70; Malone 6:299–300; *Domestic Life,* 416. For the details of Jefferson's financial problems, see Malone 6:301–5, 309–10, 473–74, 511.

48. Randall 3:537, 665–67; Malone 6:489; *Domestic Life,* 431.

49. Martha to Ellen Randolph Coolidge, Apr. 5, 1826, Ellen Wayles Coolidge Correspondence, University of Virginia Library.

50. Randall 3:543–46; Peterson, *Visitors to Monticello,* 109.

51. T. J. Randolph to Jane Randolph, June (?), July 2, 1826, Edgehill Randolph Papers.

52. Randall 3:545; *Domestic Life,* 429; photostat of the original, in Jefferson's hand, and a copy written out by Nicholas Trist, James Monroe Museum, Fredericksburg, Va.; *Jefferson's Literary Commonplace Book,* 9, 218.

53. Page to TJ, Mar. 7, 1788, Boyd 12:650–54.

54. TJ to Eliza House Trist, Dec. 15, 1786, Boyd 10:600. The eighteenth-century meaning of "character" referred directly to personal quality and "constitution of the mind" (Johnson's 1783 *Dictionary*).

55. TJ to Page, June 25, 1804, Jefferson Papers, Library of Congress; to Madison, July 31, 1788, May 9, 1791, Boyd 13:442, 20:293.

56. TJ to Angelica Church, Sept. 21, 1788, Boyd 13:623. See also TJ to Albert Gallatin, Jan. 13, 1807, Ford 9:7.

57. Jefferson offered his assessment of sexual politics as a newly wedded lawyer in 1772. See Frank L. Dewey, "Thomas Jefferson's Notes on Divorce," *William and Mary Quarterly* 39 (1982): 212–23.

58. Lewis, "Blessings of Domestic Society"; TJ to Nathaniel Burwell, Mar. 14, 1818, Ford 10:104–5.

59. Kenneth A. Lockridge, *On the Sources of Patriarchal Rage: The Commonplace Books of William Byrd and Thomas Jefferson and the Gendering of Power in the Eighteenth Century* (New York, 1992), 69–70, 125. On symbols of control more generally, see ibid., 90, 94.

60. TJ to Martha, Nov. 28, 1783, *Family Letters*, 20.

61. Cash, *Laurence Sterne: The Later Years*, 184.

62. Shackelford, *Jefferson's Adoptive Son*, 114.

63. Bullock, *My Head and My Heart*, 134, 138, 144–46.

CONCLUSION

1. Gustafson, *Representative Words*, 266.

2. Howard Anderson, "Sterne's Letters: Consciousness and Sympathy," in Anderson, *Familiar Letter in the Eighteenth Century*, 138–39.

3. Zirker, "Richardson's Correspondence," 87.

4. Spacks, *Imagining a Self*, 25, 307. See also James Engell, *The Creative Imagination: Enlightenment to Romanticism* (Cambridge, Mass., 1981), vii–viii.

5. Redford, *Converse of the Pen*, 9; Bailyn, "Boyd's Jefferson: Notes for a Sketch," 392.

6. TJ to Martha, Feb. 8, 1798, Jan. 15, 1784, *Family Letters*, 155, 23. See also Lewis, "Blessings of Domestic Society."

7. TJ to Elizabeth Wayles Eppes, Sept. 22, 1785, to Eliza House Trist, Aug. 18, 1785, Boyd 8:539–40, 404.

8. TJ to Adams, June 27, 1822, Jan. 11, 1817, Aug. 15, 1820, *Adams-Jefferson Letters*, 580, 505, 567; to Waterhouse, Mar. 3, 1818, Ford 10:103; to John Waldo, Aug. 16. 1813, in Randall 3:391–93.

9. See Daniel Walker Howe, "The Language of Faculty Psychology in *The Federalist Papers*," in Terence Ball and J. G. A. Pocock, eds., *Conceptual Change and the Constitution* (Lawrence, Kans., 1988), esp. 116–119.

10. For a discussion of the concept of a "natural aristocracy," see Wood, *Creation of the American Republic*, chap. 12; see also John Zvesper, *Political Philosophy and Rhetoric: A Study of the Origins of American Party Politics* (Cambridge, 1977).

11. Theodore Dwight, *The Character of Thomas Jefferson, as Exhibited in His Own Writings* (Boston, 1839), 17.

12. Forrest McDonald has written of Hamilton: "Though he labored brilliantly and diligently to build a system that was not dependent on men's goodness, he could not avoid the consequences of an unconscious assumption that an adequate number of virtuous men would always be available to run the system" (McDonald, *Alexander Hamilton*, 112). This analysis places him, ironically, closer in spirit to Jefferson's "optimism" than either man would have been able to acknowledge.

13. TJ to Adams, Sept. 4, 1823, *Adams-Jefferson Letters*, 596.

14. See McCoy, *Elusive Republic*, chap. 1.

15. *Notes*, 140–41; *Letters of Laurence Sterne*, 145–50.

16. TJ to Coles, Aug. 25, 1814, in *Thomas Jefferson's Farm Book*, ed. Edwin Morris Betts (Princeton, N.J., 1953), 37–39. See also Miller, *Wolf by the Ears*, esp. chap. 28.

17. See Merrill D. Peterson, *The Jefferson Image in the American Mind* (New York, 1960), 174; Charles L. Griswold, Jr., "Rights and Wrongs: Jefferson, Slavery, and Philosophical Quandaries," in Michael J. Lacey and Knud Haakonssen, eds., *A Culture of Rights* (Cambridge, 1992), 144–214; Frank Shuffelton, "Thomas Jefferson: Race, Culture, and the Failure of Anthropological Method," in Shuffelton, ed., *A Mixed Race* (New York, 1993).

18. *Notes*, 138–39.

19. Jefferson's revelation of his abortive affair with Betsy Walker may have been offered in the same mode as Benjamin Franklin's. In his *Autobiography* (50–51), Franklin wrote that he had "attempted familiarities" with the mistress of his friend James Ralph. For both men the indiscretion had occurred early in life and did not appear to cause the transgressors much self-recrimination in their later years' reflections.

20. Becker, *Declaration of Independence*, 217–19.

21. See Lerner, *Thinking Revolutionary*, 119.

22. TJ to Mazzei, Apr. 24, 1796, Ford 7:72–78; Mazzei, *My Life and Wanderings*, 14–15; TJ to Washington, Apr. 16, 1784, Boyd 7:106.

23. TJ to Adams, June 27, 1813, *Adams-Jefferson Letters*, 337.

24. Adams to TJ, July 15, 1813, TJ to Adams, Oct. 12, 1823, ibid., 358, 600.

25. TJ to Destutt de Tracy, Jan. 26, 1811, Ford 9:307. See also TJ to Joel Barlow, Jan. 24, 1810, L&B 12:351; Adrienne Koch, *Power, Morals, and the Founding Fathers: Essays in the Interpretation of the American Enlightenment* (Ithaca, N.Y., 1961), chap. 3.

26. Cicero to Lucceius, 56 B.C., *The Letters to His Friends (Epistulae ad Familiares)*, trans. W. Glynn Williams (Cambridge, Mass., 1979), 5.7.373; Peterson, *Jefferson Image in the American Mind*, 259–60.

27. Randall 3:345.

28. See Gordon Wood, "The Democratization of Mind in the American Revolution," *Leadership in the American Revolution* (Washington, D.C., 1974), 68; Wood, *Radicalism of the American Revolution*, 221; Schlereth, *Cosmopolitan Ideal in Enlightenment Thought*, chap. 1; David S. Shields, "Anglo-American Clubs: Their Wit, Their Heterodoxy, Their Sedition," *William and Mary Quarterly* 51 (1994): 293–304; Griswold, "Rights and Wrongs," 154ff.

29. Randall 1:42–44.

30. H. J. C. Grierson, "Classical and Romantic: A Point of View," in Robert F. Gleckner and Gerald E. Enscoe, eds., *Romanticism: Points of View* (Detroit, 1962), 52.

31. Lewis, *Pursuit of Happiness,* esp. 212–14.

32. Engell, *Creative Imagination,* 83, 313–16.

33. John Dewey, *Freedom and Culture* (New York, 1939), 155.

34. See also Koch, *Power, Morals, and the Founding Fathers,* 30–31.

35. Adams to TJ, May 3, 1812, *Adams-Jefferson Letters,* 303.

36. Shackelford, *Jefferson's Adoptive Son,* 167.

37. Peterson, *Jefferson Image in the American Mind,* 46–50; Vance, *Thomas Jefferson Randolph,* chap. 11; George Green Shackelford, "Jane Hollins Nicholas and Thomas Jefferson Randolph," in Shackelford, ed., *Collected Papers to Commemorate Fifty Years of the Monticello Association of the Descendants of Thomas Jefferson* (Princeton, N.J., 1965).

38. TJ to Benjamin Waterhouse, Mar. 3, 1818, Ford 10:103–4.

39. *John Dewey: The Later Works* 14:254.

Index

Adams, Abigail, 8, 88, 175; cares for Maria
    Jefferson, 175–76; disparages French,
    72; letters from TJ, 66, 72–73, 89, 179,
    243; letters to TJ, 102, 179
Adams, Henry, 147–48, 218
Adams, John, 5, 6, 19, 34, 57, 68, 71, 116, 128,
    161, 203, 220, 240, 260, 265, 288–89;
    breaks off contact with TJ, 178–79; per-
    sonality, 163, 173, 175, 177; in France,
    174; and Great Seal, 186; and *Rights of
    Man* controversy, 177, 267; as presi-
    dent, 224–25, 227, 231; letters from TJ,
    13, 15, 51, 115, 175–80, 187, 235, 244, 257–
    58, 261–62, 276, 283–84; letters to TJ,
    176, 258, 262, 283; reconciles with TJ,
    179, 185
Adams, John Quincy, 31, 69, 175, 177, 237,
    279, 283
Adams, Thomas, 26, 70
Addison, Joseph, 14
Aeneas, 106
African Americans, TJ's disparagement of,
    279–80. *See also* Slavery
Aix, 99, 106
Albemarle County, 12–15, 41, 70–71, 154–55,
    188, 222
Alien and Sedition Acts, 224, 258
American Philosophical Society, 7, 180–84,
    241
Anas, 209, 210, 220, 234–36
Anson, George, 14, 85
Aristotle, 3
Augusta County, 17
Avignon, 99, 122

Bacon, Edmund, 146, 250, 254
Bacon, Francis, 115, 127, 152
Bailyn, Bernard, 1, 274
Banister, John, Jr., 112–13, 115, 280
Bankhead, Anne Cary Randolph, 38, 190,
    250–51, 263–64
Bankhead, Charles, 264
Barbé-Marbois, François, marquis de, 4, 74,
    216

Battestin, Martin C., 51, 66
Bayard, John, 146
Becker, Carl, 281
Beckley, John, 228
Belknap, Jeremy, 40
Bellini, Charles, 115, 159, 216
Bingham, Ann Willing, 113–14
Bingham, William, 113, 163
Blair, Hugh: *Dissertation* on Ossian, 32–33,
    36, 267; *Lectures on Rhetoric and Belles
    Lettres,* 36, 127–30, 138, 203
Bolingbroke, Henry St. John, 56; on letter
    writing, 130
Bonaparte, Napoleon, 278
Book of Common Prayer, 143
Boone, Daniel, 41
Boorstin, Daniel, 184
Boswell, James, 43
Boulanviller, Henri de, 51–52
Brant, Irving, 152, 157
Brodie, Fawn, 319n
Brown, Charles Brockden, 105
Brown, Marshall, 33, 47
Brown, Mather, 175
Brown, Richard, 116
Brutus, 124
Bryan, William Jennings, 284
Buchanan, James, 50
Buffon, Georges-Louis Leclerc, 74, 217
Bullock, Helen Duprey, 76
Burke, Edmund, 89–90
Burr, Aaron, 154, 233–34, 238, 241, 266
Burwell, TJ's slave, 264
Burwell, Rebecca, 136, 229, 231

Caesar, 36
Callender, James Thomson, 167, 227–29, 231
Cappon, Lester J., 173–74
Carmichael, William, 163
Carr, Dabney, 6, 31, 48, 60, 143–44, 262,
    267
Carr, Martha Jefferson, 60, 143, 263
Carr, Overton, 144
Carr, Peter, 133, 144, 157, 169, 192, 280; let-

Carr, Peter (*continued*)
    ters from TJ, 145, 171–72, 261; and Maz-
    zei letter controversy, 222; and Sally
    Hemings controversy, 230–31
Carr, Samuel, 192, 230–31
Carrington, Edward, 210, 220
Carter, Robert, 16, 267
Cassirer, Ernst, 23
Castell, Robert, 20
Charlottesville, 14, 264
Chastellux, François-Jean, marquis de, 7–8,
    39, 63, 192, 200, 204; describes Hamil-
    ton, 207; and *Notes,* 74; visits Monti-
    cello, 32–35; writings, 73–74
Chinard, Gilbert, 73
Church, Angelica Schuyler, 8, 189, 207; let-
    ters from TJ, 108–9, 219, 268; visits
    Paris, 107
Church, Catherine, 108
Church, John Barker, 107
Cicero, Marcus Tullius, 56, 117, 149, 256,
    284; on ambition, 241–43; *Letters to
    Atticus,* 118–22, 124, 130, 135
Ciceronian ethos, 117–23, 274
Cincinnati, Society of, 221, 223
Clark, George Rogers, 199–200, 215
Clay, Henry, 133
Coles, Edward, 279
Commager, Henry Steele, 39
Condillac, Etienne Bonnot de, 51
Condorcet, Marie Jean Antoine, marquis
    de, 73, 278
Consciousness and conscience, 50–52
Coolidge, Ellen Wayles Randolph, 230, 248,
    252–53, 264
Cornwallis, Charles, Lord, 60, 198
Corny, Mme de, 73, 108, 189
Cosmopolitanism, 74–75
Cosway, Maria, 146, 163, 165, 248, 270, 280;
    handwriting, 96; "My Head and My
    Heart" letter, 18, 35, 38–39, 55, 78–95,
    106; in TJ's company, 78, 107; letters
    from TJ (other than "Head and
    Heart"), 66, 96–99, 104, 106–8, 189,
    255, 263; letters to TJ, 96, 107–9, 115;
    personal history, 76, 219, 271
Cosway, Richard, 76, 78, 97, 106, 271; paints
    Sterne's Eliza, 111
Coxe, Tench, 239
Crèvecoeur, St. John de, 71, 73

Davies, Reverend, 30
Davy, George Alan, 216
Death: eighteenth-century perspective on,
    35, 266–67; in Sterne, 48; TJ's reflec-
    tions on, 255–57, 272
Declaration of Independence, 4, 14, 57–58,
    70, 116, 138, 170, 182, 186, 225, 257
Defoe, Daniel, 39
Demosthenes, 129, 198
Destutt de Tracy, 284
Dewey, John, 1, 288, 291
Dickinson, John, 246
Diderot, Denis, 52, 75
Dinwiddie County, 29
Discourses on Davila, 177
Donne, John, 195
Don Quixote, 51
Dos Passos, John, 68
Douglas, Reverend William, 16
Draper, Eliza, *see* Sterne, Laurence
Drummond, Mrs., 25–26
Dryden, John, 51, 54
Dunglison, Dr. Robley, 264, 265
Dunlap, William, 67
Du Pont de Nemours, Pierre Samuel, 8, 89,
    153, 245
Du Simitière, Pierre, 186

Edgehill, 188, 247, 249
Edinburgh, 67, 127, 235
England, 14–15, 56, 68, 75, 96; conflict with
    France, 220; TJ's feelings toward, 113,
    162, 217–18, 222, 238, 240
Enlightenment thinking, 7, 28, 33–34, 72,
    125, 126, 195, 286
Enville, duchesse d', *see* La Rochefoucauld
    d'Enville
Epictetus, 28
Eppes, Elizabeth Wayles, 63, 275
Eppes, Francis, TJ's brother-in-law, 57–58
Eppes, Francis, TJ's grandson, 247, 253, 264
Eppes, John W., 148; marries Maria Jeffer-
    son, 188
Eppes, Maria Jefferson, 24, 59, 64, 70, 86,
    108, 179, 269, 275; death, 247; fragility,
    141, 191; letters from TJ, 5, 191–93, 247,
    249; marriage, 188
Eppes, Martha, 30
Erikson, Erik, 195
Everett, Edward, 128

Fauquier, Francis, 6, 132
The Federalist, 207, 210, 276
Fenno, John, 211
Fithian, Philip, 16
Fliegelman, Jay, 2, 28, 53, 132
Floyd, Kitty, 64, 158
Forest, the home of John Wayles, 30
Fossett, Joe, 264
France, 171, 174, 224; conflict with England, 220; TJ's arrival in, 68–71; TJ's feelings toward, 72, 225, 278
Franklin, Benjamin, 6–7, 34, 57, 72, 97, 161, 180, 183, 197, 203, 281; on friends and enemies, 243–44; influence on TJ, 170–72, 285; letter from TJ, 71; in Paris, 68–70, 74, 174
Franks, David, 163, 223
Fredericksville, 13, 17
Freeman, Joanne, 203
Freneau, Philip, 211, 214
Freud, Sigmund, 290
Friendship, and epistolography, 118–26, 267; in TJ's formative years, 131–49; within TJ's larger community, 151–87; and TJ's political alliances, 197, 201, 204, 218, 226, 243; TJ's vision of, 5, 78, 88–91, 94, 194–95, 282–83
Fry, Joshua, 14

Gallatin, Albert, 88
Garber, Frederick, 51
Geismar, Baron de, 70
George III, king of England, 4, 39, 56–57, 239
George, "King," TJ's slave, 22
Gerry, Elbridge, 159, 225, 236
Gibbon, Edward, 31
Giles, William Branch, 123, 223, 234–35, 238
Gilmer, George, 111
Girardin, 60
Gossip, 137, 163–64, 204, 206
Great Seal of the U.S., 186
Green, Reverend Enoch, 16
Gustafson, Thomas, 203
Guthrie, William, 120

Hall, Francis, 40
Hamilton, Alexander, 4, 107, 140, 151, 154, 178, 180, 200, 223, 227, 266, 276, 289; duel with Burr, 234; funding and as-
sumption plan, 209–10, 212; personal history, 206–8; TJ remonstrates about, 196, 212–19, 231, 238–40; womanizing, 228–29; writes against TJ, 211–12
Hamilton, William, 21
Hancarville, d', 79
Hancock, John, 57
Harries, Elizabeth, 46
Harvie, John, 13–14
Heller, Joseph, 43
Helvétius, Anne-Catherine, 72
Hemings, Eston, 264
Hemings, James, 68, 186
Hemings, Madison, 230, 264
Hemings, Sally, 228–31
Henry, Patrick, 134, 150, 205, 206, 215, 218, 224, 232; TJ's early esteem for, 197–98; TJ's enmity toward, 198–202, 238, 241
Herodotus, 255–56
Hocquetout, countess d', 73
Hogendorp, G. K. van, 147
Homer, 31, 36, 56, 62, 89, 129, 133, 197, 270
Hopkinson, Francis, 180, 182–83, 186–87, 242, 282
Hume, David, 28, 135
Humphreys, David, 69, 206
Hutcheson, Francis, 195
Hyperbole, TJ's use of, 112, 114, 138

Imagination: in eighteenth-century vocabulary, 34, 36, 152, 274; and romanticism, 39, 54, 288; in Sterne, 47, 66, 102; in TJ's letter writing, 26, 85, 94, 97–98, 106, 129, 135, 138, 190, 270, 279
Indians, *see* Native Americans
Isaac, TJ's slave, 3
Isaac, Rhys, 15
Ivernois, François d', 178

Jack, Ian, 43
Jay, John, 174, 204, 220, 276
Jay Treaty, 140, 196, 220, 276
Jefferson, Jane, sister, 48, 267, 272
Jefferson, Jane Randolph, mother, 12, 262
Jefferson, Lucy, daughter, 64, 69
Jefferson, Maria, daughter, *see* Eppes, Maria Jefferson
Jefferson, Martha, daughter, *see* Randolph, Martha Jefferson

Jefferson, Martha Wayles ("Patty"), wife, 32, 48–49, 57–58, 84, 118, 156, 269–71; death, 60–64; TJ courts, 24–30; TJ's memories of, 66, 90, 264

Jefferson, Peter, father, 12, 14, 16–17, 48, 85, 267, 269, 278

Jefferson, Randolph, brother, 21, 114

Jefferson, Thomas
  personal life and views: amorous inclinations, 8, 25–26, 49, 95, 97, 102, 104, 106, 109, 136, 268; as architect, 12, 18–24; autobiography, 49, 60, 205; believes Europe corrupting, 111–15, 278; classical references suggested by, 19–21, 28, 38, 66, 85, 89, 97–98, 106, 117–19, 242, 260–61, 286; death of, 264–66; dislocates wrist, 78; distinguishes "delight" from "happiness," 88–89; final retirement, 117, 246–66; funerary imagery expressed by, 22, 62, 262–64; generosity toward beggars, 91–93, 199; handwriting, 62, 96, 133; hydrophobia, 85; interaction with slaves, 21–23, 189; invents moldboard plow, 187, 282; library of, 12, 135, 152, 164, 263; love of family, 5, 24–25, 62, 148, 190–93, 248, 251, 253, 275; on moral sense, 23, 50–51, 91, 195, 238; nostalgia, 35–36, 48, 111, 253–54, 271; optimistic tendencies, 84, 90–91, 128, 153, 238, 257, 278, 284, 288–90; personal qualities, 1, 30, 59, 146–51, 173–74; physical health, 244–45, 249, 254; on "pursuit of happiness," 9, 52, 88–89, 95, 136, 148–49, 270, 288; reflects on loss and grief, 33, 48, 63–64, 82–84, 89–90, 247–48, 250, 257, 261, 267; and secrecy, 137; self-repression, 113, 195; travels on Continent, 99–100, 108; use of Sternean idiom, 45, 47, 49, 54, 66, 93, 95, 100–105, 266; wedding, 30
  public career: in Continental Congress, 4, 57–58, 63, 205; distaste for public life, 63, 165, 194, 246; governor, 4, 59–60, 156, 176, 198; in House of Burgesses, 18, 134, 144; as lawyer, 17–18, 150; manipulates political language, 277; midcareer retirement, 4–5, 178, 190, 242–43, 269; minister to France, 4, 7,
68–75; perception of intrigue, 113, 201–2, 215–16, 218, 219; president, 5, 143, 146, 160–61, 179, 226–35, 244, 246, 252, 259, 286, 290; secretary of state, 4, 166, 177, 196, 206, 210–20, 286; trust in popular will, 197, 241; vice president, 5, 165, 224–26, 242

Johnson, Samuel, *Dictionary,* 50, 81, 125–26, 276; on judgment, 54; on Ossian, 31

Johnson, William, 237

Jones, Walter, 235–36

Judgment and wit, 54–56, 92, 95

Jupiter, TJ's slave, 22

Kames, Henry Home, 28

Kentucky and Virginia Resolutions, 224

Ketcham, Ralph, 168

King, Martin Luther, 291

King Lear, 28

Knight, Richard Payne, 79

Knox, Henry, 151

Kors, Alan Charles, 72

Kosciusko, Thaddeus, 224

La Boëtie, 123

Lafayette, Marie Joseph du Motier, marquis de, 8, 60, 70, 72, 73, 154, 163; friendship with TJ, 7; letter from TJ, 101

La Rochefoucauld d'Enville, duchesse de, 73

La Rochefoucauld, Louis Alexandre, duc de, 71, 73

Laurens, John, 208

Laurentinum, 20

Lectures on Rhetoric and Belles Lettres, see Blair, Hugh

Lee, Henry, 265

Lee, Richard Henry, 58, 197

Lehmann, Karl, 21, 124, 128, 129

Lennon, John, 43

Letter writing, history of, 117–30; TJ's attachment to, 3, 5, 8, 10–11, 59, 78, 110, 116, 130–31, 141–43, 148–49, 164, 194–95, 250, 267–68, 270, 273–76, 279

Lewis, Jan, 148, 287

Lewis and Clark expedition, 184, 278

Library of Congress, 152

Literary Commonplace Book, 3; death-related passages, 255–56; Ossian passages, 31, 38; Sterne passage, 49, 56, 58, 61–62

Livingston, Robert, 58, 168
Livy, 28, 261
Locke, John, 2, 28, 66, 127, 128, 217; *Essay concerning Human Understanding,* 43, 50–52; on judgment and wit, 54–55, 95; on letter writing, 121
Lockridge, Kenneth, 269
Louis XVI, 163
Louisiana Purchase, 168, 278
Lucceius, 284

McFarland, Thomas, 38
McLaughlin, Jack, 12, 19
Maclay, William, 150–51, 206
Macpherson, Charles, 31, 36
Macpherson, James, 31, 34, 38
McWilliams, Wilson Carey, 1, 149
Madison, Dolley Todd, 167
Madison, James, 8, 88, 127, 137, 139, 174, 188, 211, 222, 238, 241, 252, 268, 276, 281; early history, 64, 152; friendship with TJ, 5, 6, 29, 152–59, 163–70, 264; Hamilton's opinion of, 210–11; letters from TJ, 5, 6, 34, 69, 93, 113, 121, 140, 144, 152–54, 156–59, 162–64, 175, 180, 200, 201, 219, 231–33, 242, 243, 246, 267; letter to TJ, 207; relations with Monroe, 159–62; TJ's particular language with, 153–54, 158, 162–63
Madison, Reverend James, 152
Malone, Dumas, 1, 14, 69, 78, 134, 184, 208
Marshall, John, 225; as TJ's enemy, 231–35, 238; as Washington's biographer, 235–37, 283
Maury, James, 16–17, 112, 143, 152
Maury, James, Jr., 253–54
Maury, Walker, 112
Mayo, Bernard, 78
Mazzei, Philip, 73, 226; as neighbor, 70–71; publishes TJ's letter, 222–23
Melmoth, William, 121
Mentoring, 132–35, 169, 193
Miller, Charles A., 2, 128
Milton, John, 49, 256
Mockingbirds, 40, 66
Monroe, Elizabeth Kortright, 62–63, 155
Monroe, James, 5, 6, 88, 137, 141, 188, 211, 229, 235, 238, 241; and Ash Lawn, 154–56, 167; early history, 154–55, 169; letters from TJ, 62, 69, 80, 118, 155–56, 164–65;

letter to TJ, 155; relations with Madison, 159–62; TJ's particular language with, 155–56, 160–62; volatility, 159–61, 165, 170
Montaigne, Michel de, 39, 47, 123–24, 127, 149
Monticello, 5, 7, 13, 32, 35, 39, 43, 58–59, 64, 70, 84, 111, 118, 135, 138, 253, 282; cemetery, 22, 62, 144, 255, 262–63; construction, 17–24; as haven for family, 10, 25, 63, 187–93, 247–49; sold, 289; as symbol of inner life, 9, 12, 29, 148, 219, 270–71; and TJ's desire for neighborhood, 5, 152–57, 169, 188, 201
Music, 282; and TJ's courtship of Patty, 26; and TJ's daughters, 190–91
"My Head and My Heart" letter, *see* Cosway, Maria

Native Americans, 14–15, 29, 74, 117, 216
Natural Bridge, 35–40, 52, 98
Nature: in TJ's thought, 38–41, 89; metaphors of in TJ's letters, 26, 69, 90, 126, 190
Newton, Isaac, 127
Nicholas, George, 198
Nicholas, Wilson Cary, 263
Notes on Virginia, 4, 18, 40, 60, 123, 140, 181, 183, 198, 205; and African Americans, 278–80; argumentation in, 216–18; publication, 74

Ogilvie, James, 25
Ong, Walter J., 2
Ossian, 31–34, 39, 56, 76, 192, 257, 270, 290
Outasette, 15
Ovid, 66

Page, John, 6, 71, 149, 166, 247; friendship with TJ, 17, 88, 135–44, 146, 164, 229, 268; letters from TJ, 25, 60, 129, 136–43; letters to TJ, 138, 139, 141, 143, 181, 266–67
Paine, Thomas, 75, 184, 233, 241; *Rights of Man,* 177
Palladio, Andreas, 19–20
Pantops, 188, 264
Paradise, John, 267
Peale, Charles Willson, 7, 9, 39, 180, 184, 251, 282

Peterson, Merrill D., 1, 64, 115, 157, 173, 189, 209, 227

Pickering, Timothy, 232

Pinckney, Charles Cotesworth, 225, 232–33

Pliny (Plinius, Caecilus Secundus), 20–21, 117, 121, 130

Plumer, William, 204, 211

Plutarch, 28, 207

Pope, Alexander, 43, 51, 56, 207

Poplar Forest, 60, 253–54, 285

Price, Richard, 75

Priestley, Joseph, 89, 124, 149, 259

Primitivism, 39, 126

Quintilian, 117

Quintus, 120

Rabelais, 42, 46

Raleigh Tavern, 17

Randall, Henry S., 26, 143, 150, 175, 230, 255, 285

Randolph, Anne Cary, *see* Bankhead, Anne Cary Randolph

Randolph, Cornelia Jefferson, 253

Randolph, Edmund, 160, 197, 211, 213

Randolph, Ellen Wayles, *see* Coolidge, Ellen Wayles Randolph

Randolph, Isham, 85

Randolph, John, father of Edmund, 205, 217–18

Randolph, John, of Roanoke, 251

Randolph, Martha ("Patsy") Jefferson, 24, 40, 64, 86, 133, 181, 182, 264; character, 191–92; letters from TJ, 190, 191, 247, 269, 275; letters to TJ, 247, 249; on loss of mother, 60–61; marriage, 188; in Paris, 68–70, 93, 275; on Sally Hemings, 230; and TJ's deathbed adieu, 265–66

Randolph, Peyton, 57, 135

Randolph, Thomas Jefferson, 133, 190, 281; discusses Hemings charges, 230; as editor of TJ's papers, 97, 277; letters from TJ, 3, 16, 96, 135, 145, 251, 263; letter to TJ, 252; personality, 251; public career, 289–90; at TJ's deathbed, 264–65

Randolph, Thomas Mann, 188, 190, 249, 251

Randolph, William, 13, 17

Reason: as Enlightenment concept, 38–39, 43, 102, 127–28, 152, 271, 276; and TJ's religious quest, 261; and TJ's view of racial inequality, 279

Redford, Bruce, 274

Religion: freedom of, 84, 139–40, 201, 213; TJ's conceptions of, 22–23, 28, 93, 258–63, 285

Reynolds, James, 228

Reynolds, Maria, 228

Richardson, Samuel, 48, 105, 125, 273–74

Richmond, 30, 57, 59, 199, 228, 234

Richmond Recorder, 228

Riedesel, Baron de, 70

Rittenhouse, David, 7, 180–82, 187, 282

Rivanna River, 13, 18

Rollin, Charles, 28

Romanticism, 38–39, 54, 287–88

Roosevelt, Franklin D., 284

"Rosalie," duchess, 75, 111, 165

Rousseau, Jean-Jacques, 39, 51

Rowanty, 29

Rush, Benjamin, 7, 67, 145, 180, 184–87, 216, 245, 251, 264, 282; debates religion with TJ, 185, 258–59; orchestrates TJ-Adams reconciliation, 185; praises Wythe, 133

Salons, 41, 72–73, 114, 126

Sancho, Ignatius, 279

Schachner, Nathan, 208, 209

Schuyler, Philip, 234

Sea metaphors, 85–88, 161, 214, 257–58, 272

Sensibility, 52

A Sentimental Journey, see Sterne, Laurence

Sexuality: in eighteenth century, 105; in Sterne, 102–4, 109; TJ's, 268, 270, 280–81

Shadwell, 12–14, 18, 25, 134, 137, 188, 269

Shaftesbury, earl of, 195

Shakespeare, William, 28, 43, 49

Shenstone, William, 266

Sherlock, William, 256

Sherman, Roger, 58

Short, William, 5, 6, 121, 155, 188, 289; affair with Rosalie, 75, 111, 270; early acquaintance with TJ, 156; letters from TJ, 99, 166–67, 256–57; letters to TJ, 115, 157; as TJ's protégé, 69, 78, 165–66

Sincerity, meaning of to TJ, 158–59, 161, 169, 179–80, 200

Skelton, Bathurst, 30

Skipwith, Robert, 26–29, 53, 92, 188, 256

Skipwith, Tabitha (Wayles), 26, 29
Slavery, 21–23, 189, 205, 279, 289; *see also* African Americans
Small, William, 6, 30, 132, 135, 136
Smith, Margaret Bayard, 14, 254, 260; characterizes TJ, 40, 146–47; describes Monticello graveyard, 262; on TJ's daughters, 192
Smith, Samuel Harrison, 146
Smith, William S., 78, 121
Socrates, 51
Spacks, Patricia, 274
Spenser, Edmund, 50
Spinoza, 23
Stamp Act, 17, 134, 183, 224
Steele, Richard, 50, 105
Sterne, Laurence, 115, 146, 148, 256, 266, 282, 290; befriends Ignatius Sancho, 279; compassion toward women, 66, 270; health of, 47–48, 102; as letter writer, 273; letters to Eliza Draper, 45, 102, 110–11; *A Sentimental Journey*, 50, 92–93, 100–102, 109; *Sermons*, 28, 49–50, 53–54, 279; *Tristram Shandy*, 42–48, 54–55, 58, 67, 104–6, 109, 110, 137, 274, 279. *See also* Death; Imagination; Sexuality
Story, Isaac, 261
Sublime, natural, 36–41, 89
Summary Journal of Letters, 3, 64
A Summary View of the Rights of British America, 4, 56–58
Swift, Jonathan, 43, 46

Tacitus, 28, 261
Tarleton, Banastre, 60, 217
Taylor, John, of Caroline, 224, 226
Telemachus, 132
Tessé, Mme de, 8, 73, 109
Thomson, Charles, 7, 112, 180, 183–84, 186–87, 260
Thoughts on English Prosody, 73, 128–29
Ticknor, George, 254–55
Tinkler, John F., 122
Tott, Mme de, 73, 109–10
Tracy, Colonel, 68
Trist, Eliza House, 8, 146, 253, 268, 270; letter from Patsy, 93; letters from TJ, 65, 82, 86, 88, 267, 275
Trist, Nicholas P., 253, 266

Trist, Virginia Randolph, 253
Tristram Shandy, see Sterne, Laurence
Trumbull, John, 39, 70, 71, 107; and Cosways, 75–79, 106; estrangement from TJ, 223–24
Tuckahoe, 13, 20, 188
Tucker, St. George, 86, 267
Turner, Nat, 289

Ursula, TJ's slave, 22

Van Buren, Martin, 223
Virgil, 129
Virginia, 12, 19, 117, 137, 200; Committee of Correspondence, 57, 144; contrasted with New England, 13, 16, 116, 204–5; during Revolution, 4, 56–59, 134, 152, 198; tidewater culture, 15–16; TJ's attachment to, 4, 35, 111
Virginia, University of, 254–55
Virginia Resolution, *see* Kentucky and Virginia Resolutions
Voltaire, 69, 75

Waldo, John, 128
Walker, Betsy, 229–30
Walker, John, 229–30
Walker, Dr. Thomas, 13
Walpole, Horace, 130
Washington, Bushrod, 222
Washington, George, 4, 6, 14, 39, 63, 71, 140, 149, 153, 167, 174, 189, 197, 199, 233; letters from TJ, 158, 210, 212–15, 283; letters to TJ, 211, 221; mediates TJ-Hamilton dispute, 221, 240; relations with Hamilton, 208; TJ assesses, 217, 220–23, 236–37; turns against TJ, 222–23
Wayles, John, 30, 42, 62
Webster, Daniel, 245
Webster, Noah, 222
West, Benjamin, 67, 70, 184
Whitcomb, Samuel, 168
White, Alexander, 224
Whitman, Walt, 290
William and Mary, College of, 15, 43, 60, 132, 135, 152, 159, 252
Williamsburg, 6, 12, 19, 30, 57–59, 133, 136
Wirt, William, 202, 284

Wythe, George, 6, 17, 25, 112, 132–35, 156, 172, 198, 267

XYZ affair, 225, 232
Xenophon, 28

Yorick, 47, 50, 92, 93, 101–2, 109, 110

Zane, Isaac, 198, 201
Zirker, Malvin R., Jr., 273